# Religion and Popular Culture in America

D1566421

# Religion and Popular Culture in America

*Third Edition*

Edited by Bruce David Forbes
and Jeffrey H. Mahan

UNIVERSITY OF CALIFORNIA PRESS

University of California Press, one of the most
distinguished university presses in the United States,
enriches lives around the world by advancing scholarship
in the humanities, social sciences, and natural sciences. Its
activities are supported by the UC Press Foundation and
by philanthropic contributions from individuals and
institutions. For more information, visit www.ucpress.edu.

University of California Press
Oakland, California

Library of Congress Cataloging-in-Publication Data

Names: Forbes, Bruce David, editor. | Mahan, Jeffrey
    H., editor.
Title: Religion and popular culture in America / edited
    by Bruce Forbes and Jeffrey H. Mahan.
Description: Third edition. | Oakland, California :
    University of California Press, [2016] | Includes index.
Identifiers: LCCN 2016030111| ISBN 9780520291447
    (cloth : alk. paper) | ISBN 0520291441 (cloth : alk. paper)
    | ISBN 9780520291461 (pbk. : alk. paper) | ISBN
    0520291468 (pbk. : alk. paper)
Subjects: LCSH: Popular culture--Religious aspects. |
    Religion and culture—United States. | United States—
    Religion—1960–

Classification: LCC BL2525 .R4613 2016 |
    DDC 201/.70973—dc23
LC record available at https://lccn.loc.gov/2016030111

Manufactured in the United States of America

26   25   24   23   22   21   20   19   18   17
10   9   8   7   6   5   4   3   2   1

# CONTENTS

# PREFACE TO THE THIRD EDITION

This third edition of *Religion and Popular Culture in America* significantly updates a volume that has become a standard text in teaching about religion and popular culture. It continues the structure of the earlier editions, exploring four different relationships between religion and popular culture and the critical approaches out of which those relationships arise. This revised and expanded edition includes updated versions of five chapters from previous editions, and fourteen new essays. This expansion gives voice to a wider range of voices and provides greater attention to the diversity of religious life in America. The third edition also gives increased attention to the implications of the emergence of digital culture, including the increasingly interactive quality of popular culture. The authors of these essays draw on a wide range of methods to tease out these relationships between religion and popular culture. Some of the chapters take their approaches from the social sciences, while others are rooted in the humanities; some bring the tools of religious or theological studies to bear on popular culture, while others use the tools of film and television studies, sociology, and cultural studies. All are interested in the ways that religion has developed in the midst of, and adapted to the demands of, a consumer-oriented, mass-mediated culture. We hope that the interaction of fields, methods, and perspectives will help students of religion and popular culture understand and appreciate the work of those trained in different disciplines, in order to deepen and enrich the conversation about religion and popular culture.

We are first and foremost grateful to the authors of the provocative essays in this volume. Their thoughtful and creative work, and their generous response to the tinkering of the editors, is much appreciated. They have been thoughtful dialogue partners whose work deepens our understanding of the complex and changing relationships between religion and popular culture. The first edition of this book grew out of the founding of what has become the Religion and Popular Culture Group at the American Academy of Religion, and most of the original essays were first presented before that group. We are grateful to those who in the intervening years have provided leadership to maintain the group as a vital place for ongoing conversation about the evolving relationships of religion and popular culture.

Our editor at the University of California Press, Eric Schmidt, has provided tireless encouragement and wise counsel as we have imagined and prepared this expanded edition. At various times through the life of *Religion and Popular Culture in America,* Morningside College and the Iliff School of Theology have provided the volume editors with sabbatical or research leaves that were critical to the development of this book, as well as staff and student assistant support. We especially thank Sherry Swan for her invaluable assistance throughout the entire process of preparing the third edition.

In this refreshed form, we hope the book will continue to provoke thoughtful study of the popular culture that surrounds us, and of the way that religion is embedded in stories, images, and rituals that express, explore, and sometimes challenge shared cultural values and beliefs.

*Bruce David Forbes, Morningside College*
*Jeffrey H. Mahan, Iliff School of Theology*

Earlier versions of the following essays have appeared elsewhere in similar form. Appreciation is expressed for permission to republish them in this volume:

"It about Faith in Our Future: Star Trek Fandom as Culture Religion" by Michael Jindra is adapted from his essay "Star Trek Fandom as a Religious Phenomenon" in the journal of the Association for the Sociology of Religion, Inc., *Sociology of Religion* 55: 27–51, 1994. © Association for the Sociology of Religion, Inc.

"Can Watching a Movie be a Spiritual Experience" by Robert K. Johnson draws on previously published material including "The Film Viewer and Natural Theology: God's 'Presence' at the Movies," in *The Oxford Handbook of Natural Theology*, ed. Russell Re Manning (Oxford: Oxford University Press, 2013), 595–610 (chap. 38), as well as to the preface and chapter 3 of *God's Wider Presence: Reconsidering General Revelation* (Grand Rapids, MI: Baker Academic, 2014), xii–xix, 42–66.

"Rap Music and Its Message: On Interpreting the Contact between Religion and Popular Culture" by Anthony Pinn is a revision of the chapter titled "Blues, Rap and Nitty-Gritty Theology" in his *Why Lord? Suffering and Evil in Black Theology* (New York: Continuum, 1995). Reprinted by permission of the Continuum Publishing Company.

"Shopping, Religion and the Sacred 'Buyosphere'" by Sarah McFarland Taylor draws on her essay "Shopping and Consumption" in *The Routledge Companion to Religion and Popular Culture* (New York: Routledge, 2015).

# Introduction

## *Finding Religion in Unexpected Places*

BRUCE DAVID FORBES

Religion appears not only in churches, synagogues, mosques, and temples; it also appears in popular culture.[1] Best-selling popular music has included U2's "I Still Haven't Found What I'm Looking For," Lady Gaga's "Judas" and "Bloody Mary," and Carrie Underwood's "Jesus Take the Wheel." For almost three decades the animated television program *The Simpsons* has regularly included religion in its episodes, either in passing or as a featured topic, with Christian, Jewish, Hindu, Buddhist, Muslim, and Wiccan characters and even personal appearances by God and the devil. Millions of Americans have embraced yoga, a practice with roots in Hinduism, as a path to improve health and well-being. Angels, demons, witches, vampires, zombies (arising from Haitian Vodou), and occult phenomena seem to be everywhere in popular culture. Superhero comic books and their associated movies and television shows portray cosmic battles between good and evil. Batman has been portrayed in a crucifix pose on the covers of at least seven comic books over the years. What does it all mean?

Other examples of intersections between religion and popular culture are quite different in character. When preaching workshops for ministers include advice that sermons should be shortened, to accommodate the television-influenced attention span of seven or eight minutes between commercials, popular culture apparently affects the shape of institutional religion. At other times, aspects of popular culture seem to become a religion: the national hoopla surrounding the Super Bowl has suggested to more than one scholar that this January event has all the trappings of a religious festival. When fans virtually organize their lives around football or basketball, might we say that sport is a religion?

All of these examples both pertain to religion and are drawn from the realm of popular culture, which some people would dismiss as trivial, faddish, or "just entertainment," but which a growing body of scholars finds to be a significant focus for reflection and analysis. This essay, and this book, are about the connections between the two: popular culture and religion. Looking at the various ways in which these two subject areas interact provides a way to reflect on religion that is quite different from studying religious institutions, their scriptures, and their formal theologians. Approaching the study of religion through popular culture can help us learn more about the role religion plays in people's everyday lives and about widespread perceptions of it. The analysis of popular culture also can provide insights into how religions change and are changed by the cultures in which they are embedded. To help frame the discussion of such avenues of inquiry, this introductory essay will attempt to define popular culture, summarize some of the basic terminology and strategies of popular culture analysis, and introduce four different ways that popular culture and religion relate to one another.

## DEFINING POPULAR CULTURE

What is popular culture? Most of us already have a rough idea from the very phrase itself, but some clarification might be helpful. Scholars in the field frequently distinguish popular culture from both high (or elite) culture and folk culture. To employ suggestive examples from the realm of food: high culture is a gourmet meal, folk culture is grandma's casserole, and popular culture is a McDonald's hamburger.[2] All three are forms of "culture," which is intended here as a neutral term that includes the whole range of human products and thoughts that surround our lives, providing the context in which we live. Although some advocates of high culture would like to use the word "culture" in a more restricted sense, arguing that the word should be applied only to those human works that are of higher sophistication and quality—so, for instance, a symphony orchestra might be an example of "culture" while a polka band would not—analysts of popular culture use the word "culture" in a wider sense, without making judgments of value, quality, or taste, so that comic books and Faulkner novels, tuxedos and torn jeans, radio talk shows and university lectures, and the three meals mentioned above are all parts of "culture."

The distinctions between the three classifications of culture (high, folk, and popular) have to do especially with the size of the respective cultures' audiences, and perhaps also the means by which they are transmitted. High or elite culture, often transmitted in written form (a literary magazine, the score of an opera, a gourmet cookbook), has a limited audience by its very intention and is addressed to persons who are perceived to have superior backgrounds or more sophisticated taste. Folk culture, often transmitted orally (family recipes, local legends, regional marriage customs), also has a limited audience, because the oral communication is roughly limited to the more immediate family, community, or other local or regional group. Popular culture might be communicated in many ways, but it most often becomes widespread, and thus popular, through mass media (television, radio, movies, books, magazines, and cyber-communication). As its very name implies, popular culture is marked by its larger audience.

At this point a disagreement has arisen among scholars of popular culture about its further definition. How indispensable are the mass media to the concept of popular culture? One circle of scholars is represented by Ray Browne, a key figure in the founding of the Popular Culture Association and the American Culture Association. They consider popular culture to be the broad "way of life of a people" that "has existed since the most primitive times": in other words, even before the advent of the printing press and other developments of mass media.[3] Athenians laughing at the plays of Aristophanes would be a historical example. This approach to the definition makes it possible to discuss the existence of popular culture throughout virtually the entire range of human history. When this definition is used, popular culture and folk culture sometimes merge and are difficult to distinguish in earlier time periods, although they still contrast with high culture.

Another circle of scholars is represented by Russel Nye, also a central figure in the development of popular cultural analysis as an academic field. They contend that truly popular culture requires a mass audience (created by urbanization and democratization) and technologies of mass distribution (the printing press and the various forms of mass media that followed). Popular culture thus "describes a cultural condition that could not have appeared in Western civilization before the late eighteenth century," Nye asserts.[4] In essence, mass mediation is a basic part of the definition for this group of scholars and not for the other. When we move beyond historical questions and consider the present, however, both perspectives agree that popular culture refers to "that which is (or has been) accepted or approved of by large groups of people," and that the mass media are today of central importance in its transmission.[5] Thus popular culture includes television programs, movies, popular music, comic books, social media, video games, magazines, popular fiction (romance, detective, graphic novels), and much more.

The question remains: how widespread must something be in order to be considered popular? For example, in previous decades, popular music often was measured in general "top forty" lists, but these have given way to more specific categories of music for more targeted audiences: adult contemporary, rock, country, R&B/hip-hop, latin, jazz, blues, and on and on. Some music may still be broadly recognized, but are not the more specific kinds of music examples of popular culture as well, within what we might call sub-universes or subcultures of the larger national or international cultures? We are dealing with spectrums of popularity, and it is difficult to draw clear lines. Yet these very degrees of popularity can be one of the subjects of our analysis: why is it that certain popular cultural forms flourish in some subgroups and not in others?

These comments, then, do not leave us with an absolutely clear definition. The contrasts between popular culture, folk culture, and high culture are instead simply a suggestive typology, and the pure types do not always precisely fit actual examples. Furthermore, an example of popular culture in one time period or geographical location might be high culture in another setting, such as medieval European morality plays, which may have been popular culture when performed by street players centuries ago but become high culture when presented in an American university theater today. In short, as Ray Browne writes, popular culture "is an indistinct term whose edges blur into imprecision,"[6] but, even with its imprecision, the notion of "popular culture" draws our attention to the widespread, common, frequently commercial, and often entertaining aspects of our cultural context as worthy of attention and reflection.

## ANALYZING POPULAR CULTURE

Why should we pay attention to popular culture, even studying it in academic settings? What could we learn? Put most simply, *popular culture both reflects us and shapes us,* and the implications of that twofold dynamic are profound.

On one hand, popular culture reflects us. This strikes many as common sense, because it is the general public that makes something popular. For example, creators and producers offer new television series to the public every year, but their manipulation of publicity and time slots cannot automatically guarantee that a show will be a hit; the public decides, sometimes surprising the pundits. "We" make something popular when it touches a chord within us, perhaps expressing our assumptions and values, or portraying our yearnings, or providing moments of escape. There has to be a reason (or reasons) why great numbers of people choose to watch one television show and not another. The trick, of course, is to figure out what the reason is. In the process, we are essentially trying to learn about ourselves.

Jack Nachbar and Kevin Lause, in their introduction to popular culture analysis at the beginning of *Popular Culture: An Introductory Text,* offer a "Popular Culture Formula" that exemplifies this approach. Their formula states simply that "the popularity of a given cultural element (object, person or event) is directly proportional to the degree to which that element is reflective of audience beliefs and values." Thus, we examine elements of popular culture "not as ends in themselves but as means of unlocking their meaning in the culture as a whole." It is a "quest for meaning" to ask "why audiences choose one cultural element over another" and try to discern what this choice says about those audiences.[7] In a widely used metaphor, popular culture is like a mirror, reflecting who we are. Yet when we look into the mirror, the images are somewhat altered or distorted, because only portions of our realities, interests, values, and desires are reflected back to us, with a selectivity that is influenced by the personal perceptions and intentions of the creative forces behind popular culture. As a result, Nachbar and Lause and others refer to popular culture as a funhouse mirror.[8]

Because popular culture surrounds us, it seems reasonable to assume that its messages and subtle themes influence us as well as reflect us. If popular culture reflects values we already hold, that reflection also serves to reinforce our values and deepen our commitment to them. If selective images emphasize certain groups or experiences and neglect others, our perceptions of reality may be altered. Television programs and commercials of the 1950s, in which African Americans seldom appeared, provide an example. Consistent viewing of such programming helped the dominant white society ignore or forget that African Americans were part of the nation's community, and let African American viewers receive and internalize the message that they were marginal.

Michael Real provides another example of how popular culture shapes us. His book *Mass-Mediated Culture* argues that

> Mass-mediated culture primarily serves the interests of the relatively small political-economic power elite that sits atop the social pyramid. It does so by programming mass consciousness.... For example, while allegedly "giving people what they want," commercial television maximizes private corporate profit, restricts choices, fragments consciousness, and masks alienation.[9]

Kenneth Myers, an evangelical Christian and a journalist, offers a different critique of the subtle influences of popular culture when he emphasizes "the erosion of character, the spoiling of innocent pleasures, and the cheapening of life itself."[10]

Almost all arguments about popular culture's influence, however, include the hope that once we analyze popular culture's subtle dynamics and raise them to a level of consciousness, they will no longer affect us, at least not as powerfully as before, making us more resistant to manipulation. Trusting in this new awareness, activists work to blunt popular culture's effects and perhaps even change the production of popular culture in directions they find more appropriate. This is an indication of a more general conflict between the creators of popular culture and their critics, which illustrates the twofold claim that popular culture both reflects us and shapes us. When crusaders argue that movies, advertisements, video games, and other products of popular culture prompt violence, or demean women, or encourage materialism, popular culture's producers often answer that they are merely reflecting society. On the much debated subject of violence, for instance, critics complain that the frequency of violence in movies or on television has helped create a more violent society, while producers argue that their programs simply express the realities of an already violent society. From the perspective of this essay, such a disagreement presents a false choice, because both claims may be true; it remains appropriate, however, to argue which claim is more significant than the other.

To examine popular culture as both a reflection and a shaping force, what specific strategies or methodologies might we employ to try to discern the underlying meanings and influences of popular culture? The essays in this book will provide examples of a variety of approaches. However, let me first make two general points.

First of all, some discussions that purport to be popular culture analysis limit themselves to a consideration of the intentions of the creators and the nature of the popular culture text or artifact itself. These discussions are valuable, and are akin to literary analyses, but unless we add a focus on audience reception, on how and why the public receives and responds to the element of popular culture, we miss the special insights that the study of popular culture can bring. For example, it may be interesting to hear the inside stories told by producers and cast members of the various *Star Trek* television series, including descriptions of their personal backgrounds and motivations, but the central question for popular culture analysis is why and how *Star Trek* became popular. What attracted the audience? What does its popularity say about the audience? How does it influence the audience?

Secondly, we are likely to discern more about the meanings of popular culture when we examine patterns rather than isolated examples. A critic might discuss a unique, groundbreaking novel by a particular mystery writer, but this novel becomes more significant for popular culture analysis when examined in light of detective fiction as a genre, particularly when it represents a continuing or changing pattern rather than a single anomaly. Single examples tend to focus upon creative uniqueness; patterns and genres point to broader themes and popular response.

## RECOGNIZING RELIGION

The academic examination of popular culture has flourished in recent decades, with the founding of the Popular Culture Association in 1971 and the American Culture Association in 1979, a number of presentations about popular culture at other scholarly conventions like the Modern Language Association and the American Studies Association, and the advent of popular culture commentators in the national media. In the early years religion often was underrepresented in these popular culture discussions. For example, an introductory undergraduate text about popular culture published by the Popular Culture Association in 1992 contained twenty-nine articles, none of which pertained directly to religion.[11] The first session of a Religion and Popular Culture group at a national meeting of the American Academy of Religion did not occur until 1995, with a theme issue in the AAR's journal the following year;[12] some of the essays presented or published there appeared in the first edition of this volume. Thereafter the quantity of scholarship exploring the topic of religion in relation to popular culture has exploded, in books, articles, presentations, and college courses too numerous to count.

Now that religion is included in the discussion, it is important to emphasize that what we call religion can be perceived at several levels. The most readily recognizable manifestation is institutional religion: major religions of the world such as Christianity, Islam, Judaism, Hinduism, Buddhism, and indigenous spiritualities, among others, plus any number of smaller groups. Beyond the institutionalized religions, one often can detect some broad societal assumptions or tendencies about what is holy or what is valued most highly. Examples might include the common assumption that wealth is a measure of success or the tension Americans feel between individualism and the assumed valued of the family. Furthermore, many individuals have their own somewhat unique, personal religious beliefs and practices that do not fit with any particular group. It has become commonplace for many to call the institutionalized groups "religions" and to use the label "spirituality" to refer to general movements and private expressions, thus the prevalent phrase "spiritual but not religious." However, many scholars in religious studies would use "religion" in a broader sense, to include the institutionalized groups, general cultural tendencies, and individual expressions as well.

Thus, some definitions of religion are very inclusive, beyond what is the ordinary meaning of "religion" for many people. When the Christian theologian Paul Tillich calls religion "ultimate concern," or when the authors of an undergraduate text define it as "any person's reliance upon a pivotal value," they see religion as the organizing principle in a person's life, whatever is most important, the value or concern to which everything else is subordinate.[13] While such a definition definitely includes major world religions, it also might include many other passions or priorities for an individual or a society, such as nationalism, or materialism, or sports. Defined this broadly, the topic of religion certainly ought to arise in the process of analyzing popular culture, because popularity is seen as an indication of what the public values, and that might be called their "religion" in its broadest sense.

Other scholars would use the word religion in a narrower way, to refer to human expressions that are closer to the traditional religions most people recognize. Julia Mitchell Corbett's working definition of religion in her textbook *Religion in America* is that a "religion is an integrated system of belief, lifestyle, ritual activities, and institutions by which individuals give meaning to (or find meaning in) their lives by orienting themselves to what they take to be holy, sacred, or of the highest value."[14] This definition still is broad enough to include unconventional religions, or twelve-step programs, or what used to be called the new age movement, but it is more restrictive than the previous definitions cited. Even when defined more narrowly, religion certainly appears frequently in popular culture.

As with our discussion of the concept of "popular culture," we need not arrive here at one conclusive definition of the term "religion," although there is further discussion of definitions in the following sections, especially when we ask whether a feature of popular culture like sports might be considered a religion. For now, it is helpful to see the spectrum of subject matter that is associated with the topic of religion.

In learning about religion and popular culture, we will find ourselves discussing not only the institutional religions we readily recognize, with rabbis, and cathedrals, and revivals. Religion also may be present in discussions of the roles superheroes play as deliverers, or reflections on the struggles of life, or in devotional acts to a celebrity, or in ritual patterns of television viewers.

## FOUR RELATIONSHIPS BETWEEN RELIGION AND POPULAR CULTURE

The topic of religion and popular culture has seen an explosion of interest in recent decades among scholars from very diverse formal educational backgrounds (e.g., theology, history, biblical studies, literature, cultural studies, anthropology, and media studies), who are often unaware of one another's work. It remains an area of study in need of definition, articulated methodologies, and fuller awareness of the diverse contributions already made. This book hopes to contribute to the process with its continuing revisions.

One step is to recognize that religion and popular culture relate to each other in at least four different ways, and each merits examination:

1. Religion in popular culture
2. Popular culture in religion
3. Popular culture as religion
4. Religion and popular culture in dialogue[15]

### *Religion in Popular Culture*

When people hear about religion and popular culture, the examples in this category probably are what first come to mind when religious characters, images, themes, language, and subject matter appear in elements of popular culture. For instance, how often do Catholic nuns, or Buddhist monks, or revivalist preachers appear in movies, and how are they portrayed? Other examples might include the redeemer role played by comic book superheroes, or the frequency of apocalyptic themes, or an apparent public fascination with witches, angels, vampires, and zombies in television series. How does religion appear in expressions of popular culture? How is it portrayed? At what points in popular culture is religion strikingly absent? What does it mean?

Movies, which have received more attention from religion scholars than any other feature of popular culture, can provide helpful illustrations of how religion might appear in popular culture, both explicitly and implicitly. First, there are those films that explicitly focus on religion: *The Passion of the Christ* (2004), *The Ten Commandments* (1956), *The Chosen* (1981), *Gandhi* (1982), and *Little Buddha* (1993) are obvious examples. In addition, many movies include explicit representations of religion or religious figures, although they may not be the focus of the films: priests, monks and nuns, rabbis, evangelists, sun dancers, gothic cathedrals, Muslim prayer rugs, exorcisms, and so on. In all such cases, one might attempt to discern patterns in these portrayals of religion, asking what the patterns reveal about the creative forces behind the images and the audiences who respond.

Religion also makes implicit appearances. For instance, many theologically oriented viewers find allegorical Christ figures in movies, such as the extraterrestrial in *E.T.* (1982), a special being with healing powers who descends to earth, is loved by many, misunderstood and feared by the authorities, and finally undergoes death and resurrection. Many of the Superman movies can be interpreted in this way, most obviously *Superman Returns* (2006). Average viewers may detect nothing religious at all in the movie, but the examples are not subtle. Zach Snyder, the director of the following Superman movie, *Man of Steel* (2013), with similar parallels, commented, "The Christ-like parallels, I didn't make that stuff up. We weren't like, 'Hey, let's add this!' That stuff is there, in the mythology. That is the tried-and-true Superman metaphor."[16] However, as an essay by Dan Clanton in this volume points out, the Jewish themes in Superman are equally strong.[17] Neo in the *Matrix* trilogy of movies (1999–2003) generated considerable debate about whether the implicit religious metaphors are Christian, Buddhist, Jewish, or Gnostic.

Such religious allegories are found not only in characters like E.T. or Superman, but also in plot structures. Robert Jewett and John Shelton Lawrence make such an argument in their book *The American Monomyth,* later republished in substantially revised form as *The Myth of the American Superhero.* They note that Joseph Campbell wrote about a "classical monomyth," a single archetypal plot in which a hero "ventures forth from the world of common day into a region of supernatural wonder: fabulous forces are there encountered and a decisive victory is won: the hero comes back from this mysterious adventure with the power to bestow boons on his fellow man." This plot is based on rites of initiation and is seen in the stories of Ulysses, Aeneas, St. George and the dragon, and countless others. Yet Jewett and Lawrence are convinced that most of American popular culture follows a different singular plot, a distinctively American monomyth: "A community in a harmonious paradise is threatened by evil: normal institutions fail to contend with this threat: a selfless superhero emerges to renounce temptations and carry out the redemptive task: aided by fate, his decisive victory restores the community to its paradisal condition: the superhero then recedes into obscurity." Western movies in which the hero rides into the sunset at the conclusion, as well as the stories of comic book superheroes, provide ready illustrations of this plot. Jewett and Lawrence note that the American monomyth is essentially a secularization of Judeo-Christian redemption dramas: "The supersaviors in pop culture function as replacements for the Christ figure, whose credibility was eroded by scientific rationalism," they write. "But their superhuman abilities reflect a hope of divine, redemptive powers that science has never eradicated from the popular mind."[18]

The American monomyth is only one example of what might be called a mythological approach, borrowing from the study of comparative religion. Films can be examined for "cross-cultural forms, including myth, ritual, systems of purity, and gods," and studied for "the ways Hollywood reinterprets, appropriates, invents, or rejects" these archetypes.[19]

Finally, in addition to characters and plot structures, there are also implicitly religious themes in popular culture stories. Theologians, often Jewish and Christian theologians, have for years been eager to discuss what they see as implicit theological themes in film: love, meaning, forgiveness, sin, and death and resurrection. Through the arts and the responses of their audiences, human beings ask questions of identity and purpose and wrestle with possible answers to these questions. Many theologians are interested in viewing movies to see how "the world" poses the questions, are intrigued when the answers seem to parallel their own faith traditions, and offer critiques when they disagree with the implicit answers. A considerable body of theological literature takes this approach. Andrew M. Greeley, a Catholic priest, sociologist, and prolific author, goes a step further, seeing popular culture in general, and film in particular, as a locus in which one may encounter God. "The film is the sacramental art par excellence; either as a fine or lively art nothing is quite so vivid as film for revealing the presence of God."[20]

Movies thus illustrate how religion might appear on several different levels: through explicit representations, allegorical parallels, and implicit theological themes. Of course, the same variety of manifestations can be found in country music, television comedies, music videos, comic strips, spy stories, science fiction, romance novels, and so forth; religion is represented or expressed in many ways in all of these popular cultural forms.

### Popular Culture in Religion

This category refers to the appropriation of aspects of popular culture by religious groups and institutions. Even more, this category considers the impact of popular culture upon traditionally recognized religious groups, influencing what they believe and how they operate. For instance, when churches or synagogues borrow popular musical styles, or organizational or advertising techniques, or popular culture slogans and icons, are the popular culture appropriations totally neutral, or do they change the religion and the message in some ways? As another example, when the Dalai Lama appears on a billboard, do the religion and the message change or not? What are the dynamics involved?

These influences can be subtle. The thesis of Neil Postman's *Amusing Ourselves to Death: Public Discourse in the Age of Show Business* provides an interesting example of a cultural influence that is both pervasive and yet largely unrecognized. Postman argues that American culture has moved from a print-dominated age to an age of television, and that the shift has literally changed our ways of thinking and the content of our culture. Echoing Marshall McLuhan's aphorism that the medium is the message, Postman maintains that print culture (the age of typography, of exposition), by the very nature of its mode of communication, encouraged coherent, orderly, serious, rational discourse with propositional content. Television, he says, shifts us to an image-based culture that features explosions of images, fragmented rather than coherent, emphasizing sensation and feeling rather than rationality. Postman calls the television era the age of show business, because entertainment is its highest value. He devotes an entire chapter to television's impact on religion, arguing that religion on television is presented simply as entertainment, not because of deficiencies in the televangelists but because of the nature of the medium itself: anything presented on television becomes entertainment. Furthermore, because the pervasiveness of television has shaped the expectations of the entire culture, even when a religious practice (such as a small local church's weekly worship service) is not on television, it is pressured to measure up to entertainment standards. When religion is presented as entertainment, does the basic content and character of religion change? "The danger is not that religion has become the content of television shows," Postman writes, "but that television shows may become the content of religion."[21]

Postman's book is a classic and has been widely influential, but it was published in 1985, and technological changes since then have been breathtaking. In an era of computers, tablets, and smartphones, is the cyber-communication in today's popular culture landscape a further extension of the characteristics of the television age Postman described, or have we entered into another new age with different dynamics? If so, how does that impact the beliefs and practices of religion?

What are other ways in which religions consciously or unconsciously borrow examples, images, language, themes, and assumptions from popular culture as tools for their own purposes? Does such borrowing influence the religion, for good or for ill, sometimes in ways it may not recognize? For example, what does it mean when the supposedly distinctive music of an evangelical Christian youth subculture is expressed in hard rock, heavy metal, alternative, or meditative ("new age") musical styles? As another example, what are the implications of the trend, currently so popular in the culture, of casting religion as a self-help program, for wellness or for prosperity?[22] One more question: when religious groups adopt "the strategies and techniques of modern marketing" from the business world, and "the audience becomes a market and the gospel is transformed into a product," should religious people view these influences as effective adaptation or a threatening transformation?[23] Of the four relationships between religion and popular culture, this one, the impact of popular culture upon religion, has been the least examined.

*Popular Culture as Religion*

A third category involves the argument that popular culture serves as religion or functions like religion for many people. Crucial to these discussions, of course, is one's definition of religion, which we already have considered in a preliminary way. Catherine Albanese has provided a helpful, concise summary of three types of definitions: substantive, functional, and formal.

Substantive definitions of religion focus on the inner core, essence, or nature of religion and define it by this thing-in-itself. They tend to emphasize a relationship with a higher being or beings (God or the Gods) and to be favored by theologians and philosophers. Functional definitions of religion emphasize the effects of religion in actual life. They stress the systems of meaning-making the religion provides and how it helps people deal with the ills, insecurities, and catastrophes of living. Functional definitions are favored by scholars in the social sciences. Lastly, formal definitions of religion look for typically religious forms gleaned from the comparative study of religions and find the presence of religion where such forms can be identified. Religious forms include sacred stories, rituals, moral codes, and communities; and formal definitions of religion tend to be favored by historians of religions.[24]

Most claims about popular culture as religion are based upon functional or formal definitions, but it is possible to find some appeals to substantive definitions as well.

One of the most common examples that might be examined in this way are various "fandoms," subcultures of fans who form communities through social networks and/or at conventions to share their enthusiasm and extend the experience, with costumes, newly created stories and videos, detailed expertise, reenactments, and more. *Star Trek* fans, Trekkies, are among the best known and are the subject of one of this volume's essays, but there are many others, surrounding Harry Potter, Twilight, Sherlock Holmes, Doctor Who, Disney, Star Wars, comic book superheroes, and the Beatles, to name a few. One might mention the devotion of those who followed the Grateful Dead from concert to concert, or Graceland as an Elvis shrine and pilgrimage site. In all of these cases, one might comment that the devotion of the fans seems almost religious, but could that be a serious claim? It would depend on the definition of religion one uses. In light of the definition chosen, do the groups provide public rituals, private rites, myths and symbol systems through which their followers interpret the world, the way traditional religions do? Do they provide meaning and purpose for participants? Are belief systems involved, with basic worldviews and values?

In the end, whether one concludes that the various examples are religions or not, the discussion sheds light on various needs, patterns, and desires of human existence.

In addition to such comparisons with specific features of popular culture, one might also assert that the sum total of American popular culture expresses an overall cultural religion. John Wiley Nelson, in *Your God Is Alive and Well and Appearing in Popular Culture*, another classic book, makes just this claim: "Popular culture is to what most Americans believe as worship services are to what the members of institutional religions believe." Nelson, a theologian, describes what he sees as American cultural religion, with a belief system regarding the nature and source of problems (evil), the source of deliverance, the nature of a resolved situation, and the proper path to the future. In his view, the beliefs of this American cultural religion are generally not consistent with the formal religions to which many Americans claim to adhere. He argues that the Western movie "is the classic ritual form, the 'High Mass,' of the predominant American belief system." Unlike high art, he says, which "challenges one's self-understanding towards self-criticism and insight," the primary function of popular culture as "worship" is "to affirm already held beliefs and values." The mythic pattern of a Western is pervasive, he believes, appearing in *Casablanca* and modern crime dramas as well as stories set in the pioneer American West. The pattern of this basic storyline is important because it reveals and reaffirms what the dominant culture really believes, such as the general public's conviction that they are relatively innocent and that evil comes from outside. "Those institutions normally called 'religions' are explicit in announcing precisely what they believe and in scheduling the ritual dramas of reaffirmation, that is, the worship services. American cultural religion is much less recognizably explicit, but no less powerfully persuasive in our lives," Nelson writes.[25]

When Nelson describes what he sees as an "American cultural religion," he focuses upon its *beliefs*, especially its assumptions about what is unsatisfactory in our present existence and the source of our eventual deliverance. Other scholars give more emphasis to the *forms* of religion, and the parallel forms that appear in popular culture: rituals, symbols, myths, and icons. Yet another approach is to notice that popular culture and traditional religions *function* in similar ways, providing meaning and helping people cope with life's problems. Whether the emphasis is upon essential religious beliefs, religious forms, or religious functions, each avenue of discussion makes it possible to suggest that aspects of popular culture (sports, weight loss programs, shopping, celebrities, and more) might constitute a religion for their most devoted followers.

## Religion and Popular Culture in Dialogue

Other interactions between religion and popular culture do not fit well in the three categories considered thus far. The issue of violence in the media, briefly mentioned earlier, is a good example. When religious leaders become involved in the debate about whether portrayals of violence in movies and on television are harmful to society, it is not a matter of representations of religion in the media (religion in popular culture), nor is it directly a matter of popular culture shaping religion (popular culture in religion). Most of the discussions do not claim that violence has become a sort of religion (popular culture as religion), although it might be possible to make that case. Rather, violence in the media and in society is an ethical issue that concerns both religions and religious people and the general population. Religion wants to take part in the broader discussion.

While this fourth category, religion and popular culture in dialogue, may seem like a catch-all to include discussions that do not belong elsewhere, if one imagines two parties in conversation with each other, there is a coherence to it. We might provisionally refer to two sides of the conversation, religion on one side and popular culture on the other, even though conceptually religion and popular culture are not totally separate entities, and neither does each side speak with one voice. Yet in a generalized sense, there is a dialogue between the two "sides," when they (a) talk to and about the other side, and (b) when they engage in conversation about issues in which they have a shared interest. The term "dialogue" here is meant broadly, including affirmations, denunciations, observations, and shared concerns.

From the religious side, denunciations often receive the most publicity, when Muslim-American leaders complain about the negative portrayal of Muslims in action-adventure movies, or when conservative Christians criticize positive depictions of LGBT relationships in television programs. Yet religious leaders also have spoken appreciatively of aspects of popular culture, for bringing greater awareness of global cultures and religious diversity, or promoting stories about the less fortunate. In the other direction, popular culture voices also speak to and about religion, as when movies like *Spotlight* (2015) portray abusive activities by religious leaders or when songwriters comment on religious hypocrisy, as we hear in Green Day's "East Jesus Nowhere." Other creators of popular culture have been affirming of religion, with country singers regularly including Christian hymns in their albums and movies and television telling heart-warming stories of conflict ending in reconciliation. In the examples cited above, when religious leaders object to or praise how they are portrayed in popular culture, this dialogue overlaps with the first category, religion in popular culture. When general cultural issues and values constitute the topic, however, it belongs more clearly under the heading of religion and popular culture in dialogue.

The dialogue is about much more than whether religious leaders approve of American popular culture or not, or whether popular cultural voices criticize or affirm religion. Popular culture represents and sometimes advances values and perspectives about gender roles, race, sexuality, economic objectives, definitions of success, the relative importance of youth and the elderly, and so on. These issues are not directly about religion, but they are ethical arenas to which religious values pertain, and thus religions of all kinds enter into dialogue with popular culture and its creative forces.

In the United States, Jewish and Christian representatives have historically been the predominant religious voices in these exchanges. The dialogues are being enriched by the addition of voices from other religious traditions, more direct (even face to face) conversations between creators of popular culture and religious representatives at conferences or workshops, and scholarly assessments of the shape of the dialogue.

## CONCLUSION

These four relationships between religion and popular culture are not exclusive categories; in fact, they might better be seen as interactive, helpful in highlighting four directions of scholarly discussion, even though discussions of one aspect can and often do shade into discussions of another. For example, R. Laurence Moore's *Selling God: American Religion in the Marketplace of Culture* describes not only how religion has borrowed commercial practices to promote religion (popular culture in religion) but also how business leaders have employed religion to advance their commercial purposes (religion in popular culture).[26] Christian theologians who highlight the presence of implicit theological themes in novels or television shows (religion in popular culture) often include comparative discussions of religious and cultural assumptions (religion in dialogue with popular culture). There is fluidity among the relationships between religion and popular culture. Though these categories are imprecise, when a person's reflection fits almost totally into one of the categories, the outline of four relationships can be useful in suggesting additional possibilities.

Many of us come to the analysis of popular culture with a particular special interest, related to our own private enthusiasms (comic books, country music, video games, science fiction, or whatever), and we sometimes hesitate to reveal our interest and even fandom to our more "sophisticated" friends. To enter into reflection on the meanings and influences of popular culture out of simple curiosity or because "it's fun" is an effective starting point that requires no apology, and it easily leads to the conviction that we have stumbled upon something that holds promise for significant insight in understanding ourselves, and in understanding religion in the context of our culture.

This volume is intended to survey and widen the discussion, which many of us know only in narrow slices. A broader view allows us to share and borrow methodologies, detect wider patterns, and stimulate our curiosity about new subject areas. The possibilities for research and reflection are endless, because the multifaceted and constantly changing nature of popular culture, and the changing faces of religion as well, assure that there will be no final word.

### DISCUSSION QUESTIONS

1. What could a person possibly learn by analyzing popular culture?

2. Do you agree that popular culture both shapes us and reflects us? If so, what are some examples? If not, explain.

3. This chapter and this book describe four different relationships between religion and popular culture. Do these four relationships make sense? Would you suggest any additional categories?

4. Various definitions of religion are mentioned in this chapter, including Catherine Albanese's three *kinds* of definitions. What definition of religion, or which kind of definition, would you support as most accurate or most helpful? Why?

### NOTES

1. This sentence echoes the title of John Wiley Nelson's classic book on the subject, *Your God Is Alive and Well and Appearing in Popular Culture* (Philadelphia: Westminster Press, 1976).

2. See Jack Nachbar and Kevin Lause, "An Introduction to the Study of Popular Culture: What Is This Stuff that Dreams Are Made Of?" in *Popular Culture:*

*An Introductory Text,* ed. Jack Nachbar and Kevin Lause (Bowling Green, OH: Bowling Green State University Popular Press, 1992), 1–35, esp. 16–17.

3. Ibid., 11.

4. Russel B. Nye, "Notes on a Rationale for Popular Culture," in *The Popular Culture Reader,* ed. Jack Nachbar and John L. Wright (Bowling Green, OH: Bowling Green University Popular Press, 1977), 10–16, quotation from 10.

5. Nachbar and Lause, eds., *Popular Culture Reader,* "Introduction," 5–6.

6. Ray B. Browne, "Popular Culture: Notes Toward a Definition," in Nachbar and Wright, eds., *Popular Culture Reader,* 1–9, quotation from 1.

7. Nachbar and Lause, eds., *Popular Culture Reader,* "Introduction," 5–6.

8. Ibid., 7; examples of the common use of the phrase "funhouse mirror" to describe popular culture include Michael Medved, *Hollywood vs. America: Popular Culture and the War on Traditional Values* (New York: HarperCollins, 1992), 253, and Melissa Ames and Sarah Burcon, *How Pop Culture Shapes the Stages of a Woman's Life: From Toddlers-in-Tiaras to Cougars-on-the-Prowl* (New York: Palgrave Macmillan, 2016), with an Introduction titled "Funhouse Mirrors— Popular Culture's Distorted View of Girl/Womanhood."

9. Michael R. Real, *Mass-Mediated Culture* (Englewood Cliffs, NJ: Prentice-Hall, 1977), xi.

10. Kenneth A. Myers, *All God's Children and Blue Suede Shoes: Christians and Popular Culture* (Wheaton, IL: Crossway Books, 1989), xiii.

11. Jack Nachbar and Kevin Lause, eds., *Popular Culture: An Introductory Text* (Bowling Green, OH: Bowling Green State University Popular Press, 1992).

12. *Journal of the American Academy of Religion* 61, no. 3 (Fall 1996).

13. Paul Tillich, *Dynamics of Faith* (New York: Harper & Row, 1957), 1–4; Robert C. Monk et al., *Exploring Religious Meaning,* 3rd ed. (Englewood Cliffs, NJ: Prentice-Hall, 1987), 3.

14. Julia Mitchell Corbett, *Religion in America,* 3rd ed. (Upper Saddle River, NJ: Prentice-Hall, 1997), 7.

15. In addition to the four relationships between religion and popular culture considered here, one might argue for a fifth possibility, religion as popular culture. If popular culture sometimes functions as religion, can the inverse be true as well? Can religious activity or production not only take on the features of popular culture, but function fully as popular culture? This might apply especially to historical situations where a single religion is central to a culture as a whole, prior to the complications of secularization and religious diversity. Pre-Lenten carnivals in medieval Europe or camp meetings in nineteenth-century America could be viewed as examples of religious activity and popular culture at the same time; the widespread wearing of crosses or Taoist

symbols as jewelry might be cited as modern examples. Yet all of these could be considered extensions of "religion in popular culture," although they near the limits of the category. We recognize the fluidity of these categories and the possibility that at various points others will find additional categories possible.

16. Jennifer Vineyard, "'Man of Steel' director Zack Snyder on Superman's Christ-like parallels," www.cnn.com/2013/06/14/showbiz/zack-snyder-man-of-steel.

17. See Simcha Weinstein, *Up, Up, and Oy Vey: How Jewish History, Culture and Values Shaped the Comic Book Superhero* (Baltimore: Leviathan Press, 2006) as one of several books about the Jewish influence on comic books in general.

18. Robert Jewett and John Shelton Lawrence, *The American Monomyth* (Garden City, NY: Anchor Press/Doubleday, 1977), xix–xx. Their quotation from Joseph Campbell is from his *The Hero with a Thousand Faces* (New York: Meridian, 1956), 30. Lawrence and Jewett's revised volume (the names are reversed for this edition) is *The Myth of the American Superhero* (Grand Rapids, MI.: Eerdmans, 2002.).

19. See the discussion of "mythological criticism" in Joel W. Martin and Conrad E. Oswalt Jr., eds., *Screening the Sacred: Religion, Myth, and Ideology in Popular American Film* (Boulder, CO: Westview Press, 1995), 6.

20. Andrew Greeley, *God in Popular Culture* (Chicago: Thomas More Press, 1988), 245–46.

21. Neil Postman, *Amusing Ourselves to Death: Public Discourse in the Age of Show Business* (New York: Penguin Books, 1985), 124.

22. Three examples from dramatically different perspectives are Leonard Sweet, *The Jesus Prescription for a Healthy Life* (Nashville: Abingdon Press, 1996); David W. Jones and Russell S. Woodbridge, *Health, Wealth, and Happiness: Has the Prosperity Gospel Overshadowed the Gospel of Christ?* (Grand Rapids, MI: Kregel Publications, 2010); Kate Bowler, *Blessed: A History of the American Prosperity Gospel* (New York: Oxford University Press, 2013).

23. Quentin J. Schultze expresses concerns about such developments in *Televangelism and American Culture: The Business of Popular Religion* (Grand Rapids, MI: Baker Book House, 1991), 14–17.

24. Catherine L. Albanese, *America: Religions and Religion* (Belmont, CA: Wadsworth, 1981), xxi.

25. John Wiley Nelson, *Your God Is Alive and Well and Appearing in Popular Culture* (Philadelphia: Westminster Press, 1976), 16, 30, 196, 19.

26. R. Laurence Moore, *Selling God: American Religion in the Marketplace of Culture* (New York: Oxford University Press, 1994).

# PART I

# Religion in Popular Culture

This book is organized around four potential relationships between religion and popular culture. Essays in the first section look at one of the most obvious relationships between religion and popular culture, which is that sometimes religion appears as a subject in popular culture. When I tell people that I study religion and popular culture, they almost always imagine this relation between the two. They want to discuss the portrayals of Hindus or Evangelical Christians in television's longest running cartoon series *The Simpsons* (1989—present), or to examine the ideas about Mormons and Mormonism in the highly successful Broadway musical *The Book of Mormon* (2011—present), and they still want to tell me why they liked or hated Mel Gibson's 2004 film *The Passion of the Christ*. The most obvious relationship between religion and popular culture is that particular religions of the world, represented by religious figures, symbols, rituals, and stories are often elements of the stories popular culture tells. This presence of religion can be quite explicit, as when a character wears a burka to signal that she is a Muslim. They can also be more subtle, as in the implicit nature worship in *Avatar* (2009). If you accept the premise that the stories we tell are important, that they are not simply entertainment but an important way to make sense of the world, then you can see why people would read them carefully, seeking to understand their structures and clarify their meanings.

Yet, not everyone is comfortable with the appearance of religion in popular culture. Some people find it inherently trivializing to see any sacred matters treated as entertainment. Others are offended by particular portrayals of religion, especially of their own religion. These groups would often prefer that religion be protected from imaginative use by non-believers or people of other faiths. But others argue that the discussion of religion is not exempt from principles of free speech. Or, they think of these uses of religion in popular culture as an important part of America's symbol system through which people think about the world, explore models of identity, present and challenge ethical systems, and articulate deeply held values. Whatever the reader's attitudes about particular portrayals of religion, the authors of these chapters think that we will better understand religion and its place in the United States if we look carefully at the stories popular culture tells about religion.

It is not surprising that many students of religion take a literary approach to the study of religion and popular culture in which they think about popular culture as a collection of stories to be unpacked. This parallels a common way of thinking about religion itself. Sacred texts and stories are treasured and preserved within religious communities as a sacred heritage. Zen Buddhist teachers tell enigmatic stories called koan, some as simple as the oft repeated Zen question, "What is the sound of one hand clapping?" Christians recount Jesus' parables such as that of "the good Samaritan." The Torah tells the story of the Hebrew people and their God, including the exciting tale of Moses leading the Hebrew people out of slavery in Egypt. Those who study religion are typically trained to think about the stories a religion tells about itself, how they reveal what the religion regards as sacred, and how it explains the origins of the world. They ask where these stories come from, how they explain our human situation. Attention to questions of race, gender, and class leads them to examine who is named and featured in stories and who is absent or unseen, who has power and privilege and who does not. They consider the way stories express moral values and norms, explaining the world we live in. Even when they are studying religious objects, spaces, or practices they often think about the way these elements are being used to tell a particular story.

These chapters draw attention to particular stories that American popular culture tells about religion. The authors ask many of the same questions they would ask about traditional religious stories. What are the literary and cultural contexts in which these stories were produced? What are the reoccurring elements, narrative patterns, characters, symbols, places and objects that are used in constructing a story? How are they used, revised or combined in unique ways within a particular story? These studies suggest nuanced readings that seek out religious elements in popular cultural stories and ask what this suggests about what is regarded as sacred and profane in American culture.

Before turning to the chapters and their particular discussions of religion in popular culture, it may be useful to acknowledge some criticisms of this literary approach to understanding religion and popular culture. First, important as sacred texts and stories are in understanding religion, religion also includes beliefs, doctrines, practices, spaces, and objects. Similarly, as important as a good story is in popular culture, focusing only on popular stories can lead us to miss other elements of popular culture. People play video games, engage in costume play, collect objects and memorabilia, create and listen to music and videos, practice yoga, get tattoos, and dress in ways that express their identities and express their opinions. Much of this may be related to stories, but it is not reducible to the stories.

Secondly, some people suggest that a literary approach, with its metaphor of reading to describe how we engage with popular culture, reduces other aesthetic forms to their narratives in a way that misses the power of sound, image, and movement. Critics of this approach ask whether these acts of critical "reading" treat film, music videos, television show, games, dances, and concerts as literary texts in ways which reduce them to summaries of their plots and miss the way that sound, image and movement contributes to the audience's experience.

Finally, these approaches are based on a model of literary or textual criticism in which a trained careful reader is assumed to be able to locate the core meaning of a text, as though that text had a single right meaning inserted by the author. Certainly a good interpreter helps us see an element of religion or an example of popular culture more clearly, to tease out its nuance. But this sometimes leads to the assumption that there is a single "right" interpretation of an example. It is well to be reminded that these are not the only readings of these stories. Sometimes critics' interpretations, while they are interesting and insightful, do not tell us much about how a popular audience uses and interprets the text. It is helpful to think about what other interpretations there might be, and how they grow out of different emphases that focus on different elements of the story. This may be particularly important when we think about the popular. We may want to know about how most readers, or readers in particularly groups, interpret a story.

The essays in this section provide rich examples of the ways that religion is presented in popular culture. They help us think about how religion informs the popular imagination, providing images and narratives that offer interpretations of the origin of particular people. They also examine how popular culture draws on and expresses particular attitudes about religion or particular religions.

In *The Origins of Superman* Dan Clanton looks at an ongoing popular story. He considers how the story of the Man of Steel has been shaped by the mythologies of two distinct religious traditions, Judaism and Christianity. Further, he invites us to consider how our own religious location and familiarities lead us to notice particular religious elements in a popular story and to miss others. Clanton's discussion of *Superman: The Movie* (1978) is a clear example of the way that the religion in popular culture may be *implicit*. While he points out that there are clear parallels between the story of Christ and the story told about Superman's origin in this movie, the connection is not explicit. The story of the Christ has a residue of meanings in Western cultures that helps us understand the claims the film makes about Superman's role in society.

In the second and fourth of these chapters, Jane Iwamura's *The Oriental Monk* and *Monstrous Muslims* by Sophia Arjana, the authors look at the stories that American popular culture has told over time about particular minority communities. These essays look at the way that particular minority communities and their religions have been portrayed in popular culture, and at the purpose they serve in the narratives dominant cultures tell about themselves and others. Both suggest that these portrayals should not be thought of as accurate presentations of the people described, their beliefs and practices, but as reflections of American attitudes, curiosities, and anxieties about religious and racial difference.

*Myth and Reality in Adventure Time* by Elijah Siegler looks at how even a form like cartoons for children seeks to establish an imaginative world that rests on a reliable system of mythology. He asks what we mean by *myth* in popular and scholarly usage and considers why the term has been important in religious and cultural studies. Finally, he makes a case for increased attention to myth within television programs as an expression of religion in popular culture.

Jason Bivins's *Religion and Heavy Metal* suggests that this subcultural form of popular music has been intertwined with religion and obsessed with God and the devil. He teases four ways heavy metal communities have represented quite different attitudes about religion and its place in society.

Jeffrey H. Mahan
Iliff School of Theology

# CHAPTER ONE

# The Origin(s) of Superman

## Reimagining Religion in the Man of Steel

DAN W. CLANTON JR.

Superman is possibly the most ubiquitous symbol of American popular culture there is. He is found in comic books, newspaper strips, graphic novels, radio and movie serials, television series, feature films, and a whole host of tchotchkes and other examples of "material culture." But in the beginning, he was just an idea cooked up by two Jewish teenagers from Cleveland: Jerry Siegel and Joe Shuster. They had a difficult time getting anyone to publish it, but when Superman saw the light of day in a new art form called the "comic book" in June 1938, he was an immediate success.

From the beginning Superman stories have contained potentially religious or scriptural references or echoes, leading interpreters to suggest that there are religious/scriptural meanings or subtexts within "Superman."[1] Surprisingly some of these interpreters see these subtexts as obviously Jewish, while others understand them as clearly Christian. In what follows, I will show that cultural artifacts like "Superman" can be *religiously multivalent,* that is, different interpreters find various kinds of symbols and themes when examining the same aesthetic product. To do so, I will examine some possibly religious elements within the 1978 Richard Donner film *Superman: The Movie* in order to demonstrate how some readers/viewers can see Superman as another in a long line of Jewish heroes, while others see him as an obvious Christ figure.

Why can people read the same stories or watch the same film and come away with very different interpretations? Where does meaning exists—is it solely in a text, or does the viewer/reader/hearer play a role in determining what something means? If they do, can texts mean anything the reader wants them to, or does the text somehow constrain or limit its potential meanings?[2] I argue that meaning emerges in the complex interaction between interpreter and text, so that meaning is negotiated between certain clues in and information about a text, and the experiences and interpretive expertise of the interpreter. Neither the text nor the reader/hearer/viewer is totally responsible for what a given story means.

One constant in the history of Superman is a preoccupation with his origin. Starting soon after his introduction in print, Superman's origin story was told and retold in different formats by different writers and artists with different details included or omitted. The significance of this is that many of these later additions can be interpreted as carrying theological significance. Below, I will briefly describe the first origin story for Superman and note how three subsequent key retellings of that story add particulars to flesh out the Man of Steel's background. Given space constraints, I will then focus mainly on *Superman: The Movie* and simply note plot components therein which could hold potentially religious and/or scriptural significance. I will also discuss several Jewish and Christian readings of this film, noting particular themes and common threads among these readings. Finally, I will assess the significance of our project for understanding popular culture and religion.

In June 1938, comic readers met a new character in the pages of *Action Comics* #1: a brightly attired alien who, remarkably, looked just like a human. This first origin story for Superman is brief and direct, consisting of only seven panels on only one page, without any of the verbosity and pomposity one finds in later iterations.[3] First, we are shown "a distant planet" that "was destroyed by old age," but not before a "scientist placed his infant son within a hastily devised space-ship, launching it toward Earth!" The narrator informs us that the child arrives safely on Earth, a "passing motorist" finds the craft, and the "sleeping babe within" is promptly deposited in an orphanage, where the child develops wondrous powers. The final panels tell the reader how Superman as an identity was formulated when "Clark decided he must turn his titanic strength into channels that would benefit mankind." The result of this decision is the creation of "Superman," who is a "champion of the oppressed, the physical marvel who had sworn to devote his existence to helping those in need!"

In the context of discussing the religious symbolism both of and in Superman's origin(s), we are forced to admit that there is precious little explicit evidence in *Action Comics* #1. That is, there are no specific scriptural citations or allusions and no obvious thematic parallels with religious or theological traditions to which Siegel and Shuster would have been exposed. All we can say confidently about the religious content of the original origin is that we see an alien being with great power make a conscious decision to use that power for the betterment, not the domination, of a people not his own. And while there are examples and paradigms within various religious traditions of powerful beings using their power compassionately and altruistically, any attempt to draw specific parallels with individual beings would result in only limited analytic usefulness. Put differently, we will have to wait for specific sacred resonances until we examine later versions of Superman's origin(s).

No one could have predicted the immense popularity of Superman.[4] Capitalizing on this, their publishers gave Siegel and Shuster what they had always dreamed of: a daily newspaper comic strip.[5] In the first twelve daily strips (published in January 1939), readers learned much more about Superman's home planet Krypton, including information about his birth parents and why they had made the decision to send him away.[6] In Strip #1 we are introduced to Jor-L and Lora, told that the former is "Krypton's foremost scientist," and shown the birth of their son, Kal-L. Suddenly, a terrifically powerful earthquake "commences to topple" the family's home. Luckily, the family survives, but Jor-L subsequently announces that "due to an internal cataclysm, Krypton will explode to fragments!" Strip #6 is an especially moving section, as both parents bemoan what the looming destruction of the planet means for their infant son. Lora's wistful desire that they "could be up there [among the stars], safe to pursue our life as we please!" gives Jor-L the "solution" to their predicament: "I'll build a ship ... An Ark of space! We'll transport our planet's entire populace to another world!" The governing Council of Krypton refuses to believe Jor-L's diagnosis and prescription, but he secretly has built a "model space-flier" that he hopes will succeed as a test flight to "the only nearby planet capable of supporting life": Earth. Before long, we witness the beginning of the final conflagration that will destroy the planet. Both Jor-L and Lara decide that Kal-L should be placed in the "flier" and sent to Earth. Strip #10 details the "self-sacrificing gesture" of the boy's parents and the explosion of Krypton. Kal-L lands safely on Earth, and a "passing motorist" plucks the child from the burning ship and takes him to "an orphan asylum."

Obviously, the language used by Jor-L to describe the craft he wants to build to ferry the inhabitants of Krypton to safety is key for our purposes: he calls it "an Ark of space." Given the context—an impending cataclysm initially known to and later only believed in by one man and his family that will prove fatal to all living creatures on a planet—and the specific use of the term "Ark," it becomes difficult to avoid the conclusion that this is an explicit reference to two stories from the Torah. First is the obvious connection with the story of Noah in Genesis 6–9, in which Noah is commanded by God to construct an "ark" (in Hebrew, *tevah*) in 6.14 in order to save a segment of the life forms on the planet, while leaving the remainder to drown (6.6). This story clearly parallels Jor-L's desire to rescue the "entire populace" of Krypton and relocate them to Earth prior to the destruction of the planet.[7] The second connection is perhaps not as obvious, since it depends on knowledge of biblical Hebrew and an awareness of a specific term whose meaning is often obscured in English. In Exodus 1, Pharaoh orders that all male Hebrew children be killed, because he is concerned about the increasing numbers and power of the Hebrews who have settled in Egypt. At the outset of Exodus 2, we are told that a Levite woman has a baby boy, whom she hides for three months. In 2.3 the narrator tells us that, no longer able to conceal the boy, she got a basket (*tevah*) put him in it, and sent him down the river, where he would eventually be found by Pharaoh's daughter and named Moses. The significance of this detail lies in (a) the fact that the Hebrew word *tevah* is only used twice in the Torah: once in the story of Noah, and once here; and (b) in the story of Moses, the word designates the vessel used by a parent in order to secure a safe future for her son in an alien culture to which he will have to acculturate to survive.[8] These echoes of Noah and Moses sounded by both the general context of strips ##1–12 and the more specific use of the term "Ark" by Jor-L signal the earliest explicit religious reference in Superman's origin(s), and as such provide us with our first important piece of data in determining how different interpreters can interpret Superman's story as resonating with different religious traditions.

With Superman's debut in newspapers, he became even more popular.[9] Nothing like this had been experienced before in the fledgling genre of comic books. In 1939, not only was a Sunday newspaper comic strip introduced, but the publishers decided to try something new: a comic book bearing his name and containing only Superman stories. The result was *Superman* #1, in which Siegel and Shuster introduced the Kents, Superman's parents here on Earth, who advise him both to use his powers to help others and to hide his alien identity and gifts from humanity.[10] Gone, though, is all the narrative elaboration regarding Krypton found in the newspaper dailies from earlier in 1939. Instead, we are simply shown an "experimental rocket-ship" speeding away from an exploding planet with no familial biographical information or cultural context provided. Next, we see the ship sitting on Earth and "an elderly couple" standing next to it in place of the "passing motorist" of the previous two origins. This couple, named the Kents, take the "poor" child to an orphanage, but at this point, a new wrinkle is introduced: the Kents later return to the orphanage and ask if they can adopt the child. The reader is soon shown the impact of the addition of the Kents to the origin: they provide "love and guidance" for the boy, which will help in "shaping his future." Pa Kent (no first name is provided here) advises him to "hide ['this great strength of yours'] from people or they'll be scared of you!" His adoptive mother, Mary, exhorts, "But when the proper time comes, you must use it to assist humanity." Including the Kents and expounding on their influence on how Clark (his name is finally provided) grows to understand his identity and decides on the altruistic use of his gifts allows for the assigning of a motive for helping humanity. The insertion of the Kents allows the reader to see and hear why Clark decides to use his powers for good, namely, because that is the way he was raised. Of the remaining content in this origin, only one panel presents new information to the reader absent from the 1938 origin: an image of Clark standing over the Kents' graves, with the narration that even though their deaths "greatly grieved" him, "it strengthened a determination that had been growing in his mind." That "determination" is to become Superman, and therefore put his Earth parents' admonitions into practice by using his strength to help humanity.

In sum, the introduction of the Kents is significant for two main reasons. First, their advice to Clark introduces an ethical theme into Superman's story that had previously been absent. Up to this point, we readers have been unsure as to why he does what he does. By providing the ethical exhortation of his mother, readers now know that the decision to behave morally was due to exposure to some—at this point seemingly generic—system of ethical thought. Later writers and scholars would spill a lot of ink trying to specify the origin and content of that ethical system for an obvious reason: if Superman acts in such and such a way, then it becomes easier to draw a parallel between that moral action and the ethical thought of a specific religious tradition. Once that parallel is drawn, Superman can be "claimed" as a symbol and/or outgrowth of that religious tradition, lending credence to its influence within American popular culture, as well as providing a powerful tool for proselytizing purposes. Moreover, the fact that Clark's adoptive mother is named "Mary" might be seen as reinforcing the larger theme that emerges with the introduction of ethics—namely, a parallel between Superman and the Christ of the New Testament. Simplifying the Gospels, one might come away with an image of the Christ as one who descends from the heavens as an alien yet has both a human presence and appearance, who wishes to help humanity via his superhuman powers ... and who has a human mother named Mary. Even so, at this point we should not make too much of these parallels; there are far too many details and plot points missing for a substantive link.

To be sure, there are other retellings of Superman's origin between 1939 and the 1978 blockbuster *Superman: The Movie*. However, this film is possibly the best known and most accessible example of adding prospective religious aspects to Superman's origin story. *Superman: The Movie* makes four narrative additions to the by then standard origin story found in the comic books and newspaper strips mentioned above, all revolving around two speeches by Superman's biological father Jor-El, which could be read as allusions to biblical texts and/or religious experiences generally.

As we try to understand the relationship(s) between *Superman: The Movie* and various Jewish and Christian interpretations of it, two key questions arise. What features of the story might signify a specific religious tradition over and against another? And, in what ways have readers/interpreters/scholars understood Superman religiously? In Jewish readings of the film, there are three themes which represent the building blocks of the argument for Superman's Jewishness: the "godlike" nature of Superman's family name; the theme of immigration for the sake of survival, including adopting a "dual identity"; and the parallels with Old Testament and/or Jewish heroes, most often Moses.[11] The Christian readings likewise emphasize four aspects of the aforementioned additions, including Jor-El as "heavenly father"; a sense that the parallels with Moses actually point to an identification with Christ; Kal-El (Clark) as the "only son" sent with a "divine mission" with a "hidden identity"; and most obviously and thoroughgoing, the view that Superman is a kind of "Christ figure."[12]

*First*, in Jor-El's farewell speech to Kal-El on Krypton, he notes, "The son becomes the father, and the father the son."[13] This language echoes the complicated theme of "residing in" one finds in Jesus' "Farewell Discourse" in the Gospel of John, chapters 14–17.[14] Here Jesus helps his disciples understand the intricate and intimate relationship between him, God, and the Holy Spirit (called the Paraclete in 14.26), and also reassures them that when he ascends to return to the Father, the Paraclete will remain with them as a substitute divine presence. To demonstrate this web of relations, Jesus employs seemingly confusing language, such as when he tells his disciples that after he departs they will know that "I am in my Father, and you in me, and I in you" (14.20). By doing so, Jesus provides a blueprint for readers to understand how to become disciples themselves.

In this scene, Jor-El is obviously "the father," which by extension makes him a godlike figure. Some Jewish interpreters pick up on this characterization and link it to the familial name "El." For example, Rabbi Simcha Weinstein discusses the significance of the name "El," which "is one of the ancient names for God used throughout the Bible." Similarly, Weinstein claims, the proper name Kal "is the root of several Hebrew words meaning 'with lightness,' 'swiftness,' 'vessel,' and 'voice.'"[15] Christian readers, too, understand Jor-El as a kind of divine father. Anton Karl Kozlovic, a specialist in religion and film, lists twelve examples of the overlap between Jor-El and God, including the name El; the cinematography of the film; and Jor-El's association with "the colour white," commonly thought to be the "iconic signature colour of the Divine."[16]

*Second*, after Clark enters the Fortress of Solitude and encounters the electronic version of his dead Kryptonian father, they embark upon a twelve-year tutelage. At its conclusion, Jor-El exhorts him to "rejoin your new world and serve its collective humanity. Live as one of them, Kal-El, and discover where your strength and power are needed. But always hold in your heart the pride of your special heritage." There is a literary form/ genre in the Hebrew Bible in which persons are singled out and commissioned for a specific task by God, that scholars creatively call "commission narratives." Most of them are in the prophetic books, such as Isaiah 6 and Jeremiah 1, but other examples include Exodus 3 (Moses) and Judges 6 (Gideon). In the New Testament, Paul has this role in Galatians 2 and Acts 9, 22, and 26. If we analyze Jor-El's speech as a commission narrative, we see both overlaps with and departures from the classic biblical model. Superman experiences most of the six observable components of the classic commissioning narrative.[17] Clark is *confronted* with the divine or the sacred when he discovers the green crystal, sets out on his journey, and witnesses the creation of the Fortress. There is an *introductory word* when Jor-El introduces himself before they embark on Clark's education. After this twelve-year period ends, Jor-El *commissions* his son using imperative or commanding verbs to indicate what he wishes him to do as a result of their encounter. Unlike many of those commissioned in the Bible, Clark/Kal-El offers no *objection* to the task Jor-El sets before him.[18] Since Kal-El offers no objection to the commission, strictly speaking a *reassurance* and *sign* are not necessary, but it seems that he still receives them in the form of his uniform and heightened powers, on the one hand, and the remainder of Jor-El's speech, on the other.

For Jewish readers, the language here regarding the "new world" coupled with the exhortation always to remember "your special heritage" brings to mind the theme of immigration. Arie Kaplan, author of *From Krakow to Krypton: Jews and Comic Books,* notes the significance of Superman's identity as a "refugee": "Superman, though an alien, can pass as one of us, even though he is an immigrant—in fact, the ultimate immigrant, the supreme stranger in the strangest land, and thus the supreme metaphor for the Jewish experience."[19] The sociologist Harry Brod is especially interested in the choice to give Kal-El a secret human identity. Like Kaplan, he posits that the significance of Superman's secret identity is connected to a gender-based stereotype of Jewish men. Siegel and Shuster's story only works psychologically, he says, if we know that people in it see Clark as "a timid, socially inept, physically weak, clumsy, sexually ineffectual quasi intellectual": "In other words, the classic Jewish nebbish."[20] But, continues Brod, "It is the combination of Superman's invincibleness and the nebbish-like characterization of Clark Kent that makes Superman such a Jewish character."[21] That is, the stereotypically Jewish Clark is emblematic of an "old world" sensibility and (anti-) masculinity, whereas Superman's physical virility and courage represents a new context, a new home in America for Jews.[22]

*Third,* in Jor-El's final speech, he states: "They can be a great people, Kal-El, they wish to be. They only lack the light to show the way." Within biblical literature, light is a multivalent symbol. The light mentioned in Genesis 1.3 as being created on the first day is clearly not sunlight, since this is not created until Day Four (1.14–19). Jewish interpreters generally see this light as reflective of "the splendor of the divine presence."[23] They often point to Psalm 104.2, which describes God as being clothed in majesty, "wrapped in light as with a garment."[24] Christians, on the other hand, tend to read the light imagery in Genesis 1.3 in tandem with the characterization of Jesus as "the light of the world" in John 8.12 and in the prologue to John, where the narrator says: "The life was the light of all people. The light shines in the darkness, and the darkness did not overcome it" (1.4–5). This light imagery in Jor-El's speech could be heard as indicating that his son will be the agent of moral change among humans via his servant leadership. In other words, Jor-El intends Kal-El to "shine his light" so as to move others to live morally and fulfill their desire to be a "great" people.[25]

This charge to be a heroic moral exemplar, along with the film's emphasis on sending the child away to protect him from harm, is addressed by Jewish interpreters in the context of discussing the parallels between Moses and Superman. Weinstein lists a number of overlaps between Moses' story in Exodus 1–15 and Superman. For example, the fate of the Kryptonians resembles that of the firstborn male Jews in Egypt; just like Kal-El's parents, Moses' mother sends him away to protect him from this fate; both Moses and Superman are "raised in foreign cultures"; both are commissioned to help people; and both hide their true identities.[26] Similarly, in his section on Superman and Moses, Brod first notes the tradition of "Jews making illustrated books" in connection with the *Haggadah,* the text, often illustrated and child-friendly, used by Jews during the religiously didactic holiday of Passover.[27] As Brod puts it, this text tells the story of

> Moses, sent off in a small vessel by his parents to save him from the death and destruction facing his people. He is then raised among people to whom he really is an alien, but who do not suspect his secret identity, and he grows up to become a liberator and champion of the oppressed, with the aid of miraculous superpowers displayed in some truly memorable action scenes. Sound at all familiar?[28]

It certainly sounds familiar to Christian interpreters like Ken Schenck, who acknowledges the parallels with Moses that Weinstein and Brod point out. However, he, like other Christian readers who see Moses as a prototype of Jesus, adapts/appropriates those parallels to reinforce the analogy between Superman and Jesus.[29] Schenck writes that Superman's

> story also resembles the early life of Moses, whose parents sent him off in a basket down the Nile in order to save him from Pharaoh, who ordered that newly born male sons of the Israelite slaves be killed. However, even this similarity echoes the early life of Jesus, whose parents flee to Egypt with the infant, escaping King Herod's edict to kill all male infants in Bethlehem. In the New Testament the early followers of Jesus believed him to be the long, awaited redeemer of God's people, just like Moses. In fact, Jesus was considered the "New Moses."[30]

The Christian educator Stephen Skelton also mentions the Moses imagery prevalent in both the comics and the films, noting that among the "pre-Christ figures" he examines, "Moses is the preeminent one, more so than Samson and Hercules combined."[31]

*Finally,* Jor-El ends his speech by saying, "For this reason, above all, their capacity for good, I have sent them you, my only son." The characterization of Kal-El as "my only son" in concert with the above three additions reinforces the possibility of reading the film messianically, that is, interpreting Superman as a kind of Christ figure.[32] Christian readings of the film's fourth and final addition focus intently on Superman as a metaphor for Christ. Roy M. Anker discusses Jor-El's farewell speech and how it engages "in sophisticated terms the mysterious notion at the heart of the Christian conception of God: the Holy Trinity."[33] Anker connects this speech with John 3.16 ("For God so loved the world that he sent his only begotten son . . . "), writing: "The language of light, redemption, spiritual aspiration, and, most of all, of biblical messiahship ... fastens clearly and tightly to the Christ story."[34]

For Anker, it is Jor-El's intention—the "commission" noted above—that demonstrates "[h]ow intentionally the filmmakers constructed the theme of the Incarnation."[35] This "one drastic departure from the story told in the original ... comic-book *Superman* series" allows the film not only to echo texts like John 1, but also to illustrate "Jor-El's steadfast resolve ... to send Kal-El to a place where he might do much good with his extraordinary powers."[36] To be sure, other Christian interpreters examine the parallels the film seems to establish between Superman and Christ. For example, Rev. Edward Mehok writes, "Both Christ and Superman represent the fulfillment—one religious and the other secular—of basic human hopes for a messiah. Both are savior figures that people of all ages and religions have dreamed about and longed for."[37] This claim is also found in Skelton's book-length Christian interpretation of Superman: "Superman is not Jesus Christ. But he is a Christ figure, a figure resembling Christ—as we all should be. That said, the story of Superman bears some incredible parallels to the story of the Super Man, Jesus Christ."[38] However, Anker delves deeper than both Schenck and Skelton, focusing on the "christomorphic" character of the plot, that is, how the film weaves a narrative that thematically emulates or "transfigures" the story of Jesus, ultimately becoming what Anker terms a parable that engenders hope.[39] He continues:

> In the case of the first two *Superman* films ... Superman as a Christ figure is not a random allusion or image simply pasted over the top of displays of special effects or old-style heroism. Rather, in what is a rare accomplishment in Hollywood, the whole of the film serves to elucidate and impart the surprise, wonder, and delight of the fantastic possibility of an incarna-

tion of divine love itself. And that characterization is no simple miracle-working trickster in a cape or spider webs but a notion of God that features an extravagantly loving servant who comes out of nowhere, be it Krypton or Kansas, to suffer and triumph for bedraggled human creatures.[40]

Anker's focus on love and servanthood clearly reinforces the claim by Christian interpreters that Superman is a "Christ figure," carrying out a commission from his heavenly father to bring light to humanity through his moral example. Of course, as we have seen, Jewish viewers could just as easily claim that this divine commission to improve humankind morally hearkens back to stories about Moses in the Torah.

We have examined four key additions *Superman: The Movie* makes to Superman's generally accepted origin story that make potentially religious and/or scriptural imagery or allusions, which were seized upon by later interpreters as data to argue that Superman has either a Jewish or Christian subtext or identity. The purpose of doing so was to demonstrate the religious multivalency of "Superman" as an aesthetic discourse. But what does this tell us about the study of religion and popular culture?

This examination of Superman reveals four issues in the discussion of religion and popular culture. *First,* it demonstrates the difficulty of the subject by displaying the interdisciplinary demands inherent in such an enterprise. This work requires scholars not only to have training in the academic study of religion, but also expertise and/or experience in other fields as well; in our case, in literary theory and comic studies.

*Second,* these disparate understandings of the same texts illustrate the variety of possible interpretations of any popular cultural text. This variety is a consequence of viewing meaning as being negotiated in the encounter between text and reader. Put differently, if both I—a straight, white, Southern-born, male Jew with a PhD. in Religious and Theological Studies—and someone with a different sociocultural background, religious beliefs, and educational experiences read the same text, we will filter its meaning through different experiential/environmental perceptive grids and understand it differently, noticing different aspects of it or allusions within the text and/or what we can know about the world behind the text.

*Third,* this study shows how important it is for interpreters to pursue knowledge of the history of how a given discourse develops. We would not have been able to comment on the way(s) in which *Superman: The Movie* alters or revises previous origin stories without knowledge of those previous stories. To understand any (popular) cultural product it is useful to understand the history of interpretive conversations about the creation(s). Of course, one does not have to be aware of all of the examples we delve into above to find pleasure in reading a Superman comic or watching a Superman cartoon. However, a viewer who knows the genealogy of the character and has some knowledge of the major story arcs in earlier comics can appreciate the artistic choices and narrative sophistication in later examples. This allows the reader or viewer to engage in a more active, holistic reading or viewing experience, whether engaging a discourse like Superman or biblical literature. Background knowledge allows the reader to notice when details are added, omitted, or referenced, and to place what one is reading or viewing within the spectrum of other aesthetic products within that discourse.

*Finally,* what I hope I have demonstrated is that all interpretations— not just of Superman, but all encounters with texts—are open to analysis and critique because of their perspectival nature. As I mentioned at the outset, meaning is created in the interaction between texts and readers and negotiated after considering signs within and contextual data behind the text utilizing the particular viewpoint and experience of the reader. There is no one, correct reading of Superman. Different interpreters understand the different texts we have surveyed differently because they all have different experiences, training, and backgrounds. All of the analyses in this book are open to critique as well from your own individual perspective, using your own unique voice. Just don't forget your cape.

### DISCUSSION QUESTIONS

1. Clanton identifies the authors of earliest versions of Superman as Jews. How does their religious identity, and their experience as immigrants, shape the stories they tell about Superman? What was going on in the world at the time that might have drawn Jews to tales about a superhero?

2. What are other examples of popular culture that contain allusions to more than one religious tradition?

3. Do you agree that meaning is not found exclusively in a text or in the reader, but, rather, is constructed in the interaction between text and reader? Why or why not? And what is at stake either way? Why does this question matter?

4. Organize a classroom debate between groups arguing that Superman is best understood as an expression of Judaism in popular culture and those who argue that the Man of Steel is best understood as an expression of Christianity in popular culture. What evidence would you cite to support your case?

### NOTES

1. This process of infusing traditionally non-sacred media with sacred images, ideas, and texts is called the "sacralization of the secular" by Conrad Ostwalt in his *Secular Steeples: Popular Culture and the Religious Imagination* (2nd ed.; London: Bloomsbury, 2012), 28–29 and 48–51.

2. I have addressed these and other questions in my "Pop Culture and the Bible," in *The Oxford Encyclopedia of Biblical Interpretation,* ed. Steven L. McKenzie (2 vols.; New York: Oxford University Press, 2013), 2: 114–23, esp. 115–17.

3. This issue is now collected in Jerry Siegel (scripts) and Joe Shuster (artwork), *The Superman Chronicles, Volume One,* ed. Anton Kawasaki (New York: DC Comics, 2006), 3–16. The origin I discuss is found on p. 4 of this collection, and all quotes in this section are taken from that page.

4. See Larry Tye, *Superman: The High-Flying History of America's Most Enduring Hero* (New York: Random House, 2012; Kindle Book), loc. 718.

5. Ibid., loc. 820–22.

6. These strips are collected in Siegel and Shuster, *Superman: The Dailies: Strips 1–966, 1939–1942* (3 vols.; New York: Sterling, 2006), 1: 12–18.

7. Noachic imagery generally fades early on in Superman continuity in favor of the Mosaic parallels. Even so, the Space Ark returns in the classic story line "Superman's Return to Krypton," found in the daily strips ##6759–6836, published from 15 August to 12 November 1960 (esp. ##6812 and 6815–16). This story arc was adapted from *Superman* #141 (November 1960) and can be found in Jerry Siegel (scripts) and Curt Swan, Stan Kaye, and Wayne Boring (artwork), *Superman: The Silver Age Dailies, Volume One, 1959–1961* (Library of American Comics Series; San Diego: IDW Publishing & DC Comics, 2013), 155–180.

8. See Nahum M. Sarna, *Exodus* (Philadelphia: Jewish Publication Society, 1991), 9. See also his *Exploring Exodus: The Origins of Biblical Israel* (New York: Schocken Books, 1986), 28, for more on the thematic importance of the overlap between Noah's Ark and Moses' basket.

9. See Tye, *Superman*, loc. 572.

10. *Superman* #1 is now collected in Siegel and Shuster, *Superman Chronicles, Volume One*, 194–204. This third origin is found on 195–96. The Kents also figure prominently in another retelling of the origin in the Sunday comic strips published from November 25 to December 16, 1945. These strips have been collected in Jerry Siegel & DC Comics (scripts); Wayne Boring & Jack Burnley (artwork), *Superman: The Golden Age Sundays, 1943–1946* (Library of American Comics Series; San Diego: IDW Publishing & DC Comics, 2013), 142–45 (Sunday Strips ##317–20).

11. Obviously, the latter two themes are clear enough from the comic and newspaper origins discussed. Some scholars also compare Superman to the Golem; see, e.g., Arie Kaplan, *From Krakow to Krypton: Jews and Comic Books* (Philadelphia: Jewish Publication Society, 2008), 14.

12. Again, several of these themes are also potentially present in the 1938–39 origin stories.

13. See Jake Rossen, *Superman vs. Hollywood: How Fiendish Producers, Devious Directors, and Warring Writers Grounded an American Icon* (Chicago: Chicago Review Press, 2008), 72.

14. For a deeper analysis of this section, see Raymond E. Brown, *The Gospel according to John* (2 vols., AB 29 & 29A; Garden City, NY: Doubleday, 1966, 1970), 2: 617–782; and Robert Kysar, *John's Story of Jesus* (Philadelphia: Fortress, 1984), 68–76.

15. Simcha Weinstein, *Up, Up, and Oy Vey! How Jewish History, Culture, and Values Shaped the Comic Book Superhero* (Baltimore: Leviathan Press, 2006), 27.

16. Anton Karl Kozlovic, "The Holy, Non-Christic Biblical Subtexts in *Superman: The Movie* (1978) and *Superman II* (1981)," *Journal of Religion and Film 6*, no. 2 (2002), http://www.unomaha.edu/jrf/supergood.htm, pars. 3, 4, and 10.

17. Norman C. Habel, "The Form and Significance of the Call Narratives," *Zeitschrift für die alttestamentliche Wissenschaft* 77 (1965): 297–323. The six components are: the Divine Confrontation; the Introductory Word; the Commission; the Objection; the Reassurance; and the Sign.

18. To be fair, not all those commissioned by God offer an objection (e.g., Abram in Genesis 12), and in these cases the obedience and even heroism of those called is highlighted by later interpreters.

19. Kaplan, *From Krakow to Krypton,* 14.

20. Harry Brod, *Superman Is Jewish? How Comic Book Superheroes Came to Serve Truth, Justice, and the Jewish-American Way* (New York: Free Press, 2012; Kindle Book), loc. 435.

21. Ibid., loc. 490.

22. See also Thomas Andrae, "*Funnyman,* Jewish Masculinity, and the Decline of the Superhero," in *Siegel and Shuster's Funnyman: The First Jewish Superhero,* ed. Thomas Andrae and Mel Gordon (Port Townsend, WA: Feral House, 2010), 55–75.

23. This is the view of Genesis Rabbah; see Nahum M. Sarna, *Genesis* (Philadelphia: Jewish Publication Society, 1989), 7.

24. See Sarna, *Genesis,* 7.

25. As in Matt. 5.14–16.

26. Weinstein, *Up, Up, and Oy Vey!* 26–27.

27. Brod, *Superman is Jewish?* loc. 394.

28. Ibid., loc. 402. For a more critical Jewish view on the parallels between Moses and Superman, see Danny Fingeroth, *Disguised as Clark Kent: Jews, Comics, and the Creation of the Superhero* (New York: Continuum, 2007), 44–45.

29. A typological interpretation of a character or event seeks to understand that character or event by comparing it to a prior character or event. Richard B. Hays calls it an "act of imaginative correlation" (*Echoes of Scripture in the Letters of Paul* [New Haven, CT: Yale University Press, 1989], 100). For example, Paul sees his Corinthian congregation in light of the generations Moses led in the wilderness, and based on their actions exhorts the Corinthians not to act as they did: "These things occurred as examples for us, so that we may not desire evil as they did" (1 Cor. 10.6). That is, Paul asks the Corinthians not to adhere to the "type" of the rebellious wilderness generation, but rather to see that behavior as discordant. As Hays notes, Paul does not thereby denigrate the wilderness generation, so that this typological reading is not supersessionist like the

typological argument in Hebrews 8. See *Echoes of Scripture in the Letters of Paul,* 95–102.

30. Ken Schenck, "Superman: A Popular Culture Messiah," in *The Gospel According to Superheroes: Religion and Popular Culture,* ed. B.J. Oropeza (New York: Peter Lang, 2005), 33.

31. Stephen Skelton, *The Gospel According to the World's Greatest Superhero* (Eugene, OR: Harvest House, 2006), 46. Skelton had previously mentioned the influence of Samson on Siegel, but claimed specifically that both Samson and Hercules—another early influence—"prefigure the person of Christ" (37).

32. Different writers mean different things when they claim a character in a film is a Christ figure. See, e.g., Lloyd Baugh, *Imagining the Divine: Jesus and Christ-Figures in Film* (Kansas City: Sheed & Ward, 1997), esp. 109–12; and William R. Telford, "Through a Lens Darkly: Critical Approaches to Theology and Film," in *Cinéma Divinité: Religion, Theology and the Bible in Film,* ed. Eric S. Christianson, Peter Francis, and W.R. Telford (London: SCM Press, 2005), 15–43.

33. Roy M. Anker, *Catching Light: Looking for God in the Movies* (Grand Rapids, MI: Eerdmans, 2004), 254.

34. Ibid., 254.

35. Ibid., 255.

36. Ibid., 255–56. The first ellipsis elides Anker's shocking error in identifying the first appearance of Superman as being in a "Marvel" comic. One can only hope that my fellow comic fans can overlook this heinous transgression.

37. Edward Mehok, "St. Clark of Krypton," in *Superman at Fifty! The Persistence of a Legend,* ed. Dennis Dooley and Gary Engle (New York: Collier Books, 1987), 128.

38. Skelton, *Gospel,* 22.

39. See Anker, *Catching Light,* 250–51. He borrows the term "christomorphic" from Neil Hurley (250n3).

40. Anker, *Catching Light,* 251.

# CHAPTER TWO

# The Oriental Monk in American Popular Culture

JANE NAOMI IWAMURA

Driving down a busy street in Oakland, California, I was met by the larger-than-life presence of the Fourteenth Dalai Lama. He appeared to me in a vision of unparalleled clarity and grace. His direct gaze was gentle, yet intent, and his spiritual repose arresting. For that one moment, the hectic pace of my life was interrupted, and I was transported to another time, another world, another possibility.

Many others who passed that same spot shared a similar vision. To each of us, the message reverberated: *Think Different.*

In olden days the unexpected appearance of such a prominent spiritual figure would undoubtedly be taken as nothing short of a miracle. But in contemporary times, a miracle it is not. The Dalai Lama's "visitation" had been made possible by the Apple Corporation and the spiritual power of advertising. The vision derived its meaning, not from a single epiphany, but rather through a series of mass media orientations: glossies in magazines; newspaper photos and references; images in film, television, and the Internet. Indeed, at times, His Holiness seemed to be everywhere at once.

The Dalai Lama has become one of the most recognizable spiritual figures of our times. As a non-Christian religious leader, the positive interest he holds for millions of Americans is unprecedented; he represents a pacifism and spiritual calm admired by many. Indeed, Americans love the Dalai Lama.

It is this American love and fascination for Eastern spiritual figures such as the Dalai Lama that I am most interested in understanding. Rather than simply recounting the religious and moral qualities these spiritual individuals possess, it is important to discuss the social context from which their attraction emerges. How did the Dalai Lama come to represent all that he does for Americans? Indeed, what exactly does he represent? How have we come to "know" him? Is our ability to embrace someone and something (Tibetan Buddhism) once considered so foreign anything other than a testimony to a newfound openness and progressive understanding?

I would like to tackle these questions by critically analyzing the history of representation that has contributed to the current image of the Dalai Lama. We "know" the Dalai Lama, not simply because of the fact that we may understand his views and admire his actions, but also because we are familiar with the particular role he plays in the popular consciousness of the United States—the type of *icon* he has become— the icon of the "Oriental Monk." To get a sense of what makes the Dalai Lama (and others like him) so popular, we need to get a sense of the history of this icon and how it has been used to express and manage our sense of Asian religions.

The Oriental Monk has enjoyed a long and prominent sojourn in the realm of American popular culture. We have encountered him under different names and guises: as Mahatma Gandhi and as D. T. Suzuki; as the self-immolating Vietnamese Buddhist monk Thich Quang Duc and the Beatles' guru Maharishi Mahesh in the 1960s; as *Kung Fu's* Kwai Chang Caine and as Mr. Miyagi in the *Karate Kid;* as Yoda in the *Star Wars* saga and Splinter in *Teenage Mutant Ninja Turtles;* and as Deepak Chopra, as well as the Dalai Lama.[1] Although the Oriental Monk appears in these various forms throughout American pop culture, we are always able to recognize him as the representative of an alternative spirituality that draws from the ancient wellsprings of "Eastern" civilization and culture.

Compared with the negative stereotypes of Asians that have historically circulated in the American media (sinister Fu Manchus, inscruta-
ble Dragon Ladies, crime-driven gangsters, Yellow Peril hordes, and so
on), the icon of the Oriental Monk seems like a noteworthy advance.
And indeed, it demonstrates an air of increasing tolerance and respect.
But to look at this representation as nothing but progress precludes us
from seeing ways in which positive images may reinscribe certain racist
notions of the Asian "other." It is important to analyze the icon of the
Oriental Monk within the phenomenon of *orientalism*—as part of a network of defining representations.[2] "Positive" or "negative," these stereotypical representations serve as filters by which we "read" Asian bodies and make sense of the world. And they often reflect our own
psychological and political preoccupations, rather than the individuals
and groups they seemingly portray.

The Oriental Monk, drawing from this network of representation,
includes within its iconic scope a wide range of religious figures (gurus,
sages, swamis, masters, teachers) from a variety of ethnic backgrounds
(South Asian, Japanese, Vietnamese, Chinese, Tibetan). Although individual figures point to a diverse field of encounter, they are homoge-
nized within American popular consciousness and culture. Racialization (more correctly, in this case, "orientalization") serves to blunt the
distinctiveness of particular persons and figures. Indeed, recognition of
Eastern spiritual guides (real or fictional) is predicated on their con-
formity to general features ideally encapsulated in the icon of the Oriental Monk: his spiritual commitment, his calm demeanor, his Asian
face, and often his manner of dress.

In an analysis of the icon of the Oriental monk within the American
context, we will see a complex dynamic unfold in which orientalist notions
of Eastern spiritual traditions and Western disillusionment and desire
converge. These notions are configured in a conventionalized narrative
with formulaic aspects that demonstrate the *specific* nature of America's
engagement with "Eastern," non-Christian traditions, and its use of the
Oriental Monk as a means to symbolically express, manage, and work

through its troubled spiritual sense of self. Hence, the Oriental Monk as pop cultural icon and narrative tells us a great deal about the religious ethos of contemporary America: he details the fears, hopes, and desires of a society undergoing spiritual turmoil and change. In the following discussion, I will follow the Oriental Monk on his journey through American popular consciousness (or rather, follow this consciousness as it journeys through him), and discuss certain highlights along his spiritual path—his mass media "origins" through silent film (D. W. Griffith's *Broken Blossoms*), his "initiation" in 1980s film and television, his rise to prominence in the form of the Fourteenth Dalai Lama, and his "legacy" in children's animation. We will discover that although the monk travels under different guises, primarily dictated by the geopolitical terrain, his basic mission and tale remain strangely the same.

### ORIGINS

The Oriental Monk makes his on-screen debut in D. W. Griffith's classic, *Broken Blossoms or the Yellow Man and the Girl*.[3] The tale begins in an undesignated Chinese port town where we find the Yellow Man—a devout individual who becomes "convinced that the great nations across the sea need the lessons of the gentle Buddha." He journeys to England to "take the glorious message of peace to the barbarous Anglo-Saxons, sons of turmoil and strife." The remainder of the movie chronicles his life in the Limehouse district of London and his encounter with Lucy, a gutter waif (played by Lillian Gish), whom he shelters from her brute of a father, Battlin' Burrows. The Yellow Man is portrayed as the only one who recognizes Lucy's "beauty which all Limehouse missed." But tragedy ensues: Battlin' Burrows discovers his daughter's whereabouts, beats her to death, and then is shot in turn by the Yellow Man. The story ends with the Yellow Man, a knife between his ribs, slumped before Lucy and his Buddhist altar.

Griffith's masterpiece, released in 1919, offers a tragic adaption of Thomas Burke's short story, "The Chink and the Girl." Griffith's changes to Burke's story are noteworthy. Most significant is the transformation of Burke's "Chink," a "worthless drifter of an Oriental," into Griffith's "Yellow Man"—noble and pious in his sense of mission.[4] Indeed, Griffith's main contribution resides in the revised introduction of the story, where he locates the Yellow Man "in the Temple of Buddha, before his contemplated journey to a foreign land." Here, the Yellow Man gains inspiration and guidance, not only from the environment of the temple, but also from Oriental Monks who provide "[a]dvice for a young man's conduct in the world—word for word such as a fond parent or guardian of our own land would give." Indeed, the motif of the temple that begins and ends the film lends spiritual overtones to the tragic tale.

In his essay, "Modernizing White Patriarchy: Re-Viewing D. W. Griffith's *Broken Blossoms*," John Kuo Wei Tchen cites the "modernized cultural patriarchy" promoted in the film. This new form of dominance and oppression, he says, channels the views and prescriptions of the cultural elite into stereotypical representations set in place and reinforced by character and plot development. Tchen exposes the view that undergirds early silent film: "Proper society should be managed so Blacks [can] be segregated and kept in their place, and poor whites, immigrants and native alike, [can] be acculturated into bourgeois society."[5] Within such a framework, *Broken Blossoms* can be read as the cultural elite's commentary on the marginalized elements of urban society. More specifically, it marks the filmic origin of a device through which this is accomplished: the figure of the "good Asian."[6]

> If anything, [Griffith] eschews the standard stereotype of the "heathen Chinee" already well established in the previous century, and adapts the alternative image of the good-for-the-West "John Chinaman." "John" was the image of the tame, aristocratic, clean, honest, and often Christianized Chinese man promoted by traders, missionaries, and the wealthy who had direct personal interests in promoting good relations with China.[7]

This positive portrayal serves a number of functions: (1) as a "symbolic foil to complain about the abusive, immature authority of lower-class white men" (Battlin' Burrows); (2) to appease China, with which the

United States has "interests" in maintaining good foreign relations; and (3) to discipline immigrant Chinese who reside in the Chinatowns of the West by providing a representative *measure* and *standard* for the moral behavior of these communities.[8] In these multiple ways, films such as Griffith's provide a means by which to manage diverse groups via cultural representation rather than through direct polemic or bodily force, a strategy that is the hallmark of a "modernized cultural patriarchy."

For our purposes, it is interesting to note that Tchen emphasizes the "Christian" nature of the Yellow Man's moral and spiritual orientation, since he is portrayed as definitively Buddhist. I think Tchen is correct in pointing out the "proto-'Christian' values" that the representation masks; at the same time, this easy identification of the Buddhist Yellow Man as Christian in essence misses a significant dimension of Griffith's film.[9] Indeed Tchen's critical analysis does not account for the brief but crucial encounter between the Yellow Man and two missionizing clergymen in the desolate Limehouse streets:

> CHRISTIAN: "My brother leaves for China tomorrow to convert the heathen."
> YELLOW MAN: "I wish him well."
> (The clergymen then offer the Yellow Man a pamphlet entitled, "Hell.")

Unbeknownst to the Christian proselytizers, the Yellow Man is a missionary himself, albeit jaded and discouraged by his own experiences in a foreign land. His well-wishing is cast in a sympathetic, yet ironic, tone. The above exchange can be viewed as a brilliant foreshadowing of the Yellow Man's tragic end ("Hell"), but it also serves as a commentary on Christian missions. The viewer is meant to identify with the Yellow Man's disillusioned response. Through this identification, one can read Griffith's (and perhaps the audience's) own relation to similar efforts on the part of institutionalized Christianity as ambivalent at best.

Hence, we must struggle with Griffith's portrayal *as such*. The fact that Griffith associates peace, gentleness, sensitivity, and altruism with the Buddha and his followers in the film constitutes a significant moment in popular consciousness. At the very least, moviegoers must assume here that a "heathen" religion stands on par with its "non-heathen" counterpart, although I believe much more can be read into this moment: *Broken Blossoms* expresses an already established disillusionment with Christianity and quite possibly a budding fascination with alternative modes of moral and spiritual understanding. As "cultural midwife," Griffith inadvertently ushers this desire into popular consciousness through the Oriental Monk figures of the Yellow Man and his Buddhist teachers.

Of course, *Broken Blossoms* concludes in tragedy, not hope. This ending reinvigorated the film's elite audience—infused them with a "sense of mission" and justified their "paternalistic efforts" within national borders and without.[10] The film's moral lesson rests on a threat: *If the Christianized West is unable to care for its children, the noble Buddhist East will.* The tone and import of this message is conveyed by the dire consequences of the Yellow Man's intervention (the deaths of the three main characters); the message is to be taken as a warning to the Christian West to "practice what it preaches." Although this is perhaps the conscious aim of Griffith's work, it does not preclude other residual effects: Eastern spirituality has been representationally idealized and operates kindly in its new Western home. In this way, *Broken Blossoms* sets the groundwork for the West's future engagements, and later spiritual identification, with the East. As we will see, the message will be transformed from one of threat and consequence to one of desire and hope: *If the Christianized West is unable to care for its children, the noble Buddhist East will!*

### INITIATION

Times have obviously changed since Griffith's day, and along with them, attitudes towards Asian religions. This transformation is for the most part due to the events of the 1960s, which embodied a refreshing challenge to the American Christian establishment (in the form of "alternative" lifestyles and spiritual experimentation) and a new tolerance toward "peoples of color" (in the form of the Civil Rights Movement and the 1965 Immigration Act). At the same time, this transformation was underwritten by a sense of loss—a loss configured by the wounds of war (World War II, the Vietnam War), the impact of technology and global capitalism, domestic racial strife, and a growing disillusionment with traditional forms of religious faith and worship. Out of this context emerged the archetype of the American religious subject as a "spiritual seeker" who journeys in search of new religious ground for reconciliation and healing.[11]

The cultures of Asia offered the unparalleled promise of finding such ground. The search for spiritual renewal in the East found expression in *Kung Fu* (1972–75), the popular ground-breaking TV series that introduced a wider American audience to Asian martial arts and their spiritual underpinnings. *Kung Fu* is thus the progenitor of both the many martial arts movies that were produced from the early 1970s through the late 1980s, and later representations, such as *The Karate Kid* (1984) and *Teenage Mutant Ninja Turtles* (1990), which transformed the adult entertainment of *Kung Fu* and its more violent martial arts successors into youth-oriented film and television programming.

*Kung Fu, The Karate Kid,* and *Teenage Mutant Ninja Turtles* all are grounded in a similar narrative: a lone monk figure—oftentimes with no visible family or community, unrecognized by the dominant culture—takes under his wing a fatherless, often parentless, child.[12] This child embodies a tension: for example, *Kung Fu*'s Kwai Chang Caine is "half-American, half-Chinese"; Daniel in *The Karate Kid* hails from an ethnic working-class background; and, of course, the turtles are mutants.[13] Although these figures half-signify the dominant culture in racial terms, they have an ambivalent relationship with that culture; this allows each to make a break with the Western tradition radical enough to embrace their marginalized half. The Oriental Monk figure seizes this half, develops it, and nurtures it. As a result of the relationship between teacher and pupil, a transmission takes place: oriental wisdom and spiritual insight are passed from the Oriental Monk figure to the occidental West through the *bridge figure*. Ultimately, the Oriental Monk and his apprentice(s) represent future salvation of the culture—they embody a new hope of saving the West from capitalist greed, brute force, totalitarian, rule, and spiritless technology.

The modernized cultural patriarchy set forth in *Broken Blossoms* becomes firmly established a half a century later. Subsequent films in this genre similarly enact a commentary on and prescription for ethnic and working-class communities built upon the ideological figure of the spiritual Asian male. But in these later renditions, the Oriental Monk travels down a path not foreseen by Griffith. If *Broken Blossoms* were rewritten in more contemporary terms according to the above narrative, the Yellow Man would be as noble and pious as before, but this time take the form of a kung fu master with magical powers. He would rescue Lucy from her unloving father, care for her, and finally train her in the martial arts practices and the spirituals ways of the East. Battlin' Burrows, now a frustrated blue-collar worker obsessed with war and guns, would then attempt to reclaim his estranged daughter, and the film would culminate in a final showdown between the two father figures and their respective forms of combat and defense. Lucy would get into the act as well, employing her new talents to disarm her father as gently as possible. The Yellow Man and the girl, through superior human insight and bodily discipline, would triumph over their unruly counterpart. After his definitive defeat, Battin would lay aside his weapon and be reunitied with his daughter; the three would join forces to fight evil and corruption in *Broken Blossoms II*. Rewritten for twenty-first-century viewers, Griffith's classic cautionary tale might thus become a narrative of spiritual hope and progress.

Indeed, it may appear as if this narrative shift represents a positive trend. Asian religions are no longer portrayed as spiritual systems incompatible with the West but rather as transformative, life-enhancing influences. But the fact that a particular narrative and representation of Asian spiritual traditions and Asian peoples has become so conventionalized attests to its ideological force. The Oriental Monk figure is portrayed as a desexualized male character, representing the last of his kind.[14] Passing on his spiritual legacy to the West through the bridge figure represents his only hope for survival. Hence, this narrative implicitly argues that Asian religions are impotent within their context of origin and are only made (re)productive if resituated in the West and passed on to white practitioners who possess the creative and daring initiative that their Eastern counterparts presumably lack. In this way, the icon and narrative of the Oriental Monk, a construction of "racist love," may be more insidious than negative stereotypes; it allows for the recognition of peoples and cultures of Asian heritage while simultaneously subjecting them to a narrative of their own obsolescence.[15]

As the *Karate Kid* and the original movie series of *Teenage Mutant Ninja Turtles* developed their franchises in the 1980s and 1990s, the Oriental Monk narrative extended its reach, with a return to the East written into their subsequent sequels. Mr. Miyagi and Daniel return to Japan in *The Karate Kid II* (1986) to prevent Miyagi's home village from being overrun by a greedy capitalist Japanese gangster; and the turtles return to seventeenth-century Japan in *Teenage Mutant Ninja Turtles III* (1993). Here we find that the East also suffers from despair and corruption and requires the help of the protagonist. Asia cannot save itself, but looks toward the powers of the newly "enlightened" Westerner: the bridge figure comes to signify salvation, not only for the West, but for "the Orient" as well. In this way, a modernized U.S. cultural patriarchy uses the Oriental Monk and his narrative to transform its disillusionment into a new spiritual imperialism and a renewed sense of mission.

## PROMINENCE

In 1989, to much acclaim, the Fourteen Dalai Lama received the Nobel Peace Prize. In the tradition of Mahatma Gandhi and Martin Luther King Jr., he continued a line of world peacemakers whose vision was shaped by a mixture of profound spirituality and political awareness. The Nobel Peace Prize hurled the Dalai Lama and the small Asian nation of Tibet into the public eye, and what happened next only solidified the Dalai Lama's status as an American popular cultural figure. The Hollywood actor Richard Gere personally adopted the Dalai Lama's spiritual and political mission as his own, promoting the cause at the 1993 Academy Awards and becoming the Founding Chair of Tibet House in New York.[16] Many of Gere's contemporaries followed suit: "the Power Buddhist / Free Tibet contingent" included Harrison Ford, Willem Dafoe, Sharon Stone, Steven Seagal, and Adam Yauch of the Beastie Boys.[17] These celebrity endorsements, along with the long history of the Oriental Monk in American popular culture, offered a Buddhist way of life unprecedented Western exposure and furthered the development of the icon of the Oriental Monk.

With the Dalai Lama, we witness how the disruptions made by actual teachers are continually minimalized by the overpowering representations that have accrued in American popular cultural consciousness. The teacher of Asian origin instantaneously enters the pop culture realm and is transformed into a celebrity; that realm then exploits the reception of his physical and spiritual presence by marketing it for mass consumption. This stage is exemplified by the big movie productions centered around Tibetan Buddhism and/or the life of the Fourteenth Dalai Lama that emerged in the 1990s: Bernardo Bertolucci's *Little Buddha* (1993), in which a small Euro-American child from Seattle is selected as one of three reincarnations of the deceased Lama Dorje; Jean-Jacques Annaud's *Seven Years in Tibet* (1997); and Martin Scorsese's biopic about the Dalai Lama, *Kundun* (1997).[18]

In his physical manifestation, the Oriental Monk is modeled after the Dalai Lama (note the Tibetan-inspired, saffron-robed versions that are part of the opening sequence of *Ace Ventura: When Nature Calls* (1995)). Psychically, this new Monk continued the work of his predecessors in its critique of American society and its religious and secular preoccupations:

> We don't need these Buddhist temples, we don't need these Christian Churches. What we need, [the Dalai Lama] says, are the values of the human heart.... There's a lot of talk about [the baby boomer] generation

being materially satisfied, but the next level of need is not satisfied and that's the spiritual level.

Buddhism is seen as one way that we might re-create a sense of spiritual meaning and purpose within a directionless society. Amid widespread despair, those who have found Buddhism have a sense of joy and inspiration.[19]

A shift in geopolitical focus and mission is apparent. The history of the icon of the Oriental Monk suggests a preference for the Japanese or Chinese model. Indeed, Japan and China were viewed as cultures possessing great spiritual richness, but their challenge in the arena of international politics and the world market in relation to the United States was perceived as fairly contained; this combination of factors made them suitable representatives of the East in the American popular imagination from the 1970s to the mid-1980s.[20]

By the late 1980s, however, Japan had come to be seen as dominating the global market and was deemed to be an economic threat to the United States and an unfair trading partner. And after the Tiananmen Square massacre in 1989, China would be viewed as "giant, powerful, [and] merciless."[21] Tibet posed no threat and offered Americans a new model. The Tibetan version of the Monk paradigmatically signified, through his dress and religious practices, a mythic spiritual past. This Oriental Monk also provided his charges with a concrete political mission: Free Tibet. As the inaugural issue of the American Buddhist periodical *Tricycle* succinctly summarized:

- 1.2 million Tibetans have died (one sixth of the population)
- 70% of Tibet's virgin forest has been clear cut
- More than 6,000 monasteries, temples and historical sites have been looted and razed
- All religious practices have been outlawed.[22]

This scenario includes a Third World people who are fighting against a global power (China) for their very physical, cultural, and spiritual existence—a noble cause with which to align oneself. Hence, the

Japanese and Chinese variations of the Oriental Monk were for the most part traded in for the less compromised Tibetan model.

But unrecognized desires underlie the American interest in this politico-spiritual mission. Tibet represents a manageable cosmos where sins, past and present, can be atoned for. The Tibetan variation of the Oriental Monk therefore enacts an exchange: a model of ethical behavior and spiritual direction for political support. But this exchange serves the West well. American gained not only psychic resolution and healing, but also influence over the Tibetan nation in exile.

## LEGACY

While the image of the Dalai Lama remains prominent in the American imagination, his legacy and the legacy of the Oriental Monk is now most evident in realm of children's entertainment. As discussed, this trend began in the 1980s, but came to fruition in the new millennium as baby boomers, who developed and embraced the Oriental Monk, had children of their own. Seeking alternatives that would encourage children's individuality and reinforce ethical behavior in an entertaining manner, movie and television producers would find a winning formula in the Oriental Monk narrative.

Although its characteristic features have remained consistent, the narrative featured significant changes and "innovations." *Teenage Mutant Ninja Turtles* would establish the pattern, as the role of the pupil would be taken on by a number of characters—a team whose youthful members represent different personalities and attitudes: Donatello (inventive nerd), Leonardo (devoted and grounded leader), Michelangelo (fun-loving "dude"), and Raphael (spontaneous "bad boy"). These different positionalities allow for a young audience to self-identify with their favorite turtle/pupil and also create marketing opportunities too irresistible for economically driven studios.[23] *Lego Ninjago: Masters of Spinjitzu* (2011–present) can be seen as the latest animated feature to exploit the Oriental Monk narrative. The roles are somewhat reversed as the pupils (Kai, Jay, Cole, Zane) are now the "Masters," albeit ones who are constantly disciplined by their Oriental Monk teacher, Sensei Wu. Splinter (*TMNT*) and Sensei Wu (*Ninjago*) share a similar narrative past: both are displaced by their evil counterparts, who have stolen their youthful love interests and therefore, have disrupted their patrilineage. Involuntarily exiled, these teachers continue their line with their adopted, spirited (and pizza-loving) pupils. As such, for a young viewer, they represent a legitimate connection to the Asian spiritual past in which no apparent connection exists.

Also evident in these animated series is the increasing lack of a religious dimension in the story lines. The Oriental Monk narrative has become increasingly condensed over time. From the more complex narratives of *Kung Fu* and *The Karate Kid* to the extremely concentrated versions found in the various *Teenage Mutant Ninja Turtles* (*TMNT*) and *Lego Ninjago*. In the original *Kung Fu,* at least half of the movie is given over to explaining Shaolin practices and philosophy. All that remains in the later versions are a few anecdotes delivered in gratuitous fashion by Splinter and Sensei Wu. The narrative that is so strikingly played out in earlier Monk story lines is almost assumed at this point. The figure of the Monk becomes increasingly overdetermined as inherently spiritual. Much of this is due to the genre and television format, as well as the obvious preference for action sequences. However, the formula works, I would argue, because the narrative is so familiar and certain cultural assumptions are so squarely in place.

*Kung Fu Panda* represents the most widely embraced contemporary example of the Oriental Monk narrative. With its latest sequel released in 2016 (*Kung Fu Panda 3*), the movie franchise follows Po, a hapless panda, through his journey from working in a noodle shop to becoming the Great Dragon Warrior. *Kung Fu Panda* is solidly grounded in the Oriental Monk narrative, with its orientalized teachers, Shifu and Master Oogway. And in line with the innovation of ensemble casting, *Kung Fu Panda* makes the most of the Furious Five (Crane, Viper, Monkey,

Mantis, and Tigress). The movies' Chinese setting (or more accurately, the filmmakers' "version of ancient China") seems to preclude the protagonist's politically charged "return to Asia." However, Po still manages to "save his own kind" in *Kung Fu Panda 3* by training the panda villagers to defend themselves—something the villagers would not have able to do without Po's help. The license to "rescue" others is limitless, as expressed in Master Oogway's exhortation to Po: "You must save the world."

I have examined the historical development and complex workings of the icon of the Oriental Monk in a variety of American popular cultural representations. Although variations are geopolitically determined, the narrative remains amazingly similar throughout. The Oriental Monk serves as a colored "spiritual caregiver" to the West.[24] And attraction to the icon on the part of American media makers and audiences alike reflect disillusionment with Western religious traditions and the hopes and fears attached with alternative spiritual traditions of the East. American consciousness plagued by the demands of modernity finds peace and resolution through the Oriental Monk. Also present in the narrative is the vision of the "new man," or more accurately, the "new West," that has learned its lessons well and combines Western initiative with Eastern spiritual know-how.[25] The bridge figure represents salvation, not only for America, but also for Asia and the world. Armed with a new consciousness and mission, the United States justifies carrying on its (imperialist) work with renewed vigor and purpose around the globe.

So what am I and others to make of our sighting of His Holiness on that busy street in Oakland? Mass media images surround us in our daily lives—inundate our imaginations and reinforce certain associations—without us really taking into account the power of their repetitive force. Religion, race, class, sexuality, and gender make the representations we encounter meaningful. Understanding these dimensions of the popular images we encounter, as well as the sociopolitical contexts in which they are lodged, will inevitably determine whether we heed the injunction to "Think different" or simply drive on by ...

## DISCUSSION QUESTIONS

1. Iwamura argues that Americans are fascinated with Oriental monks, and with eastern religion and culture. What evidence is there of this fascination? What are some other examples of the Oriental monk in recent American popular culture? If you disagree, discuss why.

2. Drawing on the chapter and your own experience of popular culture presentations of Oriental monks, describe the powers and teachings of the Oriental monk. How do white Western characters benefit from the monk?

3. What are the problems and advantages of looking at religion and religious practices through the eyes of outside observers, or inside practitioners? How do you think a practitioner of Asian religious traditions (e.g., Buddhist) might view the representations of Eastern spirituality presented in film and television?

4. The author argues that the way an Oriental monk is portrayed on American television and in the movies tells us more about Western perceptions and assumptions about the East than we learn about the reality of Oriental monks. Do you think that is true? If so, what do you think the Oriental Monk and Eastern religions and cultures represent for Americans?

## NOTES

A more extended discussion of the Oriental Monk icon can be found in Jane Naomi Iwamura, *Virtual Orientalism: Asian Religions and American Popular Culture* (New York: Oxford University Press, 2011).

1. The genealogy constructed here, which is far from complete, purposely intertwines historical persons with fictional characters. In a mass-mediated age, "real" figures can no longer be clearly distinguished from imaginary ones,

creating a "hyperreal" effect (to use Jean Baudrillard's term) in which both types of representations inform and interact with one another to form a common understanding of "Eastern spirituality" in the U.S. context. This understanding crystallizes in the icon of the Oriental Monk. For a compelling example of how iconic representation functions in the contemporary United States, see S. Paige Baty, *American Monroe: The Making of a Body Politic* (Berkeley: University of California Press, 1995).

2. See Edward Said, *Orientalism* (New York: Vintage Books, 1979).

3. D. W. Griffith, renowned as a master of early American film, gained notoriety for his visions of America in works such as *The Birth of a Nation* (1915). Although *Broken Blossoms* is set in London, it too enacts a commentary on life in the United States. Scott Simmon, in his exploration of *The Films of D. W. Griffith* (Cambridge: Cambridge University Press, 1993), discusses how Griffith posited, "Anglo-Saxon superiority through British medieval ideals" (143). This romanticized link between Britain and the United States, forged in Griffith's mind, intimates his use of *Blossom*'s London and its degeneracy as a way to reflect and comment on the woes plaguing urban America.

4. John Kuo Wei Tchen, "Modernizing White Patriarchy: Re-Viewing D. W. Griffith's *Broken Blossoms*," in *Moving the Image: Independent Asian Pacific American Media Arts,* ed. Russell Leong (Los Angeles: UCLA Asian American Studies Center, 1991), 133–43, quotation from p. 135.

5. Ibid., 143.

6. The character of the "good Asian" prefigures the myth of the "model minority" so prevalent in contemporary U.S. discourse. Similar to Griffith's deployment of the Yellow Man as a figurative device through which to lodge his commentary and critique of "unruly" sectors of society, popular media and political leaders valorize and uphold Asian Americans as "model" students and citizens that other racial-ethnic groups (including lower- and middle-class whites) are urged to emulate. In a stereotypical example, Ronald Reagan praised Asian American success and attributed it to "[Asian] values, {Asian] hard work." This assumed ethic falls closely in line with Griffith's representation of the Yellow Man as the uncompromised embodiment of the traditional values of his Asian culture. For an accessible introduction into the "model minority myth," see Ronald Takaki, *Strangers from a Different Short: A History of Asian Americans* (New York: Penguin Books, 1989), 474–84; Reagan's comment above is quoted on p. 475.

7. Tchen, "Modernizing White Patriarchy," 137.

8. Ibid.

9. Ibid., 135. The view of the United States as a "white Christian nation" certainly deserves to be dismantled. But a too-easy association between these

dimensions—"white," Christian," and "nation"—obscures the complex, changing ways in which this vision generally persists (e.g., liberal pluralism, religious tolerance, multiculturalism). In the case of *Broken Blossoms*, Tchen's reliance on this association does not allow him to recognize the contradictions in Griffith's sympathetic portrayal of the Buddhist Yellow Man.

10. Tchen, "Modernizing White Patriarchy," 141.

11. Wade Clark Roof uses the term "spiritual seeker" to refer to the "baby boomers" who came of age in the 1960s. Most notable about the religious sensibility and practice of this generation is their "pastiche-style of spirituality" that draws upon an "expanded number of religious options," including Eastern spirituality (*A Generation of Seekers: The Spiritual Journeys of the Baby Boom Generation* [San Francisco: HarperCollins 1993], 245).

12. The martial arts films that emerged in the early 1970s make passing reference to the spiritual dimension of their fighting practice, but this dimension is merely assumed and is used to distinguish the "good guys" from the "bad guys." Take, e.g., *Enter the Dragon* (1973), in which the martial arts legend Bruce Lee does battle with an evil drug lord. The superior fighting skills and heroic stance of Lee's character are taken as signs of his spiritual integrity. A brief but memorable statement affirms his moral rectitude: "You have offended my family, and you have offended a Shaolin temple." Since such films presuppose Eastern spirituality, they are less useful for my purposes of showing how this representation gets established and codified for American audiences.

13. Kwai Chang Caine's designation as "half Chinese, half American" is important to note; while the designation speaks of national origin, it is racially coded to mean, "half Asian, half white."

14. The gender and sexuality of the Oriental Monk icon are ripe for critical exploration. Richard Fung describes the construction of the Asian male in popular film as "sometimes dangerous, sometimes friendly, but almost always characterized by a desexualized Zen asceticism ... the Asian man if defined by a striking absence down there" ("Looking for My Penis: The Eroticized Asian in Gay Porn Video," in *How Do I Look? Queer Film and Video*, ed. Bad Object Choices [Seattle: Bay Press, 1991], 145–68, quotation from p. 148).

15. For a discussion of "racist love" and "racist hate" and how they operate through racial stereotypes, see Frank Chin and Jeffery Paul Chan, "Racist Love," in *Seeing through Shuck*, ed. Richard Kostelanetz (New York: Ballantine Books, 1972), 65–79.

16. For a synopsis of Gere's view, see his editorial, "Tibet a Litmus Test for U.S. Moral Resolve," *USA Today*, March 13, 1997, 15A.

17. See Edward Silver, "Finding a New Path," *Los Angeles Times*, April 11, 1995, E1, E8.

18. After the release of these pictures, references to the Dalai Lama and Tibet in magazines, newspapers, television, and the Internet were numerous. A few insightful pieces during this period: Richard Bernstein, "Hollywood's Love Affair with Tibet," *New York Times,* March 19, 1997, B1, B4; David Plotz, "The Ambassador from Shangri-La: The Dalai Lama sells the romance of Tibet. The West is buying," www.slate.com, April 18, 1997; and Richard Corliss, "Zen and the Art of Moviemaking," *Time,* October 13, 1997, 82–83. For a compelling historical account of the encounter between Tibetan Buddhism and the West, see Donald S. Lopez Jr., *Prisoners of Shangri-La: Tibetan Buddhism and the West* (Chicago: University of Chicago Press, 1998).

19. Martin Wassell, documentary filmmaker, and Steven Batchelor, British Buddhist monk and scholar, respectively, quoted in Silver, "Finding a New Path," E8.

20. It is significant to note that the production of *Kung Fu* in 1971 coincided with the U.S. rapprochement with China. President Nixon's much heralded visit to the People's Republic of China took place in 1972, the year of the television series' debut. Although China had been viewed as a "communist threat" ever since the establishment of the People's Republic of China in 1949, it was never portrayed as America's primary adversary in Cold War and post–Cold War political rhetoric, the way the Soviet Union was until the fall of the Berlin Wall. See Stephen Whitfield, *The Culture of the Cold War,* 2d ed. (Baltimore: Johns Hopkins Press, 1996).

21. Bernstein, March 29, 1997, B1. It is interesting to note how the Cold War politics have shifted from being primarily fought on the grounds of commercial representation; the conflict is no longer one expressed solely in terms of national interests (United States vs. China), but rather involves a multinational corporate proxy (e.g., Disney vs. China). See Bernard Weintraub, "Disney Will Defy China on Its Dalai Lama Film, *New York Times,* November 27, 1996, C9, and Jeffrey Ressner, "Disney's China Policy," *Time,* December 9, 1996, 60.

22. "The International Year of Tibet," *Tricycle: The Buddhist Review* 1, no. 1 (Fall 1991): 32–33, quotation from p. 32.

23. Additional examples of this phenomenon include *Xiaolin Showdown,* which aired from 2003 to 2006, and Power Rangers, which began with the 1993 series, *Mighty Morphin Power Rangers;* subsequent series continue to the present day.

24. The role of the "spiritual caregiver" is very much in tune with Sau-ling C. Wong's "ideological caregiver," who operates within a "psycho-spiritual plantation system"—"a stratified world of privileged whites and colored servers/caregivers." Such caregivers as they are portrayed in popular film and television have no other role or function than to serve and "salve the insecurities of the master/mistress." See Sau-ling C. Wong, "'Sugar Sisterhood': Situating

the Amy tan Phenomenon," in *The Ethnic Canon: Histories, Institutions, and Interventions,* ed. David Palumbo-Liu (Minneapolis: Minnesota University Press, 1995), 174–210, and "Diverted Mothering: Representations of Caregivers of Color in the Age of 'Multiculturalism,'" in *Mothering: Ideology, Experience, and Agency,* ed. Evelyn Nakano Glenn, Grace Change, and Linda Rennie Forcie (New York: Routledge, 1994) 67–91.

25. See Carol Clover, *Men, Women, and Chainsaws: Gender in the Modern Horror Film* (Princeton, NJ: Princeton University Press, 1992), 90.

# CHAPTER THREE

# *Adventure Time* and Sacred History

## *Myth and Reality in Children's Animated Cartoons*

### ELIJAH SIEGLER

Everyone knows Scooby-Doo is the worst. The original TV series, *Scooby Doo, Where Are You!* ran from 1969 to 1970 with terrible animation and witless scripts. Various iterations over the next forty years—animated TV movies; episodes embedded in cartoon anthologies for kids; the updated series *What's New Scooby Doo?* (2002–6); live action films— were of similarly poor quality. Any affection felt for the Scooby Gang, the four mystery-solving teenagers and their semi-intelligent Great Dane from the town of Crystal Cove, was due to ironic nostalgia and the memory of watching hours of bad Saturday morning cartoons while eating sugary cereal.

There was no reason to think that the latest reboot, which debuted on the Cartoon Network in 2010, would be any less terrible than its predecessors. Yet *Scooby Doo! Mystery Incorporated* was different. Like new iterations of other kids' animated franchises, from *Teen Titans* to *Looney Tunes,* it was smarter, self-aware, and intertextual.[1]

But *Mystery Incorporated* was more than its knowingness: it featured serialized storytelling and complicated backstories involving the parents of the Scooby Gang, a previous group of teenage mystery-solvers, and the secret history of Crystal Cove itself. Further, the new series links monsters from earlier Scooby eras to Lovecraftian allusions, and, in its second season and final season, to Mesopotamian deities. In short, Scooby-Doo has a mythology.

How did a 2010s reboot of a kids, cartoon show develop a mythology, when previous versions did not? And what do we mean by "mythology" when applied to a TV series anyway? This essay will answer these questions and further argue that to fully understand the role of mythology in popular culture we must take kids' cartoon series of the 2010s seriously. One in particular, *Adventure Time,* best represents a particular way of thinking about mythology.

Mythological approaches to the study of literature, film and popular culture used to be quite common, whether from a mainstream literary critic like Northrop Frye or a structuralist semiotician like Roland Barthes, who famously wrote mythic analyses of James Bond movies and wrestling matches. But these approaches have recently fallen out of favor. Here, I attempt to reclaim for scholars a mythological approach, which fan communities and creators of popular culture use more and more frequently. Myths are stories, and stories should be taken seriously. To do so, we must clarify our terms. In ordinary usage, "myth" is thought of us as a commonly accepted belief that is in fact untrue ("the myth of drinking eight glasses of water a day") or else as a tale of ancient gods and heroes ("the myth of Athena"). For scholars of religious studies, on the other hand, "myth" has a different connotation: a culturally transmitted story that gives that culture a sense of identity and meaning. In religious studies, all myths are true in the sense of revealing important cultural realities, whether they are factually and historically accurate or not. William Paden, a scholar of comparative religion, calls myth "a definitive voice that names the ultimate powers that create, maintain, and re-create one's life ... a voice that articulates the prototypical events, beings, and teachings that form the standards for all subsequent religious life."[2]

A lot of work on myth in popular culture is indebted to Joseph Campbell (1904–87), a writer and speaker who did more to popularize the study of mythology than anyone else. Campbell analyzed myths from all corners of the globe and all periods of history, seeing them as all telling the same story, the "monomyth" consisting of three major segments: departure, initiation, and return, which he further divided into stages. As Campbell argued, most famously in his 1949 bestseller, *The Hero with a Thousand Faces,* all myths are about "The Adventure of the Hero" and can be used as tools for our psychological integration.

Campbell has been criticized for ignoring myths that didn't fit the template of his "hero's journey," for rewriting myths to fit his preconceived notions, and for focusing on the psychological function of myths, instead of their political and social dimensions. Nonetheless, scholars continue to apply Campbell's monomyth to cultural products such as *Star Wars, Lord of the Rings,* and superhero movies.

What most scholars do not realize is that Campbell's ideas have been so widely accepted that Hollywood films are often purposefully crafted to follow mythic patterns by screenwriters who have read either Campbell or popular guides that use him. What Campbell meant as a description of existing mythic story patterns has become a guidebook for writers. In fact, screenwriters are taught that in order to write a successful script, they should structure it according to Campbell's twelve-stage Hero's Journey and populate it with Campbell's archetypal characters.[3] So when a scholar demonstrates that Campbell's Hero's Journey is the "key" that unlocks the meaning of a particular Hollywood film, she is probably making a circular argument.

## THE MYTHOLOGY OF TELEVISION

While the hero myth may apply well to films and comic books, TV, as an increasingly rich medium, "does not recapitulate myth so much as complexify it."[4] As we have seen, filmmakers and academic critics draw on ideas about myth to talk about film. In the case of television, the terms myth and mythology have become part of the discourse of fans. As I have argued elsewhere: "We must take seriously the word "mythology" in the way television fan communities use it, as a reference to the overarching story arc of a series (and, if presented, its pre-series "back-story"); as a television series moves forward, it also moves back, exploring this "mythology." ... The term was first used in fan communities in this way to apply to *The X-Files* (FOX 1993–2002), whose episodes revolving around an alien invasion and related government cover-up were called "mythology" or "myth arc" episodes (to distinguish them from the "stand alone"—or "monster of the week"—episodes).[5]

In the discourse of television studies and television fandom, mythology means something like serialized narrative plus backstory plus world building. In some cases, over time programs develop their own origin myths that explain their mythic worlds. So how should the scholar of religion and popular culture use myth to study television? Neither the traditional literary/semiotic approach, nor the Campbellian hero myth is appropriate. I suggest reclaiming the works of Mircea Eliade (1907–86), a founder of the modern field of comparative religion. Eliade opens his widely reprinted essay "Cosmogonic Myth and 'Sacred History'" by saying that "it is not without fear and trembling that a historian of religion approaches the problem of myth."[6] This is because scholars must be very careful about their definition and examples of myth, Eliade goes on to explain. Whereas Campbell saw myths around the world as sharing a similar structure, Eliade makes sure we understand the quantity and diversity of mythology, even in a single given culture: "[Claude] Lévi-Strauss has devoted more than 300 pages to the analysis of a group of South-American myths," and the myths of the Dayak people of Borneo, as collected by an anthropologist "if ever printed would cover 12,000 pages."[7] Furthermore, where Campbell saw myths as emerging from our common psychological makeup, Elide recognized "the role of creative individuals in the elaboration and transmission of myths."[8]

Whereas Campbell saw myths' essential function to be providing a map for individual psychological growth, for Eliade, who was deeply concerned with time as a concept, the essential function of myths was to remind us of the origins of things: myths recreate sacred time, allowing us to escape from ordinary historic time. While Campbell saw the hero's journey as the paradigmatic myth, Eliade wrote primarily about cosmogonic myths, stories about the origin of our world.[9] Cosmogonic myths are less easily applied to the study of popular culture than the Campbellian monomyth, and Eliade's theories have been less influential on popular culture than have Campbell's. However, Eliade has been more influential in religious studies scholarship and has been subject to more sustained criticism than has Campbell.[10]

### "ADVENTURE TIME, COME ON GRAB YOUR FRIENDS"

If we wanted to find a pop culture artifact to demonstrate Eliadian mythic themes, we would look for one that tells a large number of different stories with great creativity. If those stories are about origins, in particular the origin of the world created in this artifact, the stories could be a read as an invented sacred history.[11]

There is no better example than *Adventure Time,* whose very name Eliade would have approved. In theory a children's show, this animated series, which debuted on the Cartoon Network in 2010, consists, as of the end of the seventh season in mid-2016, of over 230 eleven-minute episodes. (There are also growing spin-off media: a series of comic books and guidebooks). *Adventure Time* is about two adopted brothers—a human boy named Finn and a talking, shape-shifting dog named Jake who live in the fantasy land of Ooo, but the range of characters and stories present the viewer with an unimaginable richness of mythological world-making. Like all good myths, *Adventure Time* is a pastiche of cultural influences.[12] Both its look and its highly serialized storytelling are influenced by Japanese anime but it also borrows heavily from the tabletop role-playing game *Dungeons & Dragons.* Influences include the notions of good versus evil and of law versus chaos as compass points of one's "alignment," and many of its monsters are taken from the art of the *Dungeons & Dragons* book *Monster Manual*—including monsters both minor (a gelatinous cube) and major (the Lich).

*Adventure Time*'s merits have not gone unnoticed by critics and journalists. The AV Club web site , which runs regular reviews of each episode, noted that each season "expanded the series' mythology and backstory, with more revealed about the history of Ooo, the Ice King, and the Mushroom War than had been in previous seasons."[13]

Emily Nussbaum, the *New Yorker* magazine's perceptive television critic, wrote a 1,200-word appreciation of *Adventure Time* in 2014. She too noticed that while the early episodes were more conventional and "stuck more closely to a familiar formula," later episodes grew in complexity, so much so that she called the series "a post-apocalyptic allegory full of helpful dating tips for teen-agers, or like World of Warcraft as recapped by Carl Jung." It is, she writes, "one of the most philosophically risky and, often, emotionally affecting shows on TV."[14]

In a lengthy online appreciation of the series that includes reporting on and interviews with its creators, Maria Bustillos echoes Nussbaum's language, calling *Adventure Time* a "serious work of moral philosophy," with "emotional force."[15] That combination of philosophical ideas about time and space and about how to live coupled with a core of genuine ineffable emotion defines *Adventure Time* as mythic in the Eliadian sense. Interviewed by Bustillos, Pat McHale, a storyboard artist who is a creative force behind the show, gets at that sense: "It's about the literature of—the literature of the universe, or something. Any kind of symbolism, like looking into the mythology of monsters, or of religion, and history."[16]

## "WE'RE GOING TO VERY DISTANT LANDS"

Early episodes show Finn and Jake helping the denizens of Ooo: sentient animals, objects, and fantasy creatures. Most famously, the human and the dog rescue princesses from Ice King, the series' comic villain. As the series progressed we discover that Ooo may be post-apocalyptic Earth, a thousand years hence.

Certainly, *Adventure Time* is explicitly about the hero's quest, but this surface-level of analysis is so obvious as to be uninteresting: Finn constantly states that he is a hero on a quest. One of the earliest episodes, "The Enchiridion" explicitly asks the question, "What is a hero?" Finn is indeed a hero, and he has had many identities over the years, yet he is anything but a "hero with a thousand faces." Although he may wind up saving the Land of Ooo by the time the series concludes, he is not a Campbellian savior in the mode of Luke Skywalker, Rocky Balboa, or Captain America.[17] And *Adventure Time* is anything but a monomyth. Instead it follows Eliade's advice that "it is wiser not to become bound by any formulae, nor to reduce all myths to a single prototype"[18] *Adventure Time* tells all kinds of different stories, about stones, earth, water, vegetation, the sky, and palaces (all chapters in Eliade's *Patterns in Comparative Religion*).

Any slightly attentive reader will notice that *Adventure Time* is a series of myths of origin. Each of the characters has his or her own myths. The Ice King used to be Simon Petrikov, a professor of archeology who found a cursed crown, which physically transformed him, gave him magic powers, and ultimately drove him mad. The pitiful Lemongrabs are a scientific experiment gone awry. Prismo, one of the series' godlike figures, a two-dimensional master of time and space who grants wishes, is revealed as an old man's dream.

In the first season, we learn that as an infant, Finn was alone, wrapped in a leaf, until he was found by Jake's parents, a married pair of detective dogs. Later we learn of his birth father, and the show's creators have hinted that his birth mother may become a character in the series' eighth season. But the overarching origin myth in *Adventure Time* is cosmogonic: how was the Land of Ooo created? We learn bits and pieces about a Mushroom War and its mutagenic side effects, the return of Magic to the world, a war between dogs and rainicorns, and in more recent episodes the periodic appearance of a mysterious Comet.

The mythological backstory of *Adventure Time* is rich, complex, and changes as the writers add to it over time. It will not be summarized here, but has been in many online fan sites. One aficionado who calls himself "GunterFan" has created a detailed narrative that knits together the various episodes that deal with the backstory of Ooo and put the narratives together chronologically to produce a coherent cosmogony, complete with origin myths for all the characters.[19] Alternate fan theories posted online posit revisionist histories, in particular as to when the Mushroom War took place in relation to the events of the series.[20]

## SURVIVALS AND CAMOUFLAGES OF GODS AND RELIGION IN *ADVENTURE TIME*

Critics and fans love pointing out that missiles, skyscrapers, factories—remnants of Ooo's distant past, our present—figure in the scenic background of most episodes, unremarked on by characters. GunterFan's episode reviews have a distinct section for "Mushroom War Evidence." Another online fan has searched for visual clues of survivals of our present religions—one character has a picture of Mary cradling the infant Jesus on her bedroom wall (only seen once), and in one scene Jake the Dog wears a yarmulke.[21]

Organized religion is not prominent in the land of Ooo. But characters do say, "Oh my Glob" a lot, and there is one allusion to some citizens spending Sundays worshipping at a church of Glob.[22] Glob is one of the faces of a four-faced deity named "Grob Gob Glob Grod," who lives on Mars. He is one of many divine figures in *Adventure Time*'s polytheistic universe, where many deities, odd in both appearance and name (Abraham Lincoln, Prismo, Death, Cosmic Owl, Party God, and the Lich) interact with themselves (all hanging out in the episode "Wake Up!") and with the "mortal" denizens of Ooo.

But this pantheon seems arbitrary and ever-evolving: almost certainly future episodes will introduce new gods. More important, the gods are neither immortal nor omnipotent. For example, in one episode, we learn that the mysterious Cosmic Owl, the god of dreams, lives alone in a cheap motel. We see him falling in love with an enigmatic woman he keeps seeing in other people's dreams.

Indeed *Adventure Time*'s many gods and superhuman beings are all controlled by a force larger than themselves, which we may call fate.

But if we call that force "karma," we can reasonably argue that Buddhism may be the guiding religious system of *Adventure Time*. That argument gains plausibility if we consider that Finn, like *Siddhartha Gautama*, gains knowledge of his past lives, and that the very first frame of the very first "episode" (actually an online short) finds Jake meditating in the lotus position, floating a few feet above the ground. And in other episodes, he espouses Buddhist ideas.[23]

That said, for a show whose visuals are so primary, *Adventure Time* shows no interest in Asian religious iconography. Its visuals, as we have seen, are influenced by Japanese anime and *Dungeons & Dragons*, although arguably one of the pantheon, Death, who appears as a bleached horse skull wearing a cowboy hat, often seen in the desert, owes something to the mythology of the American southwest. And the themes of experiencing past lives and of multiple deities in multiples realms may owe less to Buddhism than to a general Eliadian mythical consciousness.

For Eliade, myths are real. As he stated, "one whole series of myths, recording what gods or mythical being did *in illo tempore* [in that time], discloses a level of reality quite beyond any empirical or rational comprehension."[24] *Adventure Time* too discloses a suprarational reality. It is often funny and outrageous, but it is never ironic. This lack of irony, which would create a distance from the series' world, sets it apart from *Scooby Doo: Mystery Inc.* and a lot of other animated series. *Adventure Time*'s creator, Pendleton Ward, comments: "I don't know that there's very much intentional irony in it. I try not to reference pop culture or anything, [to] try to keep it fresh."[25]

When Finn says something like "maybe birth is the greatest creative statement in all the universe" or an episode is taken up entirely by Finn and Jake playing an elaborate board game, viewers can sense the sincerity.

Though it may seem perverse to praise the "realism" of possibly the most unrealistic TV show in the history of the medium—one featuring, for example, a sentient Jump Castle named Bounce House Princess, with a goblin, a raccoon, and a gumball bouncing inside her—I believe that is exactly the proper word. In the same sense that Eliade convinces us that for the Aranda people of Central Australia, the "chthonian beings" who lived underground and who "emerged in animal forms, or [as] men and women" are real.[26]

### CONCLUSION: "THE FUN WILL NEVER END"

The rise of "mythology" in television since the 1990s combined with the fantastical imaginative sensory experience of animation led to the situation where children's animated TV series are a site for exploring mythic structures in popular culture. Several animated series that began in second decade of the twenty-first century are concerned with the origins of their worlds. *Scooby Doo: Mystery Inc.* delves into the origin of Crystal Cove. The Disney Channel's series *Gravity Falls* (a cartoon indebted to both *Twin Peaks* and *The X-Files*) is about the origin of its eponymous town, and *Steven Universe,* created by a former *Adventure Time* writer, posits its locale, the sleepy seaside town of Beach City, as the center of a cosmic war.

What would Eliade have thought of all this? What would he have made of the fact that *Adventure Time,* a series essentially targeted at six-to-eleven-year-old boys, is a fount of creation stories? I am not arguing that a "deeper meaning" of *Adventure Time* reveals itself to us when we subject the cartoon to an Eliadean analysis. Not at all. The argument is that the creators of *Adventure Time* share a goal and a method with Eliade, though they may not know his name. The goal is a recovery of mythic ways of thinking, and the method is creative presentation of a variety of myths, in particular cosmogonic myths.

Maria Bustillos compares *Adventure Time* favorably to the Giovanni Bellini's fifteenth-century painting *St. Francis in Ecstasy*: "the mixture of self-awareness, awe, doubt, affection, kindness, humor and dread in which he confronts the world and the mysteries that may lie beyond it are all very reminiscent of the work of Pen Ward.[27]" Like Bustillos's, my argument is an aesthetic one, but the comparison I am making is between viewing this series and reading Eliade. As the historian of religion Robert Ellwood wrote, "The importance one felt in Eliade's books depended more than anything else on the stylistic and imagistic calling forth of a romantic sense of wonder associated with archaic religion."[28]

Like no other TV series before it, *Adventure Time*, with its stories of being lost in the woods or in a dream, of traveling underground or up to the sky, its stories both universal and specific, calls forth in its audience a romantic sense of wonder that may tap into something archaic and religious, but almost certainly speaks with a "voice that names the ultimate powers"; in a word, *Adventure Time* is mythic.

### APPENDIX

Here are ten episodes of *Adventure Time* that show the series at its most mythological, especially in regard to its pantheon of deities and to references to classic mythic themes. Although all these episodes are considered to be among the best of the series, of course this list is highly subjective, and the reader is encouraged to watch the entire series in sequence.

The Enchiridion!: (*Season 1, Episode 5*) Finn and Jake go on a quest to find the Enchiridion, the legendary handbook of heroes.

Memories of Boom Boom Mountain: (*Season 1, Episode 10*): Finn's vow to help anyone in need is challenged when people come to him with opposing requests. In flashbacks, we learn of Finn's origins.

Death in Bloom: (*Season 2, Episode 17*) In order to resurrect a flower that Princess Bubblegum has entrusted Finn and Jake with, the royal butler allows them passage to the Land of the Dead to confront Death.

The New Frontier: (*Season 3, Episode 18*) Jake dreams of his own death, as presaged by the Cosmic Owl, and becomes determined to face his demise, much to Finn's chagrin.

Sons of Mars: (*Season 4, Episode 15*) The trickster Magic Man, brother of a deity, in order to escape punishment, switches bodies with Jake who is transported to Mars for a trial conducted by Magic Man's brother and Abraham Lincoln.

All the Little People: (*Season 5, Episode 5*) Magic Man provides Finn with living miniatures of the citizens of Ooo, including himself, and Finn becomes obsessed with controlling their lives.

The Vault: (*Season 5, Episode 34*) Finn taps into the memories of one of his many past lives in order to cure his sleepwalking.

Wake Up: *(Season 6, Episode 1)* Prismo the Wish Master advises Finn and Jake to commit a cosmic crime in order to see Finn's human father in the Crystal Citadel.

Astral Plane: (*Season 6, Episode 25*) Finn's spirit leaves his body one night and travels through Ooo and up into space, in an attempt to observe the greatest act of creativity.

The Comet: (*Season 6, Episode 43*) When Finn follows the primordial demon Orgalorg into space, the Catalyst Comet, hurtling towards earth, gives him the option to remain on Earth or to transcend existence and start everything over.

### DISCUSSION QUESTIONS

1. Siegler defines myth as a "culturally transmitted story that gives that culture a sense of identity and meaning." Describe the mythology of *Adventure Time* and discuss the system of meaning embedded in this myth.

2. Besides *Adventure Time* and the other cartoons Siegler names, what other forms of popular culture have complex storytelling that might be described as mythological?

3. Drawing on the discussion of myth in this chapter, describe America's myth of origin? What meaning does it ascribe to the nation? How is it expressed in popular culture? Give examples. Are there competing American myths of origin? What is helpful or problematic about considering society in this way?

4. Eliade believed that the model for all myths of origin was the cosmogonic myth, the story of the origin of our world. How might that argument be supported? How might it be questioned?

NOTES

Lucinda Siegler, aged thirteen, was an essential conversation partner in my thinking about *Adventure Time*. She also wrote the summaries of the ten episodes in the appendix and found many of the online links used in the chapter.

1. When the series was broadcast in the United Kingdom, the television critic for a British newspaper wrote: "*Scooby-Doo! Mystery Incorporated* takes the heavy irony a step further. It is meant for a slightly older audience.... It is hyper-fast and relentlessly savvy." Benji Wilson, "This Children's TV Revival Is Aimed at Grown-ups, not Kids," *The Telegraph*, October 3, 2015.

2. William Paden, *Religious Worlds: The Comparative Study of Religion* (Boston: Beacon Press, 1994), 73.

3. The best-known "Campbellian" Hollywood script consultant is Christopher Vogler, the Hero's Journey tab on whose web site www.thewritersjourney.com exemplifies the popularization of Campbell.

4. Elijah Siegler "Is God Still In the Box? Religion in Television Cop Shows Ten Years Later," in *God in the Details,* 2nd ed., ed. Eric M. Mazur (New York: Routledge, 2010), 180.

5. A point I consider in more detail in my essay "Television," in *The Routledge Companion to Religion and Popular Culture,* ed. Eric M. Mazur and John Lyden (New York: Routledge, 2015). I also consider *Lost* (ABC, 2004–10) as an "example of how a series' mythology can move from the background to the foreground. Each episode of the series (which began with a plane crash on a tropical island) explores one or more of the many characters' back stories, possible futures, and interconnections." (57)

6. Mircea Eliade, "Cosmogonic Myth and 'Sacred History,'"*Religious Studies* 2 (1967): 171–83.

7. Ibid., 174–75.

8. Mircea Eliade, *Myth and Reality* (New York : Harper & Row, 1963), 146

9. Eliade makes this argument in *The Myth of the Eternal Return* (New York: Harper, 1959) and *Myth and Reality*. Which is not to say he did not write about the hero's initiatory journey as one genre of myth. He did. And he even applied this to popular culture: in the final chapter of *Myth and Reality*, in a section titled "Myths and the Mass Media" (184–87), he mentions Superman comics, detective novels, and automobile shows as examples of "camouflages of myth," but the myth in question is basically the hero myth and its modern meaning is the American success narrative.

10. Eliade has been justifiably criticized for everything from fudging his data to romanticizing "archaic" man to harboring fascist sympathies. See J. Z. Smith "To Take Place," in *To Take Place* (Chicago: University of Chicago Press,

1987); Russell T. McCutcheon *Manufacturing Religion: The Discourse on Sui Generis Religion and the Politics of Nostalgia* (New York: Oxford University Press, 1997).

11. The subtitle to this section and the subsequent quoted subtitles below are taken from the *Adventure Time* theme song.

12. See S. Brent Plate, "Something Borrowed, Something Blue: *Avatar* and the Myth of Originality," http://religiondispatches.org/something-borrowed-something-blue-iavatari-and-the-myth-of-originality/.

13. www.avclub.com/review/just-past-150-episodes-adventure-time-has-yet-hit--202278.

14. "Castles in the Air," Emily Nussbaum, *New Yorker*, April 21, 2014.

15. Maria Bustillos, "It's Adventure Time," http://theholenearthecenter oftheworld.com. The philosophical profundities of the series are not the point of my essay. Readers are invited to peruse Nicolas Michaud's *Adventure Time and Philosophy: The Handbook for Heroes* (Chicago: Open Court, 2015), one of the nearly 100 volumes of the Popular Culture and Philosophy series.

16. Bustillos, "It's Adventure Time."

17. For sustained cultural critiques of these and other American heroes, see the work of Robert Jewett and John Shelton Lawrence.

18. Mircea Eliade, *Patterns of Comparative Religion* (New York: Sheed & Ward, 1958), 416.

19. "Adventure Time Mythology 101," http://gunterfan1992.tumblr.com /post/127017400379/adventure-time-mythology-101.

20. "The *Adventure Time* Time Theory," https://www.reddit.com/r/Adventure Theory/comments/2xyznn/the_adventure_time_time_theory_spoilers/.

21. "Religion in Ooo," http://adventuretime.wikia.com/wiki/User_blog: Daihasku/Religion_in_Ooo.

22. "Adventure Time Theories: The Religion of Ooo" http://adventure timeconspiracies.tumblr.com/post/35231569156/the-religion-of-ooo

23. Ibid.

24. Eliade, *Patterns of Comparative Religion*, 417.

25. http://io9.gizmodo.com/5890128/pendleton-ward-explains-how-hes-keeping-adventure-time-weird.

26. Eliade "Cosmogonic Myth," 180.

27. Bustillos, "It's Adventure Time."

28. Robert Ellwood, *The Politics of Myth: A Study of C. G. Jung, Mircea Eliade, and Joseph Campbell* (Albany: State University of New York Press, 1999), 112.

CHAPTER FOUR

# Monstrous Muslims

## *Historical Anxieties and Future Trends*

SOPHIA ROSE ARJANA

## ISLAM, MUSLIMS, AND POPULAR CULTURE

Disney's animated film *Aladdin*, released in 1992, was both a critical success and a box-office hit, earning more than $500 million worldwide. It went on to win several awards, most notably for its music. Unfortunately, not everyone was pleased with the film. The American-Arab Anti-Discrimination Committee protested the lyrics in the opening song, which began with the lines, "Where they cut off your ear if they don't like your face."[1] Other critics pointed out the movie's portrayal of Aladdin and Jasmine, the protagonists, as characters with Anglo features that contrasted with the dark-skinned and exaggerated racial features of the villains in the film. Filled with a smorgasbord of exotic locations, dress, and objects, Aladdin is typical of what Americans associate with Islam. Many of the representations of Muslims in American popular culture are rooted in these images of the fantastic—flying carpets, magical genies, and exotic landscapes. These images and the characters that accompany them are productions of Orientalism, a system of symbols that relies on the exotic.

The majority of portrayals of Muslims found in American popular culture are of this variety—flying carpets, genies, and magic lamps, what we might call "soft Orientalism." In my 2015 book *Muslims in the*

*Western Imagination,* I detail the commodification of Orientalism, which functioned as a symbolic consumption of the Orient itself. "In many cases, the consumption was literal—seen in purchasable commodities—textiles, lighting fixtures, furniture, *objects d'art,* jewelry, and other products."[2] In addition to these products, the Orient is present in metaphorical acts, such as the viewing of an Orientalist painting by Eugène Delacroix (1798–1863),[3] reading of a romantic Orientalist novel, or seeing one of the numerous films that feature Muslim characters. The production of these films was part of the larger fad of Orientalism and Egyptology, also evident in popular architecture, that was often featured in theaters and movie houses. The films shown in these venues often highlighted Orientalist themes of the romantic sort—a dashing Arab sheik, damsels in distress, exotic locations, and of course the harem. Although less common in television, the comedy series *I Dream of Jeanie* (1965–70) provided Americans with a variety of images connected to the East and Islam, including the title character, who calls her white husband "master."

The exotic also has a dark side, seen in many of the images of Muslims in literature, film, and television that feature Arab despots, murderous Turkish sultans, and more recently, homicidal terrorists. This is the "hard Orientalism" that is contrasted to the more romantic portrayals that many Americans may be more familiar with. As Edward Said wrote, there is a stock type of Muslim character who is "backwards, degenerate, uncivilized, and retarded."[4] The analysis of Islam in popular culture is typically focused on these negative portrayals of Muslims, which include characters inspired by Orientalism and the more recent villainous types situated in political discourse, such as the hijacker and suicide bomber. Jack Shaheen notes in his study of Arab characters in Hollywood films, "Beginning with *Imar the Servitor* (1914), up to and including *The Mummy Returns* (2001), a synergy of images equates Arabs from Syria to the Sudan with quintessential evil."[5]

Muslims have been a fixture in American popular culture from the earliest days of the nation, even predating the writing of the Declaration of Independence. The United States of America has never had a friendly relationship with Islam; in fact, the earliest references to Muslims express concepts related to barbarianism, violence, and criminality. These references first appeared in stories about the Barbary Coast, where Muslims were referred to the "monsters of Africa." Muslim characters, first identified with Barbary pirates, appeared in everything from dime store novels to board games. As Paul Baepler writes, "In addition to the published historical accounts of slavery in North Africa, the Barbary captivity topos appeared in at least four early American novels, nine early plays, ten dime-store novels, and almost a dozen Hollywood movies."[6] Later, North African Muslims were replaced with Arabs, Persians, and South Asians as characters featured in comics, cartoons, advertising, movies, television, and other modes of cultural production.

Popular culture is a broad subject whose definition and scope has been much debated by scholars. As noted above, Muslim characters appear in a large corpus of materials—advertising, board games, signage, and other materials. In earlier centuries, Americans could purchase such products from a catalogue. "In the absence of a widespread ability to travel with ease, Victorian Americans could simply open the illustrated catalogues, Products from the Orient, to easily recreate the harems, bazaars, and palaces that they read about in travelogues and saw on display in fairs."[7] Today, consumers purchase movie tickets, cable television subscriptions, comic books, and other materials that feature Muslim characters and imagery. The vast majority of this imagery is negative. "Islam has become a mysterious and dangerous religion to Western audiences who continue to gain most of their information about Islam from the media," Mahmoud Eid and Sarah Khan remark.[8]

In this chapter, I will limit the discussion to movies, television, and comic books, due in part to their wide reach and their role in mediating values. The relationship between social beliefs and popular culture is an important one. In the case of Islam, around which a good deal of anxiety exists, we see the expression of these concerns in movies, television, and elsewhere where Muslim characters, images, and themes are found. The French social theorist Pierre Bourdieu described this relationship as one between the habitus (the often unconscious collection of beliefs and attitudes held by a social group) and the modes of cultural production (literature, art, storytelling, movies, television) that reflect the habitus. In America, the society's anxieties, beliefs, and values find their way into popular culture, reflecting what people believe about Islam and Muslims and giving them a tactile expression.

Since 2001, many more movies have featured stereotypical and pejorative portrayals of Arabs and other Muslims than pre-2001. Over the past decade, Muslims have appeared in ever more diverse ways in popular culture, a trend that is due to several factors—the visibility of Islam since 9/11, the growing presence of Muslims in various industries, and the popularity of social media, which provides alternative outlets for the production of imagery about Muslims. Although some of the old symbols remain, they are complemented by images of Muslims that challenge the imperial narrative. Contemporary portrayals of Muslims in pop culture range from the sheiks, terrorists, and sultans of Hollywood film to the superheroes, heroines, and social revolutionaries found in comic books.

## ISLAM IN THE WEST: A BRIEF HISTORY

Islam is a fixture of the Western imagination, attached to an important set of representations in the popular cultures of Europe and later the United States. From the beginning, Islam has been "the other, the enemy, always the disturbing faction."[9] Islam functions as a kind of metric for the way the West defines itself. "By ranking the Other, we are able to define the self, and our self identity as that which we are not."[10] In Europe, images of Muslims appeared shortly after Islam emerged as a world power. Early imaginings about Muslims, who were called Saracens throughout the Middle Ages, relied on biblical eschatology about Satan and the End of Days. The early Saracens were nothing more than "actors in the divine drama of the last days," identified with the four beasts of the Apocalypse.[11]

When these ideas became expressed in popular culture—literature, art, and drama—they were situated in anxieties about monsters, the devil, and Christian identity. Medieval representations of Muslims were largely monstrous, seen in creatures such as the *cynocephalus* (dog-headed man), Saracen giant (cannibalistic), and Black Saracen (a demonic killer of Christian saints). The idea of Muslims as non-human was situated in the medieval belief in monsters, fear of the foreign and strange, and the idea that Muslims were a "race of dogs."[12] In the Renaissance, many of these characters were replaced by Turkish villains representing the threat posed by Ottoman power, typically shown with a turban, surrounded by their Jewish co-conspirators, killing Christ or executing a Christian saint.

During the Age of Exploration, Turkish monsters persisted and were joined by the "Moorish" characters that appeared in the explorers' early imaginings about the Americas. Scholars have described these imaginings as a product of Maurophilia, a process of re-naming peoples and places in the Americas that includes descriptions of American Indians as Moors and the re-naming of Indian cities as Cairo or Baghdad. As Anouar Majid points out, "So interchangeable were Muslims and Indians in the conquistador's minds that they called Indians 'Muslims' and Indian temples 'mosques.'"[13] A few centuries later, Orientalism inspired a new generation of Muslim characters, including the decadent and cruel despot, the female seductress, and the oversexed Arab, that still persist today.

Gothic horror was heavily influenced by Orientalism. In fact, scholars have often described it as a genre that combines Orientalism, a resurrection of medievalism, and a pronounced anxiety regarding women and foreigners. Gothic literature includes a long list of Muslim villains, such as the Moorish demon Zofloya, featured in Charlotte Dacre's 1806 book of the same name, and William Beckford's homicidal sultan

Vathek (1786), who sacrifices children and has an Indian male lover with green teeth. Like mummies and zombies, after the monsters of Barbary made their way into American literary culture, they entered the cinema. Movies, then television, are the venues for many of the characters and images associated with Islam in the twentieth and twenty-first centuries. Today, Muslims are commonly featured in revenge movies like the *Taken* franchise, which includes an Arab sheik who holds young American women in a white slavery ring, and television programs like *Homeland,* which despite its harsh representation of Muslims has garnered numerous awards. The majority of the Muslim characters we see are violent men, while Muslim females are often subsidiary, occupying the role of wife, concubine, or captive of the villain. Typically cast as foreigners, these characters rarely reflect the long history of Muslims in the Americas.

## MUSLIMS IN AMERICA

The historical presence of Muslims in America is not reflected in the presentation of Muslims in popular culture. As noted above, the Muslim has historically been seen as an Other, an outside, foreign, and exotic identity that is alien to the United States. Much like non-Protestant groups like Catholics, Jews, and Mexicans, Muslims are viewed as external. John Bowen describes this as part of the larger "rhetoric of Islam-bashing."[14] Even though Muslims are constantly described as un-American, immigrant, and foreign, in reality, Muslims have been present in the Americas since the beginning of the nation, first as individuals forced into slavery, later as immigrants. One of the oldest U.S. Muslim communities is in Cedar Rapids, Iowa, founded in 1934.

Today, Muslims play many roles in American society. Malcolm X is a cultural icon, visible on everything from posters to T-shirts. The late Muhammad Ali, perhaps the best-known American Muslim, also has an iconic status as both an athlete and an activist. Ali is in the company of numerous professional athletes and entertainers. Muslim athletes include the NFL players Ryan Harris, Aqib Talib, and Isa Abdul-Quddus and the basketball players Kareem Abdul-Jabbar, Kenneth Faried, and Nazr Mohammed. Muslims in entertainment include comedians like Dave Chappelle and Maz Jobrani and rappers such as Akon, Mos Def, and Lupe Fiasco.

African American Muslim communities are particularly well established and today they make up the largest numbers of American Muslims. Immigrants also make up large communities of American Muslims, but are far more recent than African American Muslims. White converts, who compose the smallest group of American Muslims, are growing in number and are also becoming more visible as scholars, community leaders, and social activists. Shaykh Hamza Yusuf is one of the best known of these white converts, a respected scholar and co-founder of Zaytuna College, the first Islamic college in the United States.

American popular culture does not typically focus on these Muslims, nor on the long history of Islam in the United States. Instead, the focus is on non-Americans—Arabs, Iranians, and South Asians who live outside the United States. These groups represent particular anxieties about economics (such as the oil sheik, a popular character in film and television), politics (the Iranians featured in movies about hostage-taking), and violence (the Pakistani or Afghan terrorist common in both movies and television dramas). Characters identified as American Muslims have only recently started to emerge and they are few in number. Rarely do these portrayals include African Americans, in part because Islam is viewed as the antithesis to America. Identifying Muslims as Americans continues to be resisted, something seen in both political discourse and popular culture.

## AMERICAN HEROES AND MUSLIM VILLAINS

A catalogue of all of the character types, narratives, and tropes associated with Muslims in American popular culture is an immense undertaking. The remainder of this chapter focuses on two types of narratives—one that examines some of the negative depictions of Muslim men in movies and television, and one that looks at the production of positive Muslim characters in comic books and cartoons. The disparity in these representations shows that, although the vast majority of Muslims in popular culture receive a negative and stereotypical treatment, there is movement away from this standard.

The first type of narrative focuses on the rescue narrative that features an American hero and Muslim villain. Stories of savages (Indians, Africans, Mexicans, Muslims) kidnapping white women, attacking civilization, and threatening American homogeneity originate in the captivity narratives associated with the Barbary Coast and the kidnapping stories involving Native Americans. The captivity narrative is America's "first coherent mythical literature," according to the historian Richard Slotkin.[15] As Greg Siemenski has pointed out, captivity narratives have often functioned politically—against Native Americans, French "papists," and the heroes of the American Revolution held "captive" by British tyranny.[16] More recently, they have been popularized in books, films, and television shows featuring Muslim villains.

In the majority of Hollywood movies, Muslims are associated with faraway lands, harems, palaces, and other symbols of the exotic. According to Stephen William Foster, the exotic is "a great zero, a place-holder about which is elaborated complex semantic systems and cross references defying the imagination of even the most far-out science fiction novelist."[17] Films like the Indiana Jones franchise that feature a bevy of frightening characters from the Orient (including Muslims) have helped establish a particular set of ideas about Muslims that reflect American anxieties and reinforce claims of American exceptionalism. In *Indiana Jones and the Temple of Doom* (1984), the East is full of foreign dangers including poisonous drinks, giants, killer snakes, man-eating crocodiles, human traffickers, and human-sacrificing cults. This is the East that necessitates an American hero. As Ella Shohat argues, "The American hero—often cinematically portrayed as a cowboy—is an archaeologist implicitly searching for the Eastern roots of Western civilization. He liberates the ancient Hebrew ark from illegal Egyptian possession, while also rescuing it from immoral Nazi control, subliminally reinforcing American and Jewish solidarity vis-à-vis the Nazis and their Arab assistants."[18]

Arabs are also popular characters in Hollywood films outside of the adventure-fantasy genre, typically cast as some kind of villain—a rapist, kidnapper, invader, or terrorist. The Arnold Schwarzenegger movie *True Lies* (1994) is one of numerous features that involve a kidnapping, American hero, and evil Arab terrorists. In this film, the Arab villains are gunned down in such an indiscriminate and wild fashion that one loses track of the body count. In the 2008 Liam Neeson rescue-revenge fantasy film *Taken* (now a franchise with numerous installments), the main character rescues his daughter from the clutches of an obese Arab who has plans to rape her. In this film, sexual trafficking is "portrayed as stocking the harems of the Eastern world with young white women, where they will be made to serve the exotic sexual whims of the Orient."[19]

Iranian characters demonstrate the lingering anxiety surrounding the 1979–81 American hostage crisis and its aftermath. The 1991 film *Not Without My Daughter* tells the story of an American woman trapped in Iran during the Revolution who escapes with her daughter from the clutches of a malevolent husband. The movie was based on the book of the same title, which was one of many accounts (both real and fabricated) of white women marrying foreign men from whom they then had to escape. The 2012 film *Argo*, which tells the story of American embassy workers trapped in Iran after the storming of the U.S. Embassy in Tehran, also follows the formula of the captivity narrative—with a twist. The American CIA agent who rescues the Americans (who are captives of the Revolution, unable to leave Iran without his help) is an unsavory character, a kind of anti-hero. The film also includes several fabricated incidents that are indictments of American hubris, imperialism, and incompetence.

*300* (2006) is a movie that is at first appearance a story about an ancient battle between the Spartans and the Persians. As numerous scholars and film critics have pointed out, the film is really about the civilizational battle between the West and Islam. Hamid Dabashi called the Persians the "nightmares of the White Christian America," who function in a "Christological" narrative that professes "hate for being other than white, male, Christian, and heterosexual."[20] The Persians are a monstrous lot, including hunchbacks with filed teeth; deformed lesbians who are part of a sex orgy in a harem lorded over by the Persian king Xerxes, a giant who fancies men; and other scary creatures from the East. The Islamic references in the film include the harem, Persians wearing turbans, Orientalist costumes, and the use of code words about submission, the battle between democracy and barbarism, and civilization. As I have written elsewhere, "*300* is not about an ancient battle—it's about the West's advanced and modern civilization over Islam's backward and brutal culture."[21]

Muslim characters in American television predate 2001, appearing as oil barons in nighttime soap operas and in other minor roles, but there was an exponential increase in the era following 9/11. Among the television shows that scholars have described as being part of the "Terror TV" phenomenon is the Showtime drama *Homeland*, which focuses on the fallout of an American soldier ("Brody") kidnapped in Afghanistan, held and tortured, and finally released. When he returns home, it is revealed that he has gone to the dark side and become a Muslim—a cruel, sex-crazed, and terroristic Muslim. Even when his storyline fades, the main character Carrie, a neurotic CIA operative who lives on a steady diet of benzodiazepines and coffee, is challenged with bad Muslim after bad Muslim, who kidnap, terrorize, torture, and kill good Americans in many episodes.

In 2015, the producers of *Homeland* hired a team of Arabic linguists to paint graffiti on the set. In a subversive turn against the show, which is thought by many Muslims, Arabs and South Asians (including non-Muslims) to be racist, xenophobic, and Islamophobic, the graffiti team wrote Arabic phrases that criticized the show or even made fun of it such as "Homeland is a joke." As James Poniewozik wrote in the *New*

*York Times,* "Arguably, this kind of small detail is the greater problem with 'Homeland' and other American dramas set in the region: the tendency to use the signifiers of a culture—clothes, music, street urchins, unfamiliar writing—as a kind of spicy Orientalist soup of otherness. Even in a well-intended drama, if you approach another culture as set decoration, in which the alien appearance matters more than the content, you risk sending a subtle but strong message: this is a terrifying, unknowable land where everything goes squibbly."[22] The fact that no one on the production team knew Arabic, or was familiar with Urdu, Dari, or Pashto, all languages represented on the show, makes a powerful statement about who has the power to represent Muslima in popular culture.

The use of master tropes and narratives includes the white hero, villainous foreigner, and superiority of the United States, and often features a voyeuristic journey through a foreign land such as Africa, Asia, or the Orient. *Homeland* is one case where the "I/eye of empire spiraled outward around the globe, creating a visceral, kinetic sense of imperial travel and conquest."[23] The effort on behalf of the graffiti artists to reclaim the Arabic language can be seen as part of a larger struggle against this presentation of Muslims, with Americans cast in the role of "armchair conquistadors" who conquer the Orient through their televisions.[24]

## COMIC BOOKS AND OTHER HOPEFUL TRENDS

Islam is typically represented in American popular culture as a problem originating from the Middle East that poses danger to the homeland. However, relying solely on these representations ignores the positive and even transformative characters featured in several areas of popular culture. Recently, the Coca-Cola Company and others have featured Muslims in major advertising campaigns, suggesting that American Muslims are being considered a viable economic demographic. This translates to popular culture as well, since it offers a reflection of the marketplace of American sensibilities about Islam, which are mixed but perhaps on an upward trend. North of the border, this is reflected in Zarqa Nawaz's groundbreaking television show *Little Mosque on the Prairie* (2007–12). *LMP* is an important show, a production that shows Muslims as normalized North Americans. It counters the negative images in television shows like *Homeland* and *24*. Zarqa Nawaz's female characters are involved in issues that affect all North American women, including "business, personal and marital relationships, feminism," with the addition of Islam and the negotiation of one's religion in a secular society.[25] The United States has no comparable television show.

Areas of popular culture outside of movie and television merit analysis. The comic book is one such area. As an important cultural text, it has often been used to support the cultural values of the majority. Such is the case of Captain America. At the same time, the comic is a medium that can be countercultural. Comics featuring African American characters have had a presence for decades. In 1966, Black Panther appeared as a prominent character in Marvel's *Fantastic Four* series. A rich character with social significance (he emerged one year after the assassination of Malcolm X), he remains popular today—evidence of the staying power of comic book characters. The presence of minorities in comics, including as superheroes, reflects the fact that there are numerous spaces in popular culture where alternative representations of Muslims can also be enacted. The emergence of Muslim characters in American comics is so new that it has yet to be examined by most scholars.[26] Of these characters, *Ms. Marvel* (Kamala Khan) has garnered the most attention. Marvel Comics' superheroine is a Pakistani-American teenager. She has numerous adventures that include storylines that have her interacting with well-established Marvel characters like Wolverine. Created by two American Muslim women, G. Willow Wilson (the author, a white convert to Islam) and Sana Amanat (the editor of the series, a Pakistani American), Kamala Khan represents an effort to tackle issues like race and gender, which are often ignored in comic books.[27] Khan's experiences as a Muslim of color, an American, and a female are highlighted in the story. "A major development, for instance, is the publisher's conscientiousness towards issues around inclusion and intersectionality."[28]

The presence of Muslims in popular culture also includes the production of characters originating abroad that have found their way into American media. One example is *Burka Avenger,* a Pakistani-produced cartoon that has an English-language web site and has been the subject of numerous articles. Burka Avenger follows the adventures of Jiya, a schoolteacher who dons a *niqab* (a veil covering the hair and face, except for the eyes) when she takes on her alter ego Burka Avenger, fighting the Taliban with books as weapons and fighting for the educational rights of children. The popularity of *The 99,* a comic book series originating in the Persian Gulf that features a large cast of Muslim superheroes and heroines, is another example of Muslim characters entering American popular culture from abroad. Much like *Little Mosque on the Prairie, Ms. Marvel, Burka Avenger,* and *The 99* offer views of Muslims that counter the tropes dominating the landscape of popular culture. While these examples are dwarfed by the large numbers of pejorative representations of Muslims in popular culture, they may represent the beginning of a more positive trend in the portrayals of Muslims in America.

## DISCUSSION QUESTIONS

1. What are the common representations of Islam in American popular culture? What do they communicate about American identity and the idea of the foreign?

2. Like Iwamura in chapter 1, Arjana draws on ideas of Orientalism to argue that popular culture portrayals of people and religions different from us are usually inaccurate, that they tell us more about the Westerners who produced them than about the people portrayed, and that these inaccurate fictions have consequences for real people from those groups (in these chapters, Asians and Muslims). Do you agree? Why or Why not? If you agree, what

are the consequences of the way Muslims are portrayed in popular culture for actual Muslims?

3. Identify some characters and storylines from popular culture that challenge what Arjana calls the Orientalist depictions of Muslims. What alternatives ways of thinking about Islam and Muslims do they provide?

4. Imagine you are a Hollywood producer and you have been given the green light to create a project about an American Muslim superhero or heroine. What qualities would he or she have? How would you identify the hero/heroine as American and Muslim, and what would the challenges be?

## NOTES

1. This line was changed in 1993 to "Where it is flat and immense and the heat is intense."

2. Sophia Arjana, *Muslims in the Western Imagination* (New York: Oxford University Press, 2015), 103.

3. Delacroix is known for paintings of Oriental subjects that included acts of violence and cruelty. Examples can be found online.

4. Edward Said, *Orientalism* (New York: Vintage, 1979), 207.

5. Jack G. Shaheen, *Reel Bad Arabs: How Hollywood Vilifies a People* (New York: Olive Branch Press, 2001), 14.

6. Paul Baepler, "The Barbary Captivity Narrative in American Culture," *Early American Literature* 39, no. 2 (1994): 221.

7. Naomi Rosenblatt, "Orientalism in American Popular Culture," *Penn History Review* 16, no. 2 (2009): 59.

8. Mahmoud Eid and Sarah Khan, "A New Look for Muslim Women in the Canadian Media: CBC's *Little Mosque on the Prairie*," *Middle East Journal of Culture and Communication* 4 (2011): 184.

9. Jack Goody, *Islam in Europe* (Malden, MA: Polity Press, 2004), 7.

10. Eid and Khan, "New Look," 187.

11. John V. Tolan, *Saracens: Islam in the Medieval European Imagination* (New York: Columbia University Press, 2002), 45–46.

12. Debra Higgs Strickland, *Saracens, Demons, and Jews: Making Monsters in Medieval Art* (Princeton, NJ: Princeton University Press, 2003), 159.

13. Anouar Majid, *Freedom and Orthodoxy: Islam and Difference in the Post-Andalusian Age* (Stanford, CA: Stanford University Press, 2004), 74.

14. John R. Bowen, *Blaming Islam* (Cambridge, MA: MIT Press, 2012), 113.

15. Michael Sturma, "Aliens and Indians: A Comparison of Abduction and Captivity Narratives," *Journal of Popular Culture* 36, no. 2 (2002): 318.

16. See Greg Sieminski, "The Puritan Captivity Narrative and the Politics of the American Revolution," *American Quarterly* 42 (1990): 33–52. Also referenced in Abraham Michael Rosenthal, "America in Captivity," *New York Times Magazine,* May 17, 1981, 33–35.

17. Stephen William Foster, "The Exotic as a Symbolic System," *Dialectical Anthropology* 7, no. 1 (1982): 21.

18. Ella Shohat, "Gender and the Culture of Empire: Toward a Feminist Ethnography of the Cinema," in *Visions of the East: Orientalism in Film,* ed. Matthew Bernstein and Gaylyn Studlar (New Brunswick, NJ: Rutgers University Press, 1997), 35.

19. Casey Ryan Kelly, "Feminine Purity and Masculine Revenge-Seeking in *Taken* (2008)," *Feminist Media Studies* (2012): 10.

20. Hamid Dabashi, "The '300' Stroke," *Al-Ahram Weekly,* August 2–8, 2007, http://weekly.alahram.org.eg/2007/856/cu1.htm.

21. Arjana, *Muslims in the Western Imagination,* 161.

22. James Poniewozik, "'Homeland,' Graffiti and the Problem of Only Seeing Squibbly," *New York Times,* October 15, 2015, http://artsbeat.blogs.nytimes.com/2015/10/15/homeland-graffiti-racist/?_r = 0.

23. Ella Shohat and Robert Stam, *Unthinking Eurocentrism: Multiculturalism and the Media* (New York: Routledge, 1994), 104.

24. Ibid.

25. Eid and Khan, "New Look," 196.

26. My forthcoming book co-authored with Kimberly Fox looks at female Muslim superheroes.

27. Miriam Kent, "Unveiling Marvels: Ms. Marvel and the Reception of the New Muslim Superheroine," *Feminist Media Studies* 15, no. 3 (2015): 523.

28. Ibid.

# CHAPTER FIVE

# The Weight of the World

*Religion and Heavy Metal Music in Four Cases*

JASON C. BIVINS

Picture a heavy metal musician or fan. The genre's identity is partly bound up with visual associations: spandex-wearing glam rockers, denim-and-stache biker outlaws, or "corpse-painted," gauntlet-sporting musicians. But few would number among such visual associations a guitarist wearing a burqa. Surprise attended a late 2015 Reuters story featuring Gisele Marie, a Brazilian convert to Islam and professional metal guitarist.[1] Gazing at Marie's tattooed hands working her polka-dotted Flying V, many readers were struck by the improbable fusion of purportedly the most conservative Muslim female identity with the convention-flouting, ostensibly irreligious musical genre.

Yet heavy metal, in all its varieties, has been consistently intertwined with religions. As Blackie Lawless of W.A.S.P., a convert to Christianity, has opined, metal is "obsessed with the idea of God and/or the devil."[2] Since its inception, metal has proven Lawless's point in regular investigations of biblical imagery, responses to religious criticisms, or in internal debates over the music's religious (or irreligious) functions. This chapter traces these resonances through four successive cases that exemplify key moments in metal's development. The first examines metal's early fascination with religious themes and symbolism, marking the simultaneous ubiquity and elusiveness of religion.

The second case reads metal's public controversies as indices of changing expectations about religio-moral content in music. The third explores the contrast between "black metal" and "white metal" since the 1990s, one explicitly Satanic and the other openly, if complicatedly, Christian. And the final one maps newly emergent ecological and pagan sensibilities proliferating since the early 2000s. Together, they mark the significance of metal for the study of religion and popular culture, while also suggesting some possible future developments.

## INTO THE VOID: DARK THEMATICS

While many associate metal with the 1980s, its three distinguishing markers took shape in the late 1960s: heavily distorted riffs used in head-nodding repetition, an affinity for dark themes and imagery, and regular controversies alleging associations with "black magic." Led Zeppelin and Black Sabbath helped cement metal's early identity as what the musicologist Robert Walser identifies as "a 'harder' sort of hard rock."[3] Certain strains of louder, more aggressive mid-1960s rock had fed this tendency: the Who, the Kinks, and the proto-metal riffing of Blue Cheer, a significant influence on high-volume acts like Steppenwolf, Deep Purple, and Iron Butterfly. On some level, metal's emergence partook of a more general broadening of religious sensibilities in popular music, ranging from the utopian aspirations of Flower Power bands to the darker imaginings of the Velvet Underground or the Stooges. Sixties audiences often sought political authenticity and experiential enlightenment in their music and in new religious movements.[4] This did not preclude, for some musicians, a focus on the era's darker resonances: themes of war, greed, cops, and demonology seemed apt as the Summer of Love ceded to the Days of Rage. Such dystopianism was fundamental to metal, whose distinctiveness came through an embrace of tropes of religious darkness, paranoia, madness, and damnation. Sabbath was consistently engaged with such themes. With occasional commentary on religious hypocrisy and wickedness ("Would you like to see the Pope on the end of a rope?"), or on worldly evil, Sabbath regularly explored demonology: in the epochal "Black Sabbath," with its tolling bells and tritones (that once-forbidden interval) narrating a black mass; in ruminations on the devil's dominion over earth, like "War Pigs" ("Satan, laughing, spreads his wings"); or in a general foregrounding of fright, in "Electric Funeral," "Children of the Grave," or "Saint Vitus Dance." Sabbath's concerts underscored these associations, with candelabras, upside-down crosses on fire, and demonic imagery resonating with a changing tone in public life and religions, now increasingly fraught with paranoia, disillusionment, and violence. Other bands were similarly obsessed, as with Washington's Pentagram, whose early songs—like "Dying World," "Be Forewarned," and "Last Days Here"—contrasted with the stadium rock hedonism of the era in their obsession with death and judgment, where tropes of madness and self-destruction signified the sacred's absence.

There also emerged during this period a more robust affinity for occultism that both galvanized critical attention and shaped metal's subsequent developments.[5] Sweden's Black Widow and America's Coven were less tentative in their embrace of demonic imagery, and suggested they were open practitioners of Satanism. Black Widow's concerts shows "featured a mock ritual sacrifice," anticipating the play-acting of Alice Cooper and KISS (itself a key piece of the puzzle).[6] Coven went so far as to record a Satanic Black Mass and featured a nude woman being sacrificed on the cover of their debut album. While the music was not technically metal, it resonated with the dark, LaVeyian undertones of the nascent genre. Indeed, Anton LaVey once planned a "Satanic Woodstock" at which Coven was to perform.[7]

Metal's originary growth resonates with growing awareness in both culture and scholarship that religious tropes and themes circulate outside conventional institutional frameworks, establishing for metal a thematic identity achieved partly through symbolic and discursive inversions (darkness over light, doom over joy). This focus on the discursive production of meaning was predominantly an internal quality of the music at this stage, as were metal's own dark signifying practices.[8] As metal's second wave—UFO, the Scorpions, and Judas Priest—grew further from blues roots into a louder, faster sound (with lyrics that were aggressive, even confrontational), it spawned a religious critique that grew similarly. Throughout the 1980s and 1990s, this powerful current of religious reception dynamics made for an externalized struggle over the content and validity of metal's identity in terms of its political and religious merits. Whereas critics of Flower Power worried about hedonism, the ascendance of metal raised a more ontological concern that certain kinds of rock music were actual manifestations of devilry.

### EVIL FANTASIES: METAL'S SATANIC PANICS

In the 1980s, nostalgic conservatism characterized both politics and entertainment. Swirling around American popular culture was also a vigorous reassertion of apocalyptic themes. One example of these tendencies was the "Satanic panic" surrounding popular music. The influential Praise the Lord network alleged in 1982 that rock music was coded with Satanic messages using "backwards masking," referring to "hidden" messages recorded backwards and thus buried in the recordings, doing their work unconsciously on listeners.[9] This resonated with a broader condemnation of "occult" or sexually explicit themes in entertainments, a criticism that cropped up in popular evangelical ministries and in legislative assemblies. This fusion of sensationalism, commerce, and moral outrage was informed by and also enabled the era's broader neoconservative sensibilities. Few popular entertainments did as much to focus this religious critique as metal, which had grown by this time into a full-blown phenomenon. In this, a twinned obsession—one external, the other internal—characterized metal's increasing significance in and for religions.

Deena Weinstein notes that metal's neo-Gothic look was indebted to medieval art and mythological imagery as much as fantasy narrative.[10]

And the performative styles of certain metal artists began to reflect this, as well as an androgyny that was previously the domain of glam rock. Acts like Twisted Sister and Mötley Crüe played libertinism to the hilt, with the latter's *Shout at the Devil* bringing the look to a wider mainstream audience in the mid-1980s. During this period, through themes of violence, horror, and death, metal became associated with transgression and edginess.

Blended into this was a continued engagement with religious language and imagery: in band names or album and song titles referring to sin, demons, vengeance, apocalypse, and more. Iron Maiden's Eddie mascot paraded across their stage, his zombie countenance giving life to the band's obsession with ancient Egypt and songs about black masses or murder. Ozzy Osbourne played with horror imagery on his solo records *Bark at the Moon* and *Diary of a Madman* (including thematically controversial songs like "Mr. Crowley"). And while there is some evidence to suggest that metal broadly had a disdain for *institutional* religion at this point in its development, this did not necessarily entail dismissals of religious pluralism as such.[11]

But the new public religious engagement with metal, now figured as an idiom in need of legislative constraint, turned on an episode involving Judas Priest. Known for the singer Rob Halford's banshee wail, and his leather-and-chains outfit astride the Harley-Davidson he rode onstage, Judas Priest helped extend metal's symbolic language, embracing and narrating a demonological obsession in a litany of songs including "Sinner," "Let Us Prey/Call for the Priest," "Race with the Devil," "Saints in Hell," "Fire Burns Below," "Evil Fantasies," "Metal Gods," and "Devil's Child." But the band would soon become associated with legal controversies, explored below, that furthered metal's imbrications with religions. These episodes built on a kind of anti-rock industry that grew between the 1950s and 1970s, extending beyond the thematic into a public religious panic of considerable political implications.

Certainly, no era of popular music has lacked fervent detractors. This is an abiding morality play in American public life, linked to early tract literature, the Comstock Laws of the nineteenth century, and the cultural panics attending popular music throughout the era of recorded music. But because of its dark comportment and imagery, metal in particular has generated especially acute concerns. Further, the coalescence of conservative political religions in the 1980s made the growing genre a particular target for critics. In the 1980s, dozens of prominent national preachers began to announce their worries about youths exposed to aggressive, demonological music performed by "angry, lonely, defiant" musicians.[12] The music was said to promote violence, social anomie, and irreligion.[13] The Baptist critic Jeff Steele said that with its fascination with Grand Guignol imagery, lurid sexuality, and tropes of rebellion, metal was a "horrible and dangerous" assault on "Western civilization."[14] But the most potent charges suggested that, whether through the ritual efficacy of the music itself or through "backwards masking," metal was actually manifesting the material presence of dark forces.

Such allegations soon made their way into public political and religious discourse in the 1980s, creating a fascinating and often lurid juxtaposition of moral outrage and sensationalism that captured something of that decade's excessive tone. Saying, "[t]he First Amendment has been twisted into a pretext for license," the pursuit of which without limits can bring harm to the innocent, President Ronald Reagan called for wider scrutiny of entertainment that in the guise of free speech placed listeners at risk.[15] Such claims picked up on long-standing assertions by religious critics like Steele, Jeff Godwin, Jacob Aranza, and Bob Larson, who linked metal music to the moral corruption and social decline they saw across American culture, finding the genre to be a baser, more violent example of a generally perverse popular culture.

The best-known articulation of this critique was the May 1985 proposal by the Parents Music Resource Center (PMRC), formed by the wives of prominent politicians and vocally supported by conservative religionists, that the Recording Industry Association of America employ a ratings system. Echoing many of the hitherto more marginal claims about metal, the PMRC openly sought to ban some records and—in its manifesto "Rock Music Destroys Kids and We've Had Enough"—it advocated ratings and content restrictions focused on excessive sexuality, mentions of drugs or alcohol, lyrical violence, and occult themes. PMRC representatives, politicians, and religious critics traded barbs in congressional hearings with representative musicians like the metal singer Dee Snider and Frank Zappa. The PMRC singled out for special concern its "Filthy Fifteen," artists emblematic of the violations posited. Metal resounded across the categories, with Snider's band Twisted Sister accused of exhortations to violent rebellion. The subgenre black metal surfaced on the critical radar, with Venom and Mercyful Fate denounced for their occult sensibilities.

Such high-profile moral panic not only resonated with the larger role religious social criticism played in American life in the 1980s—the robust conservative engagement contrasting with the broader malaise and anomie of the 1970s—but fed a series of sensational trials accusing metal of inspiring adolescent suicides, weapon attacks, or sexual assaults.[16] AC/DC had been accused of influencing the serial killer Richard "The Night Stalker" Ramirez. But it was with sensational trials involving Osbourne and Priest that metal's social and religious detractors gained a larger audience. Aranza, Larson, and even the Religious Studies professor Carl Raschke had popularized the idea that rock music contained concealed demonic exhortations to increased crime, drug use, and cultic excitement.[17] When a California teenager committed suicide in 1988 while Osbourne's *Speak of the Devil* played, a lawsuit brought by Kenneth McKenna alleged that the track "Suicide Solution" had subliminally influenced the teen to "get the gun and shoot it." McKenna's suit was unsuccessful but in 1990, buoyed by the encouragement of Larson and other evangelical critics, he charged Priest with culpability in the 1985 suicide attempt of two Nevada teens.[18] McKenna alleged that the album *Stained Class* had employed "mind control" to urge the teens to shoot themselves. McKenna also accused the band of reckless support for "cults" that also endangered at-risk youth.[19] Redge Peifer claimed that "Satanic covens ... put a satanic curse on these records asking Lucifer to draw people into drugs and the occult as these people listen to this wicked music."[20]

Events and trials such as these continued into the 1990s, further cementing the relation between metal and its usually religious detractors. There were multiple allegations of "Satanic ritual abuse" during this period. Larson, echoing the larger criticism that metal was the soundtrack for American decline, singled out then-popular bands like Slayer and Deicide for their use of Satanic imagery and their denunciations of institutional religion.[21] There were even efforts to establish institutions, such as California's Back in Control center, to "deprogram" metalheads, as the 1970s had done with "cult" members.[22] Nine Inch Nails, White Zombie, Gwar, and Marilyn Manson received particular attention. Manson routinely displayed inverted crosses, dressed in drag, and destroyed Bibles and religious portraiture on stage.[23] Some band members were arrested for "obscenity," concerts were halted under protest, and schools often banned black t-shirts or metal paraphernalia. The Columbine High School shootings of 1999, by teens alleged to be fans of metal and industrial music, further amplified religious criticism not just by individuals like Larson but by national organizations like Focus on the Family.[24] The cumulative effect felt like a weather system that had been gathering since the genre's emergence decades earlier, drawing energy from other cultural panics and expressing itself with apocalyptic urgency.[25] The intensity of these cultural conflicts and the sensationalism of the claims seemed only to echo the music that, since the 1980s, had gotten faster, more aggressive, and more fantastical in its imaginings, as perhaps had American public life.

Metal's transgressive performances freely appropriated the tropes of the apocalyptic and used them to signify rebelliously in ways that were either explicitly anti-religious or illegible to conventional religiosities. But while the events themselves are significant in terms of religious history, what do they mean in terms of popular culture and religious identity? This episode in metal's history signals the ubiquitous association of certain religious orientations (censorious, at times almost anti-worldly) with the changing shapes of popular music, nervous about the absence of the sacred in any dimension of public or expressive culture, committed to the idea that certain kinds of harmony and rhythm and collectivities lead innocent or at-risk young people to their ruin.

This is a significant scholarly arena as surely as it is a public one. In these spectacular contests over social capital, we can also detect some broader declension narrative focused on reversing religion's purported decline by identifying sonic scapegoats. While these social critics indulged in sensationalism and what I elsewhere call the "erotics of fear," they also picked up on something within the music itself.[26] While the external focus of this criticism was on alleged demonology or lurid sexuality, something was taking shape inside metal's disparate formations that went beyond the symbolic or discursive power at play in the first two stages. Metal was amplifying its fascinations with occultism and opening pathways to new and contested forms of religious identity and practice among musicians themselves.

## A BLAZE IN THE NORTHERN SKY: BLACK AND WHITE METAL

During the same period when metal began to define itself against its religio-political detractors, a transnational underground scene was developing new ideas and practices with considerable implications for religion. The "black metal" underground performed acts of anti-Christian (and other) violence to show their disdain for social convention and also to demonstrate their own religio-racial identity. While the emergence of black metal as a distinctive subgenre first received broad public attention because of incidents in Norway in the early-to-mid-1990s, the genre's broader significance for religion lies in its own growing religiosity at the intersection of Satanism and paganism (as well as its dialectical relationship with so-called white metal).

Black metal arose following the Satanic British band Venom's recording of the same name.[27] Early black metal bands like Mercyful Fate sang of demons, hauntings, and Satanic rituals, establishing a tradition embraced by later groups such as Celtic Frost, Kreator, Mayhem, Rotting Christ, and others. These groups defined the genre's "violent opposition to Judeo-Christianity, endless blasphemy, and ... grandiose theater."[28] The blueprint for black metal's influential Second Wave was established by Bathory's *Blood Fire Death,* which marked a shift from Satanism to "the heathen mythological legacy of their own forefathers" and specifically to the Norse religion Asatru.[29] Young Norwegian musicians in the early 1990s developed this fascination with Viking culture into a xenophobic nationalism that, in its opposition to Christianity's "Semitic roots," flirted with Nazism.[30] These bands wore "corpse-paint" makeup and gauntlets, and were embroiled with a series of grisly murders, assaults, grave desecrations, and, most infamously, church burnings. Those involved in these actions, like Burzum's Varg Vikernes, embraced a neo-Nietzschean critique of the "pity morality" they associated with "meek" Christianity. The warrior cult ethos (specifically indebted to the Odinism attributed by many musicians to the Nazi collaborator Vidkun Quisling, executed in Oslo for murder and high treason in October 1945) was a natural extension of black metal's theatricality and adolescent fantasies of revenge on society, linking up with romantic-era celebrations of the "Wild Hunt" and with the rise of "heathenism" and "atavism" in European pagan circles.[31]

In the United States, Profanatica (1990–92) brought black metal's anti-Christian thematics into a scene that extended variously to isolationist militarism, racial identitarianism, and occultism.[32] Profanatica's recordings *Weeping in Heaven* and *Broken Throne of Christ* marked their intention to profane "anything sacred and holy."[33] Though cautious about identifying with institutional Satanism, the band—infamous for its onstage displays of combined blasphemy and sexuality—identified with Aleister Crowley's *Book of the Law* and claimed to be "into black perversion. We shit on God.... We put down false religions."[34] In their "sick and blasphemous" performances, the band dressed as nuns or priests and used liberal amounts of bodily fluids as props. Though devoid of any well-wrought social criticism, the band articulated a defi-antly anti-religious ethos (an important part of the story of religion) that resonated with the increased prominence of Satanism as practice rather than discourse.

As if fulfilling the darkest fears of religious critics, similar bands began to constitute an American black metal scene. Von was associated with Nazi occultism. Absu blended practical magick with tales of Sumerian or Mesopotamian demonology. Judas Iscariot explored Nietzschean social criticism alongside anti-Christian and anti-capitalist themes. Demoncy, Black Witchery, and others helped establish the Gathering of Shadows, an "annual invitation-only black metal convention" in Colorado.[35] The music ranged from caustic to atmospheric, sometimes lyrically invoking the English poet and painter William Blake (1757–1827) and romantic imagery. There was also an emphasis on "purity" and "authenticity" that seemed often to be coded racially. This resonated with the rise, in the same period, of U.S. militia movements and self-styled Christian patri-ots, with their thriving musical subcultures part of a broader anti-statist separatism. More than this, as a next wave of bands emerged—including Leviathan, Xasthur, Nachtmystium, Krieg, and Lurker of Chalice—it became apparent that these blended expressions of Satanism, paganism, and sometime misanthropy were dealing not only with darker religious archetypes but in conversation with opposing religious traditions that believed differently in the material reality of evil.

While public recognition of Christian metal is less common than spectacular outrage at black metal, the range of "white metal" bands expanded alongside black metal's between the 1980s-1990s. As Eileen Luhr shows, white metal's defiant faith set against worldliness and sin dovetailed with metal's long-standing embrace of outsiderdom and rebellion, now resonating doubly by resisting metal's traditional dark-ness and worldly evil simultaneously. Christian metal bands—whether thrash, death, or even "unblack" metal—began to develop networks and communities that were self-contained, even if many acts crossed over in the name of evangelization. As David Stowe notes, many Christian rock subcultures in America can trace their influence to the Jesus People's Resurrection Band (and Barnabas). Buoyed by these examples, perhaps the most famous Christian metal band of the 1980s was Stryper, known not only for openly evangelical lyrics but also for tossing Bibles from the stage into their audiences.

Contemporaries included Messiah Prophet, Leviticus, Saint, and King's X. Following the success of such acts, Christian bands like Trouble, Vengeance Rising, Deliverance, Believer, and Tourniquet began to explore metal's more extreme idioms in the 1980s as well.[36] But though the lyrical content focused on the heaviness of the good news, the use of thrash and death proved controversial and led to difficulties with distribution at Christian stores. Significant here was Bob Beeman's establishment, in the mid-1980s, of a ministry he dubbed Sanctuary—The Rock and Roll Refuge. This was intended to be an alternative to those other ministries that denounced rock altogether, and in this Beeman created an institutional haven for many of the bands, fanzines, and tour promoters involved in Christian metal's emergence.[37] After the 1990s there was a veritable explosion of Christian underground metal, including nü metal (P.O.D.), metalcore (Zao), death metal (Crimson Thorn), doom, and more.[38] With exposure at festivals like Cornerstone and support from labels like Tooth & Nail and Facedown, bands like Underoath, As I Lay Dying, Norma Jean, and Demon Hunter sought indie credibility and authenticity, insisting that Christianity's message was as intense as the music.[39]

In the emergence and counterpoint between black and white metal, we note the hybridization of religious identity. Unlike the preceding case, religious difference is here being worked out not around some ostensible public controversy but in musical performances and musicians' networks themselves. This case also signals both the proliferation of identities on the margins of the category "religion" (black metal) and the appropriation of ostensibly anti-religious idioms by Christians (white metal). These make for clear exempla of the viral qualities of popular expression, and the way metal both picks up on and feeds into larger cultural contests between bright and dark religious impulses.

## DARK MATTER GODS: PAGAN METAL

In 2010, Hunter Hunt-Hendrix, the American black metal band Liturgy's singer, released a widely discussed manifesto criticizing traditional black metal. Calling it "Hyperborean," Hunt-Hendrix worried that the music was "nihilistic," and not focused enough on growth. Against this, Hunt-Hendrix championed "Transcendental black metal," which he described using solar rather than lunar imagery, insisting that black metal could be remade if it focused on "affirmation" and potential.[40] Celebrating creativity, introspection, and *poesis,* the piece resonated with a fourth phase of metal's ongoing evolution in and around religions. From the tropes of evil and religious corruption, to religious social criticism of the music, to an internal contest between Satanic and Christian bands, metal has consistently picked up on broader interrogations about what counts as (proper) religion. While it is significant that metal has been fragmenting into multiple traditions, one significant development since 2000 has been the growth of nonracial paganism in American metal.

European metal has often embraced the folkloric, far from the political and racial underpinnings of some black metal. Bands like Korpiklaani and Turisias employ traditional instruments and costumes as part of their embrace of European folk narratives and song forms. With an affect midway between a Renaissance Fair and a druidic gathering, these bands focus more on cultural heritage than specifically on the religious.[41] But the widely shared fascination with pre-Christian societies makes for a fascinating comparative link with American bands (like Huntress or The Sword) embracing neo-pagan themes like nature spirituality and goddess imagery.

Oakland's Neurosis has, since the early 1990s, blended hermetic imagery with naturalism, an interest in shamanism, and the use of tribal drumming in music that, according to singer Steve Von Till, comes from "not just deep in the core of us, but deep within the core of the Earth, the stars and everything else."[42] More explicit in their embrace of nature spirituality are the Pacific Northwest's Agalloch and

Wolves in the Throne Room. On "In the Shadow of Our Pale Companion," Agalloch articulates this sensibility: "Here I gaze at a pantheon of oak, a citadel of stone / If this grand panorama before me is what you call God / Then God is not dead." Wolves in the Throne Room also embrace hermetic imagery and categories, but spend considerable time living in remote locations during their songwriting periods, seeking to translate these settings into songs like "Thuja Magus Imperium," "Subterranean Initiation," or "Astral Blood." The drummer Aaron Weaver claims that the band aspires to a sound "like the liturgical music of a cedar cult."[43] Similarly expansive notions now proliferate in metal beyond specifically neo-pagan associations, as in the growing fascination of drone/doom bands—like YOB, Queen Elephantine, and Sunno)))—with Buddhist traditions of sonic awakening and with transforming performance into a ritual that erases the boundary between performer and listener.

It remains to be seen whether these tendencies will generate an audience or a subculture as robust as those in the cases preceding. Yet we see in this network of practitioners, in their shared affinities, how metal picks up on the proliferation of religious identities, showing how these are reflected in the music, while also pointing towards possible religio-musical hybrids. These also resonate with the larger cultural growth of neo-pagan and eco-religious subjectivities (as well as the identification "spiritual but not religious").[44] While not as formally cohesive an index as, say, Wiccan military chaplaincies, metal's outsider ethos here sustains new and fragmenting religious identities as countercultural practices and sensibilities. If the third case showed a contest between transgressive rebellion and transformative rebellion, it is through the embrace of "transcendental" themes and interests that these two modes combine.

## CONCLUSION

Studies of religion and popular culture are continually alert to the representational, and to the religious overtones of "fandoms." These are important dimensions of study and participation. Attention to the development of metal in America shows additional intersections of the musical and the religious at work in the music and culture simultaneously. It is well known that religious practitioners in America (and elsewhere) establish their identities partly in relation to the popular music they consume, with all its varied statements about and implications for religions. While this is abundantly true of metal music, the four cases above shape different engagements that may have implications beyond this genre alone.

Each of the four cases marks a chronological moment that has significance for metal, for religion, and for their mutual engagement. Metal's emergence in the 1960s articulated some of the darker resonances of that decade's declining utopianism, and as it developed in the 1970s, this marked another instance of popular music representing religious themes (here those of apocalypse and social decline). The genre's flamboyance and association with public political scandal in the 1980s can be read as an index of that decade's deep religious and political conservatism, as well as an instance of ongoing censorship campaigns surrounding popular musics. Shifting into the 1990s, though, we can begin to detect in metal's changing shapes and sounds something of the broader instability of the category religion itself. In two somewhat unpredictable associations, metal's own engagements with religion open into modes of practice: black metal's Satanism challenges normative religion even as it claims its own religious authenticity against presumptions about what counts as religion, while white metal seeks to evangelize listeners from within genres largely believed to be hostile to Christianity in any form. This resonates suggestively not only with scholarly deconstructions of the category "religion" itself but also with larger public openness to religious hybridity, something that since the 2000s is increasingly part of the metal scene.

So while the genre was once written off as simply the soundtrack of fist-pumping, head-banging adolescent rebellion, we see that like other music genres metal has been both part of and counterpoint to larger cultural articulations of religion, morality, and identity formation.[45] The dynamic relation between religion and popular culture is manifest in this music, with religions thoroughly part of metal's changing identity. In the four stages of its development, we also see the dialogic relation between these mutually defining categories and the larger cultures of their housing. And perhaps most suggestively, metal music shows evidence of how thoroughly subculture and alternative identities, including sometimes anti-religious ones, are part of the story of religion. The implications for music, religion, and culture open also into further scholarly possibilities: the heaviness of religion and affect, music as an alternate religious public, or the role of social media in these processes. Regardless of the particulars in these areas, metal will riff on in all its varieties, religious and otherwise.

### DISCUSSION QUESTIONS

1. Bivin's chapter suggests four quite different ways that heavy metal music has expressed or argued with religion. What are they, and how do they differ in their attitudes toward religion? Did it surprise you that heavy metal engaged religion in these ways? Why or why not?

2. What other musical genres engage religion? How does metal compare, in terms of its musical forms and its public reception, to other musical forms with religious content?

3. Play one or more examples of the music discussed in the chapter. What is distinctive about the music, its volume, and form? What is your bodily experience of listening to this music? Do you want to dance? Turn it up, or down? How would you describe the feelings and emotions described by listening? How important is it to understand the words?

4. Who is the intended audience for this music? Does metal seem to require social tension, even social controversy, for its identity

more than other forms of music? If so, what does that suggest
about its audience and their place in society? What does it tell us
about religion's place in contemporary culture?

## NOTES

1. www.msn.com/en-us/news/offbeat/playing-heavy-metal-in-a-burqa/ss-AAeFIgT.

2. www.blabbermouth.net/news/how-blackie-lawlesss-faith-affected-making-of-w-a-s-p-s-new-album-golgotha.

3. Robert Walser, *Running with the Devil: Power, Gender, and Madness in Heavy Metal Music* (Middletown, CT: Wesleyan University Press, 1993), p. 3.

4. See Stephen Kent, *From Slogans to Mantras: Social Protest and Religious Conversion in the Late Vietnam Era* (Syracuse, NY: Syracuse University Press, 2001).

5. Christopher M. Moreman. "Devil Music and the Great Beast: Ozzy Osbourne, Aleister Crowley, and the Christian Right," *Journal of Religion and Popular Culture 5* (Fall 2003): 1–17, here p. 4.

6. Michael Moynihan and Didrik Soederlind, *Lords of Chaos: The Bloody Rise of the Satanic Metal Underground* (Port Townsend, WA: Feral House Books, 2003), 6.

7. Ibid., 7. See also James R. Lewis, *Satanism Today: An Encyclopedia of Religion, Folklore, and Popular Culture* (Santa Barbara, CA: ABC-CLIO, 2001).

8. Walser, *Running with the Devil*, 26–27.

9. Eric Nuzum, *Parental Advisory: Music Censorship in America* (New York: Perennial Books, 2001), 15.

10. Deena Weinstein, *Heavy Metal: The Music and Its Culture* (New York: Da Capo Press, 2000), 27.

11. Jeffrey Jensen Arnett, *Metal Heads: Heavy Metal Music and Adolescent Alienation* (Boulder, CO: Westview Press, 1996), 122–23.

12. Ibid., 4.

13. Walser, *Running with the Devil*, x.

14. Weinstein, *Heavy Metal*, 1.

15. Reagan quoted in David Konow, *Bang Your Head: The Rise and Fall of Heavy Metal Music* (New York: Three Rivers Press, 2002), 218.

16. Ian Christe, *Sound of the Beast: The Complete Headbanging History of Heavy Metal* (New York: HarperCollins, 2004), 292.

17. Walser, *Running with the Devil*, 141.

18. www.nytimes.com/1990/07/17/arts/2-families-sue-heavy-metal-band-as-having-driven-sons-to-suicide.html.

19. See Stan Soocher's *They Fought the Law: Rock Music Goes to Court* (New York: Schirmer Books, 1998).

20. Peter Blecha, *Taboo Tunes: A History of Banned Bands & Censored Songs* (San Francisco: Backbeat Books, 2004), 48.

21. Christe, *Sound of the Beast*, 29.

22. Ibid., 294.

23. Nuzum, *Parental Advisory*, 127.

24. Ibid., 48.

25. Ibid., 126.

26. Jason C. Bivins, *Religion of Fear: The Politics of Horror in Conservative Evangelicalism* (New York: Oxford University Press, 2008).

27. Steve Waksman, *This Ain't the Summer of Love: Conflict and Crossover in Heavy Metal and Punk* (Berkeley: University of California Press, 2009), 193.

28. Moynihan and Soederlind, *Lords of Chaos,* p. 13.

29. Ibid., 19. See also Matthias Gardell, *Gods of the Blood: The Pagan Revival and White Separatism* (Durham, NC: Duke University Press, 2003).

30. Sam Dunn, dir., *Metal: A Headbanger's Journey* (Seville Pictures, 2008).

31. Moynihan and Soederlind, *Lords of Chaos,* 196.

32. www.believermag.com/issues/200807/?read = article_stosuy.

33. Ibid., and https://en.wikipedia.org/wiki/Profanatica.

34. https://en.wikipedia.org/wiki/Profanatica. Black metal's contest in and around religion is ever expanding. See, e.g., www.theatlantic.com/entertainment/archive/2012/07/when-black-metals-anti-religious-message-gets-turned-on-islam/259680/ and www.vice.com/read/anti-religious-black-metal-band-in-saudi-arabia-666.

35. https://en.wikipedia.org/wiki/Demoncy.

36. Weinstein, *Heavy Metal*, 53–54. See also https://en.wikipedia.org/wiki/Christian_metal.

37. https://en.wikipedia.org/wiki/Christian_metal.

38. See Marcus Moberg, *Christian Metal: History, Ideology, Scene* (London: Bloomsbury Academic, 2015).

39. See Andrew Beaujon, *Body Piercing Saved My Life: Inside the Phenomenon of Christian Rock* (New York: DaCapo Books, 2006).

40. www.vice.com/read/not-fit-to-print-transcendental-metal.

41. See Helen Farley, "Demons, Devils and Witches: The Occult in Heavy Metal Music," in G. Bayer, ed. *Heavy Metal Music in Britain* (Burlington, VT: Ashgate, 2009), 73–88, and Kennet Granholm, "'Sons of Northern Darkness':

Heathen Influences in Black Metal and Neofolk Music," *Numen* 58, no. 5 (2011): 14–44.

42. www.guardian.co.uk/music/2010/dec/02/neurosis-live-at-roadburn.

43. www.heavyblogisheavy.com/2011/09/06/wolves-in-the-throne-room-celestial-lineage.

44. www.pewforum.org/religious-landscape-study/religious-denomination/spiritual-but-not-religious.

45. See Titus Hjelm, Keith Kahn-Harris, and Mark LeVine, *Heavy Metal: Controversies and Counterculture* (Sheffield, England: Equinox, 2013).

# PART II

# Popular Culture in Religion

Part I of this book looked at the way religion appears in popular culture. This section reverses the relationship between religion and popular culture. It looks at ways in which traditional religious institutions and communities are themselves influenced by popular culture, taking on popular forms and practices, and perhaps changing their substance in the process. While you still see evidence of stories from or about religion, these authors move away from a predominantly literary treatment of religion and popular culture to give greater attention to matters of religious practice. They are interested in how popular culture changes what people do with their bodies. They ask how popular culture influences the way religious people worship, dress, use technology, and think about the self and family.

At the heart of this discussion are questions about how religion, religious beliefs, and practices may change in these interactions with popular culture. How people feel about this possibility depends in large measure on certain attitudes about religion and its relationship to culture more generally. For some people, the suggestion that religion is shaped by culture is troubling. They argue that religion has a substance or essence that is not reducible to other forms of culture such as politics or play. They think of religion as something that connects us to God, gods, or to an experience of the sacred that exists apart from society as a link to an unchangeable realm of the sacred. If we think about religion in this way any cultural adaptation or influence may be seen as a dilution of religion's purity and power. The history of religions tells us that, whatever the nature of the deities they point to, the human practice of religion changes over time. We reinterpret ancient stories and develop new rituals and practices that respond to our current situation.

So, to take but one example, Judaism's identity was long centered on worship at the temple in Jerusalem. When the Babylonians destroyed the temple about 586 BCE and took the Jews into captivity they lost this religious center. Their anguish is recorded in Psalm 137:4, which asks, "How can we sing the songs of the Lord [that is the songs intended to be sung in the Temple] while in a foreign land?" (NIV). Eventually, the temple at Jerusalem was reestablished, only to be destroyed again by the Romans in the year 70 CE. The loss of the temple and the scattering of Jews around the known world was an existential crisis, and the Torah, the most sacred text of the Jews, became a new center of Jewish religious practices, one that they could carry with them into the diaspora. Understanding Judaism requires thinking about how these cultural and historical changes reshaped Jewish practice and belief.

When people move from one place to another, the religious practices they bring with them come into contact with the practices of their new neighbors and vice versa. This often leads to adaptation in practice and belief. For instance, the idea of there being a "Great Spirit" was not a significant concept within most Native American religious traditions before the European conquest. The idea emerges primarily out of an effort to see native people and their traditions through a Christian lens. In this example, the religious understandings already in the land are shaped by the arrival of Christianity. However, as Christianity spread, first within the Roman Empire and then elsewhere, it was also influenced by preexisting cultures and religious practices. The way people celebrate Christmas reveals how a conquering religion is influenced by local customs as it moves into new cultural contexts. As you will see in a chapter below, things we think of as essential to Christmas, including its midwinter date and the Christmas tree, were adopted from preexisting winter festivals.

Not only is religion changed when it comes in contact with new cultures, but cultures themselves change over time, and religions adjust to respond to the needs and challenges of that cultural change. To stay with the Christmas example, the celebration of the holiday changes in importance and emphasis over time. What was once a minor Christian festival primarily celebrated within the church becomes, for a variety of complex reasons, a celebration of hearth and home in the Victorian era. The holiday is complex; it is a midwinter festival, a Christian celebration of the birth of Jesus, and are occasion to celebrate the home and family—perhaps treating them as sacred. Its commercialization begins at least as early as the Victorian era, leading some to suggest that it is today a celebration of capitalism as a sacred system. No wonder that people today debate its "true" meaning.

New technologies of communication also change the way people think of themselves and relate to others. These changes produce new forms of popular culture and lead to new religious practices. Perhaps the most famous example of the way that changes in communications impacted religion happened with the development of the printing press. When Johannes Gutenberg printed the Christian Bible (1454 CE), he began a process that would make Christianity's sacred text vastly more accessible. It has been suggested that the Protestant Reformation, with its emphasis on the ability and responsibility of individual believers to read and interpret the scriptures for themselves, was not possible until the Bible was readily available and literacy had become common.

Above I have laid out a brief case for thinking about how culture shapes religion. These chapters look in a more focused way at how religion takes on particular forms and patterns from American popular culture. They explore examples where changing social conventions or new technologies establish opportunities for alternative expression of religion. In these examples and others with which readers will be familiar, it is obvious that religion takes on the forms of its surrounding culture. Reflect on the significance of this. Are religious truth claims something that can be repackaged in many ways without changing their core, or does the form of expression shape the content? Do you think of religions as fixed and unchanging, or as dynamic and able to adapt in response to their cultural settings?

As noted in the discussion above, Christmas has become a primary meeting place of religion and popular culture. In "Christmas Is Like a Snowball," Bruce Forbes explores the way this Christian holiday has gathered material from centuries of popular culture into itself. Rather than suggesting that there is a single "right" understanding of Christmas, he argues that, like other cultural/religious holidays, it serves different purposes for different people. Forbes's discussion of Christmas invites us to return to issues he raised in the introduction to this volume. Does popular culture shape or reflect society? Have people's Christmas celebrations changed because of the stories that popular culture tells about the holiday, or does popular culture express our anxieties and desires about what Christmas might be? He argues that both claims are true.

In a number of religions, adherents set themselves apart from the culture in a visible way by their dress. We see this in the habit of Catholic nuns and the robes of Buddhist monks, but also in lay practices of religiously distinctive dress among groups like the Amish and Orthodox Jews. In "Mipsterz: Hip, American, and Muslim," Kirsten Petersen and Nabil Echchaibi explore the interplay of traditional forms of Muslim dress and contemporary urban fashion to think about style as an expression of Islam's adaptation to modernity. Muslim women's dress, particularly the question of covering the head, has raised questions both within Islam and in Islam's relationship with various cultures. Some countries require women to wear the headscarf, and sometimes the veil, in public. Other countries have sought to ban this and other forms of religious dress in public life. Against this backdrop, the Muslim hipsters described by the authors play with dress and fashion as an expression of personal and religious identity.

In "Megachurches, Celebrity Pastors, and the Evangelical Industrial Complex," Jessica Johnson argues that megachurches and their pastors have not only taken on popular cultural styles of music, dress, and gathering spaces, leading to more informal forms of worship, but have also embraced particular cultural values that come with the embrace of celebrity and consumption. She examines and critiques the theologies and practices of two pastors and their followers who represent these developments. Often people have assumed that religion can change its cultural expressions without changing its essence. Studies like this raise questions about that assumption.

Rachel Gross suggests that America's Jewish community is ambivalent about popular culture. For Jews, producing and consuming popular culture has been a pathway for a minority community to assimilate into the mainstream, but one that many have argued has led to a loss of Jewish identity. In "People of the Picture Book: PJ Library and American Jewish Religion" Gross studies a project that seeks to use a form of popular culture, children's books, to teach Jewish tradition and put a stamp of Jewish identify on family practices.

One of the significant developments in popular culture has been the rise of interactive media, which require us to think in less passive ways about the relationship between popular culture and those who engage it. We no longer passively read, or watch; we can play with popular culture. In "Meditation on the Go: Buddhist Smartphone Apps as Video Play," Gregory Grieve looks at an example of what happens when religion, in this case Buddhism, is imbedded in new technologies of play, raising questions about what is at issue when we ask whether such practices "really" count as religion.

Jeffrey H. Mahan
Iliff School of Theology

# CHAPTER SIX

# Christmas Is Like a Snowball

BRUCE DAVID FORBES

By almost any measure, Christmas is the most popular holiday of the year in the United States, whether measured by poll results, money spent, songs sung, or parties organized. Yet it is also one of the most contested times of the year. Some voices claim there is a war on Christmas, and others are concerned that Christian practices are being imposed on an increasingly pluralistic society. Arguments arise about whether Christmas music should be included in public school concerts, or whether store clerks should greet customers with "Merry Christmas" or "Happy Holidays." Others are worried about the commercialization of Christmas, distracting from both religious meanings and family relationships.

From a scholarly angle, holidays, and especially Christmas, are an ideal subject area for reflecting in general on relationships between religion and culture in societies. This essay is an introductory historical overview of how Christmas developed, from its earliest roots to its role in the United States today, but with a special interest in how religion and culture interact and intertwine. Especially as seen through the interpretive lens of two analogies (a three-layer cake and a snowball), it should become obvious that the religious celebration of Christmas has been profoundly shaped by cultural influences from many directions.

## HOLIDAYS AS THREE-LAYER CAKES

One helpful analogy, I would suggest, is to see holidays as three-layer cakes. I do not claim that this typology applies to all holidays, but it certainly describes some of America's most culturally dominant ones, including Easter, Halloween, Thanksgiving, and especially the giant of them all, Christmas. To describe the layers briefly: the first, basic layer is a seasonal celebration, when early cultures developed observances that expressed understandable human responses to various times of the year, such as exhilaration when spring brought warmth and new life, or relief that followed the completion of a harvest, or the need for a party to cope with the darkness and cold of winter. Then a religion or a nation might arise and add a second layer, an overlay either augmenting or attempting to transform the earlier seasonal celebration with new meaning. Finally, the third layer consists of whatever changes modern popular culture brings to the first two layers. Thus, a three-layer cake:

modern popular culture

religious or national overlay

seasonal celebration

When participants argue about the true meaning of a holiday and complain that other people are not observing it properly, an understanding of the three layers may help explain why the disagreements arise, even if it does not settle the arguments.

Applied to Christmas, the first layer is all about winter. Many histories of Christmas make passing mention of its winter setting, but I am not sure most of us really understand what that means. Personally, I began to think seriously about the realities of winter while leading a student trip to Alaska. We were there in May, just before the summer tourists began to arrive, but we were told that the real challenges came in the middle of winter, when there were only four hours of daylight a day and temperatures dropped as low as forty degrees below zero—*before* calculating the wind chill. This was only in the middle of Alaska, not the far north. We heard about difficulties enduring winter in little shacks with no electricity and no running water, and we heard about the struggles some people had with depression, alcoholism, domestic abuse, and suicide, aggravated by the cold, the darkness, and the resulting isolation of winter. Because I am a historian, with perhaps an offbeat imagination, I began wondering what it would have been like to live in central or northern Europe in the Middle Ages, under somewhat similar conditions. Today we have electric lights and thermostats, but we still battle "cabin fever" and seasonal affective disorder (SAD) in the middle of winter. What must it have been like for northern Europeans in those centuries long before modern conveniences? Seen this way, it becomes clear that winter is more than beautiful snow-covered landscapes. Under some circumstances, the season is difficult to survive. Entering winter is a little like walking into death and hoping that we will come out on the other side.

What might those people in early and medieval Europe have done to cope with the difficulties of winter? One great idea would be to sponsor a big, blowout midwinter party! The logical time would be mid-to-late-December, when the days stopped getting shorter and were about to grow longer. People in snowbound villages could spend the early winter distracting themselves with preparations, and then they could have the party as a break from the cold and the dark. When the party was over, the remainder of winter would be that much shorter. It also is easy to guess some details of what the party would be like. It would be a festival of lights, with candles, and burning logs, and anything else that might help push back the darkness. It would feature evergreens as signs of life when everything else seems to have died, plus other plants that not only stay green but even bear fruit in the middle of winter, like holly or mistletoe. It probably would include gatherings of family, friends, and neighbors for meals and parties, to overcome the isolation of winter. There would be feasts, and drinking, and dancing, and maybe special songs and gifts of some kind.

As it turns out, this is not just speculation. All over central and northern Europe, early cultures had winter festivities that included almost all of these features. One notable example was Yule, or Jul, celebrated in the geographical area now called Germany, Scandinavia, and the British Isles. Today people think that the word "Yule" is a synonym for Christmas, but it actually was the name for the pre-Christian winter celebrations in that region. Scholars are unsure what the word meant. It might have been "wheel," as in the cycle of seasons, or perhaps "feast" or 'sacrifice." The seasonal activities included the slaughter of animals, a lot of drinking, candles and bonfires (including the Yule log, of course), ghost stories, and prickly evergreens around windows to keep away evil spirits.[1] An example of a winter festival further south in Europe was the Roman Saturnalia, a late harvest festival varying in length from three to seven days and held between December 17 and 23. The partying was wild and included drunkenness and all kinds of unrestrained activities, but it also featured the candles and fires, greenery, feasting, gifts, and social gatherings that would be expected of a winter party.[2]

Much of what has just been described also is a description of Christmas today: outdoor displays of lights, Christmas trees and other evergreen decorations, gatherings of family and friends, feasts, and songs. All are beloved parts of today's Christmas, but they do not necessarily have anything to do with a baby in a manger. They are predictable aspects of mid-winter parties that help people cope with the difficulties of winter. This is what is meant when some refer to "the pagan roots of Christmas." "Pagan" was a word used by Christians to refer to something that was non-Christian or pre-Christian, and it is certainly true that Europeans in central and northern Europe had winter festivals before Jesus ever walked the earth. When Christians eventually started celebrating the birth of Jesus in December and then spread their religion into central and northern Europe, they encountered preexisting winter parties and absorbed aspects of these into their Christmas observances. This first layer of the holiday three-layer cake, the seasonal celebrations, might be called folk culture or, depending on which definition of popular culture one uses, an early version of popular culture.[3]

So winter came first, and then Christmas was added later, but it took a while. Early Christians did not celebrate Christmas. For the first couple of centuries of early Christianity, there was no annual celebration of the Christ child's nativity at all. This comes as a big surprise to many Christians, because today Christmas and Easter are the two most special days of the Christian year. It was not always that way. Early Christianity was, instead, an Easter-centered religion, focused on the death and resurrection of Jesus, with an expectation that he would return soon. The Eastern church (later to become identified as Eastern Orthodox) began Epiphany observances sometime in the 200s or 300s, on January 6, to celebrate the many ways that Jesus Christ was made manifest in the world, including the baptism of Jesus, and miracles such as turning water into wine, and, yes, amazing events surrounding Jesus' birth. Epiphany included some attention to the birth story, but it was not the only focus for the day.[4] In contrast, for the Western part of the early church centered in Rome, the first extant documentary mention of a celebration of Jesus' birth is an observance on December 25, and it appears in the Philocalian Calendar, also known as the Chronograph of 354. It is a collection of documents, something like an almanac, and some of the included texts may date back to 336. Thus, by either 336 or 354, and perhaps somewhat before that, Christians in Rome were celebrating Jesus' Nativity on December 25.[5]

Why Christians eventually started a birthday celebration for Jesus, and why they chose the date of December 25, is something I have described in more detail elsewhere.[6] However, much of the discussion is speculative, because evidence is limited. One problem was the date, because neither the Christian Bible nor outside sources indicate the month or day when Jesus was born, although a number of early Christians attempted to figure it out, with no consensus result. Also, after a couple of centuries with no annual remembrance of the Nativity, why did Christians eventually start one? It would be very helpful if we had a letter or a proclamation from a pope or an emperor declaring when and why Christians were going to start an annual celebration of the birth of Jesus, but we have no such document. It is likely that the celebration began for a combination of theological and cultural reasons, but the details are unclear.

What we *do* know is that in choosing the date of December 25 to celebrate the birth of Jesus, Christians placed this annual observance right in the middle of three wildly popular preexisting Roman winter festivals. First was the Saturnalia, the Roman late harvest celebration already mentioned, in the middle of December. A couple of weeks later came the New Year's festival Kalends, which lasted for as many as five days, with feasts and additional uninhibited activities. Today's word "calendar" derives from that term. In between Saturnalia and Kalends fell December 25, the winter solstice by calendars of that time. Romans celebrated December 25 as the birthday of Sol Invictus, the Unconquered Sun, a god whose devotion had been merged with worship of the warrior god Mithras (some have said in an attempt to be clever that Christians changed the birthday of a sun god to the birthday of God the Son). All three celebrations pervaded Roman culture, so Christian leaders had to have been aware of them. It cannot have been accidental that Christian leaders chose to place the birthday observance for Jesus in the midst of these three notable Roman celebrations. As for why they did it, we can only guess. Perhaps they wanted to co-opt the popularity of the existing winter parties in order to promote the acceptance of Christianity among more people. Perhaps they disapproved of how wild the parties were and hoped that adding a Christian celebration would tame them. Perhaps they wanted to compete with the Roman religions head on. Maybe it was all three.

Whatever the motivations, Christians gave an overlay of Christian meaning to some preexisting winter festivities. An important implication of this narrative is that when Christians finally initiated an annual celebration of the birth of Jesus, it was *from the very beginning* a combination of a winter cultural party and a Christian observance. The historian Stephen Nissenbaum offers a very articulate summary of the complicated repercussions:

The decision was part of what amounted to a compromise, and a compromise for which the Church paid a high price.... In return for ensuring massive observance of the anniversary of the Savior's birth by assigning it to this resonant date, the Church for its part tacitly agreed to allow the holiday to be celebrated more or less the way it had always been. From the beginning, the Church's hold over Christmas was (and remains still) rather tenuous. There were always people for whom Christmas was a time of pious devotion rather than carnival, but such people were always in the minority. It may not be going too far to say that Christmas has always been an extremely difficult holiday to *Christianize.*[7]

Today, some Christians launch campaigns to "Keep Christ in Christmas" because of an understandable concern that all of the cultural activity distracts participants from thinking about the religious meanings of the day. However, some of the campaigners wish that Christmas could return to the pure spiritual holiday it once was, before recent developments ruined it. The point is, it never was a purely spiritual holiday. From the very first annual celebrations of Jesus' birth sometime in the 300s, it already was a fusion of preexisting winter festivals and Christian themes. The struggle to find a balance between the two has continued ever since.

## CHRISTMAS IS LIKE A SNOWBALL

The timing here is interesting. In its earliest few centuries Christianity had spread around the Roman empire, in the lands surrounding the Mediterranean Sea. Then, in the next centuries immediately after Christians began their annual celebrations of the Nativity on December 25 in the 300s, Christianity advanced further northward throughout much of the European continent, and Christmas came along for the ride. Throughout the medieval period, the center of Christian activity shifted more and more into Europe and less around some sections of the Mediterranean. Of course, the further north, the more powerful the winters, and in each new region Christians encountered winter festivals. When that happened, Christianity (and Christmas) sometimes picked up some of those winter traditions and transformed them for Christian purposes rather than conquering or replacing them.

At some points in Christian history (although not all), this was a conscious strategy. The most frequently cited example is from Pope Gregory I, called Gregory the Great, who established an explicit policy of accommodation with native traditions. On June 1, 601, he wrote a letter to Abbot Mellitus containing a message to be delivered to Archbishop Augustine of Canterbury. This was not the more famous Augustine of Hippo, one of Christianity's most influential theologians, but Augustine of Canterbury was important in his own right. He was a Benedictine monk from Rome who was sent by Gregory to evangelize England and is considered one of the founders of the English church This letter was further guidance from Pope Gregory about how to proceed. In it Gregory referred to non-Christian religions as devil worship, but he was willing to retain many of their customs while trying to change their inner meaning and wrote:

> The idol temples of that race should by no means be destroyed, but only the idols in them. Take holy water and sprinkle it in these shrines, build altars and place relics in them.... When this people see that their shrines are not destroyed they will be able to banish error from their hearts and be more ready to come to the places they are familiar with, but now recognizing and worshipping the true god.... Thus while some outward rejoicings are preserved, they will be able more easily to share in inward rejoicings. It is doubtless impossible to cut out everything at once from their stubborn minds; just as the man who is attempting to climb to the highest place, rises by steps and degrees and not by leaps.[8]

Not only did Christianity accommodate some native traditions, but Christianity's movement from one region to another also helped spread one culture's traditions to other areas. For me, the most helpful image to represent the process is a snowball. Christmas is like a snowball. I am not thinking of a snowball that is thrown but one that rolls. When you push a snowball through the yard in order to create a snowman or a fort, the growing ball of snow picks up all kinds of things: autumn leaves, a mitten dropped by a child, salt thrown on and near the side-walk, and who knows what else. In a similar way, Christmas rolled through Europe and elsewhere throughout the world, picking up winter customs as it went, incorporating them into Christmas celebrations and also spreading certain customs from one region to another. The snowball changed size, shape, and color as it rolled, adding and dropping features over time and distance. Folklorists and anthropologists often struggle to explain the exact origins and timing of various Christmas traditions, but whatever the specific details in each case, I think much of the overall process of development was quite understandable. It was a rolling snowball.

Consider the poinsettia. In this case the snowball began rolling when the Spanish brought Christianity to what is now Mexico, bringing the December 25 Nativity celebration with them (along with the related Three Kings' Day on January 6). There they encountered a beautiful winter-flowering plant, *Euphorbia pulcherima,* that was native to Mexico and known to the Aztecs. What we usually refer to as the petals of the poinsettia are actually green leaves that turn red when they experience long nights of darkness. Technically, the yellow buds in the center are the flowers. What is significant is that the plant comes to full bloom in December, responding to reduced sunlight, and thus it is an ideal symbol or decoration for winter celebrations. So, on December 25, when Christians remembered the nativity of Jesus, this flower was blooming in Mexico. A touching folktale arose about a little peasant girl who wanted to bring a gift to the Christ child but, in tears, realized that she had nothing beautiful enough to offer. Nevertheless she brought a handful of ordinary weeds to the cradle of the baby Jesus, and in a miracle he turned them into brilliant red flowers. Thus the plants received the name *flores de Nochebuena,* or flowers of the Holy Night.

It so happens that the first United States ambassador to Mexico was an amateur botanist. His name was Dr. Joel Roberts Poinsett, and he was instrumental in bringing cuttings of the plant back to the United States in about 1828. The formal botanical name for the plant is

*Euphorbia pulcherima,* but the popular American name, poinsettia, obviously recognizes the ambassador. Poinsettias were widely available in the United States by the late 1800s and became a pervasive American symbol of Christmas in the twentieth century. The poinsettia went from being a plant that grew wild in Mexico to being domesticated and mass produced in the United States. Today, according to the Society of American Florists, the December holiday season is the number one floral-buying period in the United States (more than Mother's Day and Valentine's Day), and of the flowering plants purchased then, about three-fourths are poinsettias.[9]

The poinsettia story is an example of the snowball process at work. The Spanish brought Christianity and Christmas to Mexico, where it picked up the native red flower as a Christmas symbol, which then rolled into the United States, where is has flourished as a dominant Christmas symbol, now sometimes copied in other parts of the world. The Christmas tree is another example. As already discussed, early traditions included various evergreens in winter festivals. It was Germans who first introduced the evergreen *tree* as a Christmas home decoration. The House of Hanover (of German background) brought the Christmas tree custom into England, especially through the popularity of Queen Victoria and Prince Albert, and it was soon thereafter copied in the United States. Perhaps the most fascinating snowball example is the spread of December 6 Saint Nicholas observances throughout Europe, their eventual associations with Christmas, and then the gradual metamorphosis of Saint Nicholas into Santa Claus in the United States, a story I have told elsewhere.[10]

## MODERN POPULAR CULTURE

In addition to the first two holiday layers, a winter seasonal celebration and then a Christian overlay of meaning about the baby Jesus, when it comes to the influence of the third layer, modern popular culture, one word leaps immediately to almost everyone's mind, commercialization, typically with negative connotations. As Lucy Van Pelt said in the animated television special *A Charlie Brown Christmas:* "Look, Charlie, let's face it. We all know that Christmas is a big commercial racket. It's run by a big eastern syndicate, you know." As with the previous layers, a brief historical overview can offer some perspective.

Throughout most of the history of Christmas, gifts did not play the dominating role that they do now. Prior to the past few centuries, when gifts were given they often were tokens, not major investments. In the 1700s and 1800s, industrialization led to the mass production of commodities and the development of a consumer culture, which inevitably had an impact on Christmas. A decisive shift came when businesses recognized the marketing possibilities associated with holidays. The previous business attitude was represented by Scrooge in Dickens's *A Christmas Carol,* when he complained that holidays were simply a way of picking his pocket because he had to pay people for no work. From this perspective, holidays were a time of idleness and were not productive. However, if holidays held potential for the sale of additional products, whether food, clothing, decorations, or gifts, businesses not only tolerated holidays but actively promoted them. Gift-giving traditions already existed in association with both Saint Nicholas Day (December 6) and New Year's Day (January 1). In the United States in the 1800s, for reasons we do not yet fully understand, those gift traditions migrated across the calendar and converged on Christmas. Undoubtedly the morphing of Saint Nicholas into Santa Claus, the generous gift-giver, played a role.

In the late 1800s handmade gifts also gave way more and more to manufactured goods. If you want to trace the commodification of the holiday, chart the first appearances of many of the products we now associate with Christmas; most of them arose in the nineteenth century, with further developments in the twentieth. The first Christmas card appeared in England in 1843, and use of such cards became widespread in the United States in the second half of the century. Christmas trees were sold on the streets of New York as early as 1840; light bulbs for Christmas trees first appeared in the 1880s, and glass ornaments appeared in the 1890s.

Wrapping paper appeared at the end of the nineteenth century and became more colorful in the twentieth. The list goes on and on.

In the present day, the resulting statistics are staggering. The National Retail Federation annually surveys holiday shopping expectations, and the "Winter Holiday Spending" category has become an all important segment, representing approximately 19 percent of all retail sales for the entire year. (The NRF holiday sales figures do not include autos, gas, and restaurant sales, which might be considered normal ongoing expenditures.) Winter Holiday spending is more than *three times larger* than all of the other American holiday spending *combined.* Those other holidays include Mother's Day, Father's Day, Valentine's Day, Easter, Halloween, St. Patrick's Day, even the Super Bowl and Back to School/College shopping, and winter holiday sales dwarf them all. Admittedly, the winter holiday sales statistics also include Chanukah/Hanukkah (celebrated by 4.6 percent of survey respondents) and Kwanza (1.6 percent), but 96.1 percent indicated that they were celebrating Christmas. The holiday purchases include the many products that developed in the 1800s and 1900s, such as decorations, greeting cards and postage, candy, food, and flowers, but it will come as no surprise that more than three-fourths of the spending is for gifts. The vast majority of gifts are for family, but friends, co-workers, babysitters, postal workers, and even pets receive them as well.[11]

Two observations are appropriate here. First, in light of increasing religious pluralism in the United States, including the growing number of persons who identify as "unaffiliated" or "none," the 96 percent of Americans who indicate that they celebrate Christmas is a larger percentage than those who identify as Christian. One way to explain this is to conclude that a cultural Christmas has developed alongside the more explicitly Christian Christmas, and some persons participate in one, some in the other, and many in both.

The second observation relates to a general principle in analyzing popular culture, that popular culture *both* reflects us and shapes us. It is too easy to conclude that all of this holiday spending is totally a result of manipulation by commercial interests. Retailers have tried many ideas to prompt spending for special occasions, and not all of them succeed. Customers are not mere pawns; they make choices, often because they are filling a need of one kind or another. In the case of Christmas spending, it is helpful to reflect on the motivations behind the purchases: a desire to express love and affection, or to fulfill a social obligation, or other explanations. In Christmas shopping as in other examples in the marketplace, economic success results from the push and pull of product offerings, marketing initiatives, and the very important role of consumer choices.

Alongside commercialization, however, another modern cultural trend rivals it in importance, in its impact upon Christmas: the domestication of the holiday as a family-centered and child-centered festivity. In the end, ironically, it also contributed to commercialization.

One friend recently told me that the main reason he loved Christmas was that it was such a special time for children. Another remarked, sadly, "No one warns you that when your children grow up and move away, they take Christmas with them." A Christmas revolving around children and family has become a modern American assumption, but it was not always that way. Early, medieval, and Reformation-era Christmases were mainly adult activities, mostly masses at church and festivities in the village, such as feasting and drinking at the neighborhood tavern, and the home was not the overwhelming focus. (As a side note, the word "Christmas" is an English term from perhaps the eleventh century that means Christ's Mass, referring to a special midnight mass, the worship service that marked the beginning of Christmas Day and was mainly an adult activity.)

Many point to the Victorian era in both England and America, the 1800s, as the period when the center of gravity for Christmas celebrations shifted to the home. Referring to that era, the English historian Asa Briggs wrote that "the domestic ties of the family itself were sung more loudly than at any other period of English history.... The home was felt to be the centre of virtues and emotions which could not be found in completed form outside." Numerous treatises were published to foster "happy families" and the family was seen as the basic, essential unit of society.[12] Many activists worked to ameliorate the deplorable circumstances of many children, including child labor, inadequate education, high mortality rates, and crushing poverty, and some popular culture played its part. Charles Dickens as the most popular novelist of his time championed the cause of vulnerable children in many of his works, such as *Oliver Twist* and *Bleak House.* In relation to Christmas, the phenomenal success and influence of Dickens's *A Christmas Carol* in both England and the United States helped revive and reinvent the holiday, with the family at the center. The most influential early visual image accenting a family centered Christmas was a famous illustration published in 1848 in the *Illustrated London News,* picturing the popular Queen Victoria, Prince Albert, their children and a governess, all gathered around a decorated Christmas tree that had been placed on a table, with small gifts hanging from the boughs and at the base of the tree. In 1850 *Godey's Ladies Book,* the most influential American magazine of its time, published the same illustration, but with Victoria's tiara and Albert's sash edited out, to make them look like an all-American family. Here was a perfect family Christmas, a model to emulate. (As another result, Christmas trees became the rage in England and America.)

Similar forces were at work in the United States. The historian Stephen Nissenbaum has written an important book about this very topic, well summarized in the volume's long title: *The Battle for Christmas: A Social and Cultural History of Christmas That Shows How It Was Transformed from an Unruly Carnival into the Quintessential American Family Holiday.* He describes raucous bands of lower-class youths roving the streets at Christmastime, exhibiting public drunkenness, loud singing, and even looting and extortion, behavior that could be truly frightening and dangerous. Nissenbaum argues that Christmas festivities were redirected, especially by New York's elite, to become domestic, child-centered activities in the home as a way to combat or marginalize the carousing in the streets. He gave considerable attention to the composition and influence of the famous poem "The Night Before Christmas" as part of that process, which involves the American evolution of Santa Claus.[13]

As a matter of fact, if one wants to understand modern popular culture's influence on the current American celebration of Christmas, study of the three iconic artifacts briefly mentioned here would provide quite a full view: Charles Dickens's *A Christmas Carol,* the famous Victorian illustration of a family gathered around a Christmas tree, and "The Night Before Christmas" with its associated evolution of Santa Claus. Dickens's immensely popular Christmas story helped revive Christmas in England and America, in the process emphasizing a spirit of generosity with surprisingly little mention of religion. The famous illustration of Victoria, Albert, and their family gathered around a Christmas tree promoted the holiday as a child- and family-centered occasion and established the tree as a central symbol. "The Night Before Christmas," perhaps the best-known poem in the English language, was one of several steps that contributed to the morphing of St. Nicholas into Santa Claus, with implications both for children and for the importance of gifts.

This historical narrative makes it clear that when it comes to Christmas, religion and culture are thoroughly enmeshed. Culture, whether folk culture or popular culture, has impacted Christmas from many directions. The very earliest Christian observances of Jesus' birth were planted in the midst of already existing winter festivals, which immediately influenced the spiritual experience of Christmas by surrounding it with revelry and an array of images, such as evergreens and the shared symbolism of light. When Christmas encountered other winter celebrations as Christianity expanded to new regions in Europe and the Americas, it repeatedly adopted symbols and practices from each and at times helped them spread to new cultures. In terms of more modern popular culture, two of the most obvious influences have been the general commodification of culture that in the case of Christmas threatens to eclipse spiritual meanings, and a two century cultural elevation of the importance of children and family that has formed Christmas into perhaps the most child- and family-centered holiday in the United States. For

Christians the spiritual meanings are important, but if one yearns for a purely spiritual occasion uninfluenced by culture, it is something that has never existed in the entire history of Christmas.

## DISCUSSION QUESTIONS

1. In your view, does Forbes's analogy about three-layer cakes apply to any other holidays in addition to Christmas? If so, which ones? Explain. Do you find this analogy helpful in understanding holidays?

2. How do you respond to the fact that, from the very beginning, the celebration of the birth of Jesus was fused with preexisting winter celebrations? Is it problematic for the religious meanings of the day, or not? Why?

3. Has the ongoing addition of cultural features, acquired as the Christmas snowball rolled through many regions over many centuries, changed the basic nature of the holiday? If so, in what ways?

4. Is the modern commercialization of Christmas an example of how popular culture reflects us, or how popular culture shapes us? What arguments and evidence support your view?

## NOTES

1. This essay is a distillation and recasting of the Introduction and the Christmas chapter (chapter 1) of my book *America's Favorite Holidays: Candid Histories* (Oakland: University of California Press, 2015), which is in turn based upon the fuller consideration I gave to Christmas in *Christmas: A Candid History* (Berkeley: University of California Press, 2007). Kathleen Stoker, *Keeping Christmas: Yuletide Traditions in Norway and the New Land* (St. Paul: Minnesota Historical Society Press, 2000), 6–7; E.O. James, *Seasonal Feasts and Festivals* (New York: Barnes & Noble, 1961), 292.

2. Lucian of Samosata, *Lucian VI,* trans. K. Kilburn, Loeb Classical Library (Cambridge, MA: Harvard University Press, 1959), 91–115.

3. For a discussion of high culture, folk culture, and popular culture, including a disagreement about how to define popular culture, see the Introduction to this volume, 2–3.

4. Thomas J. Talley, *The Origins of the Liturgical Year,* 2nd ed. (Collegeville, MN: Liturgical Press, 1991), 103–21.

5. Susan K. Roll, *Toward the Origins of Christmas* (Kampen, Netherlands: Kok Pharos, 1995), 83–86.

6. *Christmas: A Candid History* (Berkeley: University of California Press, 2007), 25–31.

7. Stephen Nissenbaum, *The Battle for Christmas : A Social and Cultural History of Christmas That Shows How It Was Transformed from an Unruly Carnival into the Quintessential American Family Holiday* (New York: Knopf, 1996), 7–8.

8. Bertram Colgrave and R. A. B. Rynors, eds., *Bede's Ecclesiastical History of the English People* (Oxford: Clarendon Press, 1969), 107, 109.

9. www.aboutflowers.com/flower-holidays-occasions-a-parties/christmas /christmas-statistics.html.

10. Forbes, *Christmas: A Candid History,* 69–96.

11. See https://nrf.com/resources/consumer-data/holiday-headquarters, http://research.nrffoundation.com/Default.aspx?pg = 9039#.VoHyNuTzmao, and associated pages by the National Retail Federation.

12. Asa Briggs, *The Age of Improvement, 1783–1867* (London: John Murray, 1997), 114.

13. Stephen Nissenbaum, *The Battle for Christmas:* (New York: Alfred A. Knopf, 1996), 73.

# CHAPTER SEVEN

# Mipsterz

*Hip, American, and Muslim*

KRISTIN M. PETERSON AND NABIL ECHCHAIBI

In a two-and-a-half-minute-long video released on YouTube in November 2013, a series of short clips feature a group of self-confident young Muslim women hanging out in various urban landscapes in the United States, as Jay-Z's song "Somewhere in America" plays in the background. The women parade their fashionable outfits as they walk down the street, skate in high heels, take selfies, dance and run through parks. The video appears to be a harmless and carefree expression of young women being creative with their fashion styles and enjoying the company of their friends. Within days of its release, hundreds of thousands of people had watched the video and many left scathing critiques on various online blogs and news sites. The viral video, entitled "Somewhere in America #MIPSTERZ,"[1] quickly became controversial, amid heated accusations that a "misguided" group of hipster Muslim women had gone "too far" in reappropriating modesty and staking out an edgy religious and gendered identity.

Critics specifically claimed that the video misrepresented Islam, that the women were immodest and oversexualized, and that the focus on fashion was promoting an excessive materialist culture fixated on consumption and brands. One of the most well-circulated critiques came from Sana Saeed, a writer for *The Islamic Monthly,* in which she argued that the video attempts to normalize Muslim women by fitting them into mainstream culture and reducing them to a shallow visual portrayal based exclusively on physical appearance. Saeed concedes that the video is aesthetically attractive, but she finds little substance in the images. "The video doesn't really seem to have any purpose aside from showing well-dressed, put together Muslim women in poses perfect for a magazine spread," she writes.[2] Saeed seems doubtful that sleek visuals and hip music can ever provide a deep and unproblematic representation of Muslims.

In response to these comments, several of the women who participated in the Mipsterz video argued that their intention was to prompt a larger discussion about the multiple examples of Muslim modesty and the narrow coding of Muslim women as victims of rigid religious rules. Layla Shaikley, a participant and the fashion director for the video, explains that she was tired of always having to tell her story about her faith using words, so instead she wanted to participate in what she calls a "creative action." She views the Mipsterz video as a self-portrait of her identity and an expression of the larger Mipsterz identity.[3] One of the creators of the video, Habib Yazdi, insists that the video was an effort to shift assumptions about the visual portrayal of Muslim women by creating new images. "We want to give people a different experience of what they tend to see and hear about Muslim women," Yazdi explains. "You see how easy it is to manipulate images to create an idea, so for us it was like, why don't we do the same thing? Why don't we do our commercial and manipulate the images in our favor?"[4]

The Mipsterz video provides an intriguing example of how young Muslims in post–9/11 America resist the simplistic and stereotypical narratives that largely pervade Western popular culture. Muslim women, in particular, have struggled to liberate themselves from a relentless framing that portrays them as either covered and oppressed by Islam or uncovered and sexually liberated by Western secular culture. This chapter focuses on how the women behind the Mipsterz video engage with visuals, urban styles, fashion, fun, and other forms of popular culture to subvert these frames and articulate alternative narratives of what it means to be a Muslim woman in America. We analyze how the expressive and aesthetic practices of popular culture can afford marginalized groups a critical space in which to challenge dominant social values and foster a distinct sense of cultural and religious identity. In this case, we argue, popular culture and religion intersect in productive ways, breaking free of the discourse of victimization and exoticism and helping us understand the complex, multiple frames of reference that define American Muslims' everyday lives.

## MUSLIMS AND POPULAR CULTURE

Since 9/11, it has become even more challenging for American Muslims to find media spaces that are receptive to their stories and willing to recognize the diversity of their identities. Muslim women, in particular, often find themselves trapped in a climate which has all too readily connected a popular discourse about their oppression to the moral imperative of rescuing them from the tyranny of their culture and religion. Over the past decade and a half, American Muslim women have sought to leverage the symbolic power of popular culture to address their seclusion in the larger mainstream culture and their lack of voice inside the American Muslim community. Some have turned to stand-up comedy to counter the image of the subordinate Muslim woman.[5] Others have taken to popular literature, magazines, and comic strips to chronicle the rich and complex social and cultural experiences of Muslim women in America.[6]

The Mipsterz movement we are analyzing in this chapter is not too different from these other efforts because it is equally concerned with disrupting the popular rhetoric around the suppression of Muslim women and their lack of agency. But what is perhaps most striking about the Mipsterz movement and its "Somewhere in America #MIPSTERZ" video is, not just their invocation of fashion and popular culture, but rather their defense of a particular facet of Muslim female identity through the language, aesthetics, and sensibilities of neoliberalism. In this case, consumer culture provides not only the space, but also the tools and techniques through which autonomy, resistance, and a more progressive form of Islamic piety can be imagined and affirmed. Such an intersection between market ideology, female bodies, lifestyle, and religious expression does not necessarily nullify the political value of this "creative" movement, but it raises significant questions about the relationship and possibly tensions between religion, fashion, popular culture, and social change as Muslim women seek to square their religious values with a modern urban lifestyle.

## THE MIPSTERZ MOVEMENT

The "Somewhere in America #MIPSTERZ" video was not an isolated creative expression but rather the first public presentation of the larger Mipsterz movement. The filmmakers, Habib Yazdi, Abbas Rattani, and Sara Aghajanian, worked with young women who identified as Muslim hipsters to create this video as a visual portrayal of the identities of young, hip, fashionable Muslim American women. Hajer Naili, one of the women featured in the video, said that the filmmakers and women in the video wanted to create a "joyful and realistic" profile of Muslim American women, a profile that is not often shown in Western media.[7]

The Mipsterz fashion video is one aspect of the larger movement of Mipsterz, as young Muslims connect online through social media and meet up at public events. The Mipsterz Facebook page has around 15,000 fans, and every day members post articles about Islamic topics, social justice concerns, political issues, and popular culture. Members of the Mipsterz movement are also active on a Google group listserv, sharing practical advice about housing, employment, and travel; connecting with other members and setting up social events; and discussing political issues and religious topics. Recent discussions on the listserv have revolved around formulating responses to prejudicial attacks against Islam, assisting Syrian refugees, and sharing opinions about Muslim women's attire and the headscarf.

Despite some of these more formal aspects of the group, such as the Facebook page and the listserv, the Mipsterz movement is a loosely associated group that is not concerned with official membership. The Facebook description of the Mipsterz explains that everyone is welcome to become a Mipster, Muslim and/or hipster or neither, and that the group is open to anyone regardless of assigned social categories. As the description explains, "Mipsterz is not a registered 501(c)(3) nonprofit organization; rather, it is an organic ... community and culture of individuals who want to chill with creative, critical thinking folks."[8] Members of the group are not connected by official identity markers, but instead by shared interests in religion, culture, and social change.

Besides the fashion video, other visual images of the Mipsterz movement highlight the creativity of this movement. The Facebook page features a banner image of black thick-framed glasses, symbols of the hipster movement, along with Arabic calligraphy inside the lenses. A similar drawing online shows a young woman in a headscarf, wearing thick-framed glasses. Another photograph shows three Mipsterz wearing T-shirts that say, "Keep calm and hijab on," a play on the common phrase in pop culture, "Keep calm and carry on." These visual examples illustrate how members of the Mipsterz movement blend elements of popular culture into their creative expressions.

### THE MIPSTERZ VIDEO

The Mipsterz video profiles the innovative fashion styles of several young Muslim women, as they move around urban landscapes. Throughout the video, the women do more than passively pose for the camera. They run, jump, climb, dance, skate, cartwheel, laugh, and joke around for the camera. Unlike most fashion images that portray women as objects of the viewer's gaze, some women in this video challenge the gaze by standing on top of things and looking down at the camera, starring straight into the camera, and even physically grabbing the camera.

The video was filmed in New York, Los Angeles, Boston, Washington, DC, and Hillsborough, SC. The settings are mostly urban outdoor spaces, such as parks, sidewalks, and alleyways, and the locations give the video a particularly American feel. The women wear various fashion styles that are distinct to the American context. Although the Islamic fashion industry is a large and growing business in Europe, Southeast Asia and the Gulf countries, North America is generally not considered a site of innovative Islamic fashion trends. The women in this video emphasize what is unique and creative about their own styles.

The main purpose of the Mipsterz video is to visually present the fashion styles of the Mipsterz movement. Overall, the fashion in this video indicates that the Mipsterz value creativity, hybridity, individuality, and diversity. There is no single Mipsterz fashion style. Rather, what connects these women is an emphasis on eclectic styles and creatively blending various types of fashion. The women mix mainstream fashion trends, retro clothing, urban fashion, ethnic culture, and Islamic styles.

Several distinct fashion styles are present in the video. First, there is a chic fashion style in which the women aspire to fit into mainstream high fashion trends that emphasize designer clothes. In this style, the women wear leggings, tunics, long sweaters, silk scarves, dresses with leggings or tights, collared blouses, and gold jewelry. These outfits are often colorful and attractive but are still modest, mature, and professional.

Another fashion style that is shown throughout the Mipsterz video can be loosely defined as a layering style, in which the women piece together various elements from current and retro fashion to create a more complex appearance. This style is distinct from the chic style because the women tend to incorporate looser, more flowing fabrics and integrate retro styles and ethnic styles. This layering style is practically useful for Muslim women because if they are concerned about revealing too much of their body shapes, they can dress in layers or more flowing outfits. Additionally, the layering style gives young women the chance to be more creative with their fashion. They can go to thrift stores, department stores, and their own closets to put together unique outfits.

The Mipsterz video also features a street style of fashion that incorporates darker colors and heavier materials. The women who emphasize this style wear black clothing, leather jackets, thick-soled boots, fake-fur jackets, dark makeup, and silver jewelry. This street style presents the women as tough, confident, and strong. The women reject the colorful, lightweight, flowing clothing of the other styles and instead wear darker colors and heavier materials that offer more protection.

### FASHION AS POLITICAL IDENTITY

The women in the Mipsterz video incorporate elements of hipster culture, specifically fashion trends, as a form of resistance to dominant stereotypes that categorize Muslims as backward and oppressed. Fashion, like other elements of popular culture, has often been dismissed as a frivolous practice that has no impact on the larger culture and society. On the other hand, fashion can be seen as a political statement of identity. Especially for groups like Muslim women who are often misrepresented in the mainstream public, fashion offers an opportunity to resist stereotypes. Hajer Naili, one of the women featured in the Mipsterz video, explained that "the video offers an antidote to prevailing western stereotypes of Muslim, veiled women as inactive, passive, uniform in their appearance, and hidden."[9]

In their edited volume *Islamic Fashion and Anti-Fashion: New Perspectives from Europe and North America*, Emma Tarlo and Annelies Moors focus on how fashion can be a political statement for young Muslim women in Western countries, where their voices are often unheard. They argue that "through their visual material and bodily presence young women who wear Islamic fashion disrupt and challenge public stereotypes about Islam, women, social integration and the veil even if their voices are often drowned out in political and legal debates on these issues."[10] When Muslim women use fashion to show themselves as individuals with creative styles who participate in contemporary consumer culture, they overturn common misconceptions of Muslim women as "dull, downtrodden, oppressed and out of sync with modernity."[11] Muslim women may not be able to participate in public debates, but they use their fashion, daily practices, and public dispositions to express their opinions and their identities.

Furthermore, the process of getting dressed can be understood as what Joanne Entwistle calls an "embodied activity" through which individuals present their interior selves to the social world.[12] Dress provides a way for individuals to negotiate between larger social norms, the fashion system and individual identity markers. For instance, the women in the Mipsterz video have individual agency to choose what they will wear, but these choices are restricted by social norms based on their gender, religion, and ethnicity. Susan Kaiser explains that "people create their own 'fashion statements' but are ultimately constrained by what is available in the marketplace, by dress codes and social conventions, by political regimes."[13] The fashion styles in the Mipsterz video highlight the intersections, complexities and contradictions of the identity of Muslim American women. By focusing on the hybridity of the Mipsterz fashion styles, we are able to better understand what Kaiser discusses as "the overlapping or 'in between' spaces, through which fashion subjects exercise agency and articulate more than one subject position simultaneously."[14] It is arguably politically resistive for Muslim women to create blended fashion styles that emphasize their intersectional identities and complicate stereotypes of Muslim women as one-dimensional victims.

The women use fashion styles in the Mipsterz video to create a powerful identity statement of what it means to be a Mipster—a trendy, innovative, multifaceted Muslim American. First, rather than imitating the latest fashion trends on display in malls or magazines, the women in the video highlight their creativity and individuality by wearing outfits that they put together on their own. The women combine items that emphasize the religious value of modesty (headscarves, loose clothing), their various cultural backgrounds (African American, South Asian, and Arab styles), and contemporary trends (urban, chic, and hipster styles). The fashion styles in this video specifically focus on trends in hipster culture, such as mustache-shaped jewelry, thrift store clothing, ironic T-shirts, and mismatched patterns and materials.

The women also incorporate elements from popular culture to show that they are in conversation with contemporary culture. For example, one woman wears a Marilyn Monroe T-shirt, and later on another woman is seen wearing a shirt with the phrase, "You're killin' me Smalls," which is a line from *The Sandlot,* a popular children's film in the 1990s. The video also shows the women using smart phones to take selfies or to videotape each other, as well as one scene in which a woman uses an old Polaroid camera to take a photo of her friends.

These examples illustrate how the Mipsterz women engage with pop culture trends and hipster styles in an attempt to normalize their appearance in mainstream American culture and to transgress boundaries that position them as oppressed and backward. Instead, the women incorporate hybrid styles to present themselves as complex individuals who are creative, fun, active, strong, and assertive without abandoning their faith or cultural backgrounds.

## URBAN STYLES AND AMERICAN IDENTITY

Along with the incorporation of hipster culture and hybrid styles, it seems important for the women in the Mipsterz video to emphasize the stylistic sensibilities of urban lifestyles, from rap music and trendy clothes to skateboarding and street dancing. The urban landscapes that accentuate the video are used symbolically to place veiled Muslim women at the center of an American urban environment that seldom aligns with the dominant perception of Muslim culture. The inclusion of Muslim women in a hip display of decayed and distressed urban spaces is carefully designed to normalize their presence in the heart of Americana, even if American culture is reduced to an exaggerated essentialism that emphasizes the lure of consumption, play, and chic. The purpose of this visual exposition is to push back against the repressive gaze of American mainstream culture and to challenge the viewers to accept the diversity of the Muslim American experience. Skateboarding and biking symbolize the mobility of these women and their supposed freedom to go anywhere and achieve anything. The video also celebrates the accomplishments of successful Muslim women like Ibtihaj Muhammad, a professional athlete and member of the U.S. fencing team; Sandra Shamy, a fashion and jewelry designer; Marwa Atik, a hijab designer; Hajer Naili, a journalist; Layla Shaikley, the fashion director for the film but also the co-founder of a software design company; and several other women who work in business, law, and medicine.

Setting these visuals and the women's movements to Jay-Z's song "Somewhere in America" is also choreographed, not only to highlight the compatibility of Muslim music tastes and the trendy world of hip-hop, but also to invoke the rightful place of Muslims in that diverse cultural tapestry, which is insinuated in the lyrics of the song. Jay-Z's "somewhere" is also a reference to the fact that anything is possible in this America, and the Mipsterz aptly appropriate those words to affirm that what might seem a far-fetched reality of hipster Muslims is also perfectly imaginable in this inclusive and tolerant view of America.

Equally critical for the producers of the Mipsterz video is that the women appear confident, natural and at ease in their display of their Americanness. But this effort at aestheticizing Muslim American identity quickly became a major point of contention in the massive critique that the video has provoked. While some saw this performance as necessary to defy the political and cultural boundaries of Muslim identity in America, others found it extremely vapid, noting that it essentially promotes the same kind of secular excesses that Muslim modesty vehemently disputes. As the journalist Ghazala Irshad argues, the video ends up reifying the same politics of silence by normalizing Muslim women into a secular culture that objectifies their bodies and devalues their voice. "Why spend all this time and money traveling to different locations around the US filming these intelligent women only to not hear anything from them and hear a man rapping about a girl shaking her ass in the background? Why don't we send a message about why we are different?"[15]

Telling the story of difference, however, is always fraught with difficulty and risks of misrepresentation. As Layla Shaikley, one of the creators
of the video, argued in defense of the intentions behind her effort, this
creative action was meant to be a "personal expression" reacting against
years of discrimination and exclusion, but it was interpreted by many as a
collective representation of American Muslim women and a rare opportunity for Muslim Americans to create their own responses to a long history of misrepresentations. "Muslim Americans are in many cases
wounded, marginalized, reactive, and defensive, in large part because
we're underrepresented and misrepresented in the media," Shaikley
writes. "The two and a half minute clip stirred up feelings born of years, if
not generations, of exclusion and marginalization."[16] Many Muslims
reacted to this video by envisioning this project as a unique opportunity
to address the serious political and religious issues that Muslims face in
American society. Shaikley and her collaborators may not have set out to
address those issues as much as they intended to strategically complicate
the visual frames we associate with veiled Muslim women.

The reaction to the video has indeed raised some significant questions about the transgressive nature of this visual essay by the Mipsterz. Can a self-portrait of professionally-successful and fashionable
hijabis who parade their bodies through commodities and style help
build the kind of powerful Muslim female identity that defies invisibil-
ity and marginalization? And is this intervention through fashion and
the aesthetics of urban lifestyles potentially transformative for young
Muslim women who are forced to navigate both secular and religious
contexts that seek to control and manage their bodies?

## CONCLUSION

Our argument in this chapter has been that the Mipsterz video and the
strong reactions it has engendered should be read as a dynamic site of
struggle over what it means to be an American Muslim woman. The
women engage with the aesthetic aspects of American popular culture

in an effort to challenge dominant visual framings of Muslim women as oppressed victims or exotic others, to formulate a distinct cultural and religious identity, and to assert their rightful place in the fabric of American life. Through hybrid fashion that blends elements of American fashion trends, hipster styles, international cultures, and Islamic modesty, the Mipsterz emphasize that Muslim women should be seen as creative, fashionable individuals. The Mipsterz women also incorporate urban styles such as hip-hop music, skateboarding, and street dancing to stake out a place for Muslim women within the public spaces of American cities.

The creators of the video wanted to foreground an alternative Muslim identity that straddles the two seemingly opposite worlds of secular modernity and pious modesty. Their goal was to appropriate the language, aesthetics, and logics of urban modern culture to complicate the unidimensional representation of Muslim women. Some critics, however, saw only an obsessive, trivial quest to normalize Muslim women as modern, Western, and American. Others denounced the video for its brazen, superficial portrayal of Islamic values like modesty. The video struck such a raw nerve primarily because of its provocative images and loose associations, but it also generated such a heated debate because of its combination of piety, religious identity, and popular culture. Both the women behind the video and their critics have indeed engaged in a contested conversation in social media around the terms of modesty, religious expression, the policing of women's appearance, and the depoliticization of veiling through consumer culture among the Muslim bourgeoisie.

The viral circulation of the video through YouTube and other social media platforms has also exposed taboo questions about gender and the visibility of women both inside and outside of the Muslim American community. The glamorous display of veiled hipster women and their commodification may rightly be objectionable to many, but the performative arrangement of veiling through fashion and urban culture helps demystify the veil and destabilize its closed meaning both in mainstream

American culture and in some conservative Muslim communities. Despite accusations of trivializing the religious and political function of veiling, the Mipsterz video actually succeeds in expanding the visual terrain of the veil by redeploying its symbolic power and social practice. It is true that the Muslim body in this video and the reactions to it are yet again the battleground for proper piety and devotion, but that same veiled body is also made into a site of critical contestation of the bounded, sealed narrative that dictates the behavior and the mobility of the Muslim veiled woman. The circulation of this video and the use of fashion styles may not be enough to change the conditions that produce such narrow narratives or to erase conventional racialized discourses about Muslim women, but this creative action can be meaningful in locating small and somewhat mundane acts of everyday resistance, which may or may not undermine structures of power.

Our analysis shows that the Mipsterz video and its complex message do not have a single, fixed meaning. In fact, the video requires an ambivalent reading, so we avoid celebrating this kind of action as a sign of assured empowerment and subversion or dismiss it as a case of total subordination and control. These oppositional readings do little to capture the dynamic nature of these forms of cultural production and their implications for social change. Popular culture in this case serves as a prime stage for exposing these examples of what the anthropologist Asef Bayat calls "quiet encroachments," meaning "the silent, protracted but pervasive advancement of the ordinary people on the propertied and powerful in order to survive and improve their lives."[17] The actors behind these gradual, grassroots actions strategically turn to the symbols of popular culture as tactics to insert themselves into a more inclusive narrative of an American cultural identity. Despite being embedded in a capitalist logic of consumer culture and entertainment politics, the Mipsterz video fills a gaping hole in the absence of a public space in American society where Muslim women can address critical questions about their religious expression, representation, and autonomy.

## DISCUSSION QUESTIONS

1. Watch "Somewhere in America: #MIPSTERZ" on YouTube or Vimeo. What are your reactions? Does the chapter help you interpret the video and/or put it in context?

2. Drawing on the video and the chapter, discuss the religious and cultural identities that the women portrayed. What images and understandings of Muslim women is the video attempting to counter? What are these women saying about themselves? Are the Muslim women in the Mipsterz video able to claim a position within the fabric of American society and to forge political autonomy through their use of popular culture, fashion trends, and urban lifestyles? If so, how?

3. What criticisms do Peterson and Echchaibi suggest more traditional Muslims have made of the video?

4. Are online productions like the Mipsterz video a form of popular culture? Why or why not? How are they like and different from more traditionally produced commercial videos? What does this suggest about the power of dominant voices to shape popular culture and the possibility that minority voices can be heard in popular culture?

## NOTES

1. Sheikh & Bake, *Somewhere In America #MIPSTERZ*, video, 2:29, December 2, 2013, https://youtu.be/68sMkDKMias.

2. Sana Saeed, "Somewhere in America, Muslim Women Are 'Cool,'" *Islamic Monthly,* December 2, 2013, www.theislamicmonthly.com/somewhere-in-america-muslim-women-are-cool.

3. Layla Shaikley, "The Surprising Lessons of the 'Muslim Hipsters' Backlash," *Atlantic,* March 13, 2014, www.theatlantic.com/entertainment/archive/2014/03/the-surprising-lessons-of-the-muslim-hipsters-backlash/284298.

4. Hajer Naili, "Video of Fun-Loving Veiled U.S. Muslims Goes Viral," *Women News,* December 3, 2013, http://womensenews.org/2013/12/video-fun-loving-veiled-us-muslims-goes-viral/#.UqDp-xZRg8M.

5. See the work of the comedians Negin Farsad and Maysoon Zayid in the documentary *The Muslims are Coming!* (2013), http://themuslimsarecoming.com.

6. See the work of G. Willow Wilson, such as the comic series *Ms. Marvel*, the fantasy novel *Alif the Unseen,* and her memoir *The Butterfly Mosque.*

7. Naili, "Video of Fun-Loving."

8. "Mipsterz—Muslim Hipsters," www.facebook.com/Mipsterz.

9. Naili, "Video of Fun-Loving."

10. Annelies Moors and Emma Tarlo, eds., *Islamic Fashion and Anti-Fashion: New Perspectives from Europe and North America* (London: Bloomsbury, 2013), 3.

11. Ibid., 20.

12. Joanne Entwistle, *The Fashioned Body: Fashion, Dress and Modern Social Theory* (Cambridge, England: Polity Press, 2000), 10.

13. Susan B. Kaiser, *Fashion and Cultural Studies* (London: Berg, 2012), 31.

14. Ibid., 37

15. Saeed, "Somewhere in America."

16. Shaikley, "Surprising Lessons."

17. Asef Bayat, *Life as Politics: How Ordinary People Change the Middle East* (Amsterdam: Amsterdam University Press, 2010)

# CHAPTER EIGHT

# Megachurches, Celebrity Pastors, and the Evangelical Industrial Complex

JESSICA JOHNSON

Walking into a megachurch for the first time, I immediately felt lost and at home. Upon entering the lobby, I was in need of a map. The soft eggshell tone of the walls where members' artwork hung sharply contrasted with the cacophonous buzz of the crowd before service. Groups of people swarmed around shelves of theological books and urns of free coffee. As guitar chords began to swell from inside the dark sanctuary, cueing people to take their seats, parents dropped off toddlers at the children's ministry nestled down a hallway, undergraduates flocked to rows of friends bearing the same university logo on their gear, and greeters smiled hello at everyone who made eye contact. Although I was there to listen to a sermon, the dim lighting, large screens surrounding the amphitheater, and instruments onstage affected the atmosphere of a club rather than a church. While the wrought-metal cross looming above the worship band reminded me that I was there to see a pastor preach, the pulpit looked as though I was there to see a rock star perform.

Megachurch services can feel like music concerts held in high-ceilinged sanctuaries—the sense of anticipation and spectacle is very similar. However, those who sermonize from pulpits that look as though they were made for Grammy winners rather than ministry leaders are not simply charismatic. On the contrary, celebrity pastors are created by numbers that measure success, such as growth metrics demonstrating increases in attendees, baptisms, or sermon downloads that convict Christian audiences of God's hand in congregational expansion. Profit and fame are common denominators that cut across religious and secular divides as tropes of popular culture and innovations in media technology are used to convey the Word, generate buzz, and garner tithes. From the revivals of Billy Sunday to Billy Graham, to the televangelists Pat Robertson and Jimmy Bakker, evangelism and celebrity have attracted audiences in vast numbers, generating monetary gain and cultural influence.

However, this essay argues that the accelerated ascendency of megachurch celebrity pastors is best examined and understood in terms of marketing strategy and commodification processes specific to a digital age in which social media and interactive technologies are impacting the identity formation of Christians and non-Christians alike. This analysis demonstrates how relationships between celebrity pastors and their congregants are mediated by cultural and technological shifts as church branding has become integral to evangelical purpose. Congregants who volunteer their time and talent on behalf of congregational growth are not mere "followers" who idolize celebrity pastors[1] but laborers incorporated into the marketing practices that promote them. This form of industry is having an impact on evangelical subjectivity and institutional Christianity within the United States. During this participatory branding process, audiences are not passive consumers but active contributors to an "evangelical industrial complex"[2] that thrives on elevating megachurch pastors to media elite status.

In this analysis, I compare two campaigns to market books by celebrity pastors—Mark Driscoll's *Real Marriage* (2012) and Judah Smith's *Jesus Is___* (2013). These publications earned Driscoll and Smith bestselling author status, while their marketing campaigns provided the platform for distributing free sermon guides and small group curriculums that promoted the purchase of further teaching materials. In effect, these bestselling books served as marketing tools that generated monetary capital and cultural influence on behalf of the pastor's brand. In choosing these two campaigns as case studies, I focus on how pastors have managed to gain celebrity and inspire congregational growth in what is considered one of the least churched cities in the United States—Seattle.[3] By adopting a multisite model, congregations once too unwieldy to expand beyond a single sprawling location in the suburbs are now amenable to church plants in urban centers. This transformation enables megachurches to attract a younger demographic while repurposing pop cultural trends in music, video, and social media. Rather than the shopping mall, these facilities emulate a concert stadium.

## MEGACHURCHES

The Hartford Institute for Religion Research defines a megachurch as "any Protestant congregation with a sustained average attendance of 2,000 persons or more in its worship services."[4] While large congregations have existed throughout Christian history, megachurches have proliferated in the United States since the 1970s. Megachurches typically experience a growth spurt in less than ten years under the leadership of one pastor who, according to the conservative theology commonly used to structure leadership, is male. These men are considered "personally charismatic, highly gifted spiritual leaders."[5] Through a variety of counseling ministries, opportunities for fellowship within homes, and cultural events that inspire a sense of community, megachurches incite personal commitment among devoted members, while affording new Christians or the curious a chance to maintain anonymity.[6] While these are among the general characteristics used to identify a megachurch by the Hartford Institute, it is in defining its "Protestant" character in contrast to large Catholic congregations that a more detailed description is offered:

> it is a host of characteristics that create a distinctive worship style and congregational dynamic ... most [Catholic Churches] don't have strong charismatic senior ministers, many associate pastors, large staff, robust

congregational identity that empowers 100s to 1000s of weekly volunteers, an identity that draws people from a very large area (sometimes an hour [away] or more) and across parish boundaries, a multitude of programs and ministries organized and maintained by members, high levels of commitment and giving by members, seven-day-a-week activities at the church, contemporary worship, state of the art sound and projection systems, auxiliary support systems such as bookstores, coffee shops, etc. huge campuses of 30–100 acres, and other common megachurch characteristics.[7]

The keywords that register with particular timbre in this passage are "dynamic," "robust congregational identity," and "high levels of commitment." These phrases indicate the vast amount of volunteer labor necessary to generate and maintain the distinctive worship experience through which a megachurch is branded, gains notoriety, and attracts new members. This collective and embodied labor entails self-sacrifice on the part of members who donate their time and talents to benefit the megachurch's growth and the pastor's brand. Such labor includes hours of service in support of community groups, information technology administration, and a host of ministries to counsel members in need, create and disseminate teaching content, and physically contribute to the maintenance and multiplication of facilities. Congregants not only contribute money to the megachurch by tithing but also generate capital by advertising their pastor's name and legitimizing his spiritual authority: they buy his books, share his podcasts, "like" his *Facebook* status updates, and re-tweet his tweets. In effect, the very definition of a megachurch entails a marketing prerogative that is linked to the labor and sacrifice of members whose evangelical identity is constituted by said labor and sacrifice. The congregation's ability to attract more people signals God's hand in the church's mission such that high levels of commitment and a robust, dynamic brand name become indicators of spiritual health and success.

This connection between capitalist endeavor and evangelistic spirit is furthered by the fact that "almost one half of all megachurches are independent and nondenominational ... which gives considerable freedom to individual churches." Such sovereignty affords the leaders of mega-churches a great deal of spiritual and administrative authority to proclaim what the "vision" or "calling" of the congregation is through which its identity and image are established. Inasmuch as it appears that "these are not just churches, they are corporations,"[8] what is sorely needed is an examination of how a megachurch's brand is cultivated. Its marketing entails a media industry, interactive technologies, and processes of media-tion that constitute audience members not only as individual congregants or church volunteers but also as a labor force bodily, emotionally, and spir-itually investing in the entrepreneurial evangelism of their pastor.

## THE EVANGELICAL INDUSTRIAL COMPLEX

Skye Jethani, pastor and blogger for *Christianity Today,* describes the evangelical industrial complex as a systemic economic force of the dig-ital age that has accelerated the rise and increased the number of Chris-tian media elites. Jethani helpfully contextualizes his coining of this phrase by situating its language in relation to a national address by President Eisenhower in 1961 during which he warned about the effects of a "military industrial complex"—a permanent arms industry that by design perpetuates warfare. Jethani draws analogies between America's militarism and a clerical celebrity class, while persuasively arguing that there is a self-sustaining evangelical industrial complex manufac-turing celebrity pastors. In his formulation, the media industry creates and depends on megachurch pastors with thousands of congregants who will purchase their books. Thus, ministers from small or medium-sized churches are never on the main stage at conferences, where meg-achurch leaders who boast best-selling author status predominate.[9] In effect, the concept of the evangelical industrial complex pokes holes in pat descriptions of megachurch leaders that suggest that they are inher-ently charismatic or divinely ordained leaders deserving of their stat-ure. Most people want to believe something that Jethani asserts is false, namely, that:

The most godly, intelligent, and gifted leaders naturally attract large followings, so they naturally are going to have large churches, and their ideas are so great and their writing so sharp that publishers pick their book proposals, and the books strike a nerve with so many people that they naturally become best-sellers, and these leaders are therefore the obvious choice to speak at the biggest conferences. As a result they find themselves quite naturally becoming popular, even rising to celebrity status.[10]

The keyword in Jethani's critique of the evangelical industrial complex is "naturally." The profit generated in the above hypothetical is due to "publishers eager for a guaranteed sales win offer the megachurch pastor a book deal knowing that if only a third of the pastor's own congregation buys a copy, it's still a profitable deal. The book is published on the basis of the leader's market platform, not necessarily the strength of his ideas or the book's quality."[11] Furthermore, Jethani adds, "wanting to maximize the return on their investment, the publisher will then promote the pastor at the publisher-sponsored ministry conference or other events. As a result of the pastor's own megachurch customer base and the publisher's conference platform, the book becomes a best-seller. Or if that doesn't work, sometimes sugar daddies purchase thousands of copies of the book to literally buy the pastor onto the best-seller's list where the perception of popularity results in more sales."[12] Finally, Jethani usefully breaks this system down in terms of specific figures:

> Consider the scale of the evangelical industrial complex that survives by perpetuating this system. The Christian Booksellers Association, representing 1,700 Christian stores, sells $4.63 *billion* worth of merchandise a year. And that doesn't count retailers like Amazon and Walmart. Some estimate the total evangelical market to be over $7 billion a year.... And this massive market has grown in conjunction with the rise of megachurches since the 1970s; they rely upon and perpetuate each other. Megachurch leaders offer publishers pre-existing customer bases (their own congregations), and publishers make megachurch pastors into celebrities to perpetuate and expand their bottom lines. As a result, evangelicalism is not a meritocracy where talent, gifting, character, or wisdom results in a broad-

ening influence. It is an aristocracy where simply having a platform entitles you to ever-increasing influence regardless of your talent, gifting, character, or wisdom.[13]

However, Jethani's discussion loses its critical rigor when he summarizes the social and political effects of this economic system in terms of creating an "aristocracy." Although he helpfully contextualizes the evangelical industrial complex with regards to transformations in the media industry, he does not pay the same careful attention to situating its effects. His concluding remark, "Should we be concerned? Yes, but at least they're not building nukes,"[14] is dismissive of the ways in which the congregants of megachurch pastors pay a cost for their participation in making these leaders celebrities. They are laborers socially incorporated into the process of creating media elites, affected by an evangelical industrial complex to which they are active contributors. Members of megachurches serve the evangelical industrial complex while laboring to popularize their pastor's image—volunteering as creative team members, marketing staff, musicians, or video producers—and participating in the cultural production of content that blurs distinctions between teaching and promotional material. In Jethani's analysis, not only are those supporting the evangelical industrial complex on the ground ignored and unrecognized, but the effects of their labor are unaccounted for, leaving its cultural, social, and spiritual impacts unexamined. As an antidote, the analysis that follows entails the close examination of two campaigns that successfully bolstered the celebrity of two megachurch pastors.

## MARS HILL CHURCH, MARK DRISCOLL AND THE *REAL MARRIAGE* CAMPAIGN

Mars Hill Church was co-founded in Seattle in 1996 by Pastor Mark Driscoll. By the time of its dissolution at the end of 2014, it had multiplied into fifteen facilities in five U.S. states, serving approximately 13,000 attendees. As the church multiplied into facilities and community groups that spread from Seattle neighborhoods to places including Albuquerque, New Mexico; Portland, Oregon; and Orange County, California, Driscoll's preaching on topics such as "biblical oral sex" earned him a profile in the glossy *New York Times Magazine* and international celebrity through Christian and secular channels. However, by 2014 evidence had surfaced online that supported several charges against him: the use of a marketing ploy to erroneously achieve number one best-selling author status on the *New York Times* "How-to/Advice" list; inciting a "culture of fear" among staff through bullying, micromanagement, and shunning; and promoting a "culture of misogyny" through explicit teaching on biblical gender and sexuality that instructed wives to submit to their husbands' authority.[15] In fact, the book *Real Marriage: The Truth about Sex, Friendship, and Life Together* is a detailed account of the trials and tribulations of Pastor Mark's marriage to his high school sweetheart Grace, his co-author. The book is described for promotional purposes on Amazon as such:

> [The Driscolls] believe friendship is fundamental to marriage but not easy to maintain. So they offer practical advice on how to make your spouse your best friend—and keep it that way. And they know from experience that sex-related issues need to be addressed directly.

Five chapters are dedicated to answering questions like:

> Should I confess my pre-marital sexual sin to my spouse?
>
> Is it okay to have a "work spouse"?
>
> What does the Bible say about masturbation and oral sex?[16]

As this advertising shows, the book reads like a confessional memoir that details the Driscolls sexual relationship and its effects on their marital intimacy. While the church's expansion was considered empirical proof of God's hand in Mars Hill's mission to multiply, closer investigation into the media strategy and economic purpose of the *Real Marriage* campaign demonstrates a calculated plan to enlist congregants' labor and tithes in marketing "Pastor Mark" as a brand name with spiritual authority. One month prior to the publication of *Real Marriage* in 2012, Driscoll encouraged an assembly of Mars Hill Church Community Group leaders to join a surge of support: "over 2,000 churches have signed up to follow along with us in the sermon series and receive for free hundreds of pages of research, full marketing materials, counseling and worship guides." These biblical resources were advertised as: "Air war and ground war strategies to help you permeate the message from the pulpit throughout each aspect of your church and ministry," including "full *Real Marriage* branding, design, and marketing plans and materials that you can edit for your local church for such things as postcards, posters, e-vites, video commercials, social media strategy, and more," as well as "free use of Pastor Mark's sermons for the series via DVD download if you want a week off."[17] The air war and ground war strategies advanced by the *Real Marriage* campaign had long been a staple of Mars Hill's ministry once the church went multi-site. A "Preaching and Theology Sermon Series Battle Plan" co-written by Driscoll described this air war / ground war approach to ecclesiology:

> The air war is the Sunday pulpit and the preaching series that is tied to the pulpit. At Mars Hill, we generally lead our ministry with the air war of the pulpit. The ground war works in conjunction with the air war so that such things as community groups, redemption groups, training classes, biblical counseling etc. coordinates with the preached Word so as to be as effective and unified as possible. Since most of the Community Groups are sermon-based it is imperative that the CG [community group] brand and the P&T [preaching and theology] branch collaborate on every series. This collaboration includes joint branded content online and Pastor Mark pushing CG [community group] discussion points and family devotional points each week in the sermon.[18]

This "preaching and theology sermon series battle plan" signals how crucial the global communication of Driscoll's voice was to suggesting, manipulating, and amplifying his audiences' labor in varying capacities to ensure that the church stayed on mission to multiply. If Oprah proffered "the prosperity gospel of a spiritual capitalism," by "fusing her charisma with a product's image and with connecting the message of her show to the slogan of a new brand,"[19] then *Real Marriage* was Driscoll's gambit to perform and brand his image as "authentic" so as to intensify the cultural and monetary value of "Pastor Mark" as a charismatic commodity.

In fact, the *Real Marriage* campaign was in preparation a year before the book's release, including the efficient and profitable coordination of a marketing ploy that belied Mars Hill's nonprofit status, unbeknownst to church members. Evidence concerning the strategies used to erroneously elevate Pastor Mark to best-selling author status would not surface until 2014, two years after the Driscolls embarked on their *Real Marriage* tour, which included speaking engagements in cities around the country and media appearances on programs such as ABC's *The View*. The paper trail of research that led to the public unveiling of Mars Hill's connection to a book-marketing firm started with the Christian publication *WORLD Magazine*, which announced "unreal sales for Driscoll's *Real Marriage*," noting that the company Result-Source was paid "to conduct a bestseller campaign" that included not only the *New York Times*'s "How-To Advice" list but also the *Wall Street Journal, USA Today*, Barnes & Noble, and Amazon.[20]

While the details of this business transaction are complicated, when queried, Mars Hill representatives would not say whether these book purchases were made with church funds, but the contract showed that it was important that "the make up of the 6,000 individual orders include at least 1,000 different addresses with no more than 350 per state" to circumvent metrics used to prevent authors from buying their way onto lists.[21] This schema unveils a complex and far-reaching network of participants consisting of people both self-aware and oblivious to their role in its strategy. The varied addresses required by ResultSource were seemingly culled through a "pre-sale push" during which church supporters were asked to donate $25 apiece to Mars Hill ministries in order to receive a "free" book.[22] This campaign was the first of its kind but not the last waged by Mars Hill as a way of offering free teaching content to churches throughout the world in order to enhance the media presence and spiritual legitimacy of Pastor Mark. One month prior to the publication of *Real Marriage,* Driscoll gave a video-recorded talk to an assembly of Mars Hill Community Group leaders:

> [In the New Year] by the grace of God, I hope and I pray we'll do the biggest thing we've ever done. Some years ago as we were looking at the future I got a strange idea, and that is that usually what happens is that a pastor will preach a series and then write a book about it. And I thought, what would it be like if we wrote the book first, small group curriculum first, DVDs for small group curriculum first, research for all the community leaders first? What if we put together the whole thing, and then when the book launched, we did the media tour, and we did the huge campaign, and we push, push, push all together at one time? And so January 15 we're going to start the *Real Marriage* campaign. That same day, we're going to open four churches in three states ... [and] Grace and I are doing a media trip to New York for a few days. You can pray; we're trying to get on Colbert and the Today Show ... We have what we're calling a campaign which is about 300 pages of research and statistics that we've put together, as well as preaching tips, small group tips, [and] Sunday tips for other churches and we thought, let's invite them to go through this content and curriculum together. So far, over 2,000 churches have signed up to do so, and we praise God for that. I remember still the first day the campaign director, he said, "Well, I'm praying for 50." And the first day, I said, "Where are we at?" And he said, "1,500." Well, prayer got answered.[23]

Research concerning how much Driscoll personally pocketed from the best-selling moniker has yielded evidence that a tax vehicle called a Charitable Remainder UniTrust (CRUT) named "On Mission LLC" was established in Colorado a year prior to *Real Marriage*'s publication, demonstrating a calculated plan to covertly manage a large income generated by "book royalties, printing, and publishing."[24] Subsequently, in 2016, four former Mars Hill members filed a civil racketeering lawsuit against Driscoll.[25] These charges included the misappropriation of church tithes to pay the book-marketing firm ResultSource $210,000 to acquire the buyer's lists necessary to achieve him best-selling author stature.

## THE CITY CHURCH, JUDAH SMITH AND THE
### *JESUS IS___* CAMPAIGN

While Mark Driscoll identified the Mars Hill brand as "me in the pulpit holding a bible," and church-affiliated web sites like pastormark.tv supported this assertion in their design and content, Pastor Judah Smith's stamp is markedly absent from the home page of The City Church, founded in Seattle by his pastor father Wendell Smith in 1992. Although Pastor Judah has been preaching from The City's pulpit since 2009, the only mention of his name is under announcements concerning events and locations, all five of which are in the Seattle area, except for one facility in Guadalajara, Mexico. Rather than a massive archive of sermons, only a handful of a series of past video recordings are housed under the humble invitation to "watch a message." Smith's muted presence on the church's web site seems a concerted effort to work against his reputation as a pastor to celebrities, most famously to the pop singer Justin Bieber and the Seattle Seahawks quarterback Russell Wilson. While The City may be firmly situated in Seattle, Pastor Judah flies weekly to Los Angeles in order to preach a Wednesday evening sermon to people he calls "Jesus followers"[26] rather than Christians, a distinction that disassociates him from strict doctrinal boundaries or heated theological debates. In turn, Pastor Judah's physical, cultural, spiritual, and marketing mobility prompted the Hollywood talent agency Management 360 to sign him as a client in order to support his development of "faith-based projects" to attract "millennials across all areas, including television, digital, books, and branding."[27]

Smith's image is not sutured to The City as Driscoll's was to Mars Hill, affording his brand name more fluidity on the information market as he shuttles around the world performing as a pop star in his own right. Meanwhile, the web site advertising his book *Jesus Is___*, much like Pastor Judah himself, is constantly on the move. The *Jesus Is___* campaign uses a participatory, user-friendly digital platform to simulate a perpetual process of branding that, in appearing seamless, democratic, and autonomous, serves to affirm his self-presentation as an approachably hip dude who is relatable despite his celebrity. Although that book was published in 2013, the platform advertising its campaign is "live," animated by an interactive bingo-like board filled with a dozen smaller squares alternating in hue and message. One box in the top left corner, the only one that does not change in appearance, prompts visitors to "create your own" fill-in-the-blank response to the query invited by Smith's book title. Interactivity is a consistent trope as viewer participation is elicited and demonstrated via neon squares that light up this promotional home page with pronouncements that proclaim Jesus is "the light of my life," "a myth," or "the invisible man." The words in each box shift in tone and color within seconds, as messages flash before the visitor's eyes then disappear. Responses offer testimonials—"My light in a dark place"; attempt to be clever—"The master carpenter working on my heavenly hang out pad"; proselytize—"The answer. If you do not believe me, read the Bible yourself"; serve as a forewarning—"A gateway for the church to gain money"; or take the shape of Dr. Seuss rhymes—"Like sausage if you say it backwards."[28]

While these dramatic transitions in appearance, language, and meaning may sound jarring, the palette and tenor of the boxes cultivate a soothing, authentic presentation. In effect, the web site affectively registers and visually recruits the viewer to participate in an ongoing marketing process that is at once playful and seductive. Clicking on the "create your own" prompt leads to a page that leaves any identifying information such as name or e-mail address optional while affording audiences the creative license to choose background color, text color, and upload a distinctive background such as a photo. Submissions are reviewed and must meet certain terms and conditions, but on the whole this section reassures those who contribute content that they will remain anonymous and retain their privacy. So long as a submission is not obscene or defamatory, it will meet the necessary criteria for publication on the web site, the explicit purpose of which is to give visitors a platform through which to express their opinion about who Jesus is.

For those curious, there is a "submissions" link that provides archival access to (presumably) all the messages posted—a total of 3,223 pages as of February 2016—each filled with eighteen responses. Under a link called "projects," there are submissions stamped with "done" in red, signifying their materialization into "A Jesus Is Project"—a one-time community service project done by City Groups that shows the love of Jesus to our community in a practical way. People are told to click on an individual project should they be interested in getting involved. While there are no future activities planned according to the web site, examples of former projects inspired by audience submissions include: "Jesus is serving dinner in low-income public housing"; "Jesus is helping a single parent recovering from cancer"; "Jesus is pulling ivy in the Seattle Arboretum"; and "Jesus is helping a senior widow move."[29] Thus, the viewer is shown how they contribute to the manifestation of Jesus' love and mercy in real peoples' lives by participating in this virtual tool promoting Pastor Judah's book.

A link to "stories" leads to audio-visual recordings about a minute long that testify to the generosity of The City's church community by demonstrating the motive behind particular Jesus Is projects. For example, one story called "supporting our sailors" describes how volunteers shipped care packages to sailors without family members, sending letters and sundries that expressed support and gratitude for their service.[30] While the projects and stories pages are full of completed activities, current information and events are listed on the "conversation" page powered by #tagboard, where people upload content via Twitter and Instagram. For example, this message by "consumed pastor" appeared under a picture of the cover of *Jesus Is____* "Just finished this awesome book by @judahsmith #JesusIs Read it today!!!"[31] In a video recorded message at the bottom of this website, Pastor Judah and his wife Chelsea, both of whom are listed as lead pastors of The City, respond to the question of who Jesus is. Pastor Judah states: "He is more than a good man, he is more than a miracle worker, he is the savior of the world, and he's come to set you free."[32]

However, the most prominent link is at the top of this home page, where consumer-contributors are told to buy the book *Jesus Is___* at Jesusisbook.com. One click leads to advertisements for goods offered via this site, including church curriculum and free resources, as well as endorsements of *Jesus Is___* penned by an E! news correspondent and the founder of the A21 Campaign, a nonprofit organization that advocates for victims of human trafficking. While the specific pages associated with the publication of *Jesus Is___* are no longer active, a book published by Smith in 2015 entitled *Life Is___* is also promoted on this site. Clicking on this advertisement leads to "lifeisbook.tv," where Pastor Judah's bestselling author status is noted in bold white and yellow lettering foregrounded by an automated video display in lavender sepia showing men paging through *Life Is___* and discussing it; a woman picking up the book from a coffee-shop counter; and Pastor Judah speaking animatedly onstage and passionately in interview mode. In effect, the *Jesus Is___* campaign has a life beyond its eponymous publication; it is as mobile and fluid in its promotional reach as Pastor Judah is in his celebrity.

The digital platform marketing *Jesus Is___* serves a far bigger purpose than selling Smith's books by offering potential readers and casual interlopers—Christians and non-Christians alike—a sense of ownership in defining who Jesus is to them. The site appears to provide any and all visitors with the creative license to vent against, testify to, and play with Jesus' expression not only through language but also color and imagery. In turn, this public yet anonymous forum democratizes and singularizes how people relate to Jesus, providing a social outlet and safe space through which to identify with Him. Thus, even after its promotional materials are dated, the *Jesus Is___*. campaign succeeds in sustaining the consistency of the Pastor Judah brand name as he regularly travels from his home pulpit to preach from stages in churches and stadiums throughout the world. In effect, his image conjures openness, connectivity, and relationality by virtue of the interactive platform through which viewers perpetually participate in his self-promotion by filling in the blank.

CONCLUSION

This essay has analyzed the structural and technological means through which celebrity pastors are created. By investigating how the media industry and interactive technologies enlist audience participation in their popularization, this examination offers a perspective on the dynamic relationships that link megachurches, celebrity pastors, and the evangelical industrial complex. I argue that the cultural and economic value of a given celebrity pastor's brand is dependent upon the people in the pews and at their laptops. These laborers voluntarily and inadvertently contribute to ongoing processes of production and mediation not only with monetary but also social effects. For evidence of the collective emotional and spiritual cost of serving the evangelical industrial complex, look to the testimonies of those who volunteered their time, talents, and tithes to the ministries of Mars Hill. These congregants not only supported the megachurch's expansion but also suffered in the aftermath of its fall. The swift dissolution of Mars Hill under the shadow of accusations of spiritual and administrative abuse against Driscoll by former leaders and members illustrates the importance of examining the specific ways in which relationships to megachurch celebrity pastors are negotiated by laboring and sacrificing for their brand.[33]

DISCUSSION QUESTIONS

1. How does Johnson distinguish a megachurch from other churches? In what ways is the megachurch shaped by popular culture? What does the rise of the megachurch suggest about what people want from religion?

2. What is the evangelical industrial complex and how does it create celebrity pastors?

3. How do megachurch congregants participate in the process of branding celebrity pastors?

4. Pastor Judah's site as described in this chapter is interactive. What are the limits of such interactivity?

## NOTES

1. Rachel Held Evans, "When Jesus Meets TMZ: Why Celebrity Culture Is Overtaking Our Pulpits," February 9, 2012, www.relevantmagazine.com/god /church/features/28236-when-jesus-meets-tmz.

2. Skye Jethani, "The Evangelical Industrial Complex & Rise of Celebrity Pastors, Part 1," www.christianitytoday.com/le/2012/february-online-only /evangelical-industrial-complex-rise-of-celebrity-pastors.html.

3. James Wellman, "The Churching of the Pacific Northwest: The Rise of Sectarian Entrepreneurs," In *Religion and Public Life in the Pacific Northwest: The None Zone*, ed. Patricia O'Connell Killen and Mark Silk (Walnut Creek, CA: AltaMira Press, 2004).

4. http://hirr.hartsem.edu/megachurch/definition.html.

5. Scott Thumma, "Exploring the Megachurch Phenomena: Their Characteristics and Cultural Context," http://hirr.hartsem.edu/bookshelf/thumma_ article2.html.

6. http://hirr.hartsem.edu/megachurch/definition.html.

7. Ibid.

8. Ibid.

9. Skye Jethani, "The Evangelical Industrial Complex & the Rise of Celebrity Pastors (Part 1)," www.christianitytoday.com/le/2012/february-online-only/evangelical-industrial-complex-rise-of-celebrity-pastors.html.

10. Ibid.

11. Ibid.

12. Skye Jethani, "Part 2: The Evangelical Industrial Complex & the Rise of Celebrity Pastors," www.christianitytoday.com/le/2012/february-online-only /part-2-evangelical-industrial-complex-rise-of-celebrity.html.

13. Ibid.

14. Warren Throckmorton, "Twenty-One Former Mars Hill Church Pastors Bring Formal Charges against Mark Driscoll," *Patheos*, August 2014, www .patheos.com/blogs/warrenthrockmorton/2014/08/21/former-mars-hill-church-pastors-bring-formal-charges-against-mark-driscoll.

15. www.amazon.com/Real-Marriage-Truth-Friendship-Together-ebook /dp/B005ENBA02.

16. http://pastormark.tv/campaigns/real-marriage.

17. Mark Driscoll and AJ Hamilton, Trial: 8 Witnesses from 1–2 Peter. Preaching and Theology Sermon Series Battle Plan, 2008, 3, http://wp .patheos.com.s3.amazonaws.com/blogs/warrenthrockmorton/files/2013/12/1-2_ peter_battle_plan.pdf.

18. Kathryn Lofton, *Oprah: The Gospel of an Icon* (Berkeley: University of California Press, 2011), 7.

19. Warren Cole Smith, "Unreal Sales for Driscoll's Real Marriage," www .worldmag.com/2014/03/unreal_sales_for_driscoll_s_real_marriage.

20. Ibid.

21. http://pastormark.tv/2011/12/07/inside-look-at-real-marriage (web site now defunct).

22. http://pastormark.tv/2011/12/07/inside-look-at-real-marriage.

23. James Duncan, "How Mark Driscoll Pockets the Money He Gives to MarsHill,"www.pajamapages.com/how-mark-driscoll-pockets-the-money-he-gives-to-mars-hill.

24. Emily McFarlan Miller, "Lawsuit Accuses Mark Driscoll of Misusing Mars Hill Church Tithes," www.religionnews.com/2016/03/01/mark-driscoll-reportedly-sued-to-find-out-where-tithes-went.

25. Warren Throckmorton, "Former Mars Hill Church Pastors Bring Formal Charges Against Mark Driscoll," www.patheos.com/blogs/warrenth rockmorton/2014/08/21/former-mars-hill-church-pastors-bring-formal-charges-against-mark-driscoll.

26. "Justin Bieber's Pastor Signs with Management 360," www.billboard .com/articles/columns/pop/6866952/ justin-bieber-pastor-judah-smith-signs-management-360.

27. Ibid.

27. http://jesus-is.org.

29. Ibid.http://jesus-is.org/projects.

30. http://jesus-is.org/stories.

31. http://jesus-is.org/conversation.

32. http://jesus-is.org.

33. See http://welovemarshill.com; http://repentantpastor.com.

# CHAPTER NINE

# People of the Picture Book

## *PJ Library and American Jewish Religion*

### RACHEL B. GROSS

> We don't need to tell you that reading to your children is
> important.... But finding the right books and making the
> time to read as a family can be hard. That's where PJ Library
> comes in.
>
> www.pjlibrary.org/About-PJ-Library

Since 2005, a philanthropic organization has set out to influence American Jews by reaching them in one of their most tender, intimate family
moments: parents reading to children. The program uses the materials
of popular culture—in this case, children's books—to influence Jewish
families' values and practices. The organizers of PJ Library deny that
their work is religious, but this article points to a broader understanding of American Jewish religion that includes the work of PJ Library.
The organization encourages the creation of local communities of like-
minded families, aims to strengthen individual families' connections to
Jewish organizations, and nurtures family members' perception of
themselves as part of an imagined Jewish community—all of which
should be understood as components of American Jewish religion.

Currently, PJ Library is one of the most influential Jewish organizations in North America. Founded in 2005 by the real estate mogul

Harold Grinspoon, the North American iteration of PJ (for "pajama") Library is a program of the Harold Grinspoon Foundation. PJ Library partners with local Jewish organizations, including synagogues, Jewish community centers, and Jewish Federations, to provide free books and music to Jewish and interfaith families with children.[1] Each month, through its local affiliates, it sends age-appropriate books or music to children ages six months through eight years old.[2] As of November 2015, the organization had distributed 8,238,526 books throughout the United States and Canada.[3] It prints paperback copies of its book selections, with reading guides on the front and back flaps—or on the back of board books for younger children—that explain a Jewish tradition or value related to the story. The reading guides also offer suggestions for conversations between adult readers and young listeners and follow-up activities that reinforce the highlighted Jewish tradition or value, attempting to extend PJ Library's influence beyond story time.

For all that it is based on the seemingly lighthearted material of picture books, PJ Library demonstrates the burden that American Jewish institutions place on popular culture to shape their communities. Though staff members deny that PJ Library is engaged in religious activity, the organization does, in fact, use children's books as a tool to shape American Jewish religion. It uses children's books to introduce families to or reinforce their connection with sacred rituals and Jewish customs. More broadly, PJ Library seeks to persuade American Jewish families to make Judaism an important part of their lives and to connect them, one illustrated book at a time, to networks that will help them do so.

## "WE ARE NEGLECTING OUR CHILDREN"

PJ Library arose from two related trends in the American Jewish community. First, American Jews have deliberately used popular culture, including children's books, for educational and socialization purposes throughout the twentieth century. Second, in the late twentieth century and early twenty-first century, major American Jewish donors have increasingly funded organizations that offer Jewish experiences, especially for Jewish young adults. Traditional American Jewish organizations—synagogues, Jewish community centers, and charitable organizations—still exist, but they are changing as their target audiences' needs and desires change. Jews have long moved easily between religious, cultural, ethnic, and genetic understandings of Judaism (the religion) and Jewishness (the culture), and their ways of defining themselves as individuals and organizing themselves as communities reflect these ever-shifting categories. Some Jews are looking for new ways to build Jewish communities, while others have no connection to Jewish communal institutions and may consider themselves "secular Jews," Jewish by ancestry or culture rather than religion. PJ Library attempts to draw the latter into new and existing communal structures, while fortifying the former.

Funded by major Jewish donors, "episodic Jewish culture," as the anthropologists Moshe Kornfeld and Joshua Friedman term it, attempts to have a major influence on the shape of the American Jewish community through short-term experiences.[4] Birthright Israel, founded by the Jewish philanthropists Charles Bronfman and Michael Steinhardt in 1994, which offers a free ten-day trip to Israel to young Jewish adults aged 18 to 26, is the best-known and largest organization offering these experiences.[5] With PJ Library, Grinspoon adapted this model: rather than offering a one-time new experience, his program attempts to shape the existing experience of story time in Jewish households.

Support for PJ Library and other forms of episodic Jewish culture rests on American Jews' long-standing fears of assimilation—the imagined disappearance of Jewish identity, culture, and religion into an undifferentiated American identity. Where American Christians have feared the increasing "secularization" of Americans, from religion to no religious identification, Jews have been concerned about "assimilation" from Judaism to a secular and primarily Christian society. The popular, politically conservative Jewish writer Daniel Gordis articulates these views, describing episodic Jewish culture as a response to assimilation:

"Jewish identity is ... eroded with relative ease in America, but it is also strengthened with well-defined, strategically timed interventions."[6] Such fears about assimilation are ahistorical, overlooking the diversity of Jewish practice throughout history and the ways in which Judaism has been influenced by non-Jewish culture for millennia, and has changed other cultures in return. Nonetheless, this concern has motivated American Jews' organizational and philanthropic patterns throughout the twentieth and twenty-first centuries.

Despite American Jews' general fears about lack of Jewish differentiation, Jews have rarely feared engagement with the materials of American popular culture. Popular culture on its own did not threaten Jewish continuity; failing to complement it with a firm grounding in Jewish religion, culture, and traditions did. Throughout the twentieth century, American Jews turned to the materials of popular culture, creating parallel works of Jewish popular culture to resist the perceived threat of assimilation and to strengthen Jewish family practices.

In the mid-twentieth century, many American Jews moved from urban neighborhoods to new suburban homes. Urban Jewish immigrants had depended on local networks to pass on religious and ethnic identities to their children. Suburban Jewish parents leading home lives largely undifferentiated from those of their non-Jewish suburban counterparts relied heavily upon Jewish organizations to educate their children in Jewish rituals and historical narratives. Without the dynamic, continual ethnic reinforcement of Jewish neighborhoods in the city, the maintenance of the Jewish identity of the next generation seemed imperiled.

To counter this, midcentury Jewish authors and educators sought fresh ways to interest American Jewish youth in their heritage, attempting to fill the perceived Jewish gap at home. Recognizing the limited value of formal education, too easily dismissed as stiflingly boring, they turned their attention to playtime, creating a variety of formal and informal educational materials designed to interest children in Jewish life and education. Activity books—often labeled "fun books"—along with new Jewish storybooks and biographies, were intended to foster a culture of Jewish childhood that communal leaders feared would not arise organically. In this context, the cheerful, seemingly innocuous genre of Jewish children's books has borne heavy communal expectations that continue to this day.

Nonetheless, amid all of these educational and entertainment materials, few works of Jewish children's fiction were published. At the outset of the 1950s, the Jewish educator and author Jacob S. Golub bemoaned the fact that a "bare eighteen titles" of Jewish juvenile fiction were published in 1949 and 1950. "It is obvious that we are neglecting our children," he lamented, calling for more children's books on Jewish themes.[7] Jewish children's literature subsequently developed slowly and steadily. For American Jews at midcentury and thereafter, children's literature was not merely a pastime, but an essential component in the development of children's religious identities.

## "A JEWISH TWIST"

In 2004, Harold Grinspoon heard a National Public Radio story about the Imagination Library, founded by the singer Dolly Parton to give free books to children in her native rural Tennessee. The real estate entrepreneur and philanthropist, who has long given millions of dollars to Jewish summer camps, schools, and synagogues and is a major funder of Birthright Israel, aimed to "do what Dolly does, with a Jewish twist."[8] Whereas Parton's program promotes literacy in rural Appalachia, Grinspoon's PJ Library, launched in 2005, aims to increase Jewish literacy—by sending Jewish children's books to those who could afford them but might not yet know that they wanted them.

PJ Library's Book Selection Committee accepts manuscripts submitted for review by authors and publishers and independently reviews previously published books, including titles that have gone out of print. It searches for books that will be appropriate for a diverse audience of families. "PJ Library families ... come from rural, suburban, and urban environments. They also come from many backgrounds—some are intermarried, some have little or no formal Jewish learning, some attend a synagogue and celebrate Jewish holidays, and others may be unfamiliar with Jewish practice," the organization's Book Selection Guidelines explain, "While the PJ Library program is open to all Jewish families, the committee focuses primarily on unengaged families when making selections."[9] For some families already invested in Judaism, PJ Library materials are simply one more Jewish resource, but for others, PJ Library may be an introduction to Jewish values, rituals, and communities.

PJ Library has managed to transform the once small niche market for Jewish children's books into a lucrative, growing market for mainstream publishers.[10] Searching for positive engagements with Jewish culture, religion, and history, PJ Library does not distribute Holocaust-themed books, a thriving genre of children's literature. Instead, it seeks out books that can translate to contemporary families' lives, including books that promote moral instruction, traditional values, and ritual guidance. PJ Library solicits books about Jewish summer camps, a particular interest of Grinspoon's because of their quantitative influence on participants' Jewish practices.[11] It also seeks out holiday-themed books, sending materials to families each month and encouraging them to be aware of the Jewish calendar. The organization's preferences have dramatically increased the market for Jewish books dealing with holidays not often celebrated by non-Orthodox Jews, such as Shavuot, a summer holiday commemorating God giving the Torah to the Israelites assembled at Mount Sinai, and Tu BiShvat, the "New Year of the Trees," a spring holiday often celebrated as an ecological awareness day, focusing on fruits and trees of the Land of Israel.

## "THE BOOKS ARE JUST A VEHICLE"

PJ Library has an increasingly powerful influence on American Jewish families and the institutions that impact them. Parents enrolled in the program recognize that "There's no catch. There's no reason not to do it."[12] Nonetheless, having no immediately recognizable "catch" for recipients does not mean that PJ Library has no effect. In the 2010s, Jewish newspapers have been full of stories of families who became more engaged in Jewish life because of PJ Library. Anecdotal evidence even suggests that PJ Library influences non-Jewish parents of interfaith families to convert to Judaism.[13] More quantitatively, PJ Library's 2013 Executive Summary, based on surveys of over 20,000 Jewish families—the largest survey of American Jewish families to date—demonstrated its calculable impact on American Jews. Among other findings, 57 percent of their respondents reported that PJ Library made their family more aware of Jewish holidays and life-cycle events, and 56 percent reported that it made them more aware of Jewish concepts and values.[14]

As parents are well aware, "The books are aimed at children, but they are also aimed at teaching adults."[15] The organization sends illustrated books to children through age eight, well past the age at which most children become independent readers. "We focus on the parent-child experience," explains Meredith Lewis, PJ Library's Director of Content and Engagement. PJ Library encourages parents to read and discuss the books with their children, even when their children could read them on their own. PJ Library's target is not parents or children, but the Jewish family as a unit.[16]

PJ Library encourages parents and children to see themselves in the books and also to shift their perception and behavior. Its reading guides highlight Jewish values, rituals, or traditions related to the books' content. They also provide topics parents might discuss with children or activities they might do as a family, including rituals and enactments of Jewish values. Parents report that the guides helped non-Jewish parents explain Jewish concepts to children. They also help Jewish parents explain concepts or traditions that they know implicitly but might have trouble articulating in language appropriate for their children.[17]

Occasionally, the reading guides reveal the burden of communication that they carry. PJ Library's edition of the board book *Sammy Spider's*

*First Book of Jewish Holidays,* which introduces Jewish holidays with sim-plistic sketches such as, "On Yom Kippur we say we're sorry," comes with a long explanation about the Jewish ritual year. On the back of the book, PJ Library introduces parents to the twentieth-century theolo-gian Abraham Joshua Heschel's description of the "architecture of time" built by Jewish ritual. "While your little ones won't understand these concepts—or even the order of the holidays—for some time," explains the guide, Sammy Spider's adventures help "lay a foundation" for Jewish ritual life.[18] Eager little Sammy Spider bears quite a responsibility if he requires explanation from a leading theologian of the twentieth century.

Like other "implementing partners," Jennifer Baer Lotsoff, PJ Library's liaison at the Jewish Federation of St. Louis, creates programs to connect PJ Library recipients to one another and to Jewish institu-tions. "The books are just a vehicle," Lotsoff says. Activities vary depending on the implementing partner's understanding of the commu-nity's needs and desires. Lotsoff provides ways for parents to connect with each other, as well as with PJ Library through social media plat-forms, including Facebook groups and Pinterest boards. She goes wher-ever potential participants are, sometimes hosting events in non-Jewish spaces such as public libraries. She even cosponsored a charity drive during Chanukah outside an Office Depot. Lotsoff aims to attract fami-lies who are not engaged with institutional Jewish life, such as "where you're just randomly walking into Office Depot and you have no con-nection with the Jewish community at all." She also helps parents host book clubs in their homes to spread the word about PJ Library. "Because then someone says to a friend that lives down the street, 'Okay, I know you don't do anything Jewish but they're having this fun book club at my house. Do you want to come?'"[19] These creative models encourage fami-lies to fit PJ Library materials into their preexisting routines and net-works and to recognize their home lives as Jewish ones.

Like other implementing partners in locations with large Jewish communities, Lotsoff relies on St. Louis's robust Jewish institutions to support recipients who already are interested in Jewish communal life. She focuses on connecting families who are not involved in institutional Jewish life and introducing them to other Jewish communal programs. PJ Library's co-sponsorship of a social action program for preschoolers on Martin Luther King Jr. Day at a local Jewish private school doubled the number of expected attendees.[20] Because parents felt comfortable with PJ Library programs, "people went into a space that they never would have gone to," Lotsoff explains. Reportedly, the school's director attributed several children's subsequent enrollment in the private school directly to their families' participation in the MLK Day program.[21] PJ Library succeeds as a gateway, bringing families into established Jewish institutional networks and creating new ones.

## "BOOKS SUITED FOR ME AND MY FAMILY"

As PJ Library has expanded, some parents have complained that they do not see their families reflected in the books. Early selections, in particular, featured white families with two parents of opposite sexes, represented traditional Jewish religious activities, and sometimes presupposed Jewish knowledge. As PJ Library has responded to parents' concerns, encouraging authors, illustrators, and publishers to represent a broader spectrum of American Jewish families, they have shaped depictions of American Jews. While representation of American Jews in PJ Library books remains limited, as PJ Library staff members readily acknowledge, their increasingly diverse depictions of American Jewish families validate a variety of family choices.

Laurel Snyder, a poet and author based in Atlanta, found that early PJ Library books "were fine and we were glad to have them, but I didn't see books suited for me and my family." A self-proclaimed "diversity Jew," Snyder is married to a non-Jew and does not live in a Jewish neighborhood. She had been "noodling around" with drafts of children's books for some time, and the PJ Library books pushed her to return to her writing. PJ Library has since distributed Snyder's board book, *Nosh, Schlep, Schluff,* and her illustrated books, *Good Night, Lila Tov,* about a family camping trip, and *The Longest Night,* a retelling of the exodus from Egypt from a child's perspective. Snyder's books provide PJ Library with content that is more attractive to a broader base of Jewish families, particularly less religious families. "The PJ Library made me more accountable to the Jewish part of my life," Snyder said, encouraging her to reflect on the kind of Jew she wanted to be and to create material that would help others do the same.[22]

Rather than simply encouraging families to change their behavior, PJ Library encourages families to see many of their preexisting activities as Jewish. Leslie Kimmelman's *The Shabbat Puppy* describes a grandfather's ritual of taking a quiet Shabbat walk with his grandson. Though Shabbat walks are a custom of those who are *shomer Shabbat,* observant of traditional Jewish Sabbath prohibitions, it is also a fairly neutral activity that, as the PJ Library reading guide suggests, might be emulated by families with a range of religious habits. In fact, the book describes the Shabbat walk as taking place on Saturday mornings, a time when observant Jews are likely to be in synagogue services.[23] Likewise, Jane Yolen's *How Do Dinosaurs Say Happy Chanukah,* part of her popular *How Do Dinosaurs* series, suggests a number of humorous Chanukah misbehaviors by dinosaurs, in place of children. In doing so, the book reinforces easy Chanukah home rituals that are popular with many Jewish families, such as singing prayers when lighting the menorah and playing dreidel. The reading guide encourages parents who do not own a menorah to buy a fanciful one that appeals to children. Parents who already own one are encouraged to explain the origin of their menorah to their children, making the home ritual more meaningful through family stories.

In February 2014, PJ Library expanded the range of families represented in its books by offering Elizabeth Kushner's *The Purim Superhero,* which depicts a boy's debate about what costume to wear for the carnivalesque Jewish holiday of Purim, based on the Book of Esther. Kushner matter-of-factly introduces the protagonist's two fathers, "Daddy" and "Abba" (Hebrew for father), keeping the focus on Nate's desire to dress as an alien for the holiday when all the boys in his Hebrew school class plan to dress as superheroes. Kushner's story draws on a traditional rabbinic emphasis on hiding and revelation in Purim rituals, and a central moment in the book draws together traditional holiday themes, contemporary LGBTQ issues, and childhood fears:

> "Abba?" Nate asked. "Do you ever just want to be like everybody else?"
>
> Abba looked at Nate. "You know the Purim story," Abba said. "Queen Esther saved the Jews because she didn't hide who she was. She told King Ahashuerus she was Jewish, and that her people were in danger.
>
> "Sometimes showing who you really are makes you stronger, even if you're different from other people."[24]

The story blends familiar early twenty-first-century narratives of empowerment and pluralism with traditional Jewish interpretations of the holiday of masking and unmasking.

Predictably, the fate of *The Purim Superhero* illustrates the difficulties of attempting to appeal to a wide spectrum of Jews—or perhaps a misguided evaluation of mainstream Jewish public opinion. Rather than distributing *The Purim Superhero* as part of its regular monthly deliveries, PJ Library sent parents an e-mail offering the book as an "additional gift" to interested families. The response was overwhelming; after stock ran out within thirty-six hours, PJ Library requested thousands more copies from the publisher.

Kushner had created *The Purim Superhero* as an entry in a contest for Jewish-themed books with gay, lesbian, bisexual, or transgender characters held by Keshet, an advocacy organization for LGBT Jews. Responses to the book were largely positive, but PJ Library's handling of its distribution was criticized. "This is demeaning to same-sex couples and their families—that there's something so threatening and wrong about our families that children can only see them in a book if a parent requests it," Keshet's executive director Idit Klein told *The Boston Globe*.[25] Many other parents expressed their outrage online. In response, the Harold Grinspoon Foundation trustee Winnie Sandler Grinspoon defended the institution's choice in a public letter, assuring parents that "PJ Library welcomes and embraces the diversity of our community." The unusual method of distribution was a means of "putting parents in the driver's seat," she explained.[26] Nonetheless, it seems telling that PJ Library has not repeated this method of preselection. Nor, as of 2016, have they distributed another book featuring gay Jews. Another such book may not exist yet, but PJ Library has also not encouraged the creation of such a book. To date, PJ Library has only gone so far in representing the diversity of American Jews they aim to reach and allowing families to see themselves in PJ Library materials.

### "TO HAVE IT IN THEIR HEARTS"

The goal of PJ Library is not just to impart knowledge about Jewish customs and history to parents and children but something harder to measure. The organization aims "not to have them just know the facts, but to care and to feel, to have it in their hearts, not just their heads," Lotsoff asserts.[27] PJ Library wants its recipients to see their lives as Jewish ones. "The ultimate goal of PJ Library," explains the Executive Summary, "is to enhance Jewish identity, increase engagement in Jewish life and community and, over time, build a more vibrant North American Jewish community."[28] If one understands religion as engagement with networks that provide meaning, these are religious goals. PJ Library aims to connect participants with an imagined community, shape individual worldviews and values, and inspire ritual activity in a variety of contexts, all aspects of American Jewish religion.

Lewis likens the program to the annual ritual cycle of reading the Torah scroll and traditions of Jewish biblical commentary:

> Stories are a huge, huge part of Jewish history. Every time I talk to people that are unfamiliar with . . . the rhythms of Jewish life, I explain to them the Torah reading cycle, that every year we read the same story, in the same pieces, and we read it over and over again. And our community's job over

the years has been to add commentary to that. And then I say, "And we're sending families books." So that they can read those stories over and over again and add their own family commentary to it. It's a very, very powerful parallel.[29]

In this analogy, story time is not only a family ritual. It is a Jewish ritual that draws families into the networks and traditions of Jewish religious life.

Nonetheless, PJ Library staff members are uncomfortable with the suggestion that PJ Library intends to influence families' religious lives. "I tend to veer away from [the term] 'religious life,'" Marcie Greenfield Simons, the former director of PJ Library, said. Instead, she uses particularly American, individualistic language in describing PJ Library's introduction of "Jewish choices" that families might make within and beyond their homes:

> In their home, are they going to have a *tzedakah* [charity] box and make that an active part of their family's life? Are they going to bake challah for Shabbat? Are they going to think about blessing their children? Outside of their home, are they going to consider a Jewish day camp or a Jewish preschool? ... Even if they're not members of a local synagogue, would they like to go over to be part of the Purim carnival or be part of the Megillah [Book of Esther] reading?[30]

Likewise, Meredith Lewis recounts that children frequently question gaps between Jewish rituals described in books and their own families' practices. Reading books about the week-long fall harvest holiday of Sukkot, children will ask "Why don't we have a sukkah?" (a temporary hut built during the holiday to recall the Israelites' journey through the wilderness). "And then the parents will say, 'Well, I don't know. Well, let's build a sukkah.'" Lewis continues, "I know of dozens of families that have said, 'This book provoked us to try something or to do something and to shape our involvement in Jewish life in a way that without it it never would have happened.'"[31] Although they deny any such aim, nearly all of the examples of "Jewish choices" offered by

Simons and Lewis deal with traditionally religious rituals, pointing to the religious goals of the organization.

PJ Library staff members' reluctance to label these actions as religious may spring from their own constrained definitions of religion, or from a savvy understanding that labeling PJ Library's goals as religious ones would alienate a large part of their audience, which includes Jewish families who identify across and beyond the spectrum of Jewish denominations.[32] "If you look at millennial parents, even those that are faith oriented and spiritually oriented may not be religiously oriented," Lewis observes.[33] Such vague, if common, distinctions among "faith," "spirituality," and "religion" point to confusion about the location of religion not so much by PJ Library staff but by Americans more broadly, many of whom, including Jews, identify as "spiritual but not religious." For Jews, this may involve identifying as Jewish by culture or heritage rather than by religion. Some Jews may avoid the label "religious" because they associate that term with formal organizations and mandated activities, such as belonging to a synagogue and following dietary laws. Nonetheless, despite staff members' protests to the contrary, PJ Library does intend to draw families into organized Jewish life—not necessarily limited to synagogue membership—and to influence their values, both fundamental aspects of religion.

Looking ahead, PJ Library staff members envision that, not only will their program connect families to Jewish traditions and Jewish networks, but the books will provide the basis of a new Jewish canon based on shared reading material, what the PJ Library author Tamar Fox calls a "shared cultural library."[34] As Lewis expressed it:

> In a couple years from now, when kids talk about their favorite books that they read growing up, kids that were a part of PJ Library can encounter kids ... at Hillel, and say, "Oh yeah, I remember reading *Bagels from Benny*. That book was really important to my family, and it taught me values about feeding the poor and what social justice actually meant." And you can find kids [from another] part of the country that [will] say, "Oh, we did that too."[35]

In Aubrey Davis's *Bagels from Benny*, a retelling of a classic Jewish folk-tale from Spain, young Benny decides to thank God for the delicious bagels his grandfather makes at his bakery by placing bagels in a synagogue's Ark, where the Torah scroll is kept. Each week, the bagels disappear. Finally, it is revealed that a poor man has been eating Benny's bagels, and Benny learns that feeding others was a way of praising God and improving the world.

In the religious work of PJ Library, as in *Bagels from Benny*, the medium is the message. Just as a humble bagel conveys religious lessons in Davis's story, PJ Library has taken a common American cultural activity, children's story time, and applied it to furthering Jewish religious practices and values. Even so, not just any books will do. As the organization explains on its web site, quoted in the epigraph to this chapter, PJ Library provides families with "the right books," which it intends to have a particular influence on family dynamics. In this context, children's books bear a substantial responsibility that is at once weighty, playful, and shape-shifting, depending on their use. The material of popular culture connects families to Jewish religious networks of the imagined past, present, and future, as well as with existential values.

### DISCUSSION QUESTIONS

1. How, according to Gross, have American Jews used children's books to shape their communities? PJ Library assumes that children's identities are shaped by what they read and watch. Do you agree? Why? Can you think of other examples of groups that have used children's books as a way to teach values and cultural norms to children? Are the identities of youth and adults also shaped by what they read and watch?

2. Gross argues that PJ Library is a religious institution. Do you agree? What might motivate its staff not to describe it as such?

3. What does the existence of a project like PJ Library tells us about the challenges faced by minority religions in America? What does it suggest about the challenges faced by religion vis-à-vis secularity?

4. Imagine, name, and describe a children's book intended to encourage religious identity, or one intended to encourage a secular identity. What sort of story would you tell? What sort of pictures would you include? How would you imagine children and parents using the book? How would you hope it would influence them?

## NOTES

1. A Jewish Federation is a local confederation of Jewish social agencies, volunteer programs, educational bodies, and other organizations. The umbrella Jewish Federations of North America is one of the most powerful organizations in American Jewish life.

2. Each community affiliate determines the age range of children eligible for their local PJ Library program. Beginning in 2014, PJ Library extended enrollment in PJ Library to American families who live outside the bounds of a local PJ Library affiliate; such families are entered into a "US National Community" funded by a philanthropic partnership called PJ Alliance.

3. "PJ by the Numbers," *Proof* (December 2015), 3–4.

4. "Episodic Jewish Culture" panel organized by Moshe Kornfeld and Joshua Benjamin Friedman at the Association of Jewish Studies, Boston, December 2013.

5. See Shaul Kelner, *Tours That Bind: Diaspora, Pilgrimage, and Israeli Birthright Tourism* (New York: New York University Press, 2010).

6. Daniel Gordis, "The Future of American Jewish Life," *Proof* (December 2015): 5–7.

7. Jacob S. Golub, "American Jewish Juvenile Literature, 1949–1950," *Jewish Book Annual* 9 (1950–51): 27–29.

8. Mark Oppenheimer, "Aiming to Spread Judaism One Book at a Time," *New York Times,* June 24, 2011.

9. Book Selection Committee," *PJ Library,* www.pjlibrary.org/books-and-music/book-selection-committee.aspx (text since deleted).

10. Tamar Snyder, "PJ Library Now Speaking Volumes in Publishing World," *Jewish Week* (New York), February 15, 2011.

11. Steven M. Cohen, Ron Miller, Ira M. Sheskin, and Berna Torr, *Camp Works: The Long-Term Impact of Jewish Overnight Camp* (Foundation for Jewish Camp, 2011). This study was sponsored by the Foundation for Jewish Camp (FJC), to which the Harold Grinspoon Foundation contributes.

12. Ori Parnaby, quoted in Sheila Wilensky, "PJ Library Gives Locals Treasures of Jewish Literacy," *Arizona Jewish Post,* March 6, 2009.

13. Jacob Berkman, "Reaching Out with Book Giveaway," *Jewish Telegraphic Agency,* November 20, 2007.

14. Jay Sherwin et al., "The People of the Book: An Evaluation of the PJ Library," PJ Library Executive Summary, September 17, 2013.

15. Berkman, "Reaching Out."

16. Meredith Lewis, telephone interview by the author, March 1, 2016.

17. Erika Meitner, personal communication to the author, February 14, 2016.

18. "A Note from PJ Library," back cover of PJ Library edition of Sylvia A. Rouss, *Sammy Spider's First Book of Jewish Holidays* (Minneapolis: Kar-Ben, 2013).

19. Jennifer Baer Lotsoff, interview by the author, January 27, 2104, St. Louis, Missouri.

20. A Jewish day school is a Jewish educational institution that provides both Jewish and secular education in one school on a full-time basis, in contrast to the supplementary educational programs of a Jewish religious school, also known as a Hebrew school or Sunday school.

21. Lotsoff interview.

22. Snyder, "PJ Library Now Speaking Volumes ."

23. Leslie Kimmelman, *The Shabbat Puppy* (New York: Marshall Cavendish Children, 2012).

24. Elizabeth Kushner, *The Purim Superhero* (Minneapolis: Kar-Ben, 2013).

25. Gal Tziperman Lotan, "Purim Book for Children Creates a Stir," *Boston Globe,* March 3, 2014.

26. PJ Library, "In Search of the Perfect Gifts," February 23, 2014, https://pjlibrary.org/Beyond-Books/PJBlog/February-2014/In-Search-of-the-Perfect-Gifts.

27. Lotsoff interview.

28. Sherwin, "People of the Book."

29. Lewis interview.

30. Marcie Greenfield Simons, interview by the author, January 23, 2014.

31. Lewis interview.

32. Forty-six percent of families receiving PJ Library materials identify with one of the three major North American Jewish movements, including 11 percent who identify as Modern Orthodox. 28 percent identify as "just Jewish," and 22 percent identify as "Jewish and something else." Sherwin, "People of the Book."

33. Lewis interview.

34. Tamar Fox, telephone interview by the author, February 24, 2016.

35. Lewis interview. Hillel is the largest Jewish campus organization.

# CHAPTER TEN

# Meditation on the Go

*Buddhist Smartphone Apps as Video Game Play*

GREGORY PRICE GRIEVE

This award-winning mindfulness app has over 80 guided meditations custom-made for wherever you are and whatever you're doing—traveling, at work, at home, going to sleep and much more. All for the price of a cup of coffee and with no hidden extra charges.

"Mindfulness & Meditation App for iOS & Android"

Focusing on the application buddhify², this chapter explores how people use smartphones in popular culture to practice religion. My curiosity about these devices was whetted on a recent flight from New York's LaGuardia Airport back to my home in North Carolina. I sat in seat 24B, a row behind a family of four that I imagined consisted of a mother, father, son of about seven, and daughter of approximately twelve. They were affluent, urban, and cosmopolitan, extruding unself-conscious sophistication and privilege. It was a loud, turbulent flight, notable for spilled beverages and crying babies. I was sandwiched in a middle seat between two people with too many bags, and I could do nothing for the short flight except look over the shoulder of the family members. The young son's hands danced nimbly over an iPad Pro on which he played the fantasy video game *Knights II of Pen and Paper*. The preadolescent daughter flipped quickly through a copy of *Ms. Marvel* that featured a teenage Pakistani American protagonist with shape-shifting abilities. The husband worked his way painstakingly down rows of figures, often stopping to doodle absent-mindedly in the margins.

Looking over the woman's shoulder, I could see she was wearing earbuds connected to a white Apple iPhone 6 plus whose screen displayed the meditation application buddhify².[1] The application's web site describes buddhify² as "the mindfulness app for your modern life. Practical, playful and beautifully-designed, buddhify² increases your wellbeing by teaching you mindfulness-based meditation on the go."[2] Smartphone apps are popular examples of "digital religion"—religious practices that utilize electronic devices that communicate and store content as numeric data and that almost always have an online social media component. This chapter asks, how does buddhify² work? And what does it tell us about religion and popular culture in our late-capitalist, consumer-driven, corporate free market economy, intertwined as it is with digital media?

Because digitally mediated experiences are frequently assumed to be less authentic than face-to-face interactions, popular forms of digital religion are often derided as trivial, faddish, and even toxic. The difficulty with a blanket declaration of "spiritual toxicity" is that it obscures the fact that actual people, as illustrated by the woman playing with her iPhone in seat 23A, often find digital media an authentic part of their everyday religious practice. Also, no matter what the degree of one's nostalgia, there is no turning back to before the Fall. As suggested by the Apple Computer logo on the back of each iPhone, society has taken a bite from digital media's forbidden knowledge, and it is impossible to return to the edenic pre-electronic state. Rather than judging whether video games are good or bad, students of religion and popular culture need to critically address who, where, how, and for what, people actually use apps, such as buddhify², in their everyday lives.

This chapter argues that buddhify² is authentically religious because it communicates an experience of mindfulness through a procedural spirituality that poaches from video game play. Like other digital devices, buddhify² can best be described through "user experience" and "user interface." User experience defines a person's emotions and attitudes toward an application. Buddhify² is designed to promote "mindfulness," an active state of open nonjudgmental awareness of one's thoughts and emotions. User interface indicates the junction between a person and digital devices and includes the screen elements, such as menus and commands, that lead users through an application. The app's user interface cultivates an experience of mindfulness through ritualization, a way of performing certain activities that differentiates them from more conventional ones and ties this difference into a group's ultimate reality. Consider, for instance, genuflecting to the consecrated Eucharist as ritualization. The bending of one knee to the ground differs from the norm of standing, and the act communicates a deep respect for the perceived presence of Christ.

The difference that buddhify² creates is a calm space in the middle of the hubbub of digitally saturated contemporary life. The ultimate reality engaged is a calm awareness of one's breath. While content and images are important to buddhify²'s operation, the app ritualizes through a procedure, a term that describes a step-by-step sequence that emerges from a set of rules for performing a particular operation. Imagine, for instance, punching your way through the choices of an automated phone system. Buddhify²'s procedural operations borrow from video game play, particularly gamification and modding. Gamification, as discussed below, uses game mechanics, such as points and leader boards, while modding refers to a user's ability to customize digital media to her or his own personal style.

A critical understanding of smartphone apps and other forms of digital religion is necessary, because these digital devices have reshaped the way people practice religion in popular culture. As of 2016, the average American spends 4.7 hours per day on his or her smartphone.³ While we spend much time *looking*, however, we rarely *see* our digital devices. Media are not neutral conveyers of information; they affect the messages they communicate. Buddhism spoken is not the same Buddhism as in print, which again differs from that which flickers across digital screens. Buddhify²'s procedural spirituality retards the importance of religious narratives and traditional institutions and purports to afford those seeking it personal psychological growth. Is digital spirituality an authentic religious practice? Before we answer, we need to describe, explain, and critically understand how people use religious smartphone apps in their everyday lives. It is indisputable, however, that the woman in seat 23A and many others feel that they have found something they need in popular digital Buddhism and use what they understand of this seemingly exotic tradition as a justification for fulfilling that need.

## BUDDHIFY²: MAKING THE FUTURE PRESENT IN THE MOMENT

A few days after my bumpy flight landed, I searched Apple Inc.'s app store, a digital distribution platform for mobile devices, and for $4.99 downloaded buddhify² onto my own smartphone.[4] Used at least since 1981, the term "application" (or more often simply app) describes computer software programs designed to perform one specific function. "Smartphone" is a term first used in 1995 to describe handheld devices that integrate mobile phone capabilities with features more common to personal computers. Buddhify² was created by the Glasgow-based company Mindfulness Everywhere, which is described on its web site as "the creative studio combining meditation, technology & design. We're making the future of the present moment."[5] At one time computers and other digital media seemed diametrically opposed to spirituality. In popular culture, electronics no longer, however, embody the cold emotionless rational logic of an earlier computer age but has become the fetishized epicenter of what I have called the postmodern, networked consumer society. As the creator of buddhify², Rohan Gunatillake, states, digital devices have "become a design item, a thing you wanted to have in your room and show off."[6]

Smartphones make mobile apps such as buddhify[2] available to users. An app is a software program native to mobile devices and stands in contrast to programs developed for desktop computers and web applications. The first smartphone apps appeared in 2008, and by July of 2015, over 1.5 million apps were available for download from Apple's App Store.[7] Just a few years later, in 2012, the American Internet analytic company comScore reported that more people employed apps than browsed the web.[8] Early apps usually offered information retrieval, such as for e-mail, the weather, schedules, and the stock market. As of 2016, however, over a thousand different categories of apps—from Health and Mind & Body to Games/Role Playing—were classified on the Google Developers site alone. Many of these were spiritual and/or religious. On March 15, 2016, a search for "Buddhism" yielded 547 apps, primarily in English, but also in French, German, Spanish, Chinese, Thai, Vietnamese, and Tibetan. Buddhist apps included such titles as "Buddha Quotes" by Tran Anh Khoa, "A Buddhist Podcast" by Wizzard media, "ZenTone" by Martin Hoeller, and "Meditation Timer Free" by Maxwell Software.

## USER EXPERIENCE: MINDFULNESS FOR URBAN PROFESSIONALS

User experience indicates all the aspects of how people use an application, the way it feels in their hands, how they understand that it works, how they feel while using it, how it fits the purposes they see for it, and how it meshes with the context they are using it for. After downloading the app, buddhify[2]'s home screen icon flickered a burnt orange on my smartphone screen. Clicking the lowercase slab-serif letter "b" opened a screen divided into three bands. First was an upper small burnt orange band that occupies 5 percent of the screen and has the title of the app, buddhify[2], in bold lowercase italicized white letters. Moving down the screen, the vast majority of the screen, 90 percent, is a central panel that is dark gray on the top and fades near the bottom, into the final row, which is a silhouetted city scene of three rows of buildings. The final band's back two rows of buildings are light and dark gray outlines of skyscrapers. The front row shows multistory residential buildings colored in muted tones, with details such as windows, a small yellow kite, and a blue bird, as well as trees and bicycles.

Buddhify²'s design is not arbitrary. Digital devices, like all technological tools, are made to solve particular problems for particular groups of people. Many digital media are designed to sell commodities by creating an experience of anxiety and increasing distraction, dissolving the boundary between work and private life and creating the fear that users are missing out and being left out. Buddhify² was released on January 6, 2014, and is a technological solution aimed at the cultivation of mindfulness for the urban professional to counter the disruption that digital media often create in everyday life. Such pragmatic benefits are not unusual in the way Buddhism has been appropriated by contemporary American society. As Jeff Wilson writes in *Mindful America: The Mutual Transformation of Buddhist Meditation and American Culture,* "The most important aspect of the mindfulness movement is its orientation toward practical benefits, an orientation we find present in Buddhist meditation groups, MBSR [Mindfulness Based Stress Reduction] seminars, and the self-help aisle of the nearest bookstore."[9]

Gunatillake describes buddhify² as "the best on-the-go introduction to mindfulness available today."[10] Echoing the understanding of mindfulness as "that present-moment awareness, presence of mind, wakefulness" articulated by the popular author and cofounder of the Insight Meditation Society, Joseph Goldstein, the app's "Tracking Your Experience" information screen describes mindfulness as "the ability to be aware of what is happening in your experience."[11] Users of such Buddhist-inspired digital technology report that mindfulness has nothing to do with a deity and is empty of any doctrine, institution, belief, or ideological system. Attempting to describe this state, buddhify² users speak of "awakening to experience," "not-judging," and not "letting the moment pass you by." While mindfulness is reported by both users and designers to transcend any religious tradition, there is no doubt that it is derived from the Buddhist notion of *smṛti*. It is associated with "awakening" (*bodhi*), a clear and stable attention that affords a direct insight into the true nature of the world and self and the relationship between the two.

Buddhify²'s target audience is hip young urban professionals, who, as the meditation track "Stress" puts it, are "caught in the storm of feeling and thought that makes up stress" (10:00). As Gunatillake said at a 2011 Buddhist Geeks Conference presentation titled "Disrupting the Awaking Industry," "the people I talk to are all [inaudible], they live in sort of urban centers in England, Scotland and Europe and they're digital, they're relational, and something's not landing for them."[12] The target audience can be seen in the design of the app itself. To give a small example, the buildings in the lower band of the screen resemble Manhattan seen from Brooklyn, New York, and hint that the application is aimed at urban professionals. Reviews of buddhify² also evidence its intended audience. In the blog Business Insider, Matt Johnston writes, "I've been using the meditation app on my phone for a week and it's changing my life." Johnston notes that he works in New York and that his mind "is endlessly fluctuating between sort of stressed out, and totally and completely stressed out. There are only two speeds." Johnston imagines being on a train to work, putting on headphones, and using buddhify² "to clear your mind to prepare for the day."[13]

USER INTERFACE

There are many ways to meditate. Buddhify² employs a digital user interface, a term that indicates the junction between a user and computer program and includes the screen elements, such as menus and commands, by which one communicates with the program. Eighty short, guided meditations that "help you develop mindfulness, calm and compassion in the middle of wherever you are and whatever you are doing," in the words of buddhify.com, constitute the core of the application. Buddhify²'s meditations are interfaced through a multicolored "play wheel" resembling a flower that dominates the app's middle panel. At the center of the play wheel, written text in a white circle asks, "What are you doing?" The sixteen petals are a muted color wheel of hues listing activities such as "Feeling Stressed," "Can't Sleep," "Eating," and "Being Online." Tapping an activity, such as "Feeling Stressed," opens the play wheel to reveal up to six possible meditations and their times. For instance, "Feeling Stressed" blossoms up to reveal the following meditations: "Flip," "Replace," "Rain," "Learn," "Space," and "Manage."

There seems to be a "killer app" for just about everything. While smartphone apps differ greatly in content, however, they are formally similar because of their procedural operations. A procedure, like the code of a computer program, is a step-by-step practice that emerges from a set of rules for performing a particular operation.[14] In digital media, the procedure describes the processes by which software enforces rules to generate some kind of representation. Smartphone apps, like other digital media, lead us through scripted practices that, although interactive, limit users' choices. Consider for a moment operating a bank's automatic teller machine or the frustration of navigating one's way through an automated telephone switchboard.

## PROCEDURAL SPIRITUALITY

Smartphones are place-making technologies. Buddhify² uses digital media's procedural affordance to create temporary spiritualized microplaces, small bubbles of spiritual experience in the midst of urban professionals' busy, stressed-out lives. As the app's meditation track "Stress" voices, buddhify² "creates little bits of [mindful] space from difficult experiences" (0:10). The app's individualized bubbles of sacred space are created through ritualization, a way of doing certain activities that differentiates them from more conventional ones, and ties this difference into the users' ultimate reality.[15] Compare, for instance, the Christian Eucharist, which differs from a normal meal in what one eats, when one eats, where one eats, with whom one eats, and whom one eats. Buddhify² offers a calm experience differentiated from the chaotic, overscheduled business of contemporary life in developed economies.

As evidenced by the woman in seat 23A, buddhify²'s procedural operation ritualizes smartphone use to create calm temporary quiet places within the hustle and bustle of people's busy lives. The app features liminal bubbles of spirituality, micro third spaces outside of work and home in which users are temporarily removed from everyday time and space and return renewed in spirit. It is not enough, however, for ritualization simply to do something different: these differing practices must be tied to what is perceived as a group's "ultimate reality." As Catherine Bell writes in her classic *Ritual Theory / Ritual Practice,* "ritualization always aligns one within a series of relationships linked to the ultimate sources of power."[16] While mindfulness is certainly the ultimate concern neither of all Buddhists nor even of all Buddhists using digital media, it plays this role in buddhify².

While mindfulness is communicated through images and sound, and also narratives, buddhify²'s "mindful" ultimate reality is cultivated by an awareness of breath afforded by the app's procedural operations. Media technologies, including smartphone apps, always build upon, extend, and modify people's bodies, senses, and consciousness.[17] Buddhify²'s user interface cultivates mindfulness through awareness of one's breath. For instance, the guided meditation "Manage," under the "Feeling Stressed" activity, is described on the play wheel's enlarged light blue petal as "Modulating our experience through the breath." While it has a family resemblance to the Buddhist concept of *ānāpānasmṛti,* or "mindfulness of breathing," and is informed by Protestant rejection of ritual and celebration of inner experience, the app uses game mechanics, first pioneered by video game design.[18]

POACHING GAME PLAY

Gamification, the use of game mechanics such as points and leader boards, is clear in buddhify²'s user interface. Gamification and ritualization share many formal similarities. Also it must be remembered that digital games are not mere trifles, artifacts created only to distract or to amuse. Video games are a powerful and still little explored method for doing things as well as asserting things, and ever since William Higinbotham designed *Tennis for Two* in 1958, video games have been at the forefront of popular culture and a leading innovator of digital media. For example, clicking the stats icon on the bottom of buddhify²'s home screen, which is illustrated by a line graph, brings the user over to a stat screen that allows for the tracking of data generated by use of the app. At the top of the stats screen is a white circle that mirrors the play wheel and tracks information such as how many days in a row the player has used the application, as well as one's personal record streak. Below the white stat circle the player is given the chance to rate three more abstract qualities by tapping a score of one to five. First, by a square pink button that shows cogs, is "mindfulness," which the app defines as "the ability to be aware of what is happening." Second, by a square purple mountain, is "concentration," described as "the ability of our mind to rest in one place." Third is "balance," "the ability to not be swayed by any particular sensation, thought or emotion." If the player rotates the phone into landscape mode, buddhify² displays all of these statistics in graphical form over the last, week, month, and year.

The app's tapping, touching, and shaking, as well as usage statistics and scores, share a formal resemblance to video game play. The process of applying game-like practices to nongame social fields is known as "gamification," which Nick Pelling, who coined the term, describes as the act of "applying game-like accelerated user interface design to make electronic transactions both enjoyable and fast."[19] Buddhify² uses gamification to create "spiritualized circles," micro social places demarcated from the ordinary hubbub of the everyday created by a temporary porous shield that differentiates the user from ordinary life. The term "spiritualized circle" borrows from the concept of the "magic circle," coined by Johan Huizinga, a pioneer of game theory. Like ritualization, the magic circle marks off game space from ordinary places. In *Homo Ludens: A Study of the Play-Element in Culture,* Huizinga writes, "all play moves and has its being within a play-ground marked off beforehand either materially or ideally, deliberately or as a matter of course." Huizinga acknowledges that game spaces and sacred spaces share a formal similarity. As he writes, "the arena, the card-table, the magic circle, the temple, the stage, the screen, the tennis court, the court of justice, etc., are all in form and function play-grounds, i.e. forbidden spots, isolated, hedged round, hallowed, within which special rules obtain."[20]

Modifying and personalizing digital media is one of the main methods by which users display identity in a networked consumer society. As Rachel Wagner and Christopher Accardo write, "the iPhone, with its personalized programs and noise-walling headphones, is perhaps the most poignant icon of American individualism today."[21] Modding is a type of "role-play," in which users try on and experiment with different behaviors. The psychoanalyst Donald Winnicott argues that role-play and other types of pretend are essential for the discovery and maintenance of an authentic self based on a spontaneous sense of being alive. Winnicott describes play as creative acts that occur in potential spaces, "this 'third area', that of cultural experience which is a derivative of play."[22] Buddhify² is designed to give people a personal authentic freedom, a spontaneity that counters the stress of contemporary urban life. In the meditation titled "Flip," under the category of "Feeling Stressed," it speaks of "in the midst of all the turmoil even allowing yourself to smile" (0:45).

## SPIRITUAL BUT NOT RELIGIOUS

In 20/20 hindsight, it was not surprising to find the woman in seat 23A using buddhify². Wherever people go, religion seems to follow, and the spread of smartphone applications corresponds to a growth in their use for religious purposes. Yet what type of religious practice thrives in the turbulent popular culture of networked consumer society? There was a time when the material webs of practice that constituted religious practices appeared solid and, if not eternal, at least tethered to tradition. While still highly religious, however, Americans are moving away from self-identification with specific religious traditions and instead are modifying the religious landscape for their own personal use. Looking over the shoulder of the woman using buddhify² it appeared to me that she was engaged in religious practice. Yet as we were leaving the plane, I tapped her on the arm and asked if she was a Buddhist. She smiled and replied, "I am spiritual but not religious."

What does it mean to be spiritual but not religious? I maintain that what all religions have in common are people, and that what differentiates religion from other types of discourses such as economics, politics, and art is that through religion, people engage with what they perceive as "ultimate reality," that which shapes but is also perceived as separate from ordinary reality and that is experienced as overwhelmingly valuable.²³ My understanding of religion, however, is at odds with designers, reviewers, and many users of smartphone mindful apps such as buddhify². Like the woman in seat 23A, people using such apps tend to understand religion as being opposed to spirituality and use the term "religion" to indicate oppressive forms of organized institutions that they perceive as having lost their authentic search for divine expression and reserve spirituality to designate a deeply personal, existential, unique anti-institutional focus on personal exploration and spontaneity. Smartphone apps make popular religious practice an individual affair that distances users from religious authority and institutions. The app's "Using the Play Wheel" screen gives instructions on how to utilize the application and suggests that buddhify² "can be used at any time" but that this is "best done when somewhere relatively quiet," and it is recommended to "use headphones."

Over the past twenty years there has been a rapid growth in the number of people like the woman on her iPhone in seat 23A who identify as spiritual but not religious and who are leaving mainstream churches to seek their own spiritual quests. No doubt, for most users of Buddhist apps, spirituality is perceived to be deeply personal, heterodoxic, and idiosyncratic. The "spiritual individual," however, is ultimately a social product. As shown by buddhify²'s "together" button, the "individual user" only emerges from the social aspect of the app and shares three features with other users: a focus on personal growth, anti-institutionalism, and spontaneity. First, the app's design focuses on subjective experience and personal psychological growth. The meditation "Shine," for instance, located under the category of "Waking Up," speaks of "the simple technique that we are using. Connecting with the full experience of that memory and doing that so much that you will hopefully have access to it for the rest of the day" (4:44). Second, religious institutions and traditional authority, being tangential, are perceived as casual and transient at best and detrimental at worst to spiritual goals. Buddhify²'s designer Gunatillake wants to distance the smartphone app from any organized religion. As Gunatillake explains, while the app does "instruct in techniques which have been developed through the Buddhist tradition," he did not design the app to be Buddhist. Finally, countering the alienating distractions associated with networked consumer society, an experience of mindfulness allows users to spontaneously experience what they perceive as their true selves.

## CONCLUSION: HAVE YOU TRIED BUDDHIFY²?

After one of buddhify²'s meditations ends, the user can click a button that sends an e-mail to a friend with the subject line "Have you tried buddhify?" Buddhist apps shape religion in popular culture not just because of their content but also because they are a digital communication technology. This chapter has shown that digital media technologies are not neutral conveyers of meaning but mold the messages they communicate and modify our notions of religious community, identity, and reality itself. More than its content, the smartphone app is the spiritual message because of its procedural operations. The chapter has illustrated that the smartphone app buddhify² communicates an experience of mindfulness through a procedural spirituality that creates a temporary spiritual microspace in the hubbub of urban professionals' busy, stressed-out lives. Like other digital devices, the chapter has described the app through the "user experience" of mindfulness and has shown that its "user interface" poaches from video game play.

As seen by the woman in seat 23A, smartphone apps such as buddhify[2] have wormed their way into an increasingly large swath of everyday life, and people have had to scramble to invent new ways of practicing religion. The buddhistgeeks.com website describes Gunatillake as "passionate about what happens when authentic spirituality meets 21st century urban life." "Using this framing," Gunatillake said in the keynote address to the *Generation Wise* Conference on June 3, 2012, "the history of Buddhism can be seen as a history of innovation.... we cannot afford to always look back to anachronistic practice forms if Buddhism is to continue to be relevant and of service to the world—but have to make it our own in our own culture and context."[24]

There is no doubt that digital innovation has melded together spiritual practices and entertainment, lessened traditional religious authority, and created new types of communities and religious identities. Yet does it work? Can smartphone applications be considered authentic forms of spirituality, or are they just temporary fixes, which distract users from religious practice? If authenticity refers to fidelity to an original source, then a smartphone app has at best only a family resemblance to canonical Buddhist sources. Because all religious traditions are humanly constructed, however, ultimately the original Buddhism eludes any empirical search. As the Buddhologist David McMahan reminds us, there has never been a "pure" Buddhism; even the canonical Asian traditions are a "hybrid of what were already hybrid."[25] On the other hand, if authenticity refers to a cultural model of media practices that allow users to explore and create alternative identities and communities in relation to what they perceive as divine, then the Buddhist smartphone app can be considered authentic. Such an existential approach to authenticity explores how adherents frequently adopt, integrate, and adapt media practices in particular ways so that they fit more cohesively with the moral life and expectations of the communities with which they are affiliated.

The danger of mindful smartphone apps such as buddhify² is that by poaching from Asian sources, they become a virtual orientalism. As used in contemporary scholarship, orientalism describes a European ideology that divides the globe into two unequal halves, "East" and "West," and employs this epistemological framework to dominate non-European people and places.[26] As the scholar of religion Jane Iwamura argues elsewhere in this volume, orientalism did not disappear in the postcolonial period starting after World War II. The new American orientalism just became more covert than its European predecessors, operating through a network of popular mass media that display "Asia" in print, broadcast, and now online. In the contemporary American version, which Iwamura describes as "virtual orientalism," actual Asian people and Asian phenomena become even more detached from their representations, and orientalized stereotypes begin to take on their own reality and justify their own truths.[27]

Asian lives matter. Contemporary popular culture Buddhist-inspired smartphone apps are an orientalist symptom of the networked consumer society. For many Americans who engage with Buddhism in popular culture, Asia remains deeply embedded in clichéd and shorthand forms in their practice, which often takes on a manifest destiny that overwrites and dislodges Asian American practices as well as continues racist stereotypes. I contend, however, that buddhify² is both a symptom of and response to the suffering generated by a network consumer life, and that students of popular culture and religion need to understand how the romanticized fantasy about Asia plays a key role in these practices.

Even if a form of virtual orientalism, buddhify² does something. While the other passengers and I on the turbulent flight to North Carolina seemed anxious and stressed, the woman in seat 23A seemed calm, relaxed, and even blissful. Scholars may disagree about popular forms of Buddhism on moral grounds, yet such critics should not throw out the baby with the bathwater. Like the woman in seat 23A, there are an increasing number of actual human beings behind the screens whose religious practices deserve to be fairly investigated and understood. Although digital and mostly performed by Western urban professionals, these are actual people engaging in actual religious practices that obviously satisfy a spiritual craving for those who use the app. I am not calling for students of religion simply to be caretakers and advocates of digital media. I am suggesting that an investigation requires an alternative approach to religion in popular culture, and to Buddhist practitioners more generally, which does not posit them as isolated social misfits, unknowing orientalists, or mindless consumers. Behind the exotic media stereotypes, which are often uncritically perpetuated by academics, lies a largely unexamined territory of popular forms of existentially authentic spirituality. In fact, I contend that the most effective means to counter popular Buddhism's orientalist shortcomings is not to posit a transhistorical, self-identical tradition that has moved from one culture to another, unchanged through the vicissitudes of time. Rather, the Western use of Buddhism in popular culture needs to be decentered and "de-privileged," illustrating that its form of practice, while real and authentic for those who use it, is just one of the many actors on the world stage.

## DISCUSSION QUESTIONS

1. Is using a religious phone app like buddhify[2] an authentic form of religious practice? Why or why not? How do you define authenticity? What group of people does your definition help, and whom does it harm?

2. Discuss the difference between presentation and practice of religion in interactive media like buddhify[2] and forms of media like religious television. How does the type of media affect how religion is practiced in popular culture?

3. Are people who claim to be "spiritual-but-not religious" religious? How are you defining religion? What is the difference between religion and spirituality?

4. Imagine that you had the resources to design an app for a different religion. Name and describe the app. What features would it have? What religious function or purpose would it serve? Who might be drawn to your app, and why? Who might resist the use of your app, and why?

## NOTES

1. My analysis of buddhify[2] is indebted to Joanna Piacenza's excellent, groundbreaking BA thesis, "Mobile Mindfulness: Practicing Digital Religion on Smartphones with Buddhist Meditation Apps" (University of Wisconsin–Madison, 2009), and also to Rachel Wagner and Christopher Accardo's thoughtful book chapter, "Buddhist Apps: Skillful Means or Dharma Dilution," in *Buddhism, the Internet, and Digital Media: The Pixel in the Lotus,* ed. Gregory Price Grieve and Daniel Veidlinger (New York: Routledge, 2015), 134–52. See also Heidi Campbell, and Antonio La Pastina, "How the iPhone Became Divine: New Media, Religion and the Intertextual Circulation of Meaning," *New Media and Society* (2010), doi: 10.1177/1461444810362204. I am standing on their shoulders, and the chapter would simply not have been possible without their pioneering in-depth descriptions and interpretations. Also see Gregory Grieve, *Cyber Zen: Imagining Authentic Buddhist Identity, Community and Religious Practice in the Virtual World of Second Life* (New York: Routledge, 2016); Rachel Wagner, *Godwired: Religion, Ritual, and Virtual Reality* (New York: Routledge, 2012); and Jeff Wilson, *Mindful America: The Mutual Transformation of Buddhist Meditation and American Culture* (Oxford: Oxford University Press, 2014).

2. Mindfulness Everywhere (a). iTunesPreview, "buddhify—mindfulness & meditation for modern life," https://itunes.apple.com/us/app/buddhify-mindfulness-meditation/id687421118?mt = 8.

3. Lulu Chang, "Americans Spend an Alarming Amount of Time Checking Social Media on Their Phone," http://www.digitaltrends.com/mobile/informate-report-social-media-smartphone-use.

4. Mindfulness Everywhere (a).

5. Mindfulness Everywhere (b), www.mindfulnesseverywhere.io.

6. Rohan Gunatillake, "BG 247: Disrupting the Awakening Industry," paper presented at the Buddhist Geeks Conference, 2011, www.buddhistgeeks .com/2012/02/bg-247-disrupting-the-awakening-industry).

7. MG Siegle, "Analyst: There's a Great Future in iPhone Apps," http:// venturebeat.com/2008/06/11/analyst-theres-a-great-future-in-iphone-apps.

8. "comScore Reports December 2012, "U.S. Smartphone Subscriber Market Share." www.comscore.com/Insights/Press-Releases/2013/2/comScore-Reports-December-2012-US-Smartphone-Subscriber-Market-Share.

9. Wilson, *Mindful America*, 187.

10. Mindfulness Everywhere (a). "Media Center," http://buddhify.com /mediacenter.

11. Joseph Goldstein. *Mindfulness: A Practical Guide to Awakening* (New York: Sounds True, 2013), 13.

12. Gunatillake, "BG 247."

13. Matt Johnston, "I've Been Using a Meditation App on My Phone for a Week and It's Changing My Life," *Business Insider,* www.businessinsider.com /ive-been-using-a-meditation-app-on-my-phone-for-a-week-and-its-changing-my-life-2015-3.

14. Ian Bogost, *Persuasive Games: The Expressive Power of Videogames* (Cambridge, MA: MIT Press, 2007).

15. Catherine Bell, *Ritual Theory/Ritual Practice* (Oxford: Oxford University Press, 1992), 140.

16. Ibid., 141.

17. Marshal McLuhan. *Understanding Media: The Extensions of Man* (New York: McGraw-Hill, 1964), 15–16.

18. On classical sources for mindful breathing, see Steven Hein and Dale Wright, eds., *The Zen Canon: Understanding the Classic Texts* (Oxford: Oxford University Press, 2004). On Protestantism, see Richard Bauman, "Let Your Words Be Few: Speaking and Silence in Quaker Ideology," in *Let Your Words Be Few: Symbolism of Speaking and Silence among Seventeenth-Century Quakers* (Cambridge: Cambridge University Press, 1983), 20–31.

19. Nick Pelling, "The (Short) Prehistory of 'Gamification," Funding Start-ups (& Other Impossibilities), https://nanodome.wordpress.com/2011/08/09 /the-short-prehistory-of-gamification.[20] Johan Huizinga, *Homo Ludens: A Study of the Play-Element in Culture* (New York: Routledge & Kegan Paul, 1980), 10.

21. Wagner and Accardo, "Buddhist Apps," 134; Wagner, *Godwired,* 111.

22. D.W. Winnicott, *Playing and Reality* (London: Penguin Books, 1971), 163, 120.

23. Paul Tillich, *Dynamics of Faith* (1956; New York: Perennial Classics, 2001).

24. Rohan Gunatillake, "Generation Wise—My Future Everything Keynote," paper presented in Manchester, England, June 2012, http://rohan gunatillake.com/blog/generation-wise-my-future-everything-keynote.

25. David McMahan, *The Making of Buddhist Modernism* (Oxford: Oxford University Press, 2008), 19.

26. Edward Said, *Orientalism* (New York: Vintage Books, 1979).

27. See Jane Naomi Iwamura, "The Oriental Monk in American Popular Culture," chapter 2 in this volume; and see also Iwamura, *Virtual Orientalism: Asian Religions and American Popular Culture* (Oxford: Oxford University Press, 2011), 8.

# PART III

# Popular Culture as Religion

In *Religion and Popular Culture in America,* "religion" and "culture" are presented as conceptually separate and distinct categories. Indeed the title proclaims this, and Bruce Forbes' "Finding Religion in Unexpected Places" lays out four distinct relationships between religion and popular culture that provide structure to the volume. This is really a rhetorical contrivance. There is not some ideal form of religion separable from its expressions in particular cultural locations. However by imagining religion and popular culture as distinct, we hope to see more clearly the ways in which they are in fact inseparable.

The attempt to relate religion and popular culture is a work of comparison. We understand one thing by relating it to another. Even the essays in this section, which argue that certain expressions of popular culture can be thought of as forms of religion, rest on comparison. The example from popular culture, whether it is fandom, shopping, weight loss, or sports, is argued to be religion based on comparison to other things we recognize as religion.

We can go a step further. The effort to define religion itself is a comparative work. In coming in contact for the first time with other peoples' religions, or in considering new religious movements, people often describe the elements they regard as essential to religion and then use the presence or absence of these elements as evidence of whether this new thing is in fact religion or not. Catherine Albanese's distinction between *substantive, functional,* and *formal* definitions of religion, which was cited in Bruce Forbes introduction to this volume "Finding Religion in Unexpected Places," is useful in understanding what leads someone to argue that something we think of as popular culture is, or is like, religion. Does the person who makes this argument imagine that there is some *substantive* essence of religion, typically an ability to connect us to a higher being that is the essence of religion that we also see in popular culture? Does she define religion by its *function* in human communities and notice that some forms of popular culture also seem to accomplish these same functions? Or is there a particular *form* or pattern to religion? Does it have recognizable elements such as sacred stories, places and communities, and/or moral codes, which if found in popular culture suggests the presence of religion?

There is a power in naming things, in including them in or out of the category of "religion." European colonizers often denied that the Africans, Native Americans, and Asians they colonized had religion. Dismissing their beliefs and practices as superstitions dehumanized them, making it easier to exploit their labor and lands. On the other hand, in an era when social attitudes about religion are more ambiguous, some scientists are offended by the suggestion that science might be thought of as a religion with its own beliefs, practices, and explanations of human origins. Each of these discussions of whether something is, or is not, religion rests on a prior definition of religion.

In, "Popular Culture *as Religion*," readers will find essays which most nearly collapse the distinction between religion and popular culture. Unlike the authors of other essays in the volume, who maintain the distinctions between religion and popular culture, these authors consider the possibility that cultural activities that are usually thought of as secular can function as religion, at least for some of those who participate in them. Comparison leads the authors to think that religion and popular culture are not so different. It will be helpful, in reading the essays to think about what definitions of religion are explicitly or implicitly at work in proclaiming that some example of popular culture should be understood as religion.

Another difference in approach is that these authors are less focused on the content of popular culture, on its stories, objects, images and sounds. Instead they direct the reader's attention to the audience for those stories. They do not think of the people who consume popular culture as passive recipients of content. They study how they interact with it, sometimes remaking the stories as part of their own projects of identity formation. For these authors, the evidence that popular culture might sometimes be religion is not found primarily in the content of stories themselves but in the way that people engage, discuss, and reenact them in their own imaginative lives. Most often, but not exclusively, these claims rest on formal or functional understandings of religion.

These essays raise interesting questions about religion and the nature and location of the sacred. Religions typically regard the power, being, or realm that gives their practice meaning as sacred. Things, places, or practices are sacred because they relate those who practice this religion to this sacred realm. As the term "sacred texts" suggests, religious writings are themselves often thought of as sacred and are treated as though they were themselves extensions of a deity. So for instance, in Jewish worship the Torah is treated as a holy object tied closely to the holiness of the God it reveals. When, during WWII, Nazis destroyed Torah scrolls both they and Jews regarded this as an attack on more than material objects. The essays in this section rest on a somewhat different approach to religion. The authors of the essays in this section may take religious texts quite seriously; but they assume that the sacred is not found in particular texts, objects, or spaces alone but also in what people do with them.

In this way of thinking popular cultural stories and practices are seen as potentially religious because people use them in ritual practices of meaning making, just as they do with material from more traditional forms of religion. Rather than asking what religion's core elements are and then identifying other religions by how clearly they contain the elements identified as crucial, they are more likely to ask what religion's function is. Assuming that religion serves some societal purpose, they explore what religion does for individuals and societies. Traditional answers to this question include the suggestions that religion provides social cohesion, that it answers ultimate questions (i.e., why are we here? what happens after death?), that it is a form of social control particularly of sexuality, or that it provides rites of passage. Not everyone agrees about what this function is. Some see religion as a tool of social stability and control while others believe it can function as an agent of social change. However they understand the function of religion, the authors of the chapters in this section proceed comparatively to argue that if popular culture serves these same functions for people then popular culture serves as religion.

The suggestion that popular culture fandom can be a religion is contested, even among the fans themselves. For instance, many of the very people who make *shrines* to Elvis that seem to observers to be modeled on sites of Roman Catholic devotion, or who make what they and others describe as *pilgrimages* to Graceland (the singer's home in Memphis), and who report that they find comfort and guidance in his music, deny that these are religious practices. Commentators who draw on formal definitions of religion may point out the use of religious language and parallels with religious practices. Others, using functional definitions of religion, suggest that the veneration of Elvis serves the same purpose as more traditional forms of religion. Yet, drawing on substantive understandings of religion, most Elvis fans reject this and many regard the suggestion as a sacrilege to their other, often Catholic or Evangelical, practices. Should scholars respect their reservations?

There are problems with simply letting participants decide. Some religionists think that theirs is the only true religion. Scholars do not want to define religion so subjectively; we strive for definitions that are broad enough to include a wide range of religious expressions without being so broad that everything becomes potentially a form of religion. Careful definition is crucial in arguing that something is or is not religion.

Whether working from a substantive, functional, or formalist understanding of religion, most discussions of religion and popular culture follow what can be called the "looks like a duck" school of understanding religion. That is, like the folk wisdom about the duck, if it looks like religion it probably is religion. The problem of course is to be clear about what the duck looks like, which elements of duckness, or religiousness, are most important and to be open to new forms of duckness that require us to question our original definition. Good comparison begins with clearly expressed assumptions about what we think constitutes religion, but new examples may require us to expand our definitions.

It is useful to raise the question of what the author thinks constitutes religion with any of the essays in this volume, but this is particularly helpful in thinking about these essays. In "It's about Faith in our Future" Michael Jindra examines the fandom that has grown up around the *Star Trek* movies and television series. Jindra's title points to an interest in religion's power to answer ultimate questions, which might suggest a substantive understanding of religion. Yet he also makes comparisons that seem rooted in a more functional approach to religion. In "A religion of Shopping and Consumption," Sarah McFarland Taylor explores the way that consumption itself comes to be seen as a center of meaning and value in the U.S. today and looks at shopping malls as places that are potentially sacred centers for this activity. Though shopping seems on the surface quite different from fandom, we see these authors involved in similar projects of definitions and comparison. In contrast to those who think about popular culture primarily as a matter of popular entertainments like film, music videos, and comic books, Taylor and Michelle Lelwica study popular practices. While we might argue that shopping and body image are ways of telling stories about ourselves, this seems quite different than the more overt storytelling of *Star Trek*. Lelwica is particularly attentive to the ways in which religion can be a form of social control. In "Losing Their Way to Salvation" she looks at the societal pressures which encourage women to embrace what she calls a religion of thinness. Joseph Price sees religion's ability to create social coherence and a sense of belonging in "The 'Godding Up' of American Sports." He argues that sports go beyond mere game playing. Whether we participate or watch sports, they function as a center of unity and identity much in the way that religion does. Each of these essays begins with assumptions about how religion is to be defined and understood. The section concludes with a cautionary essay. In

"Celebrity Worship as Parareligion" Pete Ward uses a study of celebrity worship to argue that careful comparison suggests that there are things religion does that popular culture does not accomplish. For him, popular culture can be *like* religion, and the comparison can clarify both how popular culture functions and the nature of religion itself, but for him they remain categorically different. What sort of definition of religion leads him to that conclusion?

Jeffrey H. Mahan
Iliff School of Theology

# CHAPTER ELEVEN

# It's About Faith In Our Future

## Star Trek *Fandom as Cultural Religion*

### MICHAEL JINDRA

Over the past century, Americans have been entertained and inspired by vivid, captivating narratives presented in new visual media, from *The Wizard of Oz* to the *Davy Crockett* series of the 1950s, to franchises such as *Star Wars, Harry Potter,* and the *Marvel* universe. Increasingly, popular culture has become an influential, even dominating, force in many areas of our society. As the essays in this volume make clear, popular culture often draws upon religious themes, but in this essay I argue that the entertainment industry also creates meanings that begin to function in religious ways for consumers of popular culture.

This should not be too surprising, for there has always been a relationship between religion and popular culture. Popular culture originally split from "learned," formal religious culture after the Protestant and Catholic Reformations,[1] but it continued to complement religious culture. The pre-Lenten Carnival was a direct product of Church culture, as were the patron saint festivals and the cults of images of early modern Europe. Because of this close connection, popular culture was not a completely distinct alternative to religious culture.

Today, however, popular culture has taken on a life of its own, creating its own stories and myths through which people find meaning and identity. Popular culture has become an independent producer of mythical narratives, a reflection of cultural themes and a producer of new ones. Though often using indirect religious themes and imagery (as in *Star Wars* or *Harry Potter),* the narratives and messages have been formally cut off from the religious traditions that have dominated Western culture over the centuries. In other words, parts of popular culture have taken their place alongside the mainstream religious traditions, ideologies, and narratives that have guided people's lives.[2]

There is no better example of this than the *Star Trek* fan phenomenon. As a television and movie production, *Star Trek* has gone through several installments, but the fan phenomenon it sparked has been going strong since the original *Star Trek* was first broadcast in 1966. Its fandom first became apparent when the original *Star Trek* television series was threatened with cancellation after its second year. Fans immediately organized a letter-writing campaign to keep *Star Trek* on the air.[3] When it was canceled after its third year, the show went into syndication, which is when its fan phenomenon started to take off. The first *Star Trek* convention was in New York in 1972, and soon noncommercial *Star Trek* fan magazines ("fanzines") and commercial *Star Trek* books, manuals, and novels were being published for fans hungry for more knowledge about the *Star Trek* universe.

Efforts to revive *Star Trek* broadcasts, in some form, continued for years. After an animated series in the 1970s, the first *Star Trek* movie was released in 1979. In 1987, *Star Trek: The Next Generation* was first aired, and during its seven-year run, this series was often the highest-rated hour-long show among males 19 to 49 years of age, and a top-rated show among other viewer categories, including females. This success led to still more spinoffs, including *Deep Space Nine, Voyager,* and *Enterprise,* which led to a sense that the franchise was overexposed.[4] The last series went off the air in 2005, yet there has been a continual stream of new movies and, of course, reruns, with a new series coming out in 2017, though some of this new material has been controversial among fans who expect *Star Trek* to be historically, philosophically, and stylistically consistent. As explained below, fans have played a major role in keeping the franchise alive and even taking it over through various fan productions of *Star Trek* installments.

No other popular culture phenomenon has shown the depth and breadth of fan activity of *Star Trek*. Other popular culture productions, such as *Star Wars*, have also sold billions of dollars in merchandise, but no other fan following has been so active in creatively filling out its alternate universe and attempting to relate it to the real world. Besides the over five hundred "official" *Star Trek* novels, fans have self-published countless "fanzines," written several dictionaries of *Star Trek* alien languages, and created institutes (e.g., www.kli.org) through which to study them. Fans have created hundreds of fan clubs, attended thousands of conventions, and engaged in endless online discussions on Facebook and other sites; they play *Star Trek* simulations with other fans over the Internet, participate in live action role-playing and computer gaming, and buy tickets to *Star Trek* "experiences" and tourist sites. They also produce their own professionally done *Star Trek* films and episodes (e.g. *New Voyages, Axnar,* and *Horizon*). The fans have been highlighted in the documentary *Trekkies* and both the franchise and fans have been parodied in innumerable places, including movies such as *Galaxy Quest* and *Free Enterprise,* and a 2002 episode of *Futurama* that projected a future in which *Star Trek's* fandom had grown into a religion. Meanwhile, reruns of various *Star Trek* installments have been broadcast in over one hundred countries. Captains Kirk, Picard, Mr. Spock, and the spaceship *Enterprise* have become household names around the world.

## STAR TREK AS A RELIGIOUS PHENOMENON?

When I first undertook research on the fan phenomenon back in 1992, my earliest intention was to focus on how *Star Trek* draws a picture of the future that is attractive to many Americans. Early on, however, I realized I was dealing with something much bigger and more complex than I had anticipated. As I will show in this essay, *Star Trek* is not limited to science fiction fans, nor is it just a pop culture phenomenon created for corporate profit.

Instead, *Star Trek* fandom seemed akin to a religious movement. It has features that parallel a religious movement: an origin myth, a set of beliefs, organizations, and some of the most active and creative members found anywhere. Fans fill out a mythological universe and keep it consistent through the formation of a "canon" of acceptable and unacceptable *Star Trek* events. Within fandom, there are also the schisms and oppositions that such movements typically engender. Finally, there is a stigma associated with *Star Trek* fans that is similar to that directed against serious devotees of other religions. To address *Star Trek* as a religious phenomenon, however, we first need to understand the place of religion in our society, how it is changing, and what it is changing into.

### RELIGION IN CONTEMPORARY AMERICAN SOCIETY

Most Americans think of "religion" as a system of private, conscious, articulated beliefs, usually expressed in churches and formal creeds, and set off from the other "spheres" of life such as work, politics, or leisure. This view of religion, however, stems from the specifically Western process of societal "differentiation,"[5] in which institutional religion was given a specific function. After the medieval era, when religious practice was more intimately connected to everyday life, the practice of Christianity became "abstracted," or disconnected from everyday life.[6] As a result, we now tend to regard "religion" as something connected to institutions such as churches and denominations. Alternatively, we view it as something personal and private, a psychological aid that is only peripherally connected to a person's public life.

This view of religion severely limits our understanding of it. A less ethnocentric definition sees religious elements throughout our society.[7] In many cultures, religion is not articulated as "belief," but is more often an ongoing experience, lived out and taken for granted.[8] But we often fail to recognize religion in our own society when it lacks an institutional and creedal form, and is instead "disguised" in various political or cultural forms. The fact that nearly every group has a religious dimension is regarded as obvious in many parts of the world, but is foreign to us, and this makes us blind to religious aspects in many areas of our lives.[9]

Since at least the nineteenth century, scholars such as August Comte have been predicting the imminent downfall of religion in society. Religion may now be more "segregated" into its own private sphere, but Christianity has remained a potent force. New forms of religion have also developed, many of which are individualistic and express belief in the power of humanity and our mastery over the environment, whether through science or quasi-scientific or mystical philosophies. These modern-day beliefs are expressed in many areas of our culture, including popular culture, as Bruce David Forbes makes clear in the introduction to this volume. "New age" groups, for example, favor smaller networks and reject large-scale organization, but have a commonality fostered by commercialization and expressed in popular culture. In this essay, I argue that *Star Trek* is also a primary location for the expression of contemporary religious impulses.

## SOMETHING TO "BELIEVE" IN: THE WORLDVIEW OF *STAR TREK*

*Star Trek* is one of the most visible locations to witness religion in popular culture. Not only does it have an identifiable belief system and vision of the future, but the activities of its adherents are oriented toward participating in that vision and bringing it to fruition. *Star Trek* is a subset of the larger category of science fiction, which itself has been called a religion with a "central myth" of progress that "helps people live in or into the future." Science and technology are the vehicles by which this future will be brought into existence "and should be understood in religious terms" as that which "breathes new life into humankind."[10]

The "positive view of the future" portrayed in *Star Trek* is one of the most common reasons fans give for their attraction to the show.[11] On *Star Trek*, problems such as poverty, war, and disease have been eliminated on Earth, and threats are normally from alien forces. Faith is placed in the ability of humanity to solve its social and technical problems through the application of reason, science, and technology.

*Star Trek* mixes the scientific and technical ideals of America with its egalitarian ideology to produce a progressive world where people from all races work together in a vast endeavor to expand knowledge. One fan, recounting his first impressions of *Star Trek*, said: "We noticed people of various races, genders and planetary origins working together. Here was a future it did not hurt to imagine. Here was a constructive tomorrow for mankind, emphasizing exploration and expansion."[12]

This utopianism can be traced back to notions of Christian eschatology that foresee, in the context of a linear history, a future perfection. Also tied in with utopian impulses is the Western notion of "order" out of which came the "project" of the West, that of universal assimilation.[13] On the heels of these beliefs have come many utopian religious movements, and political "sacred projects" like orthodox Marxism. It is this culture-wide ideological inclination toward future utopias that *Star Trek* fandom draws upon.[14]

The belief in progress and a "positive view of the future" was explicitly articulated by the late creator of *Star Trek*, Gene Roddenberry. In 1991, just months before he died, a 30-page interview with Roddenberry was published in *The Humanist*, the official magazine of the American Humanist Association, to which Roddenberry had belonged since 1986. In it, he reveals that he had a very conscious humanist philosophy that saw humans taking control of their own destiny, and thus able to control the future. Roddenberry's intention was to express his philosophy in *Star Trek*, but he had to keep this intention secret lest the network cancel his show.[15]

Others besides Roddenberry have used *Star Trek* to express their philosophy publicly. Jeffrey Mills has taught courses at various colleges on

"The Cultural Relevance of *Star Trek.*" He points to the Prime Directive (forbidding interference in another culture), the pluralistic Vulcan philosophy of IDIC (Infinite Diversity in Infinite Combination), and the cooperative governing structure of the United Federation of Planets as the kinds of ideas that we need to act on if we are to survive into the twenty-fourth century. By watching *Star Trek,* studying it, and applying its lessons, we can make the world a better place, Mills has written. "[I]n this light *Star Trek* almost becomes a sort of scripture, doesn't it? What the Bible does in 66 books, *Star Trek* does in 79 episodes.... I can't think of a series that really spoke to the future of humankind with as much clarity and vision as *Star Trek.*"[16]

In sum, *Star Trek* has strong affinities with a religious outlook, namely, an underlying ideology and mythology that ties together messages about human nature and normative statements about social life with a construction and presentation of future society.[17] Fans see *Star Trek* as a sign of hope for the future: not for personal salvation, but for the future of the collective "we," our society, our species. It is a myth about where we have come from and where we are going. Through their participation in fan activities, fans have shown they want to be a part of forming that destiny.

## THE FANDOM COMMUNITY

*Star Trek* as a religious phenomenon can be understood as a set of beliefs, but the activities of its fans give us a much fuller picture of its religious potential. *Star Trek* fandom is in part the culmination of a phenomenon that began in the post–World War I era, when science fiction pulp magazines had a small but loyal readership. From the beginning, science fiction fans formed a group set apart from the rest of society. These fans formed a community: "fans married fans and raised their children to be fans; there are third- and even fourth-generation fans beginning to show up these days at the 'cons'" [conventions]," Frederik Pohl wrote as long ago as 1989.[18]

It was out of science fiction fandom that the first *Star Trek* fans came. The story of the origin and growth of *Star Trek* fandom has itself taken on mythological proportions. A preview of the pilot episode of *Star Trek*, shown at a science fiction convention in 1966, is recounted almost in terms of a conversion experience: "After the film was over we were unable to leave our seats. We just nodded at each other and smiled, and began to whisper," Allan Asherman writes. "We came close to lifting the man [Roddenberry] upon our shoulders and carrying him out of the room ... he smiled, and we returned the smile before we converged on him."[19] From then on, according to Asherman, the convention was divided into two factions: the "enlightened" who had seen the preview and the "unenlightened" who had not.

Soon after *Star Trek* was first broadcast, fans formed organizations. Star Trek fan clubs grew into a diverse worldwide circuit of clubs, with, at the show's peak, over five hundred clubs and chapters in nearly twenty countries. Many of these clubs are modeled on Star Trek ships in a fan attempt at participation in the Star Trek universe. Hierarchy is established within each club by the titles given to leaders (Admiral, Captain, etc.). Members move up the hierarchy by being active in group events, much like in the Boy Scouts. Many fan clubs stress community service projects, which distinguishes them from a mere fan group and underlies the seriousness with which they take their beliefs about building a better world. Star Trek fans often describe their fellow fans and clubs as a "family." They celebrate personal milestones such as birthdays and anniversaries, and console each other over misfortunes and personal deaths, using Star Trek ideals to give hope.[20] Many remark that they are closer to fellow fans than they are to their own family members. Fans often meet at *Star Trek* conventions. One fan described a convention in the following way:

> If you've never been to a convention, it's an experience that is difficult to explain. It's like being ushered into another world, where every facet of the day has something to do with STAR TREK. It might be seeing the incredible variety of merchandise in the dealers' room or seeing a star of the series in

person and having the opportunity to ask questions. To describe it as a time warp would not be far from wrong. You're very much cut off from the real world in a convention. You can easily forget your own troubles as well as those of the world until the con ends and you have to come down to earth again.[21]

In other words, conventions are an opportunity to immerse oneself further in the *Star Trek* "experience," much as one is immersed in ritual. Using the religious language of "immersion" is not just a rhetorical move on my part. Witness the following response to a questionnaire I sent out over the Internet:

At a convention I went to a while back they had this thing about the "Temple of Trek." I stayed and watched—even participated in the chanting. They had some woman who was there with her baby—fairly newborn. And they "baptized" the kid into this pseudo-church. Pretty bizarre—even though it was all just a joke. But I must admit—I was kind of wondering at the time if everyone there was really taking it all as a joke.

This ambiguity over the seriousness of *Star Trek* practice reveals its underlying religious sensibility.

Fan activities that seek to promote a family atmosphere are in a sense "symbolic communities" that resist the secularization and rationalization of modern life.[22] Yet there is a paradox here if we seek to apply this to *Star Trek* fandom, because the ideology expressed in *Star Trek* and adhered to by many of the fans is an expression of rationalistic modernism itself, the progressive belief that we can construct a better tomorrow. In other words, the modernism that is exemplified by *Star Trek* is, in the final analysis, itself a faith that is practiced in the various types of communities that make up *Star Trek* fandom.

## STAR TREK TOURISM, PILGRIMAGE, AND PARTICIPATION

For fans, *Star Trek* exhibitions and tourist sites have become popular places where fans can see and experience the *Star Trek* universe up close. The Universal Studios theme park in California had a *Star Trek* set in which selected tourists were filmed, in full uniform, taking on characters' roles and acting out a *Star Trek* plot. I visited one fan who proudly showed me the video of her visit there. The scenes of role-playing tourists were spliced with actual footage from one of the movies, giving the appearance that they were actually part of a *Star Trek* film. This fan described the experience "as a dream come true," which made the 2,000-mile trip "worthwhile." "We pilgrimage out there; it's our Mecca," she told me. Another fan showed me numerous pictures of herself posing in uniform on a mock-up of the Enterprise bridge that was built for a convention. It is the fan's dream to actually be on the show, and the closest thing to it are bridge mock-ups and studio tours. The ritual act of sitting on the bridge in uniform and being photographed or filmed brings one into direct participation in the *Star Trek* universe.

Participation in the *Star Trek* universe is even more direct through "simming" (playing *Star Trek* simulations over the Internet with other fans), or live-action role-playing ("larping"). These games allow fans to take a position as a crew member on a "ship" and role-play adventures with other fans. Fans move up through the ranks as they gain experience. As one player described it, simming "allows anyone who embraces the precept of *Star Trek* and its premises of a bright future to be a part of that future," by providing "their own unique interpretations of how the future might look or how far 'we' might evolve in our quest for knowledge and our thirst for exploration."[23]

Finally, fans participate in the *Star Trek* universe by buying *Star Trek* merchandise and amassing collections of episodes and movies, a "capturing" of the *Star Trek* universe that enables fans to enter it at any time. Religion often points us to another world; *Star Trek* does the same.

## LINKING THE STAR TREK UNIVERSE WITH THE PRESENT

The *Star Trek* universe is not a totally separate, fantastical universe unconnected to the present. In various ways, the *Star Trek* universe is "linked" with the contemporary world. The lead-in to every *Next Generation* episode ("Space: the final frontier. These are the voyages of the Starship *Enterprise* ... ") begins with a close-up of Earth, and then a gradual "tour" through the other planets of the solar system, until the camera finally focuses on the *Enterprise*. This sequence orients the viewer to envision the events as taking place in his own universe.

Fans, however, have made the strongest efforts to link *Star Trek* with the present. Originally it was through *Star Trek* manuals and novels, such as *Star Trek Chronology: A History of the Future*, though much of this material is now online at places like memory-alpha.wikia.com, Reddit or Wikipedia, or in commentary such as the 2013 volume *Star Trek and History*.[24] One main activity is to compile a timeline of the universe, incorporating both actual historical events and *Star Trek* history through the twenty-fourth century. This world is a direct projection from the present into the future, as a hoped-for alternate universe. Furthermore, through time travel, many of the show's plots actually take place in twentieth-century time. One fan I talked to focused on how space and time is manipulated in time travel plots, which allows one "a second chance ... to set things right again." Time travel allows us this ritualistic recourse, in much the same way healing rituals or rituals based on origin myths do. Origin myths often take place "in the beginning," but are really a message for all time, a cosmological model to be attained, enacted through ritual.[25]

*Star Trek,* like a religion, has profound effects on fans' lives. Actors often relate how fans have been inspired by the show to do well in school and eventually become engineers, doctors, or scientists.[26] *Star Trek* has given people hope for the future, inspiring them to take control of their lives in the same way many self-help movements and quasi-religions do.[27] Fans also want to make "real" life more like *Star Trek*. *Star Trek* fans have been enthusiastic supporters of increased funding for the space program, and science fiction becomes science fact when "fans actively engineer events to make it true,"[28] such as by naming the first space shuttle prototype the USS *Enterprise*. Fans also point to devices such as the communicator, which foreshadowed today's cellphones.

234 / Popular Culture as Religion

## FILLING OUT STAR TREK AND
## MAKING IT "REAL"

*Star Trek*, like many other shows, actively encourages a "suspension of disbelief" and sets itself up as a "reality" in which fans can exist. The reality of this universe is important to many people. "I believe in *Star Trek*. It's all within the realm of possibility," Richard Weiss, former head of Phillips Labs, a California rocket-technology facility, and an "avowed trekkie," has said.[29] *"Star Trek* isn't about a television series, it's about faith in our future," according to Dale Adams, who quit his job as an aerospace engineer to sell *Star Trek* merchandise.[30]

One major fan activity has been to "fill out" the *Star Trek* universe. Reference books such as the *Star Trek Encyclopedia* and "technical manuals" with detailed specifications of starships have been among the most popular.[31] Dictionaries have been compiled for several of the languages of *Star Trek* alien species, such as Klingon and Vulcan. The entire history, geography, philosophy, and even the purported location of the planet Vulcan has been described, sometimes with the full cooperation of people at academic institutions and even NASA.[32] The *Star Trek* universe has been filled out with just about everything to make it a full, consistent reality, to enable one to live within this universe. This universe is much larger and more complex than any other fictional universe, including Tolkien's *The Lord of the Rings* and the game somewhat based on it, Dungeons & Dragons. *Star Wars* has also become an extremely popular universe, but without the relative realism and science found in *Star Trek*.[33]

The coherence of this alternate universe must be maintained in order for fans to continue their "suspension of disbelief," and fans actively work to maintain a *Star Trek* "canon." For most of its history, canon was defined as the series and movies, but this became more contentious when Paramount, the owners of Star Trek, overexposed it in the early 2000s and series like *Enterprise* (2001–5) and the first "reboot" movie (2009) were seen to contradict the established Star Trek canon/

history. Fans began to question Paramount and asserted their own authority in maintaining the canon, by among other things, producing their own installments.

The fans of *Star Trek* have taken this given universe of *Star Trek*—the canon—and filled it out in order to make a consistent, idealistic world in which science has given us control over the problems of life we experience and read about in the papers. Ironically, in order to complete the *Star Trek* universe, both the creators of the show and the fans have to rely on both science and magic. The technology used is given a veneer of scientific reality, but most fans recognize that most of the technology is made up, and is thus closer to magic. Science thus turns into magic, a state of affairs anticipated in new religions where magic/science is relied upon to provide control in areas outside our ability to master.[34]

I would argue that all of this fan creativity—the invention and filling out of an entire universe—is a creation of mythology similar to processes of mythological creation in other cultures through the ages. The anthropologist Claude Levi-Strauss uses the term *bricoleur* (French for "handyman") to illustrate the process of creating mythology: *bricoleurs* use the available "tools" and "materials" of the culture to create a mythological structure over a period of time.[35] *Star Trek* fan *bricoleurs* act, not on their own culture, but on the alternative (but related) one they have constructed. Creating new plots and stories and ironing out existing ones—discussing the canon and writing new fan literature to fill in gaps in character biographies, planet details, or technology—is essentially a way to resolve the contradictions that are an affront to the consistent universe fans so desperately want to create.

In calling the activities of *Star Trek* fandom "mythological," I do not intend to eliminate the "playful" or entertainment aspect of *Star Trek* and claim that it is only serious. Play is serious business, as Victor Turner makes clear in his discussion of the ludic aspects of ritual.[36] In industrial societies, however, play and seriousness have become separated. *Star Trek* fandom, I believe, is an example of play and ritual coming back together, back to their "natural" condition of coexistence and ambiguity, as in live-action role-playing. *Star Trek* fandom does not have the thoroughgoing seriousness of more established religions, but it is not mere entertainment. This interplay of seriousness and entertainment, I argue, is a sign of its vitality.

Religious movements are often persecuted or looked down upon because of their zealousness. And indeed, there is a stigma associated with *Star Trek* fandom.[37] Non-fans react against the "seriousness" of *Star Trek* because they believe it should remain totally in the realm of entertainment, and the fact that people take it seriously offends them. *Star Trek* fans, in turn, want to be respected and understood, and want their devotion to be recognized as legitimate, even as many of them try to distance themselves from a segment of fans whom they believe to have gone "too far" in their fan activities. *Star Trek* elicits this type of controversy because it exists in the liminal area between entertainment and seriousness. It is in this interplay between "seriousness and diversion," a common feature of religion,[38] that we see the roots of the tension over *Star Trek* between its fandom and the general public.

### CONCLUSION

Fans have become the guardians of the *Star Trek* universe through their own productions of *Star Trek* episodes and films,[39] and through their online discussions and other fan activities. In a society that has become more diverse or polarized, mass popular culture has become a new unifying element, allowing groups to coalesce around shared concerns. By providing a certain commonality and unity of purpose for a wide variety of people, *Star Trek* takes on many elements of "civil religion": a generalizing of religious belief necessary for an integrated society, as a counter to pluralizing trends that divide society. In the United States, it is expressed in a sense of national purpose and destiny, and includes notions of both moral and material progress.[40] These humanistic ideals become a model for others. This is exactly what seems to have happened by the time of *Star Trek's* United Federation of Planets, the guardian of universal peace, prosperity, and self-determination, and a direct outgrowth of twentieth-century American faith in science, humanity, and a positive future. Fans latch on to the *Star Trek* vision that these ideals will eventually triumph, and they enthusiastically continue to fill out and participate in the *Star Trek* universe.

Americans are traditionally forward-looking, and it is events like the space race that animate them. For many fans of popular culture, organized religion seems less relevant, partly because they perceive it as backward-looking rather than forward-looking. Exceptions are to be found among some conservative religious denominations that speak in specific terms about the future, but enthusiasm for mainline denominations is lacking among baby boomers, who regard them primarily as community organizations that can teach their children good values.[41]

Meanwhile, popular culture, especially television and film, attempts to fill the religious void. In the ways described above, *Star Trek* has become a "cultural religion" (as discussed in the introduction to this volume) that reflects many Americans' most widely held beliefs. *Star Trek* fandom expresses Americans' idealism and offers fans reasons for hope in the future. In this sense, it is a phenomenon born in popular culture that has taken on serious religious functions.

### DISCUSSION QUESTIONS

1. If fandom shapes the values and actions of participants, what are some examples of those values and actions among *Star Trek* fans or other fan groups you may know of?

2. Is Jindra saying that *Star Trek* fandom is a religion, or that it is like a religion? What would be the difference? What definition of religion is he using in making his argument? What do we learn about religion and about popular culture by looking at them through the lens of fandom?

3. The conclusion to this chapter claims that many people perceive organized religion as "backward-looking rather than forward-

looking." The author says that popular culture, including *Star Trek,* attempts to fill "the religious void." Do you agree with this analysis? Why or why not?

4. Imagine, describe, and discuss a fan event for a movie or television show popular with your peers. What would happen at the event? How would fans express their fandom? What values does the event express for the fans? Why do you think this particular popular culture phenomenon is popular at this time in history?

## NOTES

"It About Faith in Our Future: *Star Trek* Fandom as Cultural Religion" by Michael Jindra is adapted from "*Star Trek* Fandom as a Religious Phenomenon," in *Sociology of Religion,* the journal of the Association for the Sociology of Religion, Inc., 55: 27–51, 1994. ©Association for the Sociology of Religion, Inc.

1. Peter Burke, *Popular Culture in Early Modern Europe* (New York: Harper & Row, 1978).

2. Christian Smith, *Moral, Believing Animals* (New York: Oxford University Press, 2003).

3. Bjo Trimble, *On the Good Ship Enterprise: My 15 Years with "Star Trek"* (Norfolk, VA: Donning, 1983), 22ff.

4. Ina Rae Hark, "Franchise Fatigue: The Marginalization of the Television Series after The Next Generation," in *The Influence of Star Trek on Television, Film and Culture,* ed. Lincoln Geraghty (Jefferson, NC: McFarland, 2008), 41–62.

5. Olivier Tschannen, "The Secularization Paradigm: A Systematization," *Journal for the Scientific Study of Religion* 30 (1991): 395–415.

6. Talal Asad, "Anthropological Conceptions on Religion: Reflections on Geertz," *Man* 18 (1983): 237–59, 245.

7. Though the functional definition of religion, discussed in the volume introduction, fits ST fandom the best, scholars such as Martin Riesebrodt in *The Promise of Salvation* (2010) are turning to a tighter definition of religion. Fandom wouldn't fit this definition, but would fit into the category of "spiritual" or quasi-religion, or possibly as a "sacred project"; see, e.g., Christian Smith, *The Sacred Project of American Sociology* (New York: Oxford University Press, 2014).

8. Jean Pouillon, "Remarks on the Verb, 'to believe,'" in *Between Belief and Transgression: Structuralist Essays in Religion, History, and Myth,* ed. Michel Izard and Pierre Smith (Chicago: University of Chicago Press, 1982), 1–8.

9. For an understanding of how religion has changed its form, see Thomas Luckmann, "Religion Old and New," in *Social Theory for a Changing Society,* ed. Pierre Bourdieu and James Coleman [Boulder, CO: Westview Press, 1991], 167–82, especially 169). "Implicit religion" is another term scholars use to describe hidden religion.

10. Frederick Kreuziger, *The Religion of Science Fiction* (Bowling Green, OH: Bowling Green State University Popular Press, 1986), 84, 15.

11. Numerous fans have stated this in personal interviews with me. See also Jacqueline Lichtenberg et al., *Star Trek Lives!* (New York: Bantam Books, 1975), and David Gerrold, *The World of Star Trek* (1973; New York: Bluejay Books, 1984).

12. Allan Asherman, *The Star Trek Compendium* (1981; rev. and updated ed., New York: Pocket Books, 1989), 2.

13. Michel-Rolph Trouillot, "Anthropology and the Savage Slot," in *Recapturing Anthropology,* ed. Richard Fox (Santa Fe, NM: School of American Research, 1991), 17–44.

14. The popularity of the optimistic, progressive view of the world was stronger for several decades beginning in the 1960s, but recently a more dystopian, pessimistic view (which also goes back to biblical apocalyptic themes) has surged, perhaps as a result of 9/11, as seen in the popularity of the *Hunger Games,* the zombie genre, and the like. Given their pessimism, I believe these have less of a chance of coalescing into a popular universe than more optimistic universes like that of *Star Trek.*

15. David Alexander, "Gene Roddenberry: writer, producer, philosopher, humanist," *Humanist* 51 (March–April 1991): 5–38.

16. Steve Paulson, "Free Enterprise," *Isthmus,* 27 September 1991, 27–9, quotation from p. 29.

17. Matthew Wilhelm Kapell, ed., *Star Trek as Myth* (Jefferson, NC: McFarland, 2010).

18. Frederik Pohl, "Astounding Story," *American Heritage* 40 (September–October 1989): 42–54, quotation from p. 47.

19. Asherman, *Star Trek Compendium* (1989), 2.

20. Lincoln Geraghty, "Hope When Times Are Hard: Bereavement and Star Trek Fan Letters," in *The Star Trek Universe,* ed. Douglas Brode and Shea T. Brode (Lanham, MD: Rowman & Littlefield, 2008), 175–84.

21. James Van Hise, *The Trek Fan's Handbook* (Las Vegas: Pioneer Books, 1990), 90.

22. Ken Thompson, "Secularization and Sacralization," in *Rethinking Progress,* ed. Jeffrey Alexander and Piotr Sztompka (Boston: Unwin Hyman, 1990), 161–81.

23. Jim Rubino, "Signing on for the New Voyages," *Dateline Starfleet 21,* March 1992.

24. Nancy R. Reagin, ed., *Star Trek and History* (Hoboken, NJ: Wiley, 2013).

25. Mircea Eliade, *Patterns in Comparative Religion* (New York: Sheed & Ward, 1958), esp. 410ff.

26. See, e.g., James Doohan (with Peter David), *Beam Me Up, Scotty* (New York: Pocket Books, 1996), 209.

27. Arthur Greil and David Rudy, "On the Margins of the Sacred," in *In Gods We Trust: New Patterns of Religious Pluralism in America,* ed. Thomas Robbins and Dick Anthony (New Brunswick, NJ: Transaction Publishers, 1990), 219–32, esp. 226.

28. Van Hise, *Trek Fan's Handbook,* 14.

29. "Defense Cuts Worry Departing Scientist," *Los Angeles Times,* 21 June 1993, B14.

30. "Trekking off to Harvey," *Chicago Tribune,* June 27, 1993, "Tempo SW," 2.

31. Michael Okuda et al., *The Star Trek Encyclopedia: A Reference Guide to the Future* (New York: Pocket Books, 1997); Rick Sternbach and Michael Okuda, *Star Trek: The Next Generation Technical Manual* (New York: Pocket Books, 1991).

32. See, e.g., the letters page of *Sky & Telescope* 82, no. 1 (July 1991): 5.

33. Cf. John C. Lyden, "Whose Film Is It, Anyway? Canonicity and Authority in *Star Wars* Fandom," *Journal of the American Academy of Religion* 80 [2012] 775–86, an analysis of *Star Wars* as religion, with this chapter. *Star Trek* seems a much stronger case for its religious dimensions than *Star Wars,* even though *Star Wars* currently exceeds *Star Trek* in mass popularity.

34. William H. Swatos Jr., "Enchantment and Disenchantment in Modernity: The Significance of 'Religion' as a Sociological Category," *Sociological Analysis* 44 (1983), 330. The 1997 Heaven's Gate suicide cult members are an example of those who mix science with pseudoscience, and they were also avid watchers of *Star Trek.*

35. Claude Levi-Strauss, *The Savage Mind* (Chicago: University of Chicago Press, 1966), 16ff.

36. Victor Turner, *From Ritual to Theatre: The Human Seriousness of Play* (New York: PAJ Publications, 1982), 32.

37. Maurice Cusack, Gavin Jack, and Donncha Kavanagh, "Dancing with Discrimination: Managing Stigma and Identity" *Culture and Organization* 9 (2003), 295–310.

38. William Lessa and Evan Vogt, *Reader in Comparative Religion*, 4th ed. (New York: Harper & Row, 1979), 414.

39. Justin Everett, "Fan Culture and the Recentering of *Star Trek,*" in *The Influence of Star Trek on Television, Film and Culture,* ed. Lincoln Geraghty (Jefferson, NC: McFarland, 2008), 186–98.

40. Robert Bellah, "Civil Religion in America," in *American Civil Religion,* ed. Russell E. Richey and Donald G. Jones (New York: Harper & Row, 1974), 21–44, esp. 38–41.

41. Dean Hoge, Benton Johnson, and Donald Luidens, *Vanishing Boundaries: The Religion of Mainline Protestant Baby Boomers* (Louisville, KY: Westminster/John Knox Press, 1994), esp. 75–77, 147–50, 159.

CHAPTER TWELVE

# Shopping, Religion, and the Sacred "Buyosphere"

SARAH MCFARLAND TAYLOR

Are shopping malls sacred spaces? Is shopping a religion? Whatever the answer may be to each of these questions, the fact that so many commentators on culture (both academic and otherwise) speak of consumption and shopping in religious terms should make us sit up and take notice. What does it mean to refer to shopping "arcades," as Walter Benjamin did in describing the glass-covered Parisian shopping corridors of his time, or to contemporary shopping malls, as a number of sociologists now do, as "temples"?[1] In *Consumerism as a Way of Life*, Steven Miles identifies consumerism as not *a* religion in the late twentieth century but "*the* religion of the late twentieth century."[2] The communications scholar Julia Corbett goes one step further, contending that more than simply a "way of life" or a particular "religion," consumer capitalism in the twenty-first century indeed forms the "master logic" of *all* social relations. It constitutes what media theorist Arthur Asa Berger emphatically names an "all-powerful force."[3] That religious idiom is repeatedly used to express the nature of institutions, environments, and experiences related to shopping and consumption signals that these things are being given a certain weight or seriousness. It communicates and claims a degree of intensity or commitment to shopping and/or a heightened degree of what Ann Taves would term as "specialness" to capitalist consumption. Acts of consumerism take on a ritual import and even suggest *supernatural* aspects to the very processes and powers of consumption. These aspects or qualities contest otherwise commonplace secular categorizations of the contemporary consumer capitalist economy."[4] As with the process of defining religion in general, like a Rorschach psychological inkblot test, the naming and claiming of consumer culture, commodity society, and capitalist consumer practices as religion tells us much more about those who name and the very process of naming than it does about the phenomenon in question.

## TEMPLES OF CONSUMERISM AND THE SACRED "BUYOSPHERE"

In his history of shopping, *I Want That! How We All Became Shoppers,* the American cultural critic Thomas Hine coins the term the "buyosphere" to designate the "realm" where those in developed countries are conditioned ideally to live most of their lives: "This is, at once, a set of physical and virtual spaces, and a state of mind. The buyosphere is a series of windows through which we are eager to glimpse all sorts of possibilities."[5] Sounding positively gnostic, Hine says that we come to know ourselves not through God but through our experiences as consumers in this mystical realm: "The buyosphere is not a civic space, but it is our chief arena for expression, the place where we learn most about who we are, both as people and as individuals." What's more, this "sacred" buyosphere elicits powerful emotions in us, and like "a bee in a field of flowers," Hine writes, "the shopper in our selling-saturated world is constantly being stimulated, yet always in danger of exhaustion."[6]

Although not named as such, we get a spatially developed sense of this "sacred buyophere" in the first phenomenological religious studies analysis of enclosed shopping malls in the United States. In the 1980s, Ira Zepp Jr.'s *The New Religious Image of Urban America: The Shopping Mall as Ceremonial Center* looked at shopping mall architecture and floor plans much in the way Mircea Eliade had analyzed sacred cities of the world in his books on comparative religion.[7] Zepp theorized that planners filled the central mall atrium with beautiful displays of water and idyllic vegetation to recreate an Edenic world of perfect blissful reflection. The mall center, Zepp comments in Eliadean fashion, "with all the paths leading to the middle, is a replication of the primordial world in all its harmony and pristine order."[8] Frequently, Zepp points out, this "miniature world" features some sort of world tree or world center. A more recent example of such a feature, since the publication of Zepp's book, would be the two-story-high oak tree at the center of Northbrook Court mall in Northbrook, Illinois. When the deteriorating mall was remodeled in the 1990s to "revitalize" it, a gigantic tree was added in the atrium, complete with a treehouse for children to climb. Whereas the Northbrook mall features installations of idyllic gardens and fountains, the colossal faux "world tree" provides the distinct center of mall community and activity. Eliade termed this kind of symbolic sacred center an "omphalos" or "world navel" and associated it with the presence of an "axis mundi" or "world axis," which he theorized provided a point of sacred connection between the human world and the world of the gods.[9] Whether strategically and centrally placing Edenic fountains, cosmic mountains, or world trees, Zepp argues, mall designers "do as the gods did in the beginning," engaged in an *imitatio Dei* by crafting an idyllic environment designed to elicit feelings of sacredness and perfection. Malls had become the new "temples of worship." What's more, for Zepp, these temples possess a distinct advantage over more traditional religious spaces: "The shopping mall, open almost every day from 10 A.M. to 9 P.M.... is a more inclusive and egalitarian center [than] most churches."[10]

Looking at descriptions and photographic images of turn-of-the-century department stores in the United States, Leigh Schmidt analyzes very explicit church features and aesthetics found in the sacred buyospheres of famed grand department stores, such as Philadelphia's Wanamaker's.[11] Using historical examples of popular material culture,

Schmidt shows how, during the holiday season especially, these stores became magical wonderlands, "enchantments of consumer culture" and "Christmas cathedrals" that fostered the convergence of shopping with Protestant church aesthetics. The 1911 installation of an ornate organ in the splendid marble-trimmed atrium of Wanamaker's completed the picture of a store that was a church and its customers the faithful. Wanamaker's was eventually subsumed under other department store names, and the latter part of the twentieth century marked the decline of stand-alone department stores, but stores such as Macy's and Bloomingdale's took on new roles as "anchor" stores on either side of large-scale enclosed malls. Inside these climate-controlled retail terraria, anchor department stores (for a period of time) regained some of their mystical aura.

In *Enchanting a Disenchanted World: Continuity and Change in the Cathedrals of Consumption*, George Ritzer points to the sociological mechanisms by which shopping malls serve to "re-enchant" a "disenchanted" world:

> Shopping malls have been described as places where people go to practice their "consumer religion." It has been contended that shopping malls are more than commercial and financial enterprises; they have much in common with the religious center of traditional civilizations. Like such religious centers, malls are seen as fulfilling people's need to connect with each other and with nature (trees, plants, flowers), as well as their need to participate in festivals. Malls provide the kind of centeredness traditionally provided by religious temples, and they are constructed to have similar balance, symmetry, and order. The atriums usually offer connection to nature through water and vegetation. People gain a sense of community as well as more specific community services. Play is almost universally part of religious practice, and malls provide a place (the food court) for people to frolic. Similarly, malls offer a setting in which people can partake in ceremonial meals. Malls clearly qualify for the label of cathedrals of consumption.[12]

Much as Walter Benjamin characterized arcades as consumer "dream houses," the scholar of design Lisa Scharoun casts the construction of contemporary shopping malls as "dream spaces"—as mirrors of utopian longings rife with salvific imagery and supernatural intimations.[13] But unlike Ira Zepp, who sees malls as largely supplanting in function more traditional religious spaces, Scharoun points more to a model of convergence. In *America at the Mall: The Cultural Role of a Retail Utopia,* she draws less of a distinction than do other analysts between malls as enchanted secular spaces, or sacred buyospheres, and more traditional religious spaces, chronicling a variety of religious communities that have now infiltrated mall space.[14] Zepp cites the Mall Area Religious Council (MARC), a conglomeration of twenty-five religious groups in the area of the Mall of America that works to create connections between religious groups and malls spaces, and Scharoun further points to the blurring of these boundaries. With the growing popularity of religious storefronts in malls, rather than competing against malls as "cathedrals of consumption" that siphon off the faithful, savvy religious groups have instead integrated their storefronts and chapels into these spaces, occupying retail space where they, like their retail neighbors, capitalize on "foot traffic" and "window shopping." To use Laurence R. Moore's phrase, when "selling God," as with any other retail enterprise, the three most important things are "location, location, and location."[15]

All that glitters is not gold for the Lutheran theologian Jon Pahl, whose *Shopping Malls and Other Sacred Places* sees more sinister forces lurking in the mall. Both Ritzer and Scharoun point to malls, despite their dreamy aesthetics, as providing real and important community functions. In contrast, Pahl contends that shopping malls such as the Mall of America, in all their fantastic attributes, simulate the Kingdom of God, infusing the mall with a palpable feeling of grace that is powerful yet ultimately *false.* The mall promises its pilgrims pure happiness and fulfillment through consumption—shopping as a path to salvation—intoxicating the consumer with the euphoric prospect of a better life free of pain and discomfort. Yet, at some point, Pahl claims, these promises do not deliver and leave consumers feeling depressed and haunted by their own empty hearts. Highly critical of the mall's glittering artifice that promises salvation but delivers none, Pahl anxiously urges a reorientation instead toward "real" spaces in nature that offer authentic and sustainable spiritual nourishment.[16]

In a somewhat ironic twist to cultural commentators who have fretted about the seductive enchantments of the mall supplanting American churches, as it turns out, a number of defunct or so-called "dead malls" are being purchased and assimilated by religious organizations. After the Forest Park Mall in Illinois "died" in the 1990s, Living Word Christian Ministries bought and took over the thirty-three-acre mall in 1998.[17] The defunct Forest Park Mall has since been resurrected as Forest Park Plaza and houses the Living Word Worship Center, the Living Word Bible Training Center, and the Living Word Mission Center, among Christian retail shops, a Christian bookstore, and a Christian café. The once-deserted auditorium is now filled with high-definition "Jumbotrons" for worship services, and the once-still corridors now boom with the sounds of Christian rock bands performing live at the mall's center. Forest Park Plaza's updated slogan reads: "A place where the integrity of God creates a lasting foundation for success and changes the economic destiny of the people." Here, we see promises of salvation and altered destinies—visions of economically successful futures and transformed lives made possible by a worship and practice in which "God" has taken over the mall, and presumably has been a better marketer and manager than the previous owners. Instead of analyzing malls as "temples" or "cathedrals of consumption" that threaten to displace traditional religious institutions, a new wave of scholarship might instead examine malls themselves as "consumed" spaces, devoured and assimilated by religious institutions.

## MRIS AND BLACK FRIDAYS

Beyond the discourse on shopping malls as the new "temples" or "cathedrals," religious idiom also pervades critiques of shopping fervor. A series of shopping-crush deaths in 2005 prompted *The Guardian*'s Julian Baggini to publish a widely circulated article asking whether shopping might not be "the new religion and Mammon our new God."[18] "The kind of 'must have' mania that infects some shoppers as they close in on a good deal is more akin to the imperatives of religious devotion than those of personal finance," Baggini asserted. For him, this kind of shopping hysteria is a disease that "infects" shoppers, presumably much like the transmission mechanism for religious fanaticism. Crazed shopping is thus cast as both new "religion" and a dangerous pathogen. Baggini is certainly not the first to equate religion with "disease." According to a number of sources, including Bertrand Russell, the pre-Socratic philosopher Heraclitus of Ephesus (ca. 535–ca. 475 BCE) called religion "a disease," albeit a noble one.[19] Sigmund Freud, most notably in *The Future of an Illusion,* pathologized religion in light of psychoanalytic theory and the notion of neurosis.[20] More recently, Darrel Ray has written about "the God virus" and the ways in which "religion infects our lives and culture."[21] So, in Baggini's commentary, religious devotion is a good analogy for shopping "mania" because it, like infectious disease, is communicable, invades its host, causes nasty systemic problems or disorders, and can be "tough to get rid of."

In making a 2011 documentary titled *The Secrets of the Superbrands,* the BBC filmmakers Adam Boome and Alex Riley made this link between the disease of religion and the disease of shopping even more explicit by subjecting both "maladies" to high-tech medical diagnostic testing. Riley, who keenly observed an example of shopping "mania" when filming the opening of a new Apple store in London, writes: "The scenes I witnessed at the opening of the new Apple store in London's Covent Garden were more like an evangelical prayer meeting than a chance to buy a phone or a laptop." Riley and his producers followed up their filming by asking one ecstatic Apple devotee, who had made pilgrimage to thirty different Apple store openings around the world, to submit to an MRI diagnostic brain scan. In the film, a team of neuroscientists place the Apple fan inside the MRI scanner and show him images of Apple's logo and products. They then record his physiological responses and report that "the results [suggest] Apple was actually stimulating the same parts of the brain as religious imagery does in people of faith."[22] This is an "ah-hah" or "gotcha" moment in the film, having scientifically drawn this link using scientific medical equipment designed specifically to diagnose *disease*.

The historian Lawrence Wittner echoes these asserted links between religious devotion and shopping fanaticism. Commenting on the mob violence associated with "Black Friday" (the day-after-Thanksgiving's official start of the Christmas shopping season), Wittner observes: "The frenzied participants were not starving, impoverished peasants or product-deprived refugees from Communist nations but reasonably comfortable, middle-class Americans. Their desperation was not driven by hunger. They simply wanted ... *more!*" Wittner blames churches for "not opposing the corporate cultivation of untrammeled greed among Americans." He argues that "churches have left the door open to the triumph of America's new religion—not liberal secularism, but shopping."[23]

Across a variety of platforms, expressions of popular culture diagnose the shopping "mania" of consumer capitalism as the equivalent of religious fanaticism. What does this tell us? Is this a way to communicate irrationality, intense emotion, unhealthy obsession, extremism, and ultimately something dangerous and out of control? What's more, cultural observers anxiously evoke the specter of "real" or "authentic" religion being subsumed or taken over by a virulent consumerism run amok. Even the sociologist Sharon Zurkin (2005), in her history of how shopping has changed American culture, sounds a decidedly premature death knell for religion: "We shop because we long for value—for a virtuous ideal of value that we no longer get from religion, work, or politics."[24] No longer relevant, religion is replaced by shopping, the "new religion," as Wittner calls it. Russell McCutcheon points out that "'religion' is a wonderfully useful rhetorical tool that packs a significant rhetorical punch."[25] Classification matters. The fact that shopping is classified by a variety of public cultural commentators in a variety of media contexts as being "a religion" signals something very important about perceptions of shopping, the societal role it plays, anxieties about the place of religion and its power in society, as well as fears about religion's potential demise.

## SHOPALUJAH!

Two weeks after the horrific events of September 11, 2001, as the United States headed into war, President George W. Bush urged families to head on "down to Disney World" and to keep spending money.[26] A number of political pundits interpreted the administration's message as one that promised America salvation through consumption. If Americans stopped shopping, then the terrorists had "won." The sociologist Andrew Weigert has called this kind of mentality the American "ethic of consumption," which expresses itself best through evangelical popular culture. Ironically, he says, it is not "this-worldly asceticism ... but this-worldy consumerism" that is a sign of salvation in this "ethic." It is the American Protestant televangelist who most skillfully hammers home this message: "consuming, or helping their televangelist to consume, signals salvation, and thus provides that supreme motive that all believers seek." This "most American of messages, salvation through consumption," Weigert says, goes beyond the televangelist and audience and permeates American culture. In so doing, it effectively "takes [the sociologist Max] Weber's thesis [of Protestant ethical frugality and saving] and stands it on its head."[27] President Bush did not use the exact words, as some have claimed, "Go out and shop!" But, especially for those who share Bush's evangelical faith, his phrasing at a time of extreme crisis about a way to salvation through Disney vacations and family shopping trips came across as a resonant invocation of this "ethic of consumerism." In this extremely fraught cultural moment, the logics of capitalism (perennial growth, expansion, and profit) and the logics of evangelicalism (perennial expansion, increase, and godly reward) bore striking, very public resemblance.

If anyone "gets" the tensions between the ethereal aura of corporate retail "dream worlds" and their darker masked specters, it is the New

York performance artist and street theater activist Bill Tallen, who takes on the messianic street-corner evangelist personality of "Reverend Billy." In this *actorvist,* there is much of what David Chidester (and Lionel Trilling, Jean Baudrillard, and David Lowenthal before him) analyzes as "authentic fakes," the play and improvisation of religious forms in popular culture that nonetheless do "real religious work."[28] Reverend Billy and his "Church of Life After Shopping" (formerly the "Church of Stop Shopping") stage public shopping "interventions" at corporate retailers like the Disney Store, Starbucks, and Wal-Mart.[29] In these acts of what his group calls "ritual resistance," they exorcise cash registers, illuminate the environmental impact and labor practices used in manufacturing various products, and "snap people out of the hypnosis" or the magical enchantment they feel while shopping.[30] Identifying themselves as a "post religious church," Reverend Billy and his "Earthalujah Choir" persistently ask consumers, "What would Jesus buy?" In the 2007 documentary film *What Would Jesus Buy?*, produced by Morgan Spurlock, Reverend Billy prophesizes the "shopocalypse," a prophecy that he says has now come to fruition. That is, we are literally "shopping ourselves to death," as rampant fossil-fuel-based capitalism and obsessive consumerism have intensified climate-change-related natural disasters such as the 2012 "Frankenstorm," Hurricane "Sandy." Marking the Mayan calendar doomsday, Reverend Billy and the Life After Shopping Church held an "End of the World" ritual in Times Square, seeking to "turn back the devils of debt and destruction, rallying those of radical faith to save themselves and save us all." Reverend Billy also offers exorcism services to cast the shopping demons out of "shopaholics," who like many Americans "walk in the valley of the shadow of debt." He has performed exorcisms directly on credit cards and investment bankers and has attempted to cast the "evil spirits" and "dark soul" out of British Petroleum (BP) following the 2010 Deepwater Horizon oil disaster caused by its leaking oil well in the Gulf of Mexico. In 2008, Billy's church held a candlelight prayer vigil in the parking lot of a Long Island Wal-Mart, where employee Jdimytai

Damour was trampled to death on "Black Friday" by "out-of-control" shoppers who broke down the store doors at five in the morning and stepped over Damour's mangled dead body in order to make their way to discounted plasma television sets. As Wal-Mart employees informed shoppers over the PA system that an employee had been killed and they would have to leave the store, shoppers yelled back that they had been on line since Friday morning. Refusing to leave, they kept on shopping.[31] The killing of Damour by shopper stampede came just two months after one of the worst death tolls ever recorded from a religious stampede, when 224 pilgrims were trampled to death after 25,000 worshippers rushed the doors of the Chamunda Devi Temple in northern India during the 2008 Kumbh Mela festival.[32]

Bethany Moreton, author of *To Serve God and Wal-Mart: The Making of Christian Free Enterprise,* might not be surprised by the juxtaposition of these two stampedes and the comparison between "religious temples" and "retail temples." In her history of Wal-Mart, Moreton tells the story of how evangelical values and frameworks came to be embedded in Wal-Mart's corporate structure and management strategies. Notions of "Christian service" and male-led family "headship," concepts that employees practice in their own homes and churches, came to define Wal-Mart's workforce. Moreton observes: "Drawing on the new relationships among managers, employees, and customers in its stores and on the regional evangelical revival, the company's emerging service ethos honored [employees] as Christian servants."[33] Wal-Mart stores became inscribed or encoded with a language, imagery, and personnel dynamic that "read" like both "Christian home" and "church" to its evangelical patrons. Unlike the luxurious ornamentation of Philadelphia department stores such as Wanamaker's that simulated the aesthetics of elite Protestant churches, Wal-Mart's stripped-down frugal "warehouse" aesthetic felt more like the modest contemporary rural and/or storefront churches its evangelical customers associated with worship. Operation Rescue founder and Christian Coalition director Ralph Reed once famously advised political strategists: "If you want to reach the Christian population on Sunday, you do it from the church pulpit. If you want to reach them on Saturday, you do it in Wal-Mart."[34] In this way, Moreton says, Wal-Mart came to sanctify "Christian free enterprise," "servant leadership," folksy frugality, while (in a twist on Adam Smith) exalting the gospel of God's invisible hand in the sanctity of neoliberal globalization.

As with "dead" malls, however, Wal-Marts that have expanded too quickly, in a shrinking economy, are being consumed themselves and transformed into sites of conversion. In 2012, the Cornerstone Church took over the Wal-Mart in Marion, Illinois, and turned it into an unconventional 120,000 square-foot worship space.[35] In the same year, evangelical megachurch church purchases of Wal-Mart retail stores for conversion into worship space ranged from Wisconsin, Indiana, Illinois, and Nebraska to Florida and Louisiana.[36] When giving a media tour of Church of Eleven22's newly converted Wal-Mart home in Jacksonville, Florida, Senior Pastor Joby Martin pointed out to camera crews that the congregation's new children's safari-themed "worship center" sits right on the spot where he used to purchase his shotgun shells at Wal-Mart. "Little did Sam Walton know that when he was putting a Wal-Mart here, he was actually part of building the Kingdom of God," the pastor declared.[37] Bethany Moreton's research for her book on Wal-Mart and the Walton family suggests otherwise—that Sam Walton might be anything but surprised by connections between his commercial endeavors and efforts to hasten the Kingdom of God's arrival.[38]

## DEMONS AND ADDICTION IN THE BUYOPSHERE

Demonstrating a keen sense of the "sacred buyosphere" and its potential for sinister "possessions," Reverend Billy has performed numerous "exorcisms" in Wal-Mart parking lots and inside the retail space, charismatically casting demons out of the register with his most exuberant preacherly flair.[39] He is merely one of many doing battle with the "demons of shopping." Estimates of Americans with diagnosed "compulsive buying disorder" cite around eighteen million afflicted.[40] Debtors Anonymous (DA), founded in 1968, which identifies itself as a "fellowship" for compulsive spenders, holds more than five hundred weekly meetings in fifteen countries, using an approach modeled on Alcoholics Anonymous's twelve-step program.[41] DA testimonials frequently recount how members came to terms with their "disease." One anonymous member recalls: "I gradually came to realize my debting disease manifests every time I assume that I am so special I can have whatever I want, whenever I want it, without having to earn it or pay for it."[42] Although DA is not a religious organization per se, as with Alcoholics Anonymous, belief in a "higher power" is key, and those in recovery frequently characterize their struggle to deal with their disease in spiritual terms. In Debtors Anonymous, the strands of disease, shopping, and religion intertwine. Sophie Kinsella's best-selling *Shopaholic* novel series, made into the 2009 film *Confessions of a Shopaholic,* brought the "disease" of compulsive spending and debting into more widespread popular consciousness, employing both comedic and serious portrayals of real addiction. Shopaholic "Rebecca's" retail conquests are ecstatic experiences that she has longed for since childhood, when she would gaze into the "dreamy world of perfect things" inside shop windows. There, we are told, she would see "grown-up girls, like faeries or princesses, getting anything they wanted" because they had "magic cards." Rebecca's entrancement with the retail "faery world" is finally broken by the stark consequences of credit card debt and the prospect of homelessness in New York City. Like the twelve-steppers in "DA," Rebecca goes on a "spiritual journey," where she must confront the demons that lurk underneath pretty silk scarves and sparkling Jimmy Choo shoes. Rebecca does not quite exclaim "Revolujah!" in Reverend Billy fashion, but she does see the error of her ways and struggles to vanquish her "shopping demons."

Entering the sacred buyosphere of Oprah Winfrey might instead liberate Rebecca from struggling with the demons of addiction, redirecting her toward purchasing the "right things" and "shopping for good," thus legitimating her consumption as both socially conscious and spiritually aware. Shopping as a moral solution can conveniently solve the moral problem of consumption and license even *more* consumer spending. In the chapter on "Practicing Purchase" in her 2011 book *Oprah: The Gospel of an Icon,* Kathryn Lofton illuminates Winfrey's "spiritual capitalism" and her peddling of a "good news materialism" through purchasing recommendations and directives issued to what Lofton calls her "congregants."[43] For Lofton, Oprah's approach to her television audience, magazine readership, and online community is catechistic. Consuming the "right goods" becomes a pathway to personal growth, spiritual improvement, and a meaningful, purposeful life. "In Winfrey's capitalist modernity, this materiality is *spiritual* practice," and what "separates Winfrey's work is the soul-saving signification attached to her recommendations."[44] Oprah's congregants "are told that their purchasing power is correlated to their moral merit. Individual shopping choices offer moments of possible piety: 'Our simplest shopping decisions can protect the environment, save family farmers, lift villages from destitution, and restore dignity to war-torn communities.'"[45]

### CONCLUDING THOUGHTS

In an age of global climate crisis, scientists and philosophers have come to term the period of time we inhabit, "the Anthropocene" – an age in which human activity now constitutes the dominant geologic force affecting earth. At this time, it bears considering the very real impacts that consumer culture, commodity society, and the consumer patterns and practices of the *buyosphere* have had on the *biosphere* that supports all life on the planet.[46] Numerous environmental scientists, economists, policy wonks, and activists have recast the capitalist dreams of endless prosperity and unbridled consumption as a nightmare for planet earth.[47] When Thomas Hine says that "We live much of our lives in a realm I call the buyosphere," it also prompts us to ask who that "we" is and what populations might be most socially, economically, and environmentally devastated by the consumption acts of that "we." Hine clarifies that he is talking about consumers in the "developed world," but there is considerable disparity in consumer power and levels of consumption worldwide. More than a century ago, the economist and sociologist Thorstein Veblen's famous study *The Theory of the Leisure Class* (1899) asserted that regardless of economic situation and social standing, "No class of society, not even the most abjectly poor, forgoes all customary conspicuous consumption. The last items of this category of consumption are not given up except under the stress of direct necessity."[48] Thus, whether possessing the power and resources to purchase or not, rich or poor, we are drawn into the cosmological defining "master logic" of consumption, its social markers of identity, and into the mystical aura of the buyosphere and its ultimate promises. Returning, once again, to the image of the socio-psychological "inkblot test," the fact that this particular "inkblot" of consumption is being increasingly identified and read in contemporary popular discourse through the semantic identifiers of "religion" and the "religious" points to the ongoing cultural politics of representation. To use the language of "religion" or the "sacred" to represent shopping and consumer culture is to assert a kind of "common sense" ideology about both the nature of religion and the nature of shopping. The fact that *popular culture* has become the primary site for "naturalizing" the conflation of religion, markets, and consumption, while also a key site for critiquing this convergence, speaks to the central role popular culture plays in the contested power and politics that both reinforce hegemony and call for social change.[49]

## DISCUSSION QUESTIONS

1. Discuss your own practices of shopping and consumption. What pleasures or satisfactions do you get from visiting the mall, or other shopping sites, and from the process of acquiring things?

2. Some of the sources Taylor features in her chapter suggest in their statements or cultural productions that shopping and

consumption can be thought of as a form of religion. What do you find compelling and engaging about this suggestion? What evidence might argue against this way of thinking about consumption?

3. Drawing on the chapter and your own experience, discuss the shopping mall as a destination, a place to be visited. Discuss how malls are different from other places people might shop.

4. In the section headed "Shopalujah!" the author discusses connections between shopping and patriotism. Why is shopping potentially a patriotic act? If consumption is both a religion and a patriotic act, what does this suggest about the nature of shopping as a meaning-making activity? How do religion and patriotism interact?

## NOTES

"Shopping, Religion and the Sacred 'Buyosphere'" by Sarah McFarland Taylor draws on the essay "Shopping and Consumption" in *The Routledge Companion to Religion and Popular Culture* (New York: Routledge, 2015).

1. Walter Benjamin, *The Arcades Project,* trans. Howard Eiland and Kevin McLaughlin (Cambridge, MA: Harvard University Press, 1999). Benjamin's notes on the arcades are filled with the use of religious idiom. He refers to the arcades as "temples of commodity capital" and characterizes the design of the arcade as "Dream Houses: arcade as nave with side chapels" (37).

2. Steven Miles, *Consumerism as a Way of Life* (Thousand Oaks, CA: Sage, 1998), 1.

3. Julia Corbett, *Communicating Nature: How to Create and Understand Environmental Messages* (Washington, DC: Island Press, 2006), 94–95; and Arthur Asa Berger, *Shop 'Til You Drop: Consumer Behavior and Consumer Culture* (Lanham, MD: Rowman & Littlefield, 2005), 1.

4. For Ann Taves's discussion of religion and its quality of "specialness," see *Religious Experience Reconsidered: A Building-Block Approach to the Study of Religion and Other Special Things* (Princeton, NJ: Princeton University Press, 2011), 12. On the supernatural aspects associated with the processes and powers of consumption, see David Chidester, *Authentic Fakes: Religion and American Popular Culture* (Berkeley: University of California Press, 2005), vii and esp. chap. 3,

52–70, "Plastic Religion," on the supernatural aura of plastics consumption in Tupperware marketing and advertising.

5. Thomas Hine, *I Want That! How We All Became Shoppers* (2002; repr., New York: Harper Perennial 2003), xiv–xv.

6. Ibid., xv.

7. Ira Zepp Jr., *The New Religious Image of Urban America: the Shopping Mall as Ceremonial Center* (1986; 2nd ed., Niwot: University Press of Colorado, 1997), 51–53.

8. Ibid., 51.

9. Mircea Eliade, *The Sacred and the Profane: The Nature of Religion,* trans. Willard R. Trask (1959; new ed., San Diego: Harcourt Brace Jovanovich, 1987), 36–47.

10. Zepp, *New Religious Image,* 33–35, 80.

11. Leigh Schmidt, *Consumer Rites: The Buying and Selling of American Holidays* (Princeton, NJ: Princeton University Press, 1995), 159.

12. George Ritzer, *Enchanting a Disenchanted World: Continuity and Change in Cathedrals of Consumption* (1999; 3rd ed., Los Angeles: Sage, 2010), 10.

13. Ibid. Benjamin writes: "The arcades are houses or passages that have no outside—like the dream" (Convolute L1a,1). In Convolute L1,3, he refers to arcades, winter gardens, casinos, and train stations all as "dream houses of the collective." In Convolute L1,6, Benjamin again refers to the arcade as both "dream house" and "temple." Benjamin, *Arcades Project,* trans. Eiland and McLaughlin. 405–6. Susan Buck-Morss's work, in particular, illuminates how "[t]he Paris Arcades that so fascinated Benjamin (as they did the Surrealists whose 'materialist metaphysics' he admired) were the prototype, the 19th century 'ur-form' of the modern shopping mall. Benjamin's dialectics of seeing demonstrate how to read these consumer dream houses and so many other material objects of the time—from air balloons to women's fashions, from Baudelaire's poetry to Grandville's cartoons—as anticipations of social utopia and, simultaneously, as clues for a radical political critique." See Morss's *The Dialectics of Seeing: Walter Benjamin and the Arcades Project* (Cambridge, MA: MIT Press, 1991), 144. The quotation above is taken from Morss's "front matter" general description of the book.

14. Lisa Scharoun, *America at the Mall: The Cultural Role of a Retail Utopia* (Jefferson, NC: McFarland, 2012), 52.

15. Laurence R. Moore, *Selling God: American Religion in the Marketplace of Culture* (New York: Oxford University Press, 1994).

16. Jon Pahl, *Shopping Malls and Other Sacred Places: Putting God in Place,* Reprint edition (Eugene, Ore.: Wipf & Stock Publishers, [2003] 2009), especially the Introduction and p. 61–67.

17. Russell Working, "Church Ownership Is a Miracle for Mall," *Chicago Tribune,* May 28, 2007, http://articles.chicagotribune.com/2007–05–28/news /0705280088_1_shopping-center-church-business-school.

18. Julian Baggini, "Assembly Required," *Guardian,* February 10, 2005, www .guardian.co.uk/business/2005/feb/11/consumerissues.shopping.

19. The philologist Max Müller (1823–1900) wrote that while there is no proof Heraclitus ever actually said this, it certainly "sounds" a lot like something he might have said. For a more detailed discussion, see Elisha Mulford, *Republic of God: An Institute of Theology* (1881; 8th ed., Boston: Houghton Mifflin, 1885), 46.

20. Sigmund Freud, *The Future of an Illusion,* trans. and ed. James Strachey (New York: Norton, 1989), 54–56.

21. Darrel Ray, *The God Virus: How Religion Infects Our Lives and Culture* (Bonner Springs, KS: IPC Press, 2009).

22. Alex Riley and Adam Boome, "Superbrands' Success Fueled by Sex, Religion, and Gossip," *BBC Business News,* May 17, 2011, www.bbc.co.uk/news /business-13416598.

23. Lawrence Wittner, "America's Real Religion: Shopping," *Huffington Post,* December 12, 2004, www.huffingtonpost.com/lawrence-wittner/americas-real-religion-shopping_b_2228617.html.

24. Sharon Zurkin, 2005. *Point of Purchase: How Shopping Changed American Culture* (New York: Routledge, 2005), p. 8.

25. Russell McCutcheon, "Religion, Ire, and Dangerous Things," *Journal of the American Academy of Religion* 72, no. 1 (March 2004): 173–93.

26. Andrew Weigert, *Mixed Emotions: Certain Steps toward Understanding Ambivalence* (Albany: State University of New York Press, 1991), 111.

27. George Bush, speech at O'Hare Airport, September 27, 2001. See White House archives, https://georgewbush-whitehouse.archives.gov/news/releases /2001/09/20010927-1.html.

28. See Lionel Trilling, *Sincerity and Authenticity* (Cambridge, MA: Harvard University Press, 1972); Jean Baudrillard, *Simulations,* trans. Paul Foss and Alexander Beil (New York: Semiotext(e), 1983); David Lowenthal, "Counterfeit Art: Authentic Fakes?" *International Journal of Cultural Property* 1 (1992): 79–103; and Chidester, *Authentic Fakes,* 2–3.

29. Jill Lane, "Reverend Billy: Preaching, Protest, and Postindustrial Flânerie," *Drama Review* 46, no. 1 (Spring 2002): 70.

30. This description is drawn from the written accounts, videos, and still photos of Reverend Billy actions at his official web site. This material in particular was sourced at www.revbilly.com/about-us.

31. Joseph Mallia and Matthew Chayes, "Wal-Mart Worker Dies in Black Friday Stampede," *Long Island Newsday,* November 28, 2008, www.newsday.com/long-island/nassau/wal-mart-worker-dies-in-black-friday-stampede-1.884298.

32. "Deadly Stampedes at Religious Events in India Since 2008," *Hindustan Times,* February, 11, 2013, www.hindustantimes.com/India-news/NewDelhi/Deadly-stampedes-at-religious-events-in-India-since-2008/Article1–1010208.aspx.

33. Bethany Moreton, *To Serve God and Wal-Mart: The Making of Christian Free Enterprise* (Cambridge, MA: Harvard University Press, 2009), 89.

34. Ibid., 90.

35. www.foxnews.com/us/2012/08/26/illinois-church-finds-new-home-in-walmart.

36. Jane Ford-Stewart, "Old Greenfield's Wal-Mart's Transformation into a Church Begins," *Greenfield Now,* February 5, 2013, www.greenfieldnow.com/news/old-greenfield-walmarts-transformation-into-church-begins-nm8l440–189904121.html.

37. Erica Edwards's story "Local Wal-Mart Converted into a Church," September 21, 2012, www.firstcoastnews.com/video/1852847623001/51325884001/Local-Wal-Mart-converted-into-a-church has since been removed from the First Coast News web page where it first appeared. However, a "thank you" note to the local reporter still remains and references the story on the Church of Eleven22's Facebook page, www.facebook.com/ChurchOfEleven22/posts/278334712277515.

38. For further discussion of the mutually shaping forces of capitalism and Christianity in the United States, see Darren Grem's *The Blessings of Business: How Corporations Shaped Conservative Christianity* (New York: Oxford University Press, 2016).

39. For further scholarly work on connections between spirit possessions, hauntings, and capitalist accumulation of possessions in American culture, see Sean McCloud, *American Possessions: Fighting Demons in the Contemporary United States* (New York: Oxford University Press, 2015).

40. Letty Workman and David Paper, "Compulsive Buying: A Theoretical Framework," *Journal of Business Inquiry* 9, no. 1 (2010): 89–126.

41. See www.debtorsanonymous.org/about/about.htm.

42. See www.debtorsanonymous.org/Erstwhile.htm.

43. Kathryn Lofton, *Oprah: The Gospel of an Icon* (Berkeley: University of California Press, 2011), 22.

44. Ibid., 22–23; emphasis in original.

45. Ibid., 35.

46. The Nobel laureate Paul Crutzen proposed the term "Anthropocene" at a conference in 2000 as a way to characterize our most recent geologic era—one dominated by human-influenced or anthropogenic change. Crutzen later used the term in print in an article co-authored with Eugene Stoermer, "The 'Anthropocene,'" *Global Change Newsletter* 41 (2000): 17–18. For further discussion of Crutzen's concept, see J. Zalasiewicz et al., "Are We Now Living in the Anthropocene?" *GSA [Geological Society of America] Today* 18 (2008): 4–8.

47. See Thomas L. Friedman *Hot, Flat, and Crowded: Why We Need a Green Revolution—and How It Can renew America* (New York: Farrar, Straus & Giroux,, 2008); James Lovelock, *A Rough Ride to the Future* (New York: Overlook Press, 2015); Bill McGuire, *Global Catastrophes: A Very Short Introduction* (Oxford: Oxford University Press, 2014); Mark Maslin, *Climate Change: A Very Short Introduction* (Oxford: Oxford University Press, 2014); Bill McKibben, *Earth: Making a Life on a Tough New Planet* (New York: St. Martin's Griffin, 2011); Elizabeth Kolbert, *Field Notes From a Catastophe: Man, Nature and Climate Change* (London: Bloomsbury, 2006) and *The Sixth Extinction: An Unnatural History* (New York: Henry Holt, 2014); Naomi Klein, *This Changes Everything: Capitalism vs. The Climate* (New York: Simon & Schuster, 2014); and Gernot Wagner, *But Will the Planet Notice? How Smart Economics Can Save the World* (New York: Hill & Wang, 2011). These are just a few of the growing number of works that address the connections between levels of consumption, particularly of fossil fuels, and the climate change crisis.

48. See Thorstein Veblen's 1899 book *The Theory of the Leisure Class* (repr., Mineola, NY: Dover, 1994), 53, in which he coined the term "conspicuous consumption." I wish to thank Ipsita Chatterjea for suggesting Veblen's work on "conspicuous consumption" to me as germane to a talk I gave on the relationship of *ecopiety* and *consumopiety* in American media and popular culture at the University of Florida in January 2016. I am also indebted to Julia Corbett for the insights she provides in her illuminating chapter on "Work and Consumer Culture," in *Communicating Nature: How We Create and Understand Environmental Messages* (London: Island Press, 2006), esp. 92–99, which informs my discussions of consumerism in this chapter.

49. See Antonio Gramsci's discussions of the politics of common sense, naturalizing, and cultural hegemony in his *Prison Notebooks, Vol. 1* (London: Lawrence & Wishart, 1968).

# CHAPTER THIRTEEN

# Losing Their Way to Salvation

*Women, Weight Loss, and the Religion of Thinness*

MICHELLE M. LELWICA

## WHAT IS "RELIGION"? A FLUID, FUNCTIONAL DEFINITION

What comes to mind when you hear the word "religion"? There may be as many answers to that question as there are individuals responding to it. But I would guess that few people would respond by talking about calories, body size, and dieting. What does weight-loss weight loss — and particularly many women's preoccupation with getting thinner— have to do with religion?

To explore that question, we need to clarify what we mean by "religion." In my understanding, religion is a concept that brings into focus various systems of beliefs, stories, and behaviors through which people create and discover meaning in life. This understanding highlights the human origins and historic functions of religions. Throughout history, people have constructed and turned to religions in their quest to understand their lives and seek fulfillment against the backdrop of mystery, uncertainty, and "big questions" (e.g., Why do we exist? How should we live? Why is there suffering and what can we do about it?). Through their various teachings, images, rituals, myths, and moral codes, religious traditions give their members a shared and deeply felt sense of what's most important in life, an ultimate purpose and perspective in relation to which everything else—all problems and possibilities—can be understood.

Based on this description, religion is defined not by certain characteristics that make it categorically unique and separate from the rest of society, but by the role it plays in helping people cultivate a sense of ultimate meaning and providing a set of guidelines and tools for pursuing that sacred truth. This functional definition of religion blurs the boundaries between "religion" and "culture," "spiritual" and "secular," "sacred" and "profane." In so doing, it enables us to recognize the meaning-giving, quasi-religious aspects of seemingly nonreligious phenomena, like the stories, images, norms, and practices of popular culture—including those that comprise women's quest for thinness.[1]

### THE "RELIGION" OF THINNESS

To highlight the religious-like function of this quest, I coined the term "religion of thinness."[2] This concept is not meant to suggest that the pursuit of slenderness is, *in fact,* a religion. Rather, it aims to illuminate how this pursuit has become a profound source of meaning for many people today—especially women.[3] The idea of the religion of thinness brings into focus aspects of our culture's devotion to slenderness that functionally resemble certain features of traditional religion, especially Christianity, which has had the most power to influence Western norms and attitudes regarding appetite and body size. More specifically, the religion of thinness illuminates

- the iconography of the taut, sleek bodies of models and movie stars that create an otherworldly fantasy of physical perfection
- the daily rituals that reinforce the symbolic importance of fighting fat (e.g., counting carbs, fat grams, or calories, stepping on scales, exercising to lose weight)
- the moral codes that designate which foods (and how much) you should/shouldn't eat and that produce feelings of virtue or shame, depending on your level of observance

- the sense of community that bonding over weight-loss goals, failures, and achievements engenders
- the colonial/missionizing quality and function of the crusade to conquer "obesity"
- historical Christian beliefs about the body's pivotal role in salvation
- long-standing associations between women and carnal desire, which make control of female appetites seem necessary; and
- the salvation myth that promises happiness, health, and beauty through weight loss

The concept of the religion of thinness deliberately aims to cause confusion about the distinction between "religious" and "secular" meanings and motivations surrounding women's pursuit of weight loss, suggesting that there is no crystal-clear line delineating the two. In so doing, it calls into question deeply entrenched assumptions in and beyond the academic study of religion.

### SACRED AND SECULAR RITUALS: COMPLICATING THE DISTINCTION

In his classic essay "Religion as a Cultural System," Clifford Geertz cites the difference between ascetic fasting and dieting to illustrate the distinction between "religious" and "secular" behavior. This distinction, Geertz argues, is based on these practices' diverging ends, and thus the varying frames of meaning and dispositions they foster. Whereas weight reduction aims to achieve a "conditioned" goal, religious fasting is "directed toward an unconditioned end." Whereas dieting is tied to worldly values (presumably health and beauty), religious fasting takes its meaning and motivation in reference to transcendent values and a picture of "a general order of existence."[4]

At first glance, Geertz's distinction makes a lot of sense. You only have to watch TV for an evening, page through a popular women's magazine, listen to a schoolgirl insist she's "too fat," or have a doctor advise you to "watch what you eat" to witness the this-worldly, "secular" nature of America's pursuit of thinness. And yet, a closer reading of these weight-reduction discourses suggests that something more, something of vast importance, is being summoned, weighed, and reckoned in this pursuit, especially among its female participants. The more one probes this "something," the more the distinction between "secular" and "religious" behavior fades, and the more it becomes evident that for many girls and women, creating a slender body has become a matter of all-pervading significance, an end whose achievement feels tantamount to salvation. Marya Hornbacher captures this feeling in *Wasted,* her memoir of her struggle with anorexia and bulimia: "At school we were hungry and lost and scared and young and we needed religion, salvation, something to fill the anxious hollow in our chests. Many of us sought it in food and in thinness."[5]

In her studies of symbols and rituals, Mary Douglas noted both the constitutive role of the body in the creation of religious meanings, and the permeable line distinguishing religious from nonreligious behavior.[6] Building on Douglas's insights, Catherine Bell highlighted the role of the "ritualized body"—a body that has been socialized to look, feel, and act in culturally and religiously sanctioned ways—in the creation of such distinctions. Bell suggested that the significance of ritual practices rests not in their essential difference from ordinary behavior, but in their capacity to constitute themselves as *holier than* more mundane ways of acting by referencing both dominant social norms and "realities thought to transcend the power of human actors."[7] This theory of ritual helps explain how a gesture as mundane as refusing dessert, or an activity as ordinary as walking, can become intensely meaningful insofar as these behaviors are linked to a larger, more ultimate purpose: the goal of thinness.

Part of what makes these rituals so compelling is the opportunity they present for women to exercise agency—to feel as though they are "in control." By deciding what, how much, or whether to eat, a woman exercises a kind of self-determination that has historically been the prerogative of men. Such decisions generate feelings of power she may not experience in the rest of her life. Reflecting on her history of struggle with weight and eating, a woman writes: "Food was power and control. Food was making my own decisions about what I would eat, when I would eat, how much I would eat. Food was taking control over what I looked like."[8] Losing weight also elicits the praise of others. A former anorexic explains, "The more the clothes hung, the more the compliments grew, 'What kind of diet are you on; you haven't looked this good in ages; why, you look like you've lost ten years.'"[9] That some of the primary rituals our culture proffers girls and women for cultivating a sense of agency and worth require obedience to rigidly defined body norms suggests the limits of the empowerment that dieting produces. As Susan Bordo points out, weight loss practices reward women with a sense of control by rendering them more subservient to the dominant culture.[10] Although such rituals can foster a sense of confidence and purpose, they do so by reproducing the classic scenario of patriarchal religion, in which a woman's salvation depends on her sacrifice, self-denial, and submission.

Understanding female dieting as a popular cultural ritual illuminates both its meaning-making function and the multiple levels on which the goal of thinness generates meaning. As part of a broader system of societal norms, narratives, and practices, weight-loss rituals don't simply "improve" a woman's body; they instill/reinforce a worldview, an embodied sense of self-definition, and an accessible—if precarious—method for coping with the stresses, expectations, and uncertainties of contemporary life. "After a time," a woman who dieted compulsively writes, "the number on the scale became my totem, more important than my experience—it was layered, metaphorical, metaphysical, and it had bewitching power. I thought if I could change that number I could change my life ... I would weigh myself with foreboding, and my weight would determine how went the rest of my day, my week, and my life."[11]

The meaning-giving function of weight loss is evident in another woman's description of her pursuit of thinness as "a replacement religion ... with its own set of commandments and rituals." In fact, this woman says she was so devoted to this "replacement religion," she "was practically ready to give up [her] life for it."[12]

## PRO-ANA RELIGION AND THE CONTINUUM OF FAITH IN THINNESS

Like some traditional religious adherents, some women who worship at the altar of thinness become fanatical about their faith. Both the extremes to which some go in their efforts to reduce and the quasi-religious functions and features of their quest are evident in the online subculture known as "pro-Ana." Members this movement see anorexia and bulimia as lifestyle choices rather than dangerous illnesses. Disciples of "Ana" (short for anorexia) believe that those who risk their lives for the sake of slenderness need not to be bothered by the unexceptional standards of unbelievers, who lack the willpower to be supernaturally skinny. To motivate their crusade for thinness, pro-Anas look to an iconography of "thinspirational" images—online pictures of emaciated young women posed in ways that flaunt their protruding bones and sickly appearances. In addition, the Pro-Ana Lifestyle web site has an "Ana Religion & Lifestyle" tab on its menu, which offers various tools to support the anorexic's crusade for thinness, including:

> "Ana's Psalm" (a parody of Psalm 23: "Strict is my diet / I must not want / It maketh me lie down at night hungry / It leadeth me past the confectioners ... ")
>
> "Thin Commandments" (e.g., "Thou shall not eat without feeling guilty," "What the scale says is the most important thing," "You can never be too thin")

"Ana's Creed" ("I believe in control ... I believe in salvation trough
[*sic*] starvation ... I believe in bathroom scales as an indicator of
my daily successes and failures ..." etc.); and

Ana's Laws (e.g., "Thin is beauty; therefore I must be thin ... If I
wish to be loved. Food is my ultimate enemy ... I must be thin, at
all costs. It is the most important thing; nothing else matters")[13]

However bizarre and disturbing the pro-Ana subculture may seem,
it's just an extreme expression of our culture's veneration of thinness.
Pro-Ana represents the far end of a *continuum* of troubled eating and
body image in the United States, where many females who do not have
eating disorders identify with the beliefs and behaviors of those who
do. Studies show that as many as 80 percent of ten-year-old American
girls have dieted, and the same percentage of women in their mid-fif-
ties say they want to be thinner. More than three-quarters of healthy-
weight adult women believe they are "too fat," and nearly two-thirds of
high school girls are dieting (compared to 16 percent of boys).[14] While
only a fraction of the female population in the United States are zeal-
ously pro-Ana, the majority honestly believe they would be happier if
they were thinner. Thus the perspectives and practices of Ana's disciples—including their religious functions and features—differ in
degree, not in kind, from the thinking and habits of many "normal"
girls and women, who regularly monitor what they eat in the hopes of
becoming noticeably slim.[15]

## HISTORICAL ATTITUDES TOWARD
## FOOD AND APPETITE

How did we get to this point in history where countless American
women measure their happiness and self-worth according to the
number on the bathroom scale? To understand any religious movement—whether "cultural" or "traditional"—we need to examine the
historical and social contexts in which it evolves and makes sense.

Concerns about eating and appetite have a long history in the Christian tradition,[16] whose leaders encouraged control of carnal desires (including appetite for food) as a way to cultivate holiness, while condemning excessive eating ("gluttony") as sinful. Historically, these leaders (the vast majority of whom were men) also associated females with the unruly flesh (whereas males were identified with mind or spirit), which meant that women in particular needed to supervise and contain their physical urges in order to be virtuous. Finally, traditional Christian eschatology (ideas about the final judgment at the end of time) envisioned a heavenly afterlife in which physical desires and defects would be eliminated: saved souls would be freed of the burden of their corporeal urges, and their spiritual bodies would be anatomically perfect.[17]

Elements of these three Christian narratives—the body's pivotal role in salvation, women's association with the sin-prone flesh, and the anticipated perfection of bodies in the resurrection—were recycled for centuries, inspiring practices and attitudes toward food and eating that reflected dominant concerns and beliefs in their historical contexts. For example, the early church leader Tertullian (d. 220) suggested that emaciated bodies would have an easier time getting through the narrow gates to heaven, and that only light-weight bodies could be resurrected.[18] By the fourth and fifth centuries, ascetic Christians fasted as a means of restoring their bodies to the innocence of Eden, while preparing themselves for the incorruptible perfection of the flesh they expected to enjoy in the heavenly hereafter.[19] During the late Middle Ages (1200–1500), fasting became an especially popular method for cultivating holiness among pious women, who refused food as a way of identifying with the suffering of Christ and exercising some self-direction in a male-dominated church and society.[20]

During the modern period, fasting as a religious discipline was reinvented to include more-than-spiritual goals—especially physical health.[21] According to Bryan S. Turner, the rise of a mechanistic worldview in this era involved a "secularization of the body," whereby the body as the site of sin and salvation became the object of medical scrutiny.[22]

With the rise of scientific authority, Christian understandings of the soul as connected to the flesh and dependent on God gave way to a view of the person as comprised of a machine-like body inhabited by a rational, autonomous will. Yet traditional Christian views of the flesh as disobedient, unpredictable, and in need of taming did not entirely disappear. In the narratives of modern science, Christianity's moralizing approach to appetite merged with a modern (Cartesian) notion of the "self" as sovereign individual to create a fantasy of the ideal body as not just desirable but achievable.

## THE EMERGENCE AND CONSOLIDATION OF THE SLENDER IDEAL

In *Fat Shame,* the historian Amy Erdman Farrell shows how a confluence of cultural changes made slenderness a key feature of that fantasy during the latter half of the nineteenth century and early decades of the twentieth century. The overlapping processes of urbanization, industrialization, and the rise of a consumer-based economy (with advertising as its central artery) made lifestyles more sedentary, food more available, and body norms more visible for all but the poorest Americans. In this context, the Protestant mandate to work hard, control desire, and delay gratification clashed with market imperatives to buy more, seek pleasure, and gratify the senses.[23] A distinctly modern preference for slender bodies and disdain for fat flesh coalesced at the junction of these competing values. Restricting appetite and body size became a symbolic and practical means of navigating modernity's conflicting imperatives: refrain and indulge.

Erdman Farrell's work also illuminates how dominant views on race, ethnicity, evolution, and civilization meshed with fears about the excesses of modernity to create the thin-adoring, fat-phobic culture we know today. Based on taxonomies that positioned lean, able-bodied, elite males of northern European descent at the apex of human evolution, late-nineteenth-century men of science identified corpulence as a common physical feature of "primitive" people—a trait that manifested their lack-of-control over bodily appetites and proved their inferiority.[24] In the United States, race, gender, cultural, religious, economic, and body-size hierarchies intersected as the slender physique became associated with white, bourgeois, Protestant, Anglo-Saxon privilege, and the plump form was identified with poor, working-class, and/or ethnic immigrants (especially Jewish and Catholic women) from eastern and southern European countries or Ireland. As the historian Hillel Schwartz points out, the same lean body that had been associated with sickness, poverty, and ethnic "otherness" for much of the nineteenth century, came to symbolize health and economic, racial, and cultural/religious privilege by the end of World War I.[25]

Throughout the twentieth century, the same web of superiority complexes that generated the white, Western, Protestant preference for thinness fueled the demonization of fat flesh, which became associated with a broader range of moral evils (beyond gluttony), e.g., laziness, ugliness, stupidity, greed, criminality, animality.[26] During this time, a variety of mainstream ideologies and institutions converged to strengthen the link between slenderness and social privilege, promote weight loss as the key to happiness, health, and beauty, and create the impression that thinness is a natural, eternal, universal ideal. In her historical account of these trends, Roberta Pollack Seid astutely observes that by the closing decades of the twentieth century, the fervor with which many people sought to downsize their bodies bordered on the religious:

> If sloth and gluttony have always been condemned as sins, we have taken those sins as the cornerstone of a new faith. We believe in physical perfectibility and see its pursuit as a moral obligation. The wayward are punished with ugliness, illness, and early death. The good get their just rewards: beauty and a blessedly long, happy, and fulfilling life. The virtue that presumably will put us on this road is our ability to control one of our most fundamental instincts—eating.[27]

According to Seid, this "new religion" became so pervasive—and so *persuasive*—in the latter half of the twentieth century because it meshed so well with some of America's most cherished ideologies and systems, including faith in the objectivity of science, belief in the power of individual self-mastery, and an economy driven by the relentless pursuit of profit.

## THE ICONOGRAPHY OF FLAWLESS
## FEMALE BODIES

In the late 1960s, these ideologies and systems visibly converged in idealized images of tightly contoured female bodies. This was the time when the fashion industry began featuring ultra-skinny models, who made their average-sized predecessors look pudgy. Like the images of female saints to which historical Christians looked for inspiration, commercial/celebrity icons of femininity function as role models in the eyes of millions of girls and women, who are socialized to cultivate virtue through beauty. Unlike our historical foresisters, however, who looked to exemplary holy women with the *conscious intention* of imitating their admirable qualities, most females today view popular pictures of models and movie stars as *entertainment,* unaware of the lessons these Photoshopped prototypes quietly inculcate.[28]

Part of what makes media images so effective as tools of indoctrination is the potent combination of their homogeny (model women are *uniformly* toned and trim) and their ubiquity (mass-produced pictures of this narrow ideal are *everywhere*). But the images' power to attract our attention and admiration also stems from their use of visual cues and conventions that associate thinness with social privilege. The slender bodies of idealized women are young, able-bodied, and affluent-looking (e.g., wearing expensive clothing). Frequently depicted as the object of male desire, they quietly sanction heteronormativity (the belief that everyone is—or should be—straight). Moreover, these feminine icons are disproportionately white. Those with darker skin often have Caucasian-looking features (thin lips and nose), suggesting the need to assimilate to an Anglo-Saxon norm, and/or they are sexualized in ways that reinforce racist stereotypes of black or brown women as more animalistic and exotic.[29] Implicitly, commercial fantasies of white femininity continue the colonial legacy of the "White Lady," whose Victorian image promoted the superiority of racially-economically-religiously-culturally privileged women.[30] This legacy continued well beyond the colonial era. For example, black women were not allowed to participate in the Miss America Pageant until the early 1960s![31]

Through their omnipresence, homogenous images of slender bodies establish a *universal* standard for female body size—though this norm represents a very *specific* ideal. Thanks to the media's missionizing role, this white, Western fantasy now colonizes the imaginations of women in cultures that have traditionally affirmed a diversity of body types. A well-known study of this colonial dynamic was conducted in Fiji, where, prior to the introduction of Western TV in 1995, there were no signs of body dissatisfaction among females, and fat women were deemed attractive. Just three years after U.S. and British programs started broadcasting there, more than two-thirds of Fijian girls surveyed admitted having tried to lose weight, and three-quarters reported feeling "too fat."[32] Promoted through popular pictures that link slenderness to various forms of social privilege, the religion of thinness has become a vehicle for spreading Euro-American "civilizing" values.[33]

## THE MORALITY OF THE RELIGION OF THINNESS: CREATING A *GOOD* BODY

Both the rituals and images of the religion of thinness draw support from the moral codes this faith engenders and circulates. According to these rules, food is not primarily a nourishing and pleasurable source of energy. Food is *temptation.* Consequently, abstaining from eating produces feelings of virtue. Consuming "too much" generates feelings of shame—and, for some, the need for penance, e.g., "atoning" for the "sin" of overindulging by starving the body or purging it with laxatives, vomiting, or excessive exercise. Though bad for your health, these sacrificial rituals may be deemed necessary for the sake of a *good* body.

The very phrase, *good body*, points to the moral underpinnings of women's pursuit of thinness. These underpinnings are most obvious in Christian-based dieting. Comprised primarily of evangelical weight-loss programs, books, and products, this multi-billion dollar crusade is dedicated to helping the faithful transfigure their flesh to the one-and-only size God allegedly intended it to be: skinny. Starting in the 1950s, titles like *Pray Your Weight Away* (Charlie Shedd, 1957) and *Help Lord, the Devil Wants Me Fat* (C. S. Lovett, 1982) preached that overeating is the devil's seduction and that fat manifests an idolatrous relationship with food.[34] Many evangelical weight-loss gurus emphasize the specific importance for Christian women to remain svelte, since female attractiveness is good publicity for God. Founder of the popular Weigh-Down Workshop, Gwen Shamblin, says a lithe, delicate form proves that a woman has submitted herself to the Lord by overcoming the urge to overeat.[35] In her analysis of evangelical dieting, R. Marie Griffith notes that Christian weight-loss gurus have not been overly concerned about distinguishing between God's commands and popular culture's body norms.[36]

The same moralizing theology that blatantly supports Christian dieting is tacitly embedded in secular weight-loss rhetoric, rituals, and narratives. Recognizably religious language is common in commercials that associate low-fat or low-calorie foods with purity—for example, Weight Watcher's reduced fat cream cheese is advertised as "heavenly," and Pure Protein Bars are marketed as "sinfully delicious."[37] According to Emily Contois, weight-loss regimens as secular-seeming as the Atkins Diet and the South Beach Diet are rife with Protestant ideas and idioms. The books promoting these low-carb salvation plans use guilt, confession, and conversion tactics to motivate sacrifice and conviction in the hearts and minds of believers in thinness.[38] Perhaps the most popular example of the born-again story line of weight-loss redemption is the TV "reality" show *The Biggest Loser*, on which fat contestants compete to win cash prizes and, of course, the rewards of thinness.

Curiously, the moral imperative for every*body* to be thin ignores people's uneven access to the resources that sculpting and maintaining a "good" body requires. Healthy foods—like fresh fruits and vegetables, which tend to be lower in calories—are usually more expensive than processed products. And neither the time nor accoutrements through which bourgeois bodies are tightened and distinguished (e.g., health clubs, home work-out equipment, weight-loss spas) are affordable to low-income people. Even exercise that seems to be free (e.g., walking or jogging) is a limited option for those living in neighborhoods where being outside can be unsafe.[39] The religion of thinness fosters complicity with these injustices. By encouraging us to devote our moral energy to the project of slimming, this secular faith sanctions a social/symbolic system that privileges some bodies at the expense of others.

## THE ECONOMIC UNDERPINNINGS OF THE EXPANDING QUEST TO REDUCE

The same moral rules and sensibilities that helped make slenderness a nonnegotiable feature of the good body enabled entrepreneurs to capitalize on women's anxious yearnings to achieve that ideal. Despite signs that the profit margins of weight-loss industries may be mildly contracting,[40] the $64-billion-a-year business remains robust, feeding on the dysfunctional eating habits a profit-driven food system encourages. On the one hand, marketers urge us to indulge our appetites and satisfy our cravings. Sales for highly processed edible products—namely, foods loaded with the sugar-fat-salt combination that pushes our evolutionary buttons and makes us want to eat more—have drastically increased in recent decades, contributing to Americans' growing girth.[41] On the other hand, health officials instruct us to restrict caloric intake and avoid fast, convenient, junky foods. Diet industries cash in on this instruction by selling us products, tools, and programs that promise to help us repent and reduce.[42]

Sometimes these schizoid messages—*indulge* and *refrain*—appear side by side. For example, the cover of the March 2016 issue of *Woman's World* announces "NEGATIVE-CALORIE FOODS!" that will help you "LOSE 17 LBS in 10 days!" The large, bold-faced copy runs through the slender-but-shapely torso of the magazine's conventionally attractive cover model. Directly below this promise of miraculous weight loss, we see a scrumptious-looking chocolate cake, shamrock-shaped cookies, and a generously frosted leprechaun cupcake. Such mixed messages (i.e., shed pounds and have your cake too) may seem to be diametrically opposed, but they are deeply connected: both the pressure to trim down and the enticement to dig in are rooted in the dynamics and imperatives of consumer capitalism—an economic system that preys on and profits from our conflicted relationships with our appetites and food.[43]

Despite the "help" we receive from weight-loss companies, many of us have bodies that refuse to cooperate with the dominant cultural mandate for thinness. "I've tried everything" is a recurring theme in the painful testimonials of countless unsuccessful dieters. Studies indicate that most people who shed pounds dieting regain what they lost within four to five years, leading some scientists to suggest that the phrase "permanent weight loss" is oxymoronic.[44] Ironically, the failure of commercial slimming products and programs to help full-figured consumers stay permanently thin is crucial to the success of the dieting business. Though weight-loss companies' rhetoric supports salvation through thinness, in reality, fulfilling their promises would hurt their bottom line. The commercial underpinnings of our fat-hating/thin-worshipping culture prompts Erdman Farrell to speak of the "diet industrial complex," which she compares to the "military industrial complex" President Eisenhower warned Americans about in 1961: "just as the purpose of the military industrial complex is to maintain itself, not to seek peace, the purpose of the diet-industrial complex is to keep people dieting … rather than to seek health."[45] This analogy is especially compelling when you consider the financial boost weight-loss markets received in the late 1990s when the U.S. government officially declared "war on obesity."

## THE "WAR ON OBESITY"

This campaign enlisted mainstream medicine to foster a sense of urgency in the crusade to conquer soft, adipose tissue. The popular news media supported this mission, rallying public support for the battle with thousands of reports and stories warning Americans of the dangers of the "obesity epidemic."[46] In the wake of 9/11, when public anxiety was at an all-time high, the war's leaders galvanized citizens to get back in control by getting fit. A few months after the terrorist attacks, the U.S. secretary of health and human services urged every American to lose ten pounds "as a patriotic gesture." In the years that followed, government officials likened "obesity" to the perils posed by "weapons of mass destruction" and the "terrorist threat."[47]

However hyperbolic, this comparison reveals the war's basic premise, namely, the belief that fat is a killer—that being "obese," or even "overweight," will destroy your health. This belief is so basic to the religion of thinness, that questioning it is tantamount to heresy. And yet, a growing corpus of peer-reviewed research supports a more nuanced, unorthodox view. In *Body Respect,* the nutrition researchers Linda Bacon and Lucy Aphramor discuss this evidence, including studies indicating that "overweight" people do not die sooner than their average-size peers, that shedding pounds does not prolong life, that fat individuals do not necessarily consume more calories than their slender peers, and that *fitness* is more important than *body size* in determining health and longevity. In short, this research demonstrates that weight is not the best barometer of health (cholesterol, blood sugar, and blood pressure are more reliable indicators of physical well-being), and that while heavier weights are clearly *associated* with increased risk for some diseases, being fat does not *cause* diseases.[48]

Despite scientific evidence that calls for more nuanced understandings of the relationship between body size and physical wellness, the war's propaganda insists that health = thinness. Government and public health officials promote this "truth" by advocating faith in the Body

Mass Index (BMI) as a reliable measure of health and fitness. BMI is calculated using a weight-to-height ratio, and scores are correlated with physical well-being (i.e., a "normal" BMI is considered "healthy"). Although this formula seems straightforward, the BMI disregards variances in somatic composition (muscle, bone, fat), which explains why successful athletes are sometimes diagnosed as "overweight."[49] The BMI also ignores racial, ethnic, gender, and hereditary diversity, as well as other environmental factors (e.g., poverty, educational level, access to nutritious food and exercise, etc.) that even the government admits have a bigger impact on health than individual lifestyle choices.[50] Though many health care professionals treat the BMI as dogma, its calculations and classifications are neither infallible, nor timeless, nor objective. For example, seven of the nine scientists who decided in 1998 to lower the BMI cutoff points for defining "overweight" and "obese"— a decision that re-categorized millions of people as fat and presumably unhealthy—had financial ties to the diet industry.[51]

The power of BMI numbers and categories to distort self-perception is exemplified in the story of a college student named Annemarie, who recalls the day when, at age twelve, she and her classmates were summoned by a nurse to be weighed as part of a physical education class. She was 5'7," athletic, and had never given a second thought to her weight:

> I happily stepped up onto the scale and then stepped aside as the nurse quickly calculated my BMI, something I had never heard of. She gave me my number, which was written in red, and explained to me that I was overweight … she sternly looked at me and told me that I absolutely had to get my weight down, and I was stunned. As I walked out, I realized that there were many other kids who had never heard of BMI and they had the same staggered look on their faces that I did.

Gradually, Annemarie's initial confusion about her diagnosis as "overweight" gave way to total trust in the BMI as an index of her well-being. "I basically believed that BMI was the word of God, unwavering and immovable." Although she was a strong athlete with a self-described "solid" body throughout her school years, her above-normal BMI score remained "the source of many sleepless nights and dreadful days."[52]

In *Fat-Talk Nation,* the medical anthropologist Susan Greenhalgh explores the unseen costs of America's "war on obesity" by asking: "How do heavy people feel being the object of such visceral hatred, verbal abuse, and outright discrimination?" To investigate this question, Greenhalgh had her college students write "auto-ethnographies" in which they reflected on the ways weight issues have affected their lives.[53] Their stories reveal the damage the anti-fat crusade inflicts in heart-breaking detail. Fat students of various colors, classes, and cultural backgrounds tell of parents warning them that they'll never find love, success, or happiness unless they trim down. One describes how her mother repeatedly mocked her by falling on the floor, grabbing her chest, and pretending to have a heart attack, saying, "'That's what you will look like when you have a heart attack because you're so fat.'"[54] Some students recount incidents of vicious bullying at school—for example, a young man was called a "fat, ugly piece of shit" by his peers; a young woman had trash hurled at her as she walked through the schoolyard. Large-bodied students seek refuge from such brutality by socially withdrawing—a strategy that frequently results in anxiety and/or depression. Students of all sizes report agonizing daily over food and body image, and many resort to dangerous weight-reducing methods (e.g., drugs, starvation, compulsive exercising, vomiting, smoking) in their desperation to be thinner. One heavy-set young woman's remarks epitomize the sense of shame that pervades Greenhalgh's students' narratives: "It was hard for me to communicate effectively with boys or prettier girls, since I felt I was too ugly to speak to them.... Overall, I felt that I was inferior to everyone and that I would disgust people because I was fat."[55]

While critics of America's "war on obesity" have insightfully exposed its financial underpinnings,[56] this woman's comments point to its psychic and spiritual costs, including self-hatred. Her words—

especially her use of the term "disgust"—also point to the moral overtones and functions of the anti-fat crusade: how it identifies a common
enemy and thereby creates a shared sense of purpose, and how it gives
ordinary citizens a way to feel in control, to belong, to be good. Ultimately, the "war on obesity" is the flip side of the religion of thinness.
Both deploy beliefs, images, rituals, and moral codes to support the
pursuit of salvation through weight loss. Both promote a one-size-fits-
all mentality and mission that make happiness, health, and beauty contingent on being skinny. Both tap our existential need for a sense of
meaning, even though they shortchange that need and exacerbate the
insecurities and shame they promise to cure.

## CREATING THE ULTIMATE BODY: "IS THIS A NEW RELIGION?"

Back in the mid-1990s, when I first started studying women's quest for
salvation through weight loss, I came across a magazine ad for Avia
running shoes, whose text helped clarify and affirm my inquiry. "**Is
This a New Religion?**" the boldfaced copy asks. The central image of
the two-page ad features the lean, sweating figure of a young white
woman in a leotard, arms extended in a gesture that recalls a crucifix.
This main image is flanked by two others: on one side, the same woman
is bent over and lifting weights, muscles and bosom accentuated by a
bluish haze; on the other, there is a close-up of the shoes in the same
mystifying light. Together these images form a triptych, but the religious motifs do not stop there. In the upper corners of each page, the ad
addresses its own question:

> This is not about guilt. It's about joy. Strength. The revival of the spirit. I
> come here seeking redemption in sweat. And it is here I am forgiven my
> sinful calories. Others may never understand my dedication. But for me,
> fitness training is something much more powerful than exercise. It is what
> keeps my body healthy. It is what keeps my mind clear. And it is where I
> learn the one true lesson. To believe in myself. Avia.

On an obvious level, this text illustrates the affinities between the religion of thinness and certain aspects of traditional Christianity. More subtly, however, it suggests that women's subordination within traditional religion makes them prime candidates for this "secular" substitute. Defined through an ostensibly progressive rejection of biblical religion's most notoriously harmful features—its degradation of women and the body—this commercial alternative proffers a new ultimate point of reference: the diligently trained, tightly toned, notably slender female body. Juxtaposing a stereotypical view of Christianity (characterized by guilt, damnation, and belief in female weakness) with a vision of a supposedly liberating "new religion" (defined by joy, redemption, and affirmation of female strength), this ad speaks to those whose need for meaning remains unfulfilled by the promises of traditional religion.

Surely, there are resources both within and beyond traditional religions that can help all of us develop more peaceful, respectful, and responsible relationships with our bodies—resources that enable us to challenge the religion of thinness and create a more just society in which physical diversity is appreciated rather than feared. While there is not room to explore those resources here, I encourage you to give some thought to what they might be. For in the end, the question the Avia ad raises is not simply whether women's pursuit of salvation through thinness constitutes a new religion, but what kind of religion this pursuit turns out to be.

### DISCUSSION QUESTIONS

1. Why do you think so many girls and women in particular are drawn to the pursuit of thinness as a source of meaning, value, and purpose? Why does Lelwica suggest that this is especially a problem for women and girls? What role do you think popular culture and traditional religion play in supporting this pursuit? Can you think of examples not mentioned in this chapter?

2. After reading this chapter, are you persuaded that this pursuit serves what has historically been a religious function? Do you think secular and religious phenomena are essentially distinct, or impossible to definitively distinguish?

3. What makes a body good? What makes a body healthy? What makes a body beautiful? Where do our ideas about virtue, health, and beauty come from? What roles do traditional religion and popular culture play in shaping those ideas? How have popular culture and traditional religion shaped your own relationship with your own body and whether you see it as "good," "healthy," and/or "beautiful"?

4. What resources within traditional Christianity or other religions you know well can be harnessed to challenge the religion of thinness and the fat shame it encourages? What resources within popular culture might be used to challenge the religion of thinness and the damage it inflicts on nonconforming bodies?

## NOTES

1. I develop this fluid/functional definition of "religion" in chapter 1 of *Shameful Bodies: Religion and the Culture of Physical Improvement* (London: Bloomsbury, 2017).

2. See Michelle M. Lelwica, *The Religion of Thinness: Satisfying the Spiritual Hungers behind Women's Obsession with Food and Weight* (Carlsbad, CA: Gurze, 2009). *The Religion of Thinness* is written for a more-than-academic audience, though it draws on work I did for my dissertation, which I revised and published as *Starving for Salvation: The Spiritual Dimensions of Eating Problems among American Girls and Women* (New York: Oxford University Press, 1999).

3. My focus on women is not meant to exclude or downplay the struggles many men experience in relation to body size. Rather, this focus reflects both the overrepresentation of women in the religion of thinness, and my own scholarly training and interests in women's studies in religion.

4. Clifford Geertz, "Religion as a Cultural System," in *The Interpretation of Cultures* (New York: Basic Books, 1973), 87–125, quotations from pp. 98, 89.

5. Marya Hornbacher, *Wasted: A Memoir of Anorexia and Bulimia* (New York: HarperCollins, 1998), 118.

6. Mary Douglas, *Natural Symbols: Explorations in Cosmology* (1970; repr., New York: Pantheon Books, 1982); *Purity and Danger: An Analysis of the Concept of Pollution and Taboo* (1966; repr., New York: Routledge, 1991).

7. Catherine Bell, *Ritual Theory, Ritual Practice* (New York: Oxford University Press, 2009), 48–49, 83–90.

8. Barbara Katz, "Weighing the Cost," in *Eating Our Hearts Out: Personal Accounts of Women's Relationship to Food,* ed. Leslea Newman (Freedom, CA: Crossing Press, 1993), 189–93, quotation from p. 189.

9. Pamela Gross, "A Separation of Self," in Newman, *Eating Our Hearts Out,* 63–67, quotation from p. 65

10. Susan Bordo, *Unbearable Weight: Feminism, Western Culture and the Body* (Berkeley: University of California Press, 1993), 27.

11. Sallie Tisdale, "A Weight That Women Carry: The Compulsion to Diet in a Starved Culture," in *Minding the Body: Women Writers on Body and Soul,* ed. Patricia Foster (New York: Doubleday, 1994), 15–31, quotation from p. 17.

12. Maura Kelly, "Hunger Striking," in *Going Hungry: Writers on Desire, Self-Denial, and Overcoming Anorexia,* ed. Kate Taylor (New York: Anchor Books, 2008), 3–29, quotation from p. 9.

13. "The Pro Ana Lifestyle," http://theproanalifestyle.weebly.com/the-ana-religion—lifestyle.html. Googling "Pro-Ana" yields numerous "thinspirational" images and other web pages devoted to promoting this subculture. In addition to these "primary texts," my discussion of pro-Ana draws on George Lynell, "Nurturing an Anorexia Obsession: 'Pro-Ana' Web Sites Tout the Eating Disorder as a Choice, Not an Illness, to the Horror of Experts," *Los Angeles Times,* February 12, 2002; Jill Barcum, "The Struggle with 'Ana,'" *Minneapolis Star Tribune,* May 1, 2005; and Martha Irvine, "Worshipping 'Ana': Eating Disorders Take on a Life of Their Own for Sufferers," *Brainerd Daily Dispatch,* May 31, 2005.

14. The percentage for fourth-grade girls is based on a study conducted in the Chicago and San Francisco areas, cited in Joan Jacobs Brumberg, *Fasting Girls: The History of Anorexia Nervosa* (New York: Random House, 1988), 32; percentage for women in their fifties appears in Lindsay McLaren and Diana Kuh, "Body Dissatisfaction in Midlife Women," *Journal of Women and Aging* 16 (2004): 35–55; figures for healthy-weight adult women and high school girls are from Jean Kilbourne, *Deadly Persuasion: Why Women and Girls Must Fight the Addictive Power of Advertising* (New York: Free Press, 1999), 125, 134.

15. Susan Bordo, makes this point throughout *Unbearable Weight,* and in "The Empire of Images in Our World of Bodies," *Chronicle of Higher Education* 50

(December 19, 2003): B6–B10.

16. For an extended overview of this history, see chapter 6 of *Shameful Bodies*. For detailed discussions of historical attitudes toward food and appetite, see Susan Hill, *Eating to Excess: The Meaning of Gluttony and the Fat Body in the Ancient World* (Westport, CT: Praeger, 2011); Theresa Shaw, *The Burden of the Flesh: Fasting and Sexuality in Early Christianity* (Minneapolis: Augsburg Fortress, 1998); Carolyn Walker Bynum, *Holy Feast and Holy Fast: The Religious Significance of Food for Medieval Women* (Berkeley: University of California Press, 1987); Laura Fraser, "The Inner Corset: A Brief History of Fat in the United States," in *The Fat Studies Reader*, ed. Esther D. Rothblum and Sondra Solovay (New York: New York University Press, 2009), 11–14; Christina Less, "Reluctant Appetites: Anglo-Saxon Attitudes towards Fasting," in *Saints and Scholars: New Perspectives on Anglo-Saxon Literature and Culture in Honour of Hugh Magennis*, ed. Stuart McWilliams (Cambridge: D.S. Brewer, 2012); R. Marie Griffith, *Born Again Bodies: Flesh and Spirit in American Christianity* (Berkeley: University of California Press, 2004).

17. I discuss these three traditional Christian narratives more extensively, with historical references, in chapter 2 of *Shameful Bodies*.

18. Less, "Reluctant Appetites," 170; Lisa Isherwood, *The Fat Jesus: Christianity and Body Image* (New York: Seabury Books, 2008), 47.

19. Shaw, *Burden of the Flesh*, 25, 163; 174–76; 223–24

20. Bynum, *Holy Feast and Holy Fast*.

21. Bryan Turner, *The Body and Society: Explorations in Social Theory* (New York: Basil Blackwell, 1984) and *Regulating Bodies: Essays in Medical Sociology* (New York: Routledge, 1992). See also Griffith, *Born Again Bodies*, 23–68.

22. Turner, *Body and Society*, 36–37.

23. Amy Eardman Farrell, *Fat Shame: Stigma and the Fat Body in American Culture* (New York: New York University Press, 2011). Erdman Farrell's account builds on previous work on the history of dieting, especially Hillel Schwartz, *Never Satisfied: A Cultural History of Diets, Fantasies, and Fat* (New York: Free Press, 1986), and Peter Stearns, *Fat History: Bodies and Beauty in the Modern West* (New York: New York University Press, 1997), whose arguments she summarizes on p. 44.

24. Ibid., 59–81, esp. 62–63, 68–72.

25. Hillel Schwartz, *Never Satisfied*, 142–43. On the "Americanization" of ethnic minority and working-class cultures through monitoring body size and eating habits, see Schwartz, *Never Satisfied*, 248–49; Roberta Pollack Seid, *Never Too Thin: Why Women Are at War with Their Bodies* (New York: Prentice Hall, 1989), 91, 226; and Harvey Levenstein, *Revolution at the Table: The Transformation of the American Diet* (New York: Oxford University Press, 1988), 104. Griffith

describes the form of Christianity that most influenced Americans' pursuit of physical perfectibility as "white, middle-class Protestantism," noting that many of the "somatic disciplines and devotions" that characterize this pursuit "draw their source and momentum from specific Protestant patterns" (*Born Again Bodies,* 4, 8–9).

26. Eardman Farrell, *Fat Shame,* 4.

27. Seid, *Never Too Thin,* 18–19

28. Margaret Miles, *Image as Insight: Visual Understanding in Western Christianity and Secular Culture* (1985; repr., New York: Wipf & Stock, 2006), 7–9, 128.

29. bell hooks, *Black Looks: Race and Representation* (Boston: South End, 1992), 63–72, 21; Delores Williams, "A Womanist Perspective on Sin," in *A Troubling in My Soul: Womanist Perspectives on Evil and Suffering,* ed. Emilie Townes (Maryknoll, NY: Orbis, 1993), 143.

30. Elisabeth Schüssler Fiorenza, *Wisdom Ways: Introducing Feminist Biblical Interpretation* (Maryknoll, NY: Orbis, 2001), 26, 108; Kwok Pui-lan, "Unbinding Our Feet: Saving Brown Women and Feminist Religious Discourse," in *Postcolonialism, Feminist, and Religious Discourse,* ed. Laura Donaldson and Kwok Pui-lan (New York: Routledge, 2002), 63.

31. Cheryl Townsend Gilkes, "The 'Loves' and 'Troubles' of African-American Women's Bodies: A Womanist Challenge to Cultural Humiliation and Community Ambivalence," in *A Troubling in My Soul: Womanist Perspectives on Evil and Suffering,* ed. Emilie Townes (Maryknoll, NY: Orbis, 1993), 241.

32. A. Becker et al., "Eating Behaviors and Attitudes Following Prolonged Exposure to Television among Ethnic Fijian and Adolescent Girls," *British Journal of Psychiatry* 180 (2002): 509–14.

33. I discuss the neocolonial dynamics of the religion of thinness in depth in "Spreading the Religion of Thinness from California to Calcutta: A Postcolonial Feminist Analysis," *Journal of Feminist Studies in Religion* 25, no. 1 (April 2009): 19–42.

34. My discussion of evangelical dieting draws heavily on Marie Griffith's analysis in *Born Again Bodies,* 160–250. See also Lynn Gerber, *Seeking the Straight and Narrow: Weight Loss and Sexual Reorientation in Evangelical America* (Chicago: University of Chicago Press, 2011).

35. Isherwood, *Fat Jesus,* 77; Griffith, *Born Again Bodies,* 212–14, 222.

36. Griffith, *Born Again Bodies,* 180.

37. I analyze these and other examples of religious language used in the marketing of diet foods in *Religion of Thinness,* 174–78.

38. Emily Contois, "Guilt-Free and Sinfully Delicious: A Contemporary Theology of Weight Loss Dieting," in *Fat Studies: An Interdisciplinary Journal of*

*Body Weight and Society,* special issue ed. Lynn Gerber, Susan Hill, and LeRhonda Manigault-Bryant 4 (2015): 112–25.

39. Rosemary Bray makes these points in "Heavy Burden," *Essence* (October 1989): 53–54.

40. John Kell notes the recent slowdown in the diet industry's profits in "Lean Times for the Diet Industry," *Fortune,* May 22, 2015, http://fortune.com/2015/05/22/lean-times-for-the-diet-industry.

41. David Kessler, *The End of Overeating: Taking Control of the Insatiable American Appetite* (New York: Rodale, 2009).

42. In its 393-page study entitled, "The U.S. Weight Loss & Diet Control Market (9th edition)," Marketdata Enterprises, Inc. reports that Americans spent $58 billion trying to shed pounds in 2007, projecting a 6 percent annual growth rate for weight-loss industries, which put the figure at $68.7 billion for 2010 (www.healthyweightnetwork.com/trends.htm#9). In 2014, Marketdata Enterprises reported that the weight-loss market was $64 billion, a figure Kell discusses in "Lean Times for the Diet Industry."

43. Susie Orbach, *Bodies* (New York: Picador, 2009), 126.

44. Glenn Gaesser, "Is 'Permanent Weight Loss' an Oxymoron? The Statistics on Weight Loss and the National Weight Control Registry," in *The Fat Studies Reader,* ed. Esther D. Rothblum and Sondra Solovay (New York: New York University Press, 2009), 37–39.

45. Erdman Farrell, *Fat Shame,* 13–14.

46. Eric Oliver, *Fat Politics: The Real Story Behind America's Obesity Epidemic* (New York: Oxford University Press, 2006), 37.

47. Charlotte Biltekoff, "The Terror Within: Obesity in Post 9/11 U.S. Life," *American Studies* 48, no. 3 (Fall 2007): 29, 34; Susan Greenhalgh, *Fat-Talk Nation: The Human Costs of America's War on Fat* (Ithaca, NY: Cornell University Press, 2015) 8; Linda Bacon and Lucy Aphramor, *Body Respect: What Conventional Health Books Get Wrong, Leave Out, and Just Plain Fail to Understand about Weight* (Dallas: BenBella Books, 2014), 11; Linda Bacon, *Health at Every Size: The Surprising Truth about Your Weight* (2008; repr., Dallas: Benbella Books, 2010), xxiii.

48. Bacon and Aphramor, *Body Respect,* 12–26; Bacon, *Health at Every Size,* 68, 124, 129–30, 137–40; Marilyn Wann, *Fat! So? Because You Don't Have to Apologize for Your Size!* (Berkeley, CA : Ten Speed Press, 1998), 41, 52.

49. Greenhalgh, *Fat-Talk Nation,* 125–26, 282–84.

50. Bacon and Aphramore, *Body Respect,* 22–23.

51. Bacon, *Health at Every Size,* 151.

52. Quoted in Greenhalgh, *Fat-Talk Nation,* 116.

53. Greenhalgh, *Fat-Talk Nation,* 289.

54. Ibid., 79.

55. Ibid., 109, 102, 174, 241.

56. Oliver, *Fat Politics*; Kathleen LeBesco, *Revolting Bodies: The Struggle to Redefine Fat Identity* (Amherst: University of Massachusetts Press, 2004); Paul Campos, *The Obesity Myth: Why America's Obsession with Weight Is Hazardous to Your Health* (New York: Gotham Books, 2004); Glenn A. Gaesser, *Big Fat Lies: The Truth About Your Weight and Your Health* (Carlsbad, CA: Gurze, 2002); Michael Gard and Jan Wright, *The Obesity Epidemic: Science, Morality and Ideology* (New York: Routledge, 2005).

# CHAPTER FOURTEEN

# The "Godding Up" of American Sports

JOSEPH L. PRICE

## RELIGIOUS DIMENSIONS OF SPORTS

Each year, on a Sunday at the beginning of February, more than half the people in America, and perhaps as much as one-tenth of the entire world's population, rivet their attention to a single remote event. By then the Super Bowl has dominated public attention for weeks, and viewers turn their faces to televisions even as prayerful Muslims turn toward Mecca. In 1985, the Super Bowl exercised such power that a private ceremony for Ronald Reagan's inauguration was held in the White House on the legislated day of January 20, a Sunday, while its public celebration was shifted to the following day, a frigid Monday in Washington, DC. Meanwhile, on Sunday the 20th in Palo Alto, California, Joe Montana and his crew of San Francisco 49ers commanded full national attention as they beat the Miami Dolphins.

The ongoing national veneration of the Super Bowl is signified by several presidential rituals. Ever since President Richard Nixon telephoned the victorious Kansas City Chiefs' locker room following Super Bowl IV in 1970, the president has routinely telephoned congratulatory messages to the championship game's winning coach. A decade later, President Jimmy Carter welcomed the Super Bowl champion Pittsburgh

Steelers to the White House for a reception that has now become an annual recognition event.[1]

The social allure and spiritual power of the Super Bowl are more particular than its national appeal to NFL fans and its celebration by American presidents. It has the power to create a groundswell of intense, cultic devotion among residents in the vicinity of the winning team's home city. In the 2014 season following the Seattle Seahawks' first appearance in the Super Bowl—a loss to the Steelers—fans in Seattle twice set world records for noise at a sporting event, and the combination of their stomping and jumping registered on the Richter scale. Regional fans there have so fervently identified with the team that they consider their vocal support and visible dress as necessary expression of their role as the "12th Man" on the team. Even months after the end of an earlier season when the Seahawks failed to reach the Super Bowl, the numeral 12 in Seahawk colors was prominently displayed in retail centers, at construction sites, and on T-shirts throughout the region to signify folks' allegiance to the team. Simply, reference to and representation of "12" express the cohesive identity of Seattleites that is generated and sustained by their professional football team.[2]

Throughout its first fifty years, the Super Bowl has steadily extended its impact beyond championship football contests, national political rituals, and distinct affiliation symbols. Economic exchanges, entertainment performances, and media programs have also become dominated by the event. In fact, fans' spending on the Super Bowl—purchasing tickets and making a pilgrimage to the game; attending sponsored parties in the host city and remote gatherings bedecked with official Super Bowl paraphernalia; placing bets in office pools and elsewhere—rivals the amount that Americans donate to traditional religious congregations and communities during a typical month. For Super Bowl 50, Nevada sportsbooks reported that more than $132 million was legally wagered in Las Vegas, and estimates of casual and illegal bets on the game exceeded $4 billion.[3]

The religious impact of sports, however, extends beyond the popular fascination with this most prominent national sporting event. Every week during intercollegiate sports seasons, fans orient their schedules toward their team's game, devote their attention to plays and players, and put on masks (painting their faces and bodies, dyeing their hair, and wearing color-coordinated jerseys, jackets, and sweatshirts) to increase their identification with their team. The religious significance of their activity is described succinctly by the American philosopher George Santayana, who thought of religion as "another world to live in." Yet Santayana "could not have anticipated how, for many millions of [Americans] ... what he meant by 'religion' would one day be displaced in the most immediate, existential and emotional sense by organized spectator sports."[4] For tens of millions of devoted fans throughout the country, sports constitute a popular form of religion, shaping their world and sustaining their ways of engaging it. Indeed, for many, sports are elevated to a kind of divine status, effecting an American apotheosis or what the legendary sportswriter Red Smith called "the godding up" of American sports.[5]

The *Sports Illustrated* journalist Frank Deford was among the first to identify the kind of religious hold that sports exert on modern Americans. Deford suggests that if Marx had lived today in the United States rather than in Victorian England, he would have declared that sports is the opiate of the people, anesthetizing them to class struggle and focusing their hopes on events that project fulfillment through a vicarious form of participation and through an often delayed form of gratification.[6] This poignant critique of sports and culture also indicts the decline of traditional religion's influence at the end of twentieth century. Other critics have drawn this conclusion more explicitly: "The decline of religion as a source of significant meaning in modern industrialized societies," Joyce Carol Oates avers, "has been extravagantly compensated by the rise of popular culture in general, of which the billion-dollar sports mania is the most visible manifestation."[7]

The fusion of sports and religion is neither eccentric nor particular to modern America. Throughout history, and across multiple cultures in today's world, mythic and ritual significance has often been recognized in a number of sports events and play activities. In ancient Greece, the Olympic Games were only one set of sporting events performed in honor of the gods—for their entertainment, since the gods were thought to be too serious to engage in recreational play and physical exercise, which they nonetheless enjoyed. In Central America, Mayans played ball games officiated by priests, on courts attached to temples, and with victory perhaps demanding the sacrifice of the team captain. Among other tribes and nations in precolonial America, the game of lacrosse bore religious weight in its ritual enactment of conflict and combat between contestant tribes, and perhaps in the use of its rackets to forecast or foresee future events; and for the Oglala Sioux, the seventh sacred rite of Tapa Wanka Yap, or "the throwing of the ball," combined spiritual and sporting dimensions. In Japan, sumo wrestling tournaments still utilize the Shinto purification rituals of throwing salt, and the space for the matches and the hierarchy of wrestlers reflect certain Shinto values; and a Zen approach to archery recognizes the sport as a spiritual exercise: the archer seeks to become unified with the bow and the target, precisely by not focusing on the athletic aspects of shooting an arrow. Throughout Asia, the physical and mental control demanded by karate and other martial arts can be understood as a spiritual discipline. And especially in South America and Europe, soccer promotes a sense of national identity that can rightly be considered religious.[8]

In America, sports have been identified as a form of civil religion (by the theologian Michael Novak), folk religion (by the sociologist James Mathisen), and cultural religion (by the religious historian Catherine Albanese).[9] However, several other scholars—trained in literary critical procedures or historical methods, rather than in religious studies or theology—have questioned whether sports really constitute a religion, which, they insist, is characterized by transcendental, sacramental, and inspirational social elements. The sociologist Harry Edwards hesitates to call sports a popular form of religion, suggesting instead that it is "essentially a secular, quasi-religious institution" that does not "substitute for formal sacred religious involvement."[10] Concurring with Edwards, the literary scholar Edwin Cady examines the ways in which collegiate football games provide a cultural spectacle for intensifying and celebrating rivalries. Cady claims that the "Big Game," which he calls "the most vitally folklorist event in our culture" is not in itself fundamentally religious, since it is not essentially sacramental, but he allows that it might feel sacred in approximately the same way that good art does.[11] On different grounds, the historian Joan Chandler refuses to classify sport as religion, since both priests and believers, on the one hand, and fans and players, on the other hand, would probably not identify the objects of their devotion as addressing or meeting the same spiritual needs.[12] Voicing yet another set of concerns, the cultural critic Robert J. Higgs contends that "sports are like religion in many ways just as they are like war in some ways, but they are not equatable with either."[13]

Addressing these critiques about classifying sports as religion, scholars have increasingly pursued theological, sociological, and historical analyses that build upon the recognition of sports as religion. In 2006, my treatise *Rounding the Bases: Baseball and Religion in America* appeared in the "Sports and Religion" series published by Mercer University Press, and it was followed shortly thereafter by Craig A. Forney's survey of major team sports in *The Holy Trinity of American Sports: Civil Religion in Football, Baseball, and Basketball* and Eric Bain-Selbo's examination of collegiate football in *Game Day and God: Football, Faith, and Politics in the American South*. In 2011, the American Academy of Religion began to devote sessions of its annual national meeting to sports. Subsequently, introductory textbooks featuring perspectives on sports as religion Rebecca T. Alpert's *Religion and Sports: An Introduction and Case Studies* and Eric Bain-Selbo and D. Gregory Sapp's *Understanding Sport as a Religious Phenomenon: An Introduction,* have been published by the sessions' organizers:.[14]

Even though sports do not manifest all the characteristics often associated with religion, neither do many religious traditions conform completely to the comprehensive set of characteristics that comprise the ideal norms against which historic religions are measured. And although Charles Lippy avoids calling sports a religion in his study of popular religiosity in America, he does identify a crucial contemporary factor for considering sports as a form of popular religion: the media. The incredible growth of spectator sports, he observes, has corresponded to, if not emerged out of, the expansion of media coverage of sports events.[15] Before the 1970s, when ABC began to telecast Monday Night Football and ESPN was founded, the only sports events regularly televised during weekdays and prime time were World Series games and Olympic events, and triple-header coverage of football games was restricted to the college bowls on New Year's Day. With cable systems providing increased coverage of college sports, it is now possible to view at least five football games on most Saturdays in season, and throughout each day its possible for sports junkies to watch live contests and recorded games on the NFL, NBA, and MLB networks, along with dedicated networks for the SEC, PAC 12, and Big 10 conferences.

When the telecasts of Sunday sports events began to increase in the mid-1970s, the journalist Frank Deford observed that "the churches have ceded Sunday to sports.... Sport owns Sunday now, and religion is content to leave a few minutes before the big games."[16] Not only do the overwhelming majority of Americans identify themselves as sports fans, but "sport, in its spectatorial and participatory forms, permeates our technological society to the extent that few are left untouched by it."[17] And the public's attraction to broadcast sports events represents more than merely the pursuit of entertainment, for "sports affect people, and their lives, far more deeply and for a longer time than mere diversion would."[18]

Harry Edwards was one of the first scholars to align aspects of sports with characteristics of religions, identifying their common concern with deity, authority, tradition, beliefs, devotees, ritual sites, and material elements. Superstar athletes correspond to religions' gods and deceased players serve as saints; commissioners and referees make and interpret rules like religious patriarchs and high councils; reporters and broadcasters who chronicle sports events and tabulate their statistics mirror scribes of religious traditions; sports trophies and memorabilia correspond to religious icons; dicta of common sports wisdom are like religious dogmas; sports stadiums and arenas function like houses of worship; and not only national sports halls of fame but trophy cases—the most local of sports reliquaries—resemble religious shrines. Finally, he identifies the faithful or devoted fans of sports with the true believers of a religious tradition.[19] With these perceptive points, Edwards prompts further reflections on how aspects of sports indeed correspond to elements of religions.

Most of Edwards's connections are drawn from a comparison of sports with theistic, scriptural religious traditions. In particular, his association of superstar athletes with gods calls the accuracy of his comparison into question, because the sports heroes are living, physical, visible actors, while gods, for all their presence and potency, remain invisible and nonmaterial.[20] Yet the historian of religion Charles S. Prebish supports Edwards's contention that sports heroes function as gods. "The child's worship of [baseball great] Ted Williams," Prebish offers, "is no less real than his or her reverential adoration of Christ, and to some, Williams's accomplishments and capabilities in baseball were unquestionably godly."[21]

The reverence and respect accorded to sports heroes and events are not restricted to children or to fans unfamiliar with characteristics of religion. One Saturday afternoon in late November 1993, more than seven thousand professors of religious studies convened at a hotel in Washington, DC, for their annual, professional meeting. Midway through the afternoon's sessions, a televised event claimed the attention—nay, devotion—of many of the professors. Initially, observers might have thought that the Notre Dame–Boston College football game was quite unlike the religious rituals that the professors studied. But as time wound down in the game, more than a hundred scholars spontaneously gathered around a lobby television set to watch its end. During the timeout called before the last-second field goal attempt, several of them fell to their knees, while others sat with hands clasped as though in prayer. When the winning kick went through the goal posts, players on the field and fans in stands leapt into each other's open embraces and cried with tears of ecstasy. Simultaneously, in the hotel lobby, Boston College supporters turned their faces upward, thrust their arms up, and shouted and whooped with joy. Their posture, volume, and spirit resembled a display of spirit-filled believers shouting, "Hallelujah!" As Michael Novak notes, the joy of victory in an athletic contest often prompts such a religious response, for winning games generates a feeling that "the gods are on one's side, as though one is Fate's darling, as if the powers of being course through one's veins and radiate from one's action—powers stronger than non-being, powers over ill fortune, powers over death," which is sampled in defeat. Victory, Novak asserts, "is abundant life."[22]

In contrast to the jubilation of the Boston College followers, dejected fans of the Fighting Irish reacted with rituals of mourning, first expressing shock that such a "tragedy" (as some of them put it) could occur, then denying defeat by proposing scenarios and plays that could have altered the outcome, and finally acknowledging the game's loss and their acute pain. Their grief was real, because a sports' defeat, as Novak avers, "symbolizes death, and it certainly feels like dying; but it is not death"; and he compares this rehearsal of death to the Christian sacraments of baptism and Eucharist, wherein the communicants symbolically experience death and rebirth.[23]

The religious promise of sports involves more than their substituting sports superstars for gods, or their supplanting religious rites and doctrines with sports rituals and rules. For the possible religious impact of sports derives from their basic spiritual dimensions and from the public's potential engagement with them. Addressing fundamental questions about the nature of religion and its exemplification in sports, Novak, like Edwards, draws up a list of correspondences between sports and religion. But unlike Edwards, Novak specifically affirms that "sports is, somehow, a religion." Throughout his 1976 book *The Joy of Sports: End Zones, Bases, Baskets, Balls, and the Consecration of the American Spirit,* he celebrates the spiritual dimensions and impact of sports, revels in various acts of sporting competition and in the admiration of sports heroes, and specifies the institutional correspondence between sports and religion—that they are "organized and structured." Like religions, which "place us in the presence of powers greater than ourselves, and seek to reconcile us to them," sports help participants confront the uncertainties of "Fate" by playing out contingencies in games, and by recognizing the role that chance plays in the outcome of contests. Religions regularly help people confront their anxieties and dreads about failure, aging, betrayal, and guilt, while competitive sports consistently engage participants in situations that "embody these in every combat." Furthermore, because both athletes and believers espouse a self-imposed subordination of their physical bodies to their wills, they develop a more determined "character through patterns of self-denial, repetition, and experiment."[24]

Novak also identifies sports with religion in the sense that both establish high standards of expectation, demand discipline, and strive toward perfection. Such pursuit of excellence creates and cultivates a climate of reverence—in religious traditions, manifest in devotion to saints; in sports activities, evident in celebration of heroes. In addition, Novak notes, religions normally create a sense of belonging by focusing initially on the bonding of local communities. This sense of affiliation becomes a paradigm for the germination and nurture of larger commitments—from local to national, from earthly to universal. Sports similarly generate a sense of identity with "the home team" and the loyalty that such a self-understanding entails. One of the means for generating this group identity is through rituals common to both religions and sports: just as religions use chants and songs and certain gestures, sports bond teammates and fans together through cheers ("Two bits, four bits, six bits, a dollar: All for our team, stand up and holler") and songs ("Take Me Out to the Ball Game," which features the call to "root, root, root for the home team," during the seventh inning stretch, or the school "fight song" at football games) and bodily movement (clapping, giving "high fives," slapping each other on the back, and so on). With each of these forms of acting and interacting, fans and players unite as a single body.

## THE SPIRITUALITY OF SPORTS

Underlying these common facets of religion and sports is the experience of *flow,* which the Hungarian psychologist Mihaly Csikszentmihalyi defines as "the state in which people are so involved in an activity that nothing else seems to matter; the experience itself is so enjoyable that people will do it even at great cost, for the sheer sake of doing it." Applying his insights on the psychology of optimal experience to participation and performance in sports and games, Csikszentmihalyi recognizes that such opportunities go beyond the boundaries and expectations of ordinary experience. Temporarily set apart from ordinary folks during sports contests and performances,

> players and spectators cease to act in terms of common sense, and concentrate instead on the peculiar reality of the game.
>
> Such *flow activities* have as their primary function the provision of enjoyable experiences.... Because of the way [that sports] are constructed, *they help participants and spectators achieve an ordered state of mind* that is highly enjoyable.[25]

"The peculiar reality of the game," as Csikszentmihalyi refers to it, constitutes the core of the spiritual power and religious significance of sports, and develops out of their ritual aspects—the game's time, space, rules, and purposes. In ritual and in play, the Dutch historian Johan Huizinga noted, performance space is set aside, demarcated as the "field of play" wherein a certain set of rules applies. During play or ritual, performance takes shape in a time of its own, certainly surrounded or engulfed by the chronometric measure of ordinary time but set off in such a way that the duration of the game conforms to a different standard of temporal computation, as in the play of baseball with its "innings" or in tennis with its sets and matches. Even the games that utilize a clock, such as football and basketball, run the clock and stop it at appointed times, measuring game time according to a different set of rules than those that govern the calculation of ordinary time. Finally, special rules within the designated space and time for play, such as rules regulating tackling (allowed in football but impermissible in ordinary relations) and taunting (forbidden in basketball, but not in ordinary affairs), create a microcosm, an area and time within whose confines an order is established.[26]

Like Huizinga, the historian of religions Mircea Eliade recognized the world-making functions of ritual, although he had a somewhat different perspective on their purpose. Eliade applies the concepts of ritual space and time to his analysis of humans as *homo religiosus*: for him, the categories of time and space provide the orientation for "cosmicization," or the development of a worldview, construing and maintaining one's way of being in the world. All such acts of cosmicization are fundamentally religious, because the establishment of order in a new world—even one such as that of a game—replicates the cosmogonic act of the gods in the creation of the world. And sacred time, like play time, is discontinuous with ordinary time. It is reversible and replicable, a different realm of time, in which one might forget ordinary time.[27] Like priests performing and laypersons attending religious rites, athletes and spectators lose track of ordinary time when the game is good— when the intensity of play fully engages the participants. They experience a realm of time that is satisfying in itself, because the actions that take place within it are intrinsically meaningful, although they may also connote other ideas and stimulate experiences beyond the distinct time of the game.

Obviously, American sports do not constitute a religion with a similar history to Christianity or Islam, Buddhism, or Taoism. But sports are "a form of religion," as Novak simply puts it, because they provide "organized institutions, disciplines, and liturgies" and because they "teach religious qualities of heart and soul. In particular, they recreate symbols of cosmic struggle, in which human survival and moral courage are not assured."[28] Through their symbols and rituals, sports provide occasions for experiencing a sense of ultimacy and for prompting personal transformation.

The kinds of personal and social transformations that sports proffer do not depend upon winning a game or achieving a personal best performance in a contest, although both may certainly generate religious experiences. Instead, the transformative potential of sports extends to all participants and involves, as Prebish puts it, "redemption as well as rebirth into a new type of reality, separated from ordinary reality by its sense of being permeated with ultimacy and holiness, with beauty and freedom."[29] The ultimacy or holiness of the religious experience derives from its location, not in a remote realm of transcendence, but in a sense of alterity generated by the freedom and beauty of the sports activity itself.

When considering the significance of sports as religion, one can distinguish between the sport's spiritual presence and power for athletes, and fans' allegiance to teams and heroes. In established religious traditions, it is not uncommon for priests and laypersons to enjoy various levels of engagement and enrichment in their religious exercise; so too with sports, wherein athletes experience dimensions of selfhood and the quest for perfect performance in ways strikingly different from the experiences of fans.

In her examination of the spiritual experiences of athletes in competition, even when that competition is simply a struggle with oneself to achieve a "personal best" performance, Carolyn Thomas draws inspiration from Jean-Paul Sartre's assertion in *Being and Nothingness* that a person's goal is "to attain himself [or herself] as a certain being, precisely the being, which is in question to his [or her] being." For athletes, Thomas claims, "sport is a lived experience that, despite teammates or fans, is ultimately a solitary quest that reflects highly individual, personal, and subjective intents." Serious athletes, she asserts, "often unknowingly ... enter the world of sports in search of self, in search of the reality of a given moment, in search of truth."[30] To engage the most profound level of truth requires that one become introspective and meditative, opening oneself to the Other that resides at the innermost dimension of self. In this sense, then, sports constitute an essential, spiritual pursuit—seeking truth and self-awareness.

> When performers voluntarily enter sport and commit their whole beings to the sport experience, they transcend, or go beyond, outside distractions to a fusion of subject and object that allows them to know both the sport and self in an authentic, profound, special, and very individual way. It is this kind of "knowing" that has the potential to provide a source of meaning, a sense of purpose, and a basis for self-understanding.[31]

Although an athlete might articulate this self-understanding following a performance, he or she might not be conscious of this "knowing" dimension during the performance itself. In fact, the opposite is probably the case, according to Phil Jackson, former coach of the Chicago Bulls and Los Angeles Lakers, son of Pentecostal ministers, and student of Zen Buddhism. The secret of playing basketball well, he says, is *not thinking*: a Buddhist sense of being aware of what everyone on the court is doing and responding to, interacting with, and directing the flow of the game, precisely by *not* thinking.[32] The self-awareness that, upon reflection, leads to an articulation of self-understanding and disclosure of truth is the experience of flow.

A casual observer, of course, would be unlikely to perceive the pursuit of self-awareness and truth in an NCAA Division I intercollegiate contest because of the frequency of poor sportsmanship by players and coaches, the history of institutional cheating, and the self-destructive actions of players getting carried away by the intensity of competition. "Often portrayed in terms of greed, egocentricity, and immorality, these [Division I] forms of sport ... that focus on competitive ends ... seem a far cry from a historic dependence on religion." But even in such contexts, Thomas concludes, sport "provides a place where people can dominate fear and passion; a place where adventure and purpose and commitment can remove a sense of dread that may otherwise prevail."[33]

The spiritual experience of athletes in their performance of sport is not only the introspective pursuit of personal, foundational truths, but also includes their appreciation of simplicity and harmony in team play, and their quest for a perfectly synchronized performance. While this quest for perfection arises out of the fundamental dissatisfaction and uneasiness that constitute the human condition, "sports nourish this drive [toward perfection] as well as any other institution in our society."[34] Even when the pursuit of a perfect performance in sports becomes corrupted or distorted—when it moves toward selfish goals rather than the joy and disclosive possibilities of play itself—it still manifests the fundamental human desire for fulfillment. The willingness to subject personal preferences to the good of a team constitutes the basic religious aspect of team sports. "Even for those who don't consider themselves 'spiritual' in a conventional sense, [the process of] creating a successful team—whether it's an NBA champion or a record-setting sales force— is essentially a spiritual act," Phil Jackson asserts. "It requires the individuals involved to surrender their self-interest for the greater good so that the whole adds up to more than the sum of its parts."[35]

## DEVOTION TO SPORTS

In contrast to an athlete's experience of spiritual harmony in team play, fans manifest the religious power of sports in their expressions of allegiance and respect. The most explicit recent example of this devotion was the "religious overtone," as Phil Jackson put it, of the press coverage when Michael Jordan contemplated returning to the Bulls following his first retirement. "Perhaps it was just a reflection of the spiritual malaise in the culture and the deep yearning for a mythic hero who would set us free," Jackson mused. "Whatever the reason, during his hiatus from the team, Michael had somehow been transformed in the public mind from a great athlete to a sports deity." And yearning for the possibility of his return—expecting almost an eschatological second coming of sorts—some of the most fervent fans made their way to the United Center, where the Bulls play their home games, and knelt and prayed at the foot of Jordan's statue—a shrine to his transcending the court, his being "Air Jordan."[36]

Certainly, sports fans exhibit a kind of devotion that often is described in terms of religious dedication or passion. They express their fervor not only in the religious rituals of supplication for success, but also in the negative expressions of prayer for others' destruction or failure. In the Puerto Rican town of San Germán, Jackson recalls, "the fans hated the Gallitos [Jackson's team] so much that they lit candles the night before we arrived and prayed for our death."[37] Two extreme expressions of this hateful attitude are the documented death threats to Hank Aaron during his pursuit of Babe Ruth's career home-run record and the assassination of the Colombian soccer star Andres Escobar for having accidentally scored a goal against his own team in the 1994 World Cup competition. Most fans do not resort to death threats and murder, of course, but they express their dedication and devotion by the size of their wagers on favorite teams, the extent to which they will go—the sacrifices that they will make—in order to make a pilgrimage to an important game, and the ludic masking that they often assume in order to establish full identity with their favorite team or its mascot.

One of the most vivid displays of a fan's devotion to a sport occurs in the popular romantic baseball movie *Bull Durham*. The opening sequence behind the credits features sepia tones of baseball photographs from the collection of Annie Savoy, whose wall gallery serves as a sort of shrine to the sport's bygone stars and their seemingly cosmic feats. The spiritual significance of the scene is intensified by its soundtrack, which features soul-jazz organist and singer Shirley Scott wailing "Yes, yes, yes" (a secular rendition of "Amen," which translates "so be it"). As the mournful improvisation ends, Annie confesses:

> I believe in the Church of Baseball. I've tried all of the major religions and most of the minor ones. I've worshipped Buddha, Allah, Brahma, Vishnu, Síva, trees, mushrooms, and Isadora Duncan.
>
> I know things. For instance, there are 108 beads in a Catholic rosary and there are 108 stitches in a baseball. When I learned that, I gave Jesus a chance. But it just didn't work between us. The Lord laid too much guilt on me.

> I prefer metaphysics to theology. You see, there's no guilt in baseball, and it's never boring....
>
> I've tried 'em all, I really have. And the only church that truly feeds the soul day in and day out is the Church of Baseball.[38]

Annie's experience of awe toward and sustenance by baseball is not merely aligned with her annual romantic liaison with one of the Durham Bulls. Her enduring love is for baseball, the game itself, and the way that it makes sense out of life.

What Annie senses in her devotion to baseball is that somehow the game of baseball dramatizes a myth, a set of contingent relations or a display of possible outcomes that make life meaningful. Scholars have also proposed that baseball enacts elements of a myth whose meaning often corresponds to the hopes of its athletes and fans. For example, A. Bartlett Giamatti, former commissioner of Major League Baseball, suggests that baseball's space and rules correspond in many respects to the ancient omphalos myth, which reflects upon the creation and ordering of the world from the center of the earth, often a cosmic mountain.[39]

In addition to personal acts of fan devotion such as Annie Savoy's, the group behavior of fans also has religious import. According to a *Sports Illustrated* survey in the 1970s, three-fourths of Americans identified themselves as sports fans.[40] In 1990, the Indiana State High School tournament's championship game hosted 41,046 fans, a national record, in the Hoosier Dome at Indianapolis. "Hoosier Hysteria"—Indiana's obsessive love of basketball, especially at the high school level—has been called the state's religion; "and indeed it is the church and the team," Barry Temkin observes, "that stand as the two most important institutions in many a town—and not necessarily in that order."[41]

Especially in small towns and cities throughout America, the percentage of people devoted to the hometown team often exceeds the national average of sports fandom because the team provides folks with a dynamic symbol of hope, a living image of the possibility for success. One of the memorable scenes in the popular basketball film *Hoosiers,* the headlights on a caravan of cars light the town's pilgrimage to an "away game" on a Friday night, reflecting such devotion by an entire community. Nearby in Kentucky, the reverence, hope, and community bonding associated with high school basketball can also be seen in the way that high school gymnasiums are often the most elaborate structures in the community; for instance, the Metcalf County High School gym seats more fans than the population of Edmonton, the town where it is located. A similar phenomenon has been chronicled by Buzz Bissinger in his 1990 book *Friday Night Lights: A Town, a Team, and a Dream,* an analysis of a season in the life of the Permian Panthers (Odessa, Texas), and of the community's dreams of justification and validation in terms of the success of the high school football team. In Kentucky, part of a community's dream is that the local high school stars might become immortal by playing for the vaunted University of Kentucky Wildcats. When at the start of his junior year of high school, Metcalf County star point guard J. P. Blevins signed a letter of intent to attend Kentucky, the gymnasium was filled as the entire community celebrated his accomplishment, not merely as a rite of passage for a budding star's achievement but as an enduring validation of their own way of life and their love of Kentucky Wildcats basketball.[42]

## CHALLENGES FOR SPORTS AND FAITH

There are several points of continuing concern for those who wrestle with comparing the religious creed with the code of the sports cult. The first issue is a theological one. Although religions do not necessarily involve the worship of "God" or "gods," they do orient their followers toward an ultimate force or pantheon of powers, whether personalized as "gods" or identified in abstracted ways: for example, Buddhism's path of enlightenment or Shinto's abiding sense of family and tradition. One of the primary challenges for religious studies scholars who undertake theological analysis of sports is to identify within sports the sources of power for evoking and inspiring radical transformation among participants and faithful spectators.

A second issue emerges out of ethical concerns about the inculcation and transmission of values. Challenging the naive notion that sports inherently promote the building of admirable character, a number of critics pinpoint the frequency of exposés about athletes' corruption, their appreciation and practice of violence, their cultivation of bodily deformation as a way to achieve success (as with the use of performance-enhancing drugs), and their turn to cheating in order to win at any cost.[43] It should be noted, however, that not all religions adopt and encourage humanistic, pacifist, and compassionate values; so the critique of sports on the grounds that they promote violence, bodily abuse (including concussions), and an aggressive competitive spirit does not, of itself, separate sports from established religious traditions.

In any case, many celebrate the beneficent aspects of sports, in contrast to these more negative portrayals of the potential evils in store for sports devotees. Michael Novak, for instance, writes: "Sports are our chief civilizing agent. Sports are our most universal art form. Sports tutor us in the basic lived experiences of the humanist tradition."[44] Thus, a challenge for students and scholars who pursue a religious studies critique of sports is to identify and classify the values in sports that motivate the actions of players and interactions among faithful fans.

Adjunct to these issues about the values promoted by sports is a related set of ethical and theological concerns about the development of technological enhancements of sports equipment and of legal prosthetics that make possible the participation of some athletes in games and events. For instance, Oscar Pistorius required prosthetic legs to run in a relay event in the 2012 Summer Olympics. An ethical issue raised by his participation is whether the sophisticated design and production of his artificial limbs provided a competitive advantage beyond those of human skeletal structure and muscular development. Simply proposing this inquiry about whether or not Pistorius should have been allowed to compete generates theological questions about what it means to be human, not simply as an athlete but also as a spectator who might applaud his effort to overcome a physical disability.[45]

Finally, some theological critics have been reluctant to consider sports as religion since they recognize that many traditionally pious persons are also avid sports participants and fans. "Is it possible to maintain multilateral religious affiliations? Can the proponent of sport religion also retain standing within his or her traditional religious affiliation?" Prebish asks. "Ostensibly no!" he responds, reasoning that anyone who identifies sports as his or her religion would be "referring to a *consistent pursuit* that is also the *most important pursuit* and a *religious pursuit*. If this individual were to then state that he or she is also a Jew or a Protestant or a Catholic or whatever," Prebish concludes, "he or she would be referring to *cultural heritage only*, to the complex series of factors that are essentially ethnic and locational rather than religious."[46] This conflict arises most frequently out of a monotheistic perspective, since in monotheistic traditions true believers can adhere to only one form of faith. However, if we recognize, with historians of religion like Mircea Eliade, that it is possible to be simultaneously religious in apparently competing ways, then a new respect for pluralism might arise, and we could consider ways to appreciate the rhythmic or antagonistic forces of allegiance among devoted fans who are also faithful followers of an established religious tradition.

In short, although difficulties exist in trying to specify exactly the nature and extent of sports as religion, sports do exhibit many of the characteristics of established religious traditions. Most important, they exercise a power for shaping and engaging the world for millions of devoted fans throughout America; they enable participants to explore levels of selfhood that otherwise remain inaccessible; they establish means for bonding in communal relations with other devotees; they model ways to deal with contingencies and fate while playing by the rules; and they provide the prospect for experiencing victory and thus sampling, at least in an anticipatory way, "abundant life." In America, quite simply, sports constitute a form of popular religion.

## DISCUSSION QUESTIONS

1. When Price argues that sports can be thought of as a religion, what definition(s) of religion is he suggesting? In thinking about this, it may be helpful to review those suggested in the Introduction.

2. Drawing on the chapter and your own experience of playing and/or watching sports, what evidence suggests that sports is a religion, at least for some people? What does it add to our understanding of sports to think of it as a religion? Does the analogy add to our understanding of religion?

3. Price acknowledges that some people might make a distinction in this respect between athletes and sports fans. Is it easier to make the case that sports is a religion more for one group than for the other? Or is it the same for both? Is this similar to the distinction between priests and laypeople in a traditional religion?

4. Write a description of a sports event, perhaps a game on your campus, or one played by a professional team, as though it were a religious gathering or service. What religious language would you use to make the analogy? What elements of the sport would you stress? Are there rituals in sports that are similar to those in religion? What activities of players, coaches, and/or fans would be important?

### NOTES

1. Bob Moore, "Gridiron Glory at Union Station: 'The Call from the President,'" www.chiefs.com/news/article-2/Gridiron-Glory-at-Union-Station-The-Call-from-the-President/fd18obae-1fbd-47eb-8o1c-46333d9c684e. Thomas Neumann, "Why White House Visits by Champions Are a U.S. Tradition," http://espn.go.com/college-football/story/_/id/14870667/how-white-house-visits-championship-teams-became-american-tradition.

2. "Bring on the 12s," www.seahawks.com/spirit-of-12/history-of-the-12s.

308 / Popular Culture as Religion

3. See Joseph L. Price, "The Super Bowl as Religious Festival," *Christian Century*, February 22, 1984, 190–91. Statistics about the extent of gambling on the Super Bowl appear in Bill Christine, "The Big Gamble," *Los Angeles Times*, February 3, 1999, D1, D6, and David Purdum, "Record $132 Million Bet on Super Bowl 50 at Nevada Sportsbooks," http://espn.go.com/chalk/story/_/id/14742837/record-132-million-bet-super-bowl-50-nevada-sports-books-doing-well.

4. Joyce Carol Oates, "Lives of the Latter-Day saints," *Times Literary Supplement*, 12 July 1996, 9. And according to Ninian Smart, "the heart of the modern study of religion is the analysis and comparison of worldviews," which include the "history and nature of the beliefs and symbols which form a deep part of the structure of human consciousness and society." *Worldviews: Crosscultural Explorations of Human Beliefs* (New York: Scribner's, 1983) 3, 2.

5. Quoted in Jim Naughton, *Taking to the Air: The Rise of Michael Jordan* (New York: Warner Books, 1992) 134.

6. Frank Deford, "Religion in Sport," *Sports Illustrated*, April 19, 1976, 91. Although Deford himself does not draw the analogy in quite the way that I have laid it out, his remark sparked several subsequent interpretations in the manner that I have suggested.

7. Oates, "Lives of the Latter-Day Saints," 9.

8. For an excellent introduction to the religious functions of the Greek Olympiad, see Judith Swaddling, *The Ancient Olympic Games* (1980; repr., Austin: University of Texas Press, 1984). For an explanation of the Mesoamerican game of ball, see S. Jeffrey K. Wilkerson, "And Then They Were Sacrificed: The Ritual Ballgame of Northeastern Mesoamerica through Time and Space," in Vernon L. Scarborough and David R. Wilcox, eds., *The Mesoamerican Ballgame* (Tucson: University of Arizona Press, 1991), 45–71. For information about the religious significance of lacrosse, see Stewart Culin, *Games of the North American Indians* (New York: Dover, 1975 [ (repr. of the *Twenty-fourth Annual Report of the Bureau of American Ethnology to the Smithsonian Institution, 1902–1903]*), 563ff. For an exploration of the religious origins of the rite of throwing the ball, see *Black Elk Speaks. The Sacred Pipe: Black Elk's Account of the Seven Rites of the Oglala Sioux*, recorded and edited by Joseph Epes Brown (New York: Penguin Books, 1971), 127–38. For a discussion of the spiritual dimensions of the martial arts, see, e.g., Peter Payne, *Martial Arts: The Spiritual Dimension* (New York: Crossroad, 1981). For an imaginative literary exploration of the connections between discipline, spirituality, and one of the martial arts, see Harry Crews, *Karate Is a Thing of the Spirit* (New York: William Morrow, 1971). For an examination of the spiritual challenge of archery, see Eugen Herrigel,

*Zen in the Art of Archery,* trans. R.F.C. Hull, with an introduction by D.T. Suzuki (New York: Vintage Books, 1971). For an analysis of Brazilian soccer as a civil religion, see "Sports *in* Society: *Futebol* as National Drama," in Gregory Baum and John Coleman, eds., *Sport,* (Edinburgh: T & T Clark, 1989), 57–68.

9. Michael Novak, *The Joy of Sports: End Zones, Bases, Baskets, Balls, and the Consecration of the American Spirit* (New York: Basic Books, 1976), 18–34; James A. Mathisen, "From Civil Religion to Folk Religion: The Case of American Sport," in *Sport and Religion,* ed. Shirl J. Hoffman (Champaign, IL: Human Kinetics Books, 1992), 17–33, esp. 21–24; Catherine Albanese, *America: Religions and Religion* (Belmont, CA: Wadsworth, 1981), 322.

10. Harry Edwards, *Sociology of Sport* (Homewood IL: Dorsey Press, 1973), 90.

11. Edwin Cady, *The Big Game: College Sports and American Life* (Knoxville: University of Tennessee Press, 1978), 78.

12. Joan Chandlers, "Sport is Not a Religion," in *Sport and Religion,* ed. Shirl J. Hoffman (Champaign, IL: Human Kinetics Books, 1992), 55.

13. Robert J. Higgs, "Muscular Christianity, Holy Play, and Spiritual Exercises: Confusion about Christ in Sports and Religion," *Arete* 1, no. 1 (1983): 63. Since publishing his essay in the initial issue of *Arete,* the journal sponsored by the Sports Literature Association, Higgs has published a more expansive study of the convergence of sports, religion, the military, and education, *God in the Stadium: Sports and Religion in America* (Lexington: University Press of Kentucky, 1995). Rather than focusing on issues pertaining to the exercise or perception of sports as religion, however, the work studies the development of "muscular Christianity" or "Sportianity" in America.

14. Rebecca T. Alpert, *Religion and Sports: An Introduction and Case Studies* (New York: Columbia University Press, 2015), and Eric Bain-Selbo and D. Gregory Sapp, *Understanding Sports as a Religious Phenomenon* (London: Bloomsbury, 2016).

15. Charles H. Lippy, *Being Religious, American Style: A History of Popular Religiosity in the United States* (Westport, CT: Praeger, 1994), 228.

16. Frank Deford, "Religion in Sport," *Sports Illustrated,* April 19, 1976, 92, 102.

17. Carolyn Thomas, "Sports," in Peter Van Ness, *Spirituality and the Secular Quest* (New York: Crossroad, 1996), 506.

18. Novak, *Joy of Sports,* 26.

19. Harry Edwards, *Sociology of Sport* (Homewood, IL: Dorsey Press, 1973), 261–62. Cf. M.C. Kearl, quoted in Mathisen, "From Civil Religion to Folk Religion," 24: "Like religion, professional sports use past generations as referents for the present and confer conditional immortality for their elect through statistics and halls of fame." Mathisen comments:

In our desire to fix in time the achievements of those we look back upon as our representatives for time immemorial, we attribute a sense of sanctity to them and their accomplishments.... When a record is broken in sport, we are both happy and sad. Not only has immortality been achieved, but previous immortality proves to have been conditional and so has been stolen from our midst. Maybe we should place an asterisk next to the new record, just to ensure that we do not lose sight of the former one and of the hero who established it."

For a specific connection of superstar Michael Jordan with a kind of deific projection, see Naughton, *Taking to the Air*, 134. Naughton suggests that, with Jordan's "air" quality, he embodies the nearest thing to transcendence that we are likely to see.

20. Cf. Oates, "Lives of the Latter-Day Saints," 9: "For the 'sports fan' the team or idolized athlete provides a kind of externalized soul: there to be celebrated or reviled but, as the God of the ages apparently was not, *there* in full public view."

21. Charles S. Prebish, *Religion and Sport: The Meeting of Sacred and Profane* (Westport, CT: Greenwood Press, 1993), 64.

22. Novak, *Joy of Sports*, 47–48.

23. Ibid., 21.

24. Ibid., xi (emphasis added), 29–30.

25. Mihaly Csikszentmihalyi, *Flow: The Psychology of Optimal Experience* (New York: Harper & Row, 1990), 4, 72.

26. Johan Huizinga, *Homo Ludens: A Study of the Play-Element in Culture* (Boston: Beacon Press, 1955), 1–27. In an effort to connect modern sports to its origins in play and ritual, then, Allen Guttmann has written three distinct volumes that always implicitly, and occasionally explicitly, comment on the religious significance of American sporting events, especially for the fans. Guttmann's earliest work, *From Ritual to Record: The Nature of Modern Sports*, includes the trenchant observation that "one of the strangest turns in the long, devious route that leads from primitive ritual to the World Series and the *Fussballweltmeisterschaft* is the proclivity of modern sports to become a secular kind of faith" (Guttmann *From Ritual to Record* [New York: Columbia University Press, 1978], 25). See also Allen Guttmann, *Sports Spectators* (New York: Columbia University Press, 1986), and id., *A Whole New Ballgame: An Interpretation of American Sports* (Chapel Hill: University of North Carolina Press, 1988), esp. chaps. 2, 5, and 6, in which Guttmann treats "The Sacred and the Secular" in Native American games, "The National Game" (implying a national identity—and perhaps civil religion—associated with baseball), and "Muscular Christianity."

27. Mircea Eliade, *The Sacred and the Profane,* trans. Willard R. Trask (New York: Harcourt, Brace, 1959), chaps. 1–2, esp. pp. 30–34.

28. Novak, *Joy of Sports,* 31, 21.

29. Ibid., 70.

30. Thomas, "Sports," 498–99.

31. Ibid., 509–10.

32. Phil Jackson and Hugh Delehanty, *Sacred Hoops: Spiritual Lessons of a Hardwood Warrior* (New York: Hyperion, 1995), 115.

33. Thomas, "Sports," 502, 508.

34. Novak, *Joy of Sports,* 27.

35. Jackson, *Sacred Hoops,* 5, 11–12.

36. Ibid., 16–17.

37. Ibid., 70–71.

38. Ron Shelton, *Bull Durham* (Los Angeles: Orion Home Video, 1989).

39. A. Bartlett Giamatti, *Take Time for Paradise: Americans and Their Games* (New York: Summit Books, 1989), 86ff. For an alternate application of the omphalos myth to baseball, see my essay "The Pitcher's Mound as Cosmic Mountain" in Joseph L. Price, ed., *From Season to Season: Sports as American Religion* (Macon, GA: Mercer University Press, 2001). An interpretation of football as reflecting distinct American myths can be found in my brief essay "The Super Bowl as Religious Festival," *Christian Century,* February 22, 1984. And myths, although they are more ambiguously suggested, also underlie basketball, according to Phil Jackson, *Sacred Hoops,* 7.

40. Cited in Prebish, *Religion and Sport,* xiii.

41. Barry Temkin, "Indiana's 'Impossible Dream' May Soon Be No More," originally published in the *Chicago Tribune* and reprinted in the *Denver Post.* February 11, 1996.

42. Mark Woods, "Basketball Prodigy a Kentucky Blueblood," originally published in the *Louisville Courier-Journal* and reprinted in the *Denver Post,* February 2, 1997), 11C. Cf. H.C. Bissinger, *Friday Night Lights: A Town, a Team, and a Dream* (Reading, MA: Addison-Wesley, 1990).

43. Cf. Mathisen, "From Civil Religion to Folk Religion," 22.

44. Novak, *Joy of Sports,* 27. In another essay in his collection, he promotes the potential good in sports even more hopefully. Novak testifies: "What I have learned from sports is respect for authenticity and individuality (each player learning his own true instincts, capacities, style); for courage and perseverance and stamina; for the ability of enter into defeat in order to suck dry its power to destroy; for harmony of body and spirit.... In sports, law was born and also liberty, and the nexus of their interrelation. In sports, honesty and

excellence are caught, captured, nourished, held in trust for the generations" ("The Metaphysics of Sports," 43).

45. Cf. Tracy J. Trothen, *Winning the Race? Religion, Hope, and Reshaping the Sport Enhancement Debate* (Macon, GA: Mercer University Press, 2015).

46. Prebish, *Religion and Sport*, 72.

# CHAPTER FIFTEEN

# Celebrity Worship as Parareligion

*Bieber and the Beliebers*

PETE WARD

They were trying to carry on as if it was just a normal day at the Lutheran Seminary in Oslo, Norway. Students training for the ministry attended their classes in the usual way, but the noise coming from outside was starting to make things difficult. There had been a warning that there might be some disruption, but the reality was still quite overwhelming. Justin Bieber was to stop off in Oslo for a special performance that day. The televised special was to be filmed in a student venue right next door to the Norwegian School of Theology, and as a result the ministerial students found themselves staring out of the windows at a different kind of devotion altogether. The event was to make international headlines in 2015, because after just one song, a stripped-down version of his song "Boyfriend," Bieber stormed off stage leaving the fans both inside and outside the venue distraught.[1]

## BIEBERMANIA

The kind of fan chaos that took place in Oslo has characterized Justin Bieber's career from the very start. It's crazy but it's "Biebermania" the singer explained when asked by local television about a particularly chaotic appearance at a mall in 2009.[2] The events in Oslo and elsewhere are not unusual. In fact, it is not entirely an accident that Bieber's fans have developed a particular connection to their idol, such that they cause a disturbance wherever he appears. A particular "intimacy" with the singer has been cultivated and encouraged by his use of social media. Almost from the start he adopted a strategy of connecting directly with his fan base using YouTube, Instagram, and Twitter. In 2016, he had over seventy-five million followers on Twitter, making him the second most followed person on the social networking site, after Katy Perry. Bieber has said that he sees the Internet as the "best way to reach your fans," and he uses his account both to promote his music and to offer a reaction to events and situations in his professional and personal life.[3]

Merging "Bieber" with "believer," Bieber's fans have adopted the term "Belieber" to describe their devotion to the Canadian singer. The name encapsulates the dynamics of celebrity worship. A Belieber according to Chas Newkey-Burden is someone who "believes in Justin, a Bieberholic [is]someone who is addicted to the Bieb."[4] "Belieber" neatly articulates with the pop song "I'm a Believer," first performed by another teen sensation, the Monkees. This has led to fan merchandise such as the "I'm a Belieber" T-shirt and to a Facebook page, "Then I saw his face now I'm a beleiber."[5]

In 2012 after a flash mob event, the German magazine *Newstars* recorded a YouTube video with the title "I'm a Belieber" performed by German fans of the singer. The lyrics reflect the devotion of these fans in the face of their perception of general disapproval of their attachment to the singer.

They say that I should better
Stay away from you oh baby
They say that I should better
Learn for school all night and day
They say that you are so untouchable
And I won't reach you

But I say NO NO,NO,NO NO,NO,NO—because
I'm a Belieber

Let's say hello
Here come the Beliebers'
1, 2, 3, 4 Beliebers go.[6]

Devotion here is presented as transgressive.[7] It is an act of defiant faith. Belief, according to the pop music critic Ben Rayner is a central tenet of the Justin Bieber mythology. *Believe* was the title of Bieber's third studio album, and of his second world tour, which started in 2012. Beliebers, Rayner argues, are expected to have faith, faith that one day they might have Justin as their boyfriend. Of course, this isn't going to happen, but "[f]aith in the illogical is a big part of worship, though, and in a culture where celebrity worship has arguably become religion for many people it's perfectly logical that the question should be asked again and again: 'Are you still a Belieber?'"[8] It was precisely this Biebermania that came onto the streets in Oslo.

## CELEBRITY WORSHIP

The encounter between seminary students and Beliebers encapsulates a key dynamic in the study of religion and popular culture. On one side of the window, there are those who are being inducted into a formal and authorized religious life in the Christian ministry; on the other, there is the deregulated personal devotion of the Beliebers. The use of religious language to describe the relationship between fans and celebrities has become commonplace. Pop singers are regularly referred to as icons or idols. Musicians are rock gods, and opera singers are divas. The relationship between celebrities and their followers is routinely described as worship part of the cult of celebrity. The word "fan" has religious roots; it comes from the Latin *fanaticus,* meaning "of the temple": so the fan is one who is excessively enthusiastic or taken up with a zeal that is most usually seen in religious fervor.[9] As is evident with the examples so far given, fan culture itself is not immune to the borrowing of religious language. Wearing an "I'm a Belieber" T-shirt is a statement of identity and devotion, and it appears that for some fans, it is an act of defiance in the face of it disapproval and even perhaps ridicule in some social settings.

The connection between celebrity and religion is more than a discursive trope in popular media or in fan cultures. In academic literature it has become commonplace interpretative category. Roland Barthes's essay on the face of Greta Garbo in *Mythologies* speaks of the image as divinization. "The name given her, the divine, probably aimed to convey less a superlative state of beauty than the essence of her corporeal person, descended from a heaven where things are formed and perfected in the clearest light."[10] In 1958, Malcolm Boyd used very similar language speaking of the metamorphosis of stars into a pantheon of legends in his groundbreaking book *Christ and the Celebrity Gods*.[11] The religious significance of celebrity culture is frequently connected in academic literature to a perceived decline in formal religion. Celebrity icons, Gary Laderman says, "use the religious passions of followers in modern society." With the "stranglehold of mainline Protestantism" on public life on the wane, and individuals growing more distant from God, celebrities offer a source of "spiritual meaning, personal fulfilment, and awe inspiring motivation."[12] "The decline of formal religious traditions forms the backdrop to Chris Rojek's argument concerning the rearticulation of fragmented religious sensibilities, behaviors, and rituals around mass media celebrities. What emerges, he says, is a new kind of cultic worship in which celebrities take on a shamanic character in media representation and in fan cultures, replacing traditional religious sources of identity and authority.[13] The worship of celebrity giving rise to new kind of religion is explored in depth by the film critic Edgar Morin, who writes:

> Worshipped as heroes, divinized, the stars are more than objects of admiration. They are also subjects of a cult. A religion in embryo has formed around them. This religion diffuses its frenzies over most of the globe. No one who frequents the dark auditoriums is really an atheist. But among the movie going masses can be distinguished the sect of the faithful who wear relics and otherwise consecrate them selves to worship, the fanatics, the fans.[14]

For Morin the cult of the stars has become something more like a religious system with Gods and Goddesses, temples and worshippers. This is a more developed religious framing of celebrity than, for instance, Rojek or Laderman's sense that religious behavior and sensibilities are becoming rearticulated in popular culture as more traditional religious forms are in decline. Here celebrity represents a reformulation in fragmented form of the sacred. The use of religious metaphors and analogies by the media and also by fans themselves is suggestive that something along the lines of a shifting religious sensibility is taking place. At the same time the relationships that are generated between celebrities and fans are shaped in ways that are distinctive and particular, such that they may not perhaps be quite as reverent as might be expected from true worshippers.

## BIEBER AND THE BELIEVERS

The chance encounter between seminary students and Beliebers encapsulates the issues around the nature of religion associated with celebrity worship. What is at stake is not simply a two-way dynamic with traditional religion on one side and a new fragmented and embryonic spirituality of the fans on the other. Justin Bieber can be read as a significant complicating factor around the possible religious significance of celebrity culture.

In recent years there have been a number of media stories that report that Justin Bieber has embraced the Christian faith. In the title track "Purpose," he speaks of giving his heart into the hands of God so that his soul can be kept. This is a God who is not hard to reach who forgives sins and blesses with the best gift. This is the gift of purpose. At the end of the song Bieber offers a personal message.

> You can't be hard on yourself
> For these were the cards that you were given so you have to under-
>     stand that these, like ...
> That's not who you are
> You're trying to be the best you can be but that's all you can do

If you don't give it all you got, you're only cheating yourself
Give it all you got
But if it ends up happening, it ends up happening.

That's what it's.... that's what's happening with me
It's like God I'm giving it all I got, sometimes
I'm weak and I'm gonna do it, and it's like I'm not giving myself grace
I'm just like understanding, that's just how it is.[15]

Here Bieber offers both advice and apology to his listeners. Faith is offered as part of the struggle. According to the singer sometimes "it happens" that things don't work out as they should but despite his weakness he still offers himself to God. The "you" addressed in this voice operates at a number of levels. On the face of it, this is a personal confession. The various problems and scrapes that Justin Bieber has found himself dealing with are close to the surface in this acknowledgement of failing. But the "you" here also functions to make this a word of counsel for his fans. The "you" then connotes a sense that fans and singer are part of a similar struggle, and it is from this position of apparently acknowledging his own problems that Bieber offers the advice "If you don't give it all you got, you're only cheating yourself, / Give it all you got." Sharing his Christian faith with his fans has become a frequent event for Justin Bieber. He has used his Instagram account to post a series of Bible studies for his followers.[16] The concerts on the "Purpose" tour have also cultivated a religious atmosphere, such that some critics have observed that they appear now to resemble something akin to a Christian worship service.

Justin Bieber's advocacy of evangelical Christianity is perhaps not as unexpected as it might at first appear. His mother was a committed Christian who prayed that her son would one day become a youth pastor or a Christian recording artist.[17] On his early tours he regularly prayed backstage before performing.[18] The evangelical commitments of the singer have given a new orientation to his interaction with fans such that he not only advocates faith as a way of life but also addresses the apparent worship that many Beliebers seem to manifest. Justin is concerned that he is not worthy of faith, "I would really suggest to people: Don't put your faith in me. Because I'm gonna disappoint you every time."[19] The singer is here again aware of his failings but he also wants to make it clear that he is not worthy of worship because he is no sense divine.

> But I want them to know that I'm not going to be able to solve their problems. I'm not that higher power. I'll never be. I'm not perfect. I've made so many mistakes. I just want to get to a place where … I just want people to know humans aren't meant to be worshipped. We're just not. So when a human is being worshipped, this is dangerous. 'Cause it does nothing but give you pride.[20]

Bieber's insistence that human beings should not be worshipped is an interesting contribution to the debate around celebrity worship. His objection is theological at root. To worship human beings, he says, is not only ineffectual it is dangerous because of the effect that it has in generating pride. This pride is not so much a problem for the fan as it is for the celebrity. Yet at the same time that he is objecting to the celebrity worship of his fans, his Twitter messages use the semi-religious language of the Belieber. So on the occasion of the Grammys in 2016, Bieber's account tweeted a celebratory message to his followers: "Belieber's. We did it I love you. Now get ready for the show. Not done yet."

This juxtaposition of simultaneously warning against celebrity worship and yet also seeming to encourage it exists at a number of levels in fan worship. Fans themselves are often critical of overtly religious language to describe their relationship to a celebrity.[21] Erica Doss found in her research into the religious culture of Elvis Presley fans that when they were asked directly about the religious dimensions of their relationship to Elvis, they were very likely to reject the idea with some vehemence. As one fan quoted by Doss says, "Elvis did not die for our sins, nor is he Jesus Christ and it is very wrong to even try and draw comparisons."[22] . Very similar reactions were found in research into the Sydney-based Cliff Richard Fan Club. In this research, many of the respondents identified as "devout Christians," a trait they share with their chosen celebrity. The researcher observed that "Most view Cliff as human rather than god-like."[23] These examples are significant because the fans' behavior and language appears to treat their chosen celebrity as of some kind of religious significance, but when they are confronted with this idea, they are clear that their attachment, though deeply significant to them, is not religious. Religion for the fan of Elvis and Cliff Richard is synonymous with traditional Christian practice and belief. This is precisely the position that Justin Bieber is advocating.

## PARASOCIAL RELATIONSHIPS IN
## CELEBRITY CULTURE

There is a tension that runs throughout celebrity culture. This tension exists around the kind of relationships that fans feel they enjoy with their celebrities. On the one hand, these relationships appear to be very real, in that they can mean a great deal to individuals and to groups. They become a source of identity and common feeling. At the same time, there is the obvious point that most fans have never met the person who has become the object of their devotion. The media processes that develop narratives of revelation and seeming intimacy between celebrities and fans both facilitate connection while ensuring that this connection is at a distance. This sleight of hand is exaggerated with the development of social media, where Twitter and Instagram appear to offer informal and immediate photographs and comment from "behind the scenes." This glimpse of the personal and private made public heightens a key ingredient in celebrity culture, the making public of private life for the consumption of fans. This invitation into intimacy should, however, be tempered by the realization that these insights are being shared with seven and a half million people on Twitter. Social media above all are a powerful means to generate sales and much of the content will be in the hands of publicity agents and managers.

Media communication facilitates relationship between celebrities and fans, but these relationships are circumscribed, inasmuch as they are largely one-way. Such relationships have been described as "parasocial." Ellis Cashmore sees the idea of the parasocial relationship as capturing "the way we think and feel about people we don't know and who don't know us but sometimes and unwittingly and unknowingly move us to act, occasionally in erratic and irrational ways."[24]. For the fans, one-way parasocial interactions are experienced as significant and authentic; in fact, such interactions are so common they are hard to avoid. "Even if we wanted to insulate ourselves for a while," Cashmore says, "we couldn't escape over-hearing chats, glancing at newspaper or magazine covers, or resisting switching on the TV, even if only for the news."[25] Parasocial interactions are an intimacy that is "at a distance."[26]

Theories of a parasocial relationship do not, however, account for every aspect of the fluid and irreverent world of celebrity culture. Celebrity culture operates as a complex area, where fans may in turn identify or disidentify with celebrities. Identification relates to the way that celebrities may offer significant models for lifestyle and behavior. Disidentification is the opposite. Here fans may actually disapprove of the choices made by celebrities. The irreverent dynamic in celebrity culture plays out in the way that disapproval or even disdain operates as part of the process of identity construction. Disdentification recognizes that there are deep pleasures in seeing how celebrities mess up and fail. These make it possible to locate an identity in opposition rather than one that is in tune with the celebrity. Disapproval is located in sensibilities that find enjoyment in not making that kind of mistake or choice. Here celebrity culture is focused on the poor decisions and wastefulness of many celebrity lifestyles. For the fan the pleasure is in realizing that with the same amount of money or fame, he or she would not have done that particular thing or broken up with that partner, or got that drunk and been photographed. Graeme Turner calls this aspect of celebrity culture "playfulness." He argues that the construction of identity is as much play as it is work. As he puts it, "When a women's magazine offers its readers advice on how to 'celebritize' their wardrobe, then it is important to recognise that this offer is likely to produce a playful and imaginative form of cultural consumption."[27] Fans have a "give and take" with a range of media figures and relate to celebrities by including them in the construction of "imaginary worlds."[28] These practices may in turn involve a rejection of the behavior or lifestyle choices of celebrities as much as admiring and choosing to follow their lead. The point is that parasocial relationships enable the freedom to disidentify as well as identify and both might operate as a means to play with the sense of self.

## PARARELIGION

Making a direct connection between religion and celebrity culture is somewhat problematic. There is something to be said for seeing the connection as being primarily semantic. This is the point that Laderman makes when he observes that "[c]elebrity culture, the cult of celebrity, celebrity worship—these and other phrases are regularly used to capture the elusive, irreducible power of celebrity in the present and recent past."[29] There are, however, significant problems with the idea that celebrity culture is actually a religion. Most approaches to religion involve at least one of the following ideas: a belief in a supernatural power, the significance of religion to generate community life or some kind of church, or a divine power's influence on people's lives. Celebrity culture in almost all of these respects falls significantly short of what is required of a formal religion. Celebrity worship has no reference to a transcendent divine other. There is no regular gathering or community of celebrity worshippers, and the extent to which celebrities may or may not be a resource for meaning making is less than clear. Yet rather than dismissing celebrity worship as not religiously significant, it might be possible to cast new light on how, through the action of the media, and through the agency of audiences and fans, something like (and not like) religion is starting to emerge. My term for this is "parareligion."

Parareligion is based on the premise that celebrity worship is not a religion but has religious parallels. Like the concept of parasocial inter-action, parareligion suggests that religious elements are present but that they are presented ambiguously. These religious elements are often contradictory and open to a variety of different understandings. Para-religion is an attempt to account for the irreverence and ambiguities that appear in celebrity culture. In celebrity worship there are moments when the sacred appears to be present, but this is often subverted or interrupted by the irreverent. In celebrity culture the sacred appears to be present, but it has somehow been (sub)merged in the profane. In pop-ular culture the processes of representation seem to appropriate theo-logical analogies yet are twisted and altered in the process. Articulation lifts these theological metaphors and forms of expression from their relationship to any kind of formal religious community or tradition and relocates them in a conflicted, contested, contradictory, and fluid arena of meaning making. This seems to describe a new form of religious con-text, but unfortunately these forms of representation and the kinds of identification that they support and elicit are all mixed up with a heavy dose of irony. So any attempt to dignify celebrity worship as religion must somehow accommodate the pervading impression that it is some-how ephemeral and rather silly. Parareligion is an attempt to reconcile these various elements by developing a theory of a "sort of" religion.

## JUSTIN AND THE SACRED SELF

While celebrity worship may not be regarded as in any way a formal religion, the relationships that fans develop with celebrities suggest a shift in the nature of the sacred in contemporary society. Paul Heelas and Linda Woodhead have identified what they see as a "subjective turn in contemporary religion."[30] This is a shift away from objective authority based religious understandings toward more personal and intimate approaches to religion. This accords with the notion that a renegotiation of the self is taking place within celebrity worship. This renegotiation is not directly concerned with the celebrity; rather, it arises within the fan. When, in parasocial relationships, fans choose to identify or disidentify, they are actively engaged in a construction of the self. It is this practice that signifies the sacred. This is a sacred, however, that is not located in the celebrity but in the fan. It is the fan who is seeking to make the most of him or herself, and is afraid of letting go. It is the fan who is working on his or her self-image. The celebrity in this sense is simply the focus for this personal engagement with the self. "Post-God celebrity is now one of the mainstays of organizing recognition and belonging in secular society," Rojek observes.[31]

It is the collective "us" in the celebrity that is being worshipped. So celebrities are "deities" only to the extent that they are carrying the projected identifications of fans. We are worshippers with short attention spans and a tendency to a slightly cynical take on the characters that fill our news media. The theological metaphors and religious analogies in celebrity culture allow a glimpse into the processes of the sacralization of the self in popular culture. "As the media plays an ever more active role in the production of identity; as our consumption practices increasingly reflect choices that privilege the performance of identity; and as celebrity becomes an increasingly common component of media content; it is not surprising that celebrity should become one of the primary locations where the news and entertainment media participate in the construction of cultural identity," Turner notes, arguing that celebrity culture is now one of the main resources for the construction of the self.[32]

The nature of religion is brought into focus in the encounter between the seminary students and Beliebers. The idea of parareligion could be seen as suggesting that "real" religion rests with the traditional faith of the Lutheran Seminary. This would leave the Beliebers as somewhat mistaken and perhaps deluded. Bieber himself seems to indicate that this is not entirely true. For while the singer is clear that real religion lies in the worship of God, and that this religion is the only one that is to be trusted, he also points to the shifting nature of the sacred in society. The song "Purpose" makes this clear: "You're trying to be the best you can be but that's all you can do / if you don't give it all you got, you're only cheating yourself." Bieber understands that what is really at stake in celebrity worship is the sacred self.

## DISCUSSION QUESTIONS

1. In contrast to the other authors in this section, Ward resists the suggestion that popular culture can be religion. Using the suggestion that fans "worship" celebrities as an example, he argues that while popular practices may sometimes look like religion, they are better understood as something less than fully religion, which he calls "parareligion." What distinction is the author making between religion and parareligion? In what way does the author suggest that celebrity worship is like religion? What is it that he believes religion does that popular culture cannot?

2. How does this author's definition of religion differ from those of the other authors in this section? What is it about religion that he argues is unique, that cannot be replaced with other cultural stories and practices?

3. Is celebrity worship a new form of religion or is it, as Ward argues, a parareligion? Why?

4. Do an Internet search for discussions of the "belieber" phenomenon. In what ways do the activities of the beliebers seem to be forms of religious devotion? You will also find some people, including Justin Bieber himself, arguing against the worship of Bieber. What are their arguments?

NOTES

1. www.vg.no/nyheter/innenriks/justin-bieber-leaves-the-stage-in-rage-after-yelling-at-his-fans/a/23551961.

2. Marc Shapiro, *Justin Bieber: The Fever!* (New York: St. Martin's Griffin, 2010), 9–12.

3. Chas Newkey-Burden, *Justin Bieber: The Unauthorised Biography* (London: Michael O'Mara Books, 2010), 161

4. Ibid., 10.

5. www.facebook.com/Then-I-saw-his-face-now-Im-a-Belieber-162539797089983.

6. https://www.youtube.com/watch?v=se6BezB1IQo.

7. See, e.g., Valerie Tweedle and Robert J. Smith, "A Mathematical Model of Bieber Fever: The Most Infectious Disease of Our Time?" http://storage.thoroldedition.ca/v1/suns-prod-images/file/1297270790461_BieberFever.pdf.

8. www.thestar.com/news/insight/2014/02/01/justin_bieber_are_you_still_a_belieber.html.

9. Ellis Cashmore, *Celebrity Culture* (Abingdon, England: Routledge, 2006), 79.

10. Roland Barthes, *Mythologies* (St. Albans, England: Paladin, 1973), 57.

11. Malcolm Boyd, *Christ and the Celebrity Gods: The Church in Mass Culture* (Greenwich, CT: Seabury Press, 1958), 8.

12. Gary Laderman, *Sacred Matters: Celebrity Worship, Sexual Ecstasies, the Living Dead, and Other Signs of Religious Life in the United States* (New York: New Press, 2009), 64.

13. Chris Rojek, *Celebrity* (London: Reaktion Books, 2001), 53.

14. Edgar Morin, *The Stars,* trans. Richard Howard (Minneapolis: University of Minnesota Press, 2005), 57. Originally published as *Les stars* (Paris: Seuil, 1957).

15. www.directlyrics.com/justin-bieber-purpose-lyrics.html.

16. www.christiantoday.com/article/justin.bieber.shares.bible.devotional.on.how.to.worship.god.drawing.raves.from.millions.of.his.fans/78593.htm.

17. Newkey-Burden, *Justin Bieber,* 19.

18. Shapiro, *Justin Bieber,* 4.

19. www.christiantoday.com/article/justin.bieber.tells.fans.dont.put.your.faith.in.me.because.im.gonna.disappoint.you/80533.htm.

20. Ibid.

21. SLyvetteRob, comment on "So Do We All Have Celebrity Worship Syndrome? Lol," Michael Jackson Fan Club, comment posted September 2, 2009, www.mjfanclub.net/mjforum373/showthread.php?t = 13261.

22. Quoted in Erika Doss, *Elvis Culture: Fans, Faith, & Image* (Lawrence: University Press of Kansas, 1999), 73.

23. Marylouise Caldwell and Paul Henry, "Living Dolls: How Affinity Groups Sustain Celebrity Worship," study presented at the Association for Consumer Research (ACR) Asia-Pacific Conference, Hyderabad, India, January 4, 2009, http://neumann.hec.ca/aimac2005/PDF_Text/CaldwellM_HenryP.pdf, 8.

24. Cashmore, *Celebrity Culture*, 39.

25. Ibid., 80.

26. Ibid., 80.

27. Graeme Turner, *Understanding Celebrity* (Thousand Oaks, CA: Sage, 2004), 102.

28. Neil Alperstein quoted in Cashmore, *Celebrity*, 82.

29. Laderman, *Sacred Matters*, 71.

30. Paul Heelas and Linda Woodhead, *The Spiritual Revolution: Why Religion Is Giving Way to Spirituality* (Oxford: Blackwell, 2005), 2.

31. Rojek, *Celebrity*, 58.

32. Turner, *Understanding Celebrity*, 102.

# PART IV

# Religion and Popular Culture
in Dialogue

The first two sections of *Religion and Popular Culture in America* treat religion and popular culture as provisionally distinct from each other and examine ways in which the one is shaped by the other. "Religion in Popular Culture," looks at the ways popular culture draws on religious images and practices and portrays religious figures, institutions, and movements. "Popular Culture in Religion" studies the way religions are shaped by the cultures in which they are imbedded. The third section, "Popular Culture as Religion," considers the possibility that religion and popular culture are not such neatly distinguished phenomena, arguing that popular culture might be thought as being a form or religion, or at least similar to religion in significant ways.

Like those in the first two sections, the essays in "Religion and Popular Culture in Dialogue" treat religion and popular culture as separate phenomena that are in conversation with each other. Where those earlier essays suggest that their interactions inevitably mean that one phenomena reforms, transforms, or perhaps distorts the other, this is not necessarily the case with dialogue. Here they remain distinct, while carrying on a conversation about things like the purpose of religion, the nature of society—its values and limits, and the moral life.

As we have seen throughout this volume, religion is not one thing but many. It does not enter into dialogue with a single voice or take a single position or perspective in its conversation with popular culture. This complex conversation both reflects and shapes us. We could logically, if inelegantly, have titled this section "Religions and Popular Cultures in Dialogues."

Not everyone agrees that popular culture also speaks with multiple voices. When people say that "the media promotes violence" or "attacks religion" or that "popular culture perpetuates sexist and racist assumptions," they speak as though "the media" and "popular culture" were single entities. The impression conveyed is that each speaks with just one voice.

Several factors contribute to this assumption. Much of popular culture is produced in a culture industry made up of a limited number of large film, television, music, and publishing companies. The profit motive often leads them to seek the widest possible audience, and this results in a popular culture that expresses a fairly limited number of commonly accepted cultural attitudes and ideas. Moreover, popular storytelling is expressed in familiar genres such as the action/adventure film, reality show, love song, or mystery novel that have recognizable reoccurring characters and narrative patterns that lead to certain typical resolutions. Finally, there is a logic to the assumption that popular culture confirms widely shared attitudes and understandings. If it did not, why would it be popular? Therefore, one of the things people study about popular culture is its sameness, the way it leads to particular expected resolutions that express social norms and values. Observing this sameness, popular culture critics ask whether popular culture shapes society by teaching these norms and values, or whether it reflects already existing societal and individual assumptions and understandings.

In various combinations these understandings lead some people to focus on the ways in which popular culture supports society as it exists, confirming existing attitudes and values and justifying and perpetuating injustice. Others, who focus more on the way popular culture changes, consider the way aesthetic forms develop over time. They often suggest that popular culture can also challenge existing norms and values. They are likely to look at the way popular culture is shaped by niche creators and audiences who use it to tell stories of transgression that question cultural norms. In fact, popular culture doesn't serve just one function or have a single meaning. To understand the complexity of popular culture we must pay attention to both the varied purposes of different producers and, as argued in the introduction to the first section, to the way audiences and individuals make meaning out of these.

Here the approach called "reader-response criticism" is helpful. It challenges both the assumption that a story or other art form has a single meaning and the assumption that the author is the source of that meaning. Reader-response critics argue that meaning is created in the interaction between the reader and the story. Readers bring a variety of perspectives that produce different questions about a story that lead to different insights. The same reader may even experience the story differently at different times. Further, as we saw most clearly in the examples of "Popular Culture as Religion," the meaning of popular culture is not simply established by the assumptions and intentions of those who create it; "consumers" play with, revise, and talk back to popular culture in their own practices. In fan activities and gaming, fans remake popular culture to serve their own purposes. If we think about popular culture in this way, we see that every "reading" of popular culture is a dialogue between the creator, the object, and the audience.

Even when the underlying assumptions of popular culture seem self-evident we have to pay attention to how particular images and stories are presented and interpreted. Sometimes producers appropriate popular culture forms rooted in particular cultural assumptions to create a dialogue with and about those assumptions. For instance, 1950s family comedies like *Father Knows Best* (1954–63) were clearly rooted in traditional gender norms. Later, television programs such as *Married … with Children* (1987–97) and *The Simpsons* (1989–present) were in conversation with the tradition of the family comedy, pointing out and commenting on its patriarchal assumptions. Moreover, consumers may embrace examples of popular culture at odds with their own values, such as refrigerator magnets depicting a 1950s housewife at the stove, with her husband seated at the dinner table, captioned "Maybe I'll marry my stove"—a feminist critique ironically embedded in nostalgia.

All this suggests that popular culture itself exists as a dialogue between producers and multiple audiences, and in this section we expand this dialogical understanding to suggest a relationship between religion and popular culture in which they are also in conversation with each other. Here, as Bruce David Forbes says in the Introduction, "Finding Religion in Unexpected Places," they comment on each other, debate cultural changes, and engage questions of value and social vision.

In Shreena Niketa Gandhi's "Yoga in Popular Culture: Controversies and Conflicts," yoga and yoga pants serve as an example of the shifting conversation between religion and popular culture. Yoga has historically been understood as a spiritual practice, a form of embodied prayer, and it came to United States as part of the nation's fascination with the East. Today, it is often practiced as a form of exercise and mindfulness in settings ranging from Christian churches to gymnasiums. Gandhi engages the dialogue between Hindu religionists and middle-class white yoga practitioners over who has the right to define yoga. Is it rightly understood as a spiritual practice tied to a particular Eastern tradition or a popular American activity without a religious location?

In "Mirror, Mirror on Ourselves," Stephanie Brehm and Myev Rees look at dialogue between religion and popular culture that happens around what they call the Disney Universe. They first trace the way both liberal and conservative voices have used religion to raise ethical questions about Disney stories, theme parks, and corporate policies and practices. They demonstrate how religious leaders sometimes debate with other citizens over the values expressed in particular stories or social practices at Disney; and they see places where differing religious communities debate each other about whether it is appropriate for them to participate in particular forms of popular culture. The authors go on to look at the way Disney embodies these cultural and religious tensions, telling stories that express emerging understandings of gender and race, while at the same time expressing traditional assumptions about these matters.

Although some in the evangelical wing of the Christian church continue to be suspicious of the dominant culture, Robert K. Johnston, an evangelical theologian, shows that evangelical responses to popular culture are hardly monolithic. In "Can Watching a Movie Be a Spiritual Experience?" he suggests that faith and culture are always in dialogue. He explores the way his students' conversation with movies, even seemingly secular ones, can be a spiritual experience.

There are lots of examples of religious critiques of popular culture, often but not exclusively, of its sex, violence, and the valorization of consumption. Anthony Pinn's "Rap Music and Its Message" comes from the other direction. He argues that embedded in rap's articulation of what he calls a "nitty-gritty hermeneutic" is an implicit critique of the black church, an accusation that the church has been consumed with a moralism that fails to take seriously the realities of African American suffering. Though rap has been criticized by some religious voices, Pinn argues that it fills a spiritual void and engages in a needed dialogue about the situation of many black lives.

In "Broadswords and Face Paint," Curtis Coats and Stewart Hoover study the use that evangelical pastors and men's groups have made of the Mel Gibson film *Braveheart* in their dialogue about masculinity, the roles and assumed responsibilities of men. They examine the way the film provides language and images through which these men imagine and articulate what it means for them to be evangelical husbands and fathers. Implicit here is an argument similar to Pinn's, that popular culture provides language and images that more adequately or honestly get at the struggles of particular communities. Pinn explores how rap might be an alternative place for dialogue about suffering among African Americans disaffected from the black church; Coats and Hoover focus on the way some white men who remain within the church find its language and images inadequate and turn to a particular example of popular culture to explore their roles and responsibilities.

Jeffrey H. Mahan
Iliff School of Theology

# CHAPTER SIXTEEN

# Yoga in Popular Culture

*Controversies and Conflicts*

SHREENA NIKETA GANDHI

Yoga has clearly become a part of U.S. popular culture. *Yoga Journal* does a survey every few years to gauge yoga's popularity. This is self-serving—the magazine needs to know that it has a viable audience—and its survey model is biased, because it has a monetary interest in the findings. Nonetheless, the results are revealing: in its 2012 survey, *Yoga Journal* found that 20.4 million U.S. adults practiced yoga, that they spent $10.3 billion a year on "yoga classes and products, including equipment, clothing, vacations and media," and that 44.4 percent of nonpracticing Americans were also interested in trying yoga.[1]

In my own study of the cultural history of yoga in the United States, I examine how yoga has been constructed as "Eastern" and mystical; as non-Hindu, universal, and scientific; and as a practice for better health. This 150-year process has helped Americans imagine yoga as a secular practice, which has been gendered, racially categorized, and socially classed in a particular way, free from the entanglements of any religious traditions or beliefs. This categorization involves both buy-in and push-back, and in this chapter, I examine three examples of this buy-in and push-back, and the ensuing conflicts and dialogues that arise. Looking at the phenomenon of yoga pants, the practice of Christian Yoga, and the protests of the Hindu American Foundation (HAF), will show how popular culture and religion interact and create pockets of cooperation and conflict.

## YOGA PANTS

The practice of yoga in the United States exposes the fuzzy lines between the religious and secular (and in fact calls into question the many ways in which religion is defined). There are debates over whether yoga is a part of any one religion, and whether it can be practiced by just anyone. These questions will be examined in the latter two parts of this chapter. However, first, I would like to look at the way in which many readers may have encountered yoga—the comfortable yoga pants that many of us wear even when we are not doing yoga. Material and visual exploration of yoga pants exposes how they reify categories and norma-tivities of gender, class, and race. In other words, while the practice of yoga is not easily categorized as religious or secular, the practice and products of yoga are most available to white/Euro-American, upper-middle-class women; and the visual culture of yoga in the United States reflects and reproduces this construction of yoga. Examining yoga pants in popular culture can best illustrate this phenomenon.

If you to do a quick Google search for "yoga pants" and click on "images," what is the gender and race of most of the people depicted wearing yoga pants? What body part do most of these images focus on? How many of these images actually show someone practicing yoga? Do you notice similar or different images in regards to race and gender? What do you notice in terms of prices—how much are the most expen-sive and least expensive yoga pants? Now just for fun, Google "male yoga pants." What are some of the similarities and differences you notice in regard to the style of pants, how the body is portrayed and the prices? What I notice when I conduct this search is that most of images are of white, thin women, and that these images focus on the lower half of her body. Furthermore, these pants are tight, and can range in prices from $14 to $120. In contrast, many of the men's pants are loose, though similarly, the images predominately portray white, very fit, muscular men, and the price range is about the same.

In recent years, Lululemon has been the company most identified with the yoga pants, primarily because of their popularity and prices. It does not manufacture men's yoga pants, but does sell kung fu pants for men. Its women's yoga pants cost anywhere from $88 to $118. When women complained about their expensive yoga pants pilling, Lululemon's co-founder, Chip Wilson responded: "Frankly some women's bodies just don't actually work for it. They don't work for some women's bodies. It's really about the rubbing through the thighs, how much pressure is there over a period of time, how much they use it."[2] So the Lululemon customer not only has to have plenty of disposable income but also a thigh gap. Wilson has also said that it takes 30 percent more fabric to create plus-size clothes, so Lululemon does not make pants larger than a size 12. In an attempt to be empathetic, he said, "It's a money loser, for sure. I understand their plight, but it's tough."[3] Over the past few years, women of color have started appearing in Lululemon's catalogues, but the visuals and staff in any of its stores make it clear that the customer aimed at is a white, thigh-gap-thin woman who can afford to drop at least $200 dollars for yoga pants, top, and bra.

Lululemon's marketing (to thin women only) and high prices are not the only way in which the company is controversial. Allegedly unethical labor practices have caused some people to question its popularity. Lululemon started out in 1998, making its clothing at a nonunion shop in Vancouver, Canada, but since then it has moved much of its production overseas, mainly to China. Chip Wilson is reported as saying at a business conference in Vancouver that "third world children should be allowed to work in factories because it provides them with much-needed wages." Moreover, "[n]inety-five per cent of the factories I've seen in the Orient are far better than ones in North America," he said. "In China, many people come from the western provinces and their goal is to work seven days a week 16 hours a day, because in five years they want to have a pile of money to go home with and start a business."

And he added: "In Canada for instance, 99 per cent of our factory workers are Chinese women sewers. If you were to work them eight-hour days, they will be mad at you. If you only work them five days a week for only eight hours, they'll say, 'What are you doing? I don't want to work for you.' If you do only work them that much, they walk out of their shift at 4 o'clock and walk across the street to another factory and work another six hours. This is in Vancouver, in Canada."[4] Wilson said nothing about wages, working conditions, unions, or benefits. Such business practices have proved controversial, and they have earned Lululemon less-than-stellar publicity. They are also a challenge to the yoga community, whose members are often socially and politically liberal. The knowledge that a self-proclaimed libertarian whose labor practices might be construed as abusive makes their beloved yoga pants has opened the door for other brands.

Lululemon does not have a corner on the yoga pants market—as our Google search demonstrated, one can buy yoga pants for $14, thus making them accessible to a wide variety of women, and since they are comfortable, many women of all ages, shapes, and sizes choose to wear them. This, however, is not without its own set of conflicts regarding women's bodies. Yoga pants can be tight, and schools are implementing policies to ban them. In 2014, the administrators at Devils Lake High School in North Dakota had a girls-only assembly to explain the new dress code, during which they showed clips of *Pretty Woman* to demonstrate the different ways in which women could be perceived, depending on the clothes they wear.[5] Devils Lake High School is not the exception. In 2015 at Cape Cod Regional Technical High School, yoga pants and leggings were banned unless a skirt or shorts covered them, because the school felt that students should be dressing more professionally; however, the students were not convinced. Female students are being told that their comfortable clothing is a distraction to male students and teachers, and in response they are protesting. When a middle school in Evanston, Illinois, banned leggings and yoga pants, "Hundreds of students signed a petition, and several marched—one carrying a poster that asked 'are my pants lowering your test scores?'"[6] Some students started #iammorethanadistraction to protest the monitoring and sexualizing of girls' bodies. Given that female bodies have always been a contested site, this debate over yoga pants is not surprising, just illustrative of how pervasively mainstream yoga and yoga products are becoming in the United States.

Yoga can be practiced in anything—I've seen women in saris perform *asanas,* or poses, that I can only dream of doing. However, over the past fifteen years, yoga pants have become U.S. women's standard garb in which to do yoga. It's almost as though the material and sensation of wearing yoga pants mentally prepare one for the practice of yoga and better health—or perhaps simply to be comfortable.

In American popular culture, however, we simultaneously deal with the objectification/sexualization of the female body and the desire to keep that body pure, along with messages that it has to be fit, thin, and shapely. Yoga pants have become a new site for this dialogue. The issue here is not so much who should and should not be wearing yoga pants, as who should be practicing yoga—and how.

## CHRISTIAN YOGA

The relationship between Christianity and yoga is not new. It was the Unitarians who organized the World Parliament of Religion in 1893 that brought Swami Vivekananda and *raja* yoga to the United States. Twenty-seven years later, they organized the International Congress of Religious Liberals, and through that conference, the United States was introduced to Paramahansa Yogananda and *kriya* yoga. Throughout his *Autobiography of a Yogi,* following in the footsteps of Vivekananda, Yogananda refers to Christian scripture and uses Christian imagery to position *kriya* yoga as an interdisciplinary practice. Both Vivekananda and Yogananda came to the United States partly to raise money for their projects in India—they had to make yoga appealing to and nonthreatening for Christians and their beliefs. Yoga, specifically *pranayama* (yogic breathing), was seen as a supplement to, not a substitute for, Christian practice.[7] Starting in the 1940s and 1950s, yoga practice in the United States started to become more a physical exercise, signaling a shift away from *pranayama* toward *asanas* (yogic poses/postures). Starting in the 1950s and 1960s, yoga was reaching U.S. living rooms via books and daily television programs. The market was transforming yoga into a secular exercise.

Hindu yogis continued, however, to promote yoga as a practice "compatible with all of the world's great religions." In the summer of 1971, a Catholic Women's College, Annhurst, hosted the second annual Yoga Ecumenical Retreat, where nuns, priests, monks, rabbis, and "long haired young people" all came together to learn yoga based on the teachings of Swami Satchidananda. "Deep prayer always involves transcending the body and the senses," a Sister Maria said. "Yoga is a definite help in doing this. It helps to relax the body and mind and integrate your whole person". Sister Rose Margaret Delaney felt that yoga was not prayer, but rather a preparation for it: "I don't use a mantra.... I meditate on the Gospel of the day and use Yoga as a way of disposing myself to prayer," she explained.[8]

Today, Christians also are drawing on their biblical roots to reformulate yoga. Many practicing Christians take yoga classes at gyms or yoga centers, but some do not like the overtly Hindu references, meditation, and chanting. Parishioners at New Community Church in Washington, DC, chant "Sha-LOM," not "OM" or "AUM."[9] Like Sister Rose Margaret Delaney, many Christian yoga classes recite Bible verses during certain poses and keep their minds focused on God and Jesus Christ, rather than Isvara, the Hindu Lord of Yoga. The Suryanamaskara, or Sun Salutation, is a twelve-step combination of asanas and pranayamas. In many Christian yoga classes, "Sun," S-U-N, is changed to "Son," S-O-N. Thus, when they do the twelve steps, it is not in worship of Surya but to show devotion to Jesus. At St. Andrew's Lutheran Church in Minnesota, the practice of Christian yoga is called "Yogadevotion," and although there are some members who are skeptical, one of the pastors, John Keller, is supportive, because "it draws potential converts through the church's doors"; "about a quarter of Yogadevotion students are not churchgoers."[10]

Not all agree with this blending of practice. Many Christian critics of yoga feel discomfort over the blending of Christianity and yoga. One critic says that using yoga to lure people to church is not innocent, but "dancing with the devil."[11] There are a growing number of books warning Christians about the mixing of yoga and Christian practice. In his book *Yoga and the Body of Christ*, Dave Hunt writes, "Yoga originated in India as part of the paganism practiced there" and claims that yoga is one way in which the West is being conquered.[12]

Perhaps the most creative and interesting criticism of Christian yoga comes from Laurette Willis, founder of "PraiseMoves," a Christian alternative to yoga, which along with "Fitness to His Witness" is a trademarked system of exercise for good health, plus the benefit of Jesus. Willis, a former "New-Ager" who found God in 1987, grew up practicing yoga with her mother, but says, "from experience I can say that yoga is a dangerous practice for the Christian and leads seekers *away* from God rather than to Him." Like the Hindu critics of Christian yoga, Willis argues that yoga cannot be separated from Hinduism, for all of the "yoga postures are *offerings* to the 330 million Hindu gods." And Christian yoga, for Willis, is an "oxymoron" that is an example of *syncretism,* which by her definition, is "an attempt to blend conflicting belief, religions or philosophies." So, as an alternative to Christian yoga and Hindu yoga, Willis has started the patented "PraiseMoves," which is not Christian yoga but a "*Christ*-centered *alternative* to the practice of yoga". Willis argues that even though this might seem like yoga, and the class is organized like many yoga classes in the United States and India, it is really not. She acknowledges that some of the PraiseMoves postures resemble yoga postures, because she's "discovered there's not an *infinite* number of ways the human body can move", and informs us that these postures have been created by God, and that PraiseMoves is "a way to untwist these beneficial postures back to glorify God."[13]

Willis's trademarked technique thus purports to strip away yoga's Hindu rhetoric to reveal an intrinsically Christian practice.

The ironic thing about this particular conflict over yoga in popular culture is that when Indian yogis first came to the United States, they courted Christian practitioners. And many Christians today do not see a conflict with practicing yoga—they happily do it in gym classes, church basements, retirement communities, and community centers. Since yoga was constructed as non-Hindu, universal and scientific, and as a practice likely to promote better health, it appeals to a larger population. However, Christians like Dave Hunt and Laurette Willis show that in this country, the mixing of religious or spiritual or foreign beliefs and practices can cause conflict and discomfort. What does the addition of yoga do to Christianity? Does it add or take away from Christian commitment? Does it create less devout Christians or does it enable Christians to delve deeper into their religion? It is not only Christians who discuss questions of purity and origins regarding yoga; Hindus have also pursued this line of inquiry in some interesting ways.

## THE HINDU AMERICAN FOUNDATION AND "TAKE BACK YOGA"

While Christians debate about whether they should practice yoga or not, one particular Hindu advocacy group argues that yoga is explicitly Hindu and started a "Take Back Yoga Campaign" in 2009. This Hindu advocacy or lobbying group, the Hindu American Foundation (HAF), describes itself as

> An advocacy group providing a progressive Hindu American voice. The Foundation interacts with and educates leaders in public policy, academia, media, and the public at large about Hinduism and global issues concerning Hindus, such as religious liberty, the misportrayal of Hinduism, hate speech, hate crimes, and human rights. By promoting the Hindu and American ideals of understanding, tolerance and pluralism, HAF stands firmly against hate, discrimination, defamation and terror.[14]

HAF has involved itself in quite a few controversies in the past decade. It protested the National Book Award nomination of Wendy Doniger's book *The Hindus,* charging that it was biased and inaccurate, and is the first to respond when a clothing company or designer uses Hindu iconography in "inappropriate" ways. And most notably, before the "Take Back Yoga" campaign, HAF filed suit contesting the means by which Hindu history and practice were written about in California social studies textbooks. The suit was denied in court, but the battle over the content in California textbooks is ongoing, and the HAF has launched #donteraseindia to spread the word.

Arguably, the "Take Back Yoga" campaign is what put HAF on the popular culture map. It started with a 2009 blog entry, "Let's Take Yoga Back," posted on the HAF blog. In this post, a young Hindu-American woman, Sheetal Shah, laments that the yoga taught in this country is devoid of the Hindu label. In particular, she is dismayed that *Yoga Journal* avoids using the word "Hindu" in promoting yoga, that there are no Hindus in her yoga classes, and that she was able to find many yoga teachers, but none that were explicitly Hindu. She writes,

> How can we maintain and promote the Hindu origin of yoga if the majority of yoga studios don't have Hindu students, forget the idea of Hindu yoga teachers? Our Hindu forefathers understood the unique benefits of yoga and shared yoga with the Western world. The West understood, fell in love with yoga, morphed it into a physical and "spiritual" practice—thereby removing any religious association—and proclaimed their expertise. And while so many non-Hindu Americans delve into yoga with passion, the majority of Hindu Americans seem to have forgotten its importance in uniting their mind, body, and soul and relinquished their knowledge and ownership of this life changing practice....
>
> ... I urge you, as a Hindu American, to reclaim yoga by once again becoming an expert in its practice.... I urge you to take a beginners' yoga class at a local studio and encourage your children, siblings, parents and friends to do the same. Many of our local Hindu temples offer free yoga classes taught by instructors who are born Hindu, and some of you already attend them ... next week, bring a friend or family member with you. If you

practice basic *asanas* at home, move your practice to the next level and take an intermediate yoga class at a studio.[15]

Shah's call was taken up in full force by HAF. Later in 2009, after Shah's blog post, HAF issued a position paper on yoga's Hindu origins:

> The Hindu American Foundation (HAF) reaffirms that Yoga ... is an essential part of Hindu belief and practice. But the science of yoga and the immense benefits its practice affords are for the benefit of all of humanity regardless of personal faith. Hinduism itself is a family of pluralistic doctrines and ways of life that acknowledge the existence of other spiritual and religious traditions. Hinduism, as a non-proselytizing religion, never compels practitioners of yoga to profess allegiance to the faith or convert. Yoga is a means of spiritual attainment for any and all seekers.[16]

Starting in April 2010, HAF co-founder and board member, Aseem Shukla engaged pop guru Deepak Chopra in a debate over yoga's ownership in the *Washington Post*'s "On Faith" blog. Chopra argued that yoga did not originate with Hinduism, writing,

> Beneath Shukla's complaints one detects the resentment of an inventor who discovered Coca-Cola or Teflon but neglected to patent it. Isn't that a rather petty basis for drawing such a negative picture? Most Indians, when they contemplate the immense popularity of yoga in the U.S. may smile at the pop aspects of the phenomenon but feel on the whole that something good is happening. Shukla regards the same scene with a withering frown.[17]

Shukla retorted that while Chopra materially benefits from Hinduism (what Chopra calls Vedic knowledge) and calls himself an Advaita Vedantin, he fails to credit the religion in any of his platforms. This back and forth gained attention on many explicitly Hindu blogs, anti-yoga Christian blogs, and non-Hindu yoga blogs—each view siding with either Shukla or Chopra, depending on whether they wanted or needed yoga to be Hindu or not. This debate eventually garnered the attention of the national press; the *New York Times* and *CNN* both did stories profiling the major players in this campaign.

While many have opinions on whom yoga belongs to, the HAF has clearly taken steps to frame the debate. While it maintains that anyone can practice and reap the benefits of yoga, they are adamant that Hindu roots of yoga be acknowledged. When boiled down and simplified, as Internet debates often are, the questions become, "Is yoga Hindu?" or "To which religion does yoga belong?" Scholars can debate the Jain or Buddhist legacies of yoga or even argue that yoga is more European and a colonial construction than Hindu, but in the long run, these are of little relevance in a postcolonial world dealing with boundaries between religions. In popular culture, labels have consequences, and the growing popularity of yoga among Hindu South Asian Americans, along with being made into an issue by HAF, has made the label, history and ownership of yoga one with religious, sociopolitical, and economic consequences.

The larger issue is why "ownership" is even an issue. We live in a world where people become billionaires based on patents and copyrights and phantom mortgages. Religion, spirituality, simple exercise—none of these are exempt from the reaches of capitalism and a society that values material stability and domination over all else. Thus, perhaps it was just a matter of time before yoga became a ground for battle of labels and histories. Deepak Chopra used the word "fundamentalist" in reference to Aseem Shukla. Non-Hindu yoga teachers, who liberally employ "OM" in their instruction also oppose this HAF campaign, and it is easier to brand them as fundamentalists, and thus dismiss them, than to have a frank conversation about the effects, consequences, and benefits of colonialism, about cultural appropriation and the contours of power. In other words, I do not think that we can or should simply brush off the conversation about yoga's place or ownership. Rather, I think it might be an interesting moment for us to examine our assumptions about Hindus and Hinduism. Because of colonialism, capitalism, and racism, white Europeans and Euro-Americans are able simultaneously to appropriate parts of colonized cultures and impose their values onto colonized communities, some of which have moved to Europe and the United States. Yet there are no consequences for this subjugation and appropriation; thus when groups get to react, they react in ways that seem to uphold colonial values of separation and origins regarding religion and popular culture.

At the same time, we should think about other Hindu traditions that middle-class Hindus in India and the United States have tried to forget and forsake. The HAF web site mentions tolerance, karma, dharma and Brahman as central tenets of Hinduism, but no mention is made of Tantra, sacrifice, possession, mosque bombings, female feticide, or dowry burnings. These are as much a part of Hinduism as yoga. The religious boundaries of the Protestant British have never made sense in India, so it was perhaps inevitable that yoga, Tantra, and even Hindu worship spaces defy categorization, belonging, and neat histories. Yet HAF has chosen to hone in on yoga, which again shows the ways in which yoga has become a part of the U.S. religious and cultural landscape.

CONCLUSION

The three examples highlighted in this chapter show that yoga is a contested site in modern America, one where controversy and conflict play out over the production of yoga pants, over the bodies of females wearing yoga pants, over who can/should practice yoga, and over the origins and identity of yoga. These controversies show the border between the religious and the secular to be fuzzy, and often arbitrary, and it is thus important to openly discuss this messiness. Is yoga a part of a religion or is it is secular practice, and how have yoga pants become part of our everyday secular wardrobes? Also, how does looking at race, gender, and class show us how yoga has been marketed and constructed in this country primarily for one group of people? And why is it important to look at the intersections of popular culture, the sexualization of female bodies, and yoga pants—how that can that help us understand larger conflicts in U.S. popular culture? Finally, how and why do religions mix? Is this a phenomenon local to the United States or is it global?

And, finally, to whom does culture belong, and how do we determine the lines between cultural appropriation and appreciation?

## DISCUSSION QUESTIONS

1. Why do you think yoga is popular in the United States? What factors do you think are contributing to its rise in popularity?

2. Is yoga a religious or secular activity in America today? Is the boundary between the sacred and the secular fuzzy when it comes to yoga? How do you understand the argument of some Hindus that yoga should not be separated from its role in the veneration of Hindu gods?

3. What are the roles of gender, race, and class in the constructions and practices of yoga and other parts of popular culture in the United States?

4. Do people practice yoga in your community? Look for ads or announcements promoting yoga. Is it marketed as a spiritual practice, or as a form of exercise? Who is it marketed to?

## NOTES

1. "New Study Finds More Than 20 Million Yogis in U.S.," www.yogajournal.com/uncategorized/new-study-finds-20-million-yogis-u-s.

2. Harry Bradford. "Lululemon's Founder Blames Yoga Pants Problem on Women's Bodies," www.huffingtonpost.com/2013/11/05/lululemon-founder-some-wo_n_4221668.html.

3. "Lululemon Founder Chip Wilson Resigns from Board," *Financial Times*, February 2, 2015, www.ft.com/cms/s/0/5d16fdd8-aaf2-11e4-81bc-00144feab7de.html#axzz4Eljmik03.

4. Scott Deveau, "Yoga Mogul Has Critics in a Knot," *The Tyee*, February 17, 2015, http://thetyee.ca/News/2005/02/17/LuluCritics.

5. Lindsay Ellis, "Yoga Pants Too Distracting for Boys? A N.D. School Cracks Down on Girls," *Christian Science Monitor*, October 1, 2014, www.csmonitor.com/USA/Society/2014/1001/Yoga-pants-too-distracting-for-boys-A-N.D.-school-cracks-down-on-girls-video.

6. Ellis. "Yoga Pants Too Distracting for Boys?"

7. According to Patanjali there are eight limbs of yoga: *yama* (moral principles), *niyama* (observances), *asana* (postures), *pranayama* (breath control), *pratyahara* (withdrawal of senses), *dhyana* (meditation), and *samadhi* (pure contemplation) (*Yoga Discipline of Freedom: The Yoga Sutra Attributed to Patanjali*, trans. Barbara Stoler Miller [Bantam, 1998], 52). Only two of the eight, breath control and postures, are overtly popular in the practice of modern Hatha yoga (though there are allusions to *yama*), partially due to the influence of those that brought new exposure to yoga starting in the nineteenth century. Further, it seems that both *pranayama* and *asana* were latched onto by modern yoga "exporters," for they were easiest to translate into a modern ethos—one that focused on health, control, and ecumenism.

8. Edward B. Fiske, "Priests and Nuns Discover Yoga Enhances Grasp of Faith," *New York Times*, July 2, 1971, 35, 55.

9. Phuong Ly, "Churches, Synagogues Mingle Yoga with Beliefs," *Washington Post*, January 1, 2006, C1.

10. Lisa Takeuchi Cullen, "Stretching for Jesus," *Time Magazine*, August 29, 2005.

11. Trayce Gano, "Contemplative Emerging Church Deception: Christian Yoga, Innocent Activity or Dancing With the Devil?" http://emerging-church.blogspot.com/2007/02/christian-yoga-innocent-activity-or.html.

12. Dave Hunt, *Yoga and the Body of Christ: What Position Should Christians Hold?* (Bend, OR: Berean Call, 2006), 23.

13. Laurette Willis. "Why a Christian ALTERNATIVE to Yoga?" http://praisemoves.com/about-us/why-a-christian-alternative-to-yoga.

14. "Hindu American Foundation," https://plus.google.com/HafsiteOrg/about.

15. Sheetal Shah, "Let's Take Yoga Back," www.hinducurrents.com/articles/19969/lets-take-yoga-back.

16. "Yoga beyond Asana: Hindu Thought in Practice," www.hafsite.org/media/pr/yoga-hindu-origins.

17. "Shukla and Chopra: The Great Yoga Debate," OnFaith, April 30, 2010, www.faithstreet.com/onfaith/2010/04/30/shukla-and-chopra-the-great-yoga-debate/4379.

# CHAPTER SEVENTEEN

# Mirror, Mirror on Ourselves

*Disney as a Site of Religio-Cultural Dialogue*

STEPHANIE BREHM AND MYEV REES

Disney is arguably one of the most significant creative and commercial ventures in American history. It may have "all started with a mouse," as Walt Disney was fond of saying, but "the wonderful world of Disney" has grown into a universe of narrative generation, media production, digital practice, material culture, capitalist consumption, political action, and far more. Indeed, it is difficult to even pin down what is being referred to with the term "Disney." The Walt Disney Company is a publicly traded multinational corporation, but Disney also exists in the collective zeitgeist of American culture and in individual hearts and minds. In this chapter, we use "Disney Universe" as an umbrella term to refer to that expansive understanding of Disney, which moves beyond its corporate identity. When we are referencing the corporate entity alone, we refer to the Walt Disney Company. In that same vein, we use "Disney texts" to refer to specific cultural artifacts under examination, like films or theme parks.

In the late 1990s and 2000s, scholars on the left, like the Marxist cultural theorist Henry Giroux, argued that the Disney Universe's seemingly wholesome appearance draws children into its agenda of white American supremacy, globalization, and corporate power.[1] On the right, conservative Christian groups protested the Walt Disney Company's embrace of LGBTQ families in the 1990s and created moral panic around alleged sexual imagery hidden in Disney films.[2] Many studies and criticisms of the Disney Universe from the left and the right imagine it as a unified entity with a consistent message and particular vision (often perceived as sinister).[3] Critics often imagine these messages and visions of the Disney Universe very differently. What their interpretations have in common, though, is the view that the Disney Universe explicitly or subliminally harms Americans under the masquerade of childhood innocence and wholesome family fun. The mouse, unbeknown to us, has teeth. Whether from the right or the left, critics consider the Disney Universe as a monolith, often reducible to the policies and practices of the Walt Disney Company. Such stances flatten a far more complex cultural reality. The following analysis is not an attempt at Disney apologetics but problematizes the image of the Disney Universe as a sinister cultural puppeteer with a unified message.

In this chapter, we provide an analysis of Disney films and theme parks, which we take as "texts" that can be examined or "read." Our analysis challenges the view that religion and popular culture are top-down power structures inflicting their agendas on passive individuals. This view gives too little credence to the power we have to use cultural or religious narratives as tools for making and unmaking our identities and worlds. If we imagine individuals as having such agency, religion and popular culture can be understood as constant processes of negotiation and dialogue. Rather than viewing the Disney Universe as a prescriptive, constructive force, we imagine Disney "texts" as places where that dialogue might be taking place. With that in mind, we ask, What are Disney texts (for example, films and theme parks) *revealing* about religion and popular culture in America? What does the Disney Universe reveal about the broader religious and cultural anxieties of the present moment?

Rather than thinking of media, popular culture, and religion as forces that act on powerless consumers, we take them to be phenomena with which people interact. With that as our starting point, religion and media become things people *do* rather than agendas or doctrines they are subject *to*.[4] This approach requires a tolerance for complication, but it undermines the flawed assumption that media producers' intentions and values dictate the effects media texts have on the social world.[5] People do not swallow religions whole and then become perfect embodiments of those religious systems. They use religious ideas and practices to figure out how to best live in their various contexts. Similarly, people do not absorb media messages and then parrot them back unthinkingly. They may resist or subvert them, or incorporate them often in unexpected ways into their already existing lives. As a multi-platform media producer in a consumer capitalist economy, the Disney Universe holds a rich archive of religious and cultural dialogue. In the effort to reflect changing cultural norms without alienating audiences who are less responsive to such change, Disney inevitably presents texts that are rooted in audiences' cultural and religious ambivalences.

In this chapter we focus on two significant tensions revealed in Disney texts. The first tension is between the sacralization of futuristic technological progress and the idealized return to nature religion. The second tension is between initiatives to empower girls and women and the ambivalences and anxieties caused by dismantling "traditional" gender norms and systems. Before we can explore these tensions however, it is important to understand that Disney has since its inception produced texts that reveal and reflect cultural and religious dialogues and anxieties. We may see clearer contestation in today's Disney texts, but even in the 1950s the Disney Universe was about far more than animation and the "magic" of childhood.

The Disney Universe has always reflected and contributed to the political and religious dialogues happening in a particular historical moment. For example, in 1955, Disneyland opened in Anaheim, California, with a grand ceremony. Walt Disney stood center, flanked by the governor of California, the mayor of Anaheim, and three military chaplains representing the Protestant, Catholic, and Jewish faiths. While three religions were represented that day, only the Protestant chaplain, Walt Disney's nephew Rev. Glen D. Puder, spoke. He proclaimed that his uncle had "spiritual motivations" for creating the theme park. Calling for attendees and television viewers to move beyond the "creeds that divide us," Puder led the assemblage in a silent prayer that Disneyland might "prosper at God's hands."[6] Therefore, Disneyland was presented to the American public as an extension of American state power—a power bestowed and sanctioned by God. What happened in 1955 was far more than a ribbon cutting. It was a consecration. In the rhetoric of the opening ceremony, we can hear the echoes of the seventeenth-century Puritans who came to the "new world" in the hope that their New England settlement would fulfill the biblical mandate to become "a light unto the nations" and "a city on a hill."[7] The opening ceremony in 1955 seemed to position Disneyland as an inheritor of that holy mission—it would be a theme park on a hill.

That same year, the sociologist Will Herberg published *Protestant, Catholic, Jew,* an iconic, and now roundly rejected, treatise on American religion.[8] Herberg argued that the three dominant religions could and should be seamlessly woven together to create national "unity." This was not as much observation as it was aspiration. The Cold War period was marked by an urgent desire to unify all religions in opposition to "heathen" or "godless" communists. One example is the addition of "In God We Trust" on U.S. paper currency in 1957, a move that symbolically and literally sacralized capital and capitalism.[9] Disney himself demonstrated his Cold War fears a decade earlier. Unlike many of his Hollywood contemporaries, he was a friendly witness for the House Un-American Activities Committee. He assured the committee that his films and activities would promote the ideals of wholesome American families who were virtuous, industrious, and righteous.[10]

The Disney Universe contributed to this effort by creating a consumer-driven "universal" pilgrimage site that celebrated a mythic America and was sanctioned by Protestant, Catholic, and Jewish military chaplains. The fact that the three religions were "united" under a

Protestant prayer reflected the cultural and religious tenor of the time, as did the fact that the prayer invoked God's blessing over what was a business venture as much as anything else. Disneyland therefore was imagined as a place where Cold War Americans could act out their devotion to God-sanctioned capitalism by engaging with new mythic narratives of American civil religion and purchasing Mickey Mouse hats and souvenir cups. In the Cold War period, the Disney Universe reflected and became a site for negotiating the particular political and economic tensions of the day. Tomorrowland, in particular, attempted to mitigate the fear surrounding the space race and the threat of nuclear war by depicting a romanticized technology-driven future.

Of course, not everyone agrees with Walt's assessment that the company he created was (or is) "wholesome" and "righteous." As the Disney Universe has grown over time, both through its success and through the wider and more complex influence afforded by globalization and expanding media worlds, its texts have drawn criticism from both the left and the right. Academic and liberal scholarship, in particular the study of religion and popular culture, has generated a wealth of scholarship on Disney's religious and cultural footprint. In an increasingly neoliberal climate,[11] scholars have taken up the economic implications of Disney consumerism, the Walt Disney Company's role in globalization, Disney texts' efforts to sanitize/Protestantize or otherwise "Disneyfy" literature and folklore, and its revisionist (or fictionalized) approach to history ("Distory").[12]

Critics on the left have pointed out that Disney texts have the power to whitewash and to flatten significant cultural difference as they fashion "a small world after all." For example, cultural studies scholars like Johnson Cheu have upbraided Disney for reinforcing pejorative stereotypes of Native American, Asian, and black characters in its earlier films like *Peter Pan, Lady and the Tramp,* and *Song of the South.*[13] In the same vein as Henry Giroux, Cheu goes on to argue that Disney's "small world" vision of global unity is predicated on Eurocentrism and white supremacy.

Critics like Giroux and Cheu illustrate a Marxist interpretation of the complicated Disney Universe, but others have seen very different agendas at work. In June 1996, the Southern Baptist Convention (SBC) voted to boycott the Walt Disney Company for its "anti-Christian and anti-family direction,"[14] citing the Walt Disney's Company's acceptance of homosexuality, namely, the creation of "Gay Days" at the theme parks (a weekend specifically set aside for welcoming same-sex visitors and their children), and the company's decision to grant same-sex partners the same health benefits as those offered to heterosexual employees. The SBC eventually voted to abandon the boycott in 2005 when it became painfully obvious that it was largely ineffective by all traditional standards. However, the SBC boycott and the attention it generated may have further galvanized evangelicals and spurred them to invest more in their own alternative media.[15]

Another source of tension between the Disney Universe and conservative evangelicals came in 1995 when rumors emerged that Disney animators had hidden phallic images and erotic subliminal messages in *The Lion King, Aladdin,* and *The Little Mermaid.* The allegations gained national attention when the American Life League, a conservative evangelical organization, sounded the alarm in its monthly newsletter and the *Associated Press* picked up the story.[16] The American Life League's claims that *The Little Mermaid's* animation was rife with hidden penises, for example, were the stuff of Freudian jokes. The Walt Disney Company flatly denied such content existed. However, the fact that the American Life League succeeded in creating a moral panic underscored the distrustful and ambivalent relationship American conservative evangelicals had with mainstream popular media throughout the 1990s. By the time millennials became the primary audience of the Disney Universe, all that had changed.

Today most conservative evangelicals find it more effective and less isolating to be savvy curators rather than media purists. Rather than defining themselves against popular media texts, they have found ways to make "secular" media producers responsive to their needs and values. Disney's decision to take on the work of C. S. Lewis with its *Chronicles of Narnia* franchise reflects that cultural trend. Over the past thirty years, American and British evangelicals have all but canonized Lewis's work. Disney's *Narnia* films signal that the boundaries between evangelical culture and mainstream popular culture are growing ever more porous.

In the early 2000s, when Disney began targeting millennial teens and tweens, conservative Christians' relationship with the Disney Universe underwent another significant change. Characters like the Jonas Brothers, Selena Gomez, and Miley Cyrus were candid about their faith and their decisions to wear purity rings symbolizing their commitment to sexual abstinence until marriage.[17] As a result, the Disney Universe quickly became an engine of normalization for what was once considered an extreme, conservative evangelical preoccupation with displaying virginity. It used the young stars' religious expression to tap into the profitable teen market without alienating parents. For some fans, these religious expressions were irrelevant. Other devotees donned rings to mimic their celebrity idols without fully committing to, or perhaps even understanding, the religious implications of "true love waits."[18] Still other groups of young people may have taken up purity rings as tools for discerning, hiding, or relating to their burgeoning sexualities. And, of course, many used them as powerful weapons in the so-called culture wars.[19]

Here we see that Disney is not a monolithic corporate puppeteer but a site of negotiation and a reflection of our own attempts to navigate social change. The Walt Disney Company surely wants to avoid alienating large swaths of consumers. However, the Disney Universe is far more than a product of corporate strategy. It does reflect and follow larger cultural currents, but like American religious life, like American popular culture, and like our own identities, the Disney Universe is a complicated site of contradictions. It embraces LGBT families with one hand while it slips purity rings on the other.

## TOMORROWLAND AND NATURE RELIGION

The Disney Universe is a contested space that reveals and capitalizes on our internal and social ambiguities, ambivalences, and anxieties. One such ambivalence concerns the promise of a technology-saturated future and the fear that such a future would permanently sever humanity's connection to the mysterious powers of nature—powers we can only experience by looking to the past. In his work on religion and ecology, Bron Taylor observes that with regard to nature and technology, Disney appears to be "at war" with itself.[20] Taylor correctly asserts that recent Disney narratives reflect the deep ambivalence toward the ever-present technology we have come to love and fear. The Disney theme parks Tomorrowland and EPCOT idealize technologically driven "progress," while films like *WALL-E* and *Pocahontas* warn us about the dehumanization a tech-saturated future may hold and urge us to return to a romantic, nature-oriented past.

Disneyland's Tomorrowland is the gleaming manifestation of postwar American fantasy—automation, flying cars, and lunar colonies. But even Walt could not have imagined a world where children create their own narratives using his characters on interactive apps, or where sea levels are rising to catastrophic heights, or where we fight wars with unmanned drones. We can no longer imagine technology as a purely benevolent force.

During the Cold War, many Americans were similarly afraid of technology's consequences, but Walt Disney and others confronted those fears by attempting to show that technology was the key to a utopian, conflict-free global society. The Disney Universe, as well as other cultural, political, and economic actors, sacralized "progress," particularly in the burgeoning fields of engineering, chemistry, and nuclear energy, and, therefore, braided science into American civil religion.[21] Thus, the space race became both a scientific endeavor and a new expression of manifest destiny. Tomorrowland, with its futuristic monorail and "Rocket to the Moon" ride, expressed Walt Disney's optimistic vision of the future. As Bron Taylor writes, exhibits such as the "Carousel of Progress" paint an "unambiguously positive picture of modern, industrial civilization."[22]

Similarly, Disney World's EPCOT, or Experimental Prototype Community of Tomorrow, reflects mid-twentieth-century optimism that science and capitalism would bring out the best in humanity. As Walt Disney envisioned it, EPCOT would be "a showcase to the world for the ingenuity and imagination of American free enterprise."[23] EPCOT was to be a place where new ideas and emerging technologies developed, where solutions to humankind's problems could germinate and grow, leading to global peace and understanding.[24] He imagined a pluralistic liberal endeavor undergirded by American exceptionalism and progress that could effectively demolish communism once and for all. The vision, of course, fell far short. Today, EPCOT is less about global problem solving and more about corporate sponsors vying for tourists' attention. One can, however, "drink around the world," from Norwegian aquavit to Mexican tequila.[25]

Today, there is a sinister ring to the mid-twentieth-century scientific optimism of DuPont's longtime slogan "Better Living through Chemistry" and Penn Salt Chemicals" 1947 ad proclaiming "DDT is good for me-e-e!"[26] Profoundly disappointed and fearful that our advances might actually be killing us, more and more young Americans (particularly white middle- and upper-class Americans) now equate authenticity with the absence of industrialization. There is increasing demand for "artisanal" and "organic" food and products—but of course people use their phones to find and buy them. The Tomorrowland fantasy is not dead, as evidenced by the American obsession with technology and our continued curiosity about space and the future. We are just anxious about its apparent inevitability. The Disney Universe keeps the space-age dream alive through films like *Tomorrowland* (2015) and the Star Wars franchise. Only now the texts have a cautionary undertone. Those mixed messages demonstrate that the Disney Universe is not a unified monolith, but exhibits the ambiguous dialogues occurring in American society, religion, and popular culture.

*WALL-E,* a 2008 Pixar animated film, painfully captures the feeling of trapped ambivalence many Americans feel as a result of technological saturation. Released by Walt Disney Pictures, *WALL-E* presents our competing impulses toward technological advancement and an idealized return to the land.[27] The titular robot WALL-E (or "Waste Allocation Load Lifter—Earth-class") roams the Earth cleaning up the garbage left by humans, who have long since abandoned the planet to live in a megacorporation's fully automated spaceship. Earth is depicted as an "uninhabitable wasteland" whose "ecosystems ... have been virtually eliminated."[28] This future is free from war and work, but by organizing life around automation, technology, and mass consumerism, the now obese humans are easily manipulated and stupid. Capitalist "progress" has turned out to be a poison pill, not a magic potion. In the corporatized future, human romantic relationships have become little more than common interests in consumer products. Meanwhile, WALL-E is presented as mindful and appreciative, longing for a sense of connection that the humans do not seem to miss. The robots know more about relationships, love, and reverence than their inventors.

Despite the film's bleak beginning, the world does not end with a whimper and a Big Mac. It is, after all, a Disney film. WALL-E and his paramour robot EVE discover a plant seedling on Earth and bring it to the humans, who then realize the error of their ways. The film ends with a back-to nature revival as the humans return to Earth to clean it up and form agrarian co-operatives.

*WALL-E* shines a spotlight on contemporary fears of technology that lead to a desire to return to a romanticized pre-technology world. But *WALL-E* is not just about environmental degradation; it is about the loss of meaning and a sense of the sacred. The idealized natural world we often turn to is idyllic precisely because it carries within it deeply religious qualities some feel are no longer accessible to "moderns" in the global West. In the field of Religious Studies, scholars have intensively investigated the category of "modernity" and its problematic trappings, especially its connection to race and secularism.[29] One force imagined to be in opposition to modernity is religion—but more acutely, totemic, tribal, or animist religions that can be categorized as "nature religion."[30]

Nature religion encompasses all groups, peoples, or movements who consider the natural world to embody sacrality, divine qualities, and/or supernatural characteristics.[31] Of course, such an overarching term obscures the differences between paganism, Wicca, Native American religions, fetishism, animism, and many other religious systems. However, a commonality does exist. In many of these religious imaginations, nature religion is positioned as a corrective to the consequences of modernity, such as industrialism and white male Christian hegemony.

The 1995 animated Walt Disney feature film *Pocahontas*, exemplifies the romanticized return to nature religion and illustrates the push for pluralism and political correctness of the 1990s. In a story that takes flagrant liberties with American colonial history, Pocahontas, a young daughter of the Powhatan chief, falls in love with an English captain, John Smith. The narrative hinges on the tension between nature religion and the colonial project. The Powhatans are presented as an unchanging, historyless people who live their lives "as steady as the beating drum" as "seasons go and seasons come." Conversely, their English counterparts are constantly moving forward, building, exploring, and conquering for "glory, God and gold." For John Smith and his English crew, "the Earth is just a dead thing you can claim," but the animist Powhatans "know every rock, and tree, and creature, has a life, has a spirit, has a name."[32]

The movie depicts Pocahontas as having "sacred interconnections within the web of life." She can "paint with all the colors of the wind," she counts woodland creatures as her friends, and she receives wise counsel from Grandmother Willow—a talking willow tree.[33] The sacrality and power of nature also seem to free Pocahontas from other cultural expectations. The "wild" woman reverses the gender script by saving John Smith with a bravery and defiance that, it would seem, no white woman could possibly muster.

The most significant reversal, however, reveals white anxiety about how to confront the crimes of colonialism. *Pocahontas* spotlights colonial strategies of dehumanization when, for example, the mysterious beauty balks at John Smith's use of the terms "savage" and "uncivilized." The movie appears to offer a corrective, but one dependent on the notion that white moderns can be saved by a romantic return to nature religion. Pocahontas eventually "saves" the Western colonizers from themselves and their relentless pursuit of progress by showing them the magic of nature. With this romanticized image of not only native people, but colonialism itself, audiences are free to imagine how they might reconnect with sacred, magical nature, without any risk of cultural appropriation.

If the Disney Universe could be defined by a singular vision, it would be a persistently utopian one. After all, Disney all but invented the happy ending. The examples above are not inconsistencies in the Disney Universe; rather, they reveal an ongoing dialogue. Examining the Disney Universe as a religio-cultural site, we often see mutually exclusive utopias. One presents a gleaming metal tomorrow where nature is either absent or put to human use, and where science, progress, and innovation provide all the "magic" we could ever want. The other is a cautionary utopia, or perhaps post-dystopian utopia, that corrects the dangers and destruction "civilization," technology, and science have caused. In this utopia, we reclaim the romantic "wild" by rejecting "the future," we become historyless, and we embrace sacred nature. These competing utopias reveal tensions currently felt in religion and popular culture.

## FEMALE POWER AND POWERLESSNESS

Aside from the racial and colonial implications of *Pocahontas,* it is also a story about a woman. In addition to being Native American, Pocahontas's femaleness undergirds her role as the "mysterious other." Her gender underscores her "wildness," and unlike previous princesses, she loses the man she loves. The approach to women, gender performance, and female power we see in Disney texts reveal deep cultural ambivalences about the gains of the feminist movement.

From a twenty-first-century perspective, the first Disney princesses, in *Snow White and the Seven Dwarfs* (1937) and *Cinderella* (1950), are powerless beauties who wait for men to rescue them from their unhappy lives.[34] By the 1990s, however, Disney princesses like Ariel in *The Little Mermaid* (1989); Belle in *Beauty and the Beast* (1991); and Jasmine in *Aladdin* (1992), have become smart beauties, admired for their minds and strong will, but whose purpose is ultimately to save the men who deceive, abandon, or abuse them.[35] Today, however, narratives like *Brave* (2012) and *Frozen* (2013) feature women in leadership positions who defy and criticize the gendered tropes evident in the earlier Disney princess films.

As Disney texts reveal the constant, conflicting dialogue of contemporary life, these newer narratives feature women who empower and save other women, but they also reveal a deep anxiety over who is responsible for female disempowerment and the consequences of unmitigated female power. *Brave* is a story about women limiting other women and the "problem" of being female and a political leader. *Frozen* presents a clearer picture of female leadership but it posits a self-sacrificing sisterhood, rather than independence or political power, as the "real" source of female fulfillment.

Narratives like *Brave* and *Frozen* are part of a larger "empowerment" trend in media and advertising aimed at American girls and women.[36] One example is the Disney Princess franchise, a multiplatform creation that removes female protagonists from their original film contexts and places them in a kind of princess pantheon. Through interactive web sites, apps, and material culture, the Disney Princess franchise recasts passive characters like Cinderella as paragons of "girl power" and encourages girls to claim the mantle of their preferred, now reimagined, princess. This empowerment discourse arises out of feminist critiques of how women are represented in media texts. However, it often disregards social mechanisms of female disempowerment.[37] By ignoring the social systems that create and sustain male privilege and focusing instead on individual solutions, these discourses imply that sexism is what happens when women fail to empower *themselves*.[38]

*Brave* (2012) exemplifies the focus on individual women rather than the system. It tells the story of Merida, an accomplished young Scottish archer and the daughter of the powerful Highland king. In accordance with tradition, Merida is expected to marry a son of a Highland lord. She is not terribly keen on the idea, and insists that she is worthy of her father's throne with or without a husband.[39]

However, the primary resistance to Merida's self-determination does not arise from her addled, hot-tempered father, or the pathetic gaggle of would-be suitors. Merida's greatest opponent is her mother, who sees her daughter's rejection of tradition as a threat to the kingdom's stability and Merida's own happiness. *Brave* rejects the evil-stepmother trope by representing Merida's mother as loving and well-meaning—but what ultimately thwarts the patriarchy is the two women's love and acceptance of each other's perspectives. The male supremacy in the fictional Highland kingdom is depicted as ridiculous chest-beating rather than part of a pervasive misogynistic system. By pretending that they do not to exist, patriarchal religious and cultural systems, male privilege, and the men who actively work to police female agency are exonerated. Audiences and critics applauded *Brave* for putting forward such a gutsy, self-possessed heroine.[40] It would seem that the next generation of American girls could grow up unfettered by sexist cultural traditions— if only their mothers would get with the program.

Disney's 2013 mega-hit *Frozen* can be read as an anti-princess movie, about the problems of female leadership and the magical power of familial love between women. It offers a substantive critique of the old princess narrative, which centered on female fulfillment through heteronormative marriage. As Queen Elsa quips, "You can't marry someone you just met," which is exactly what previous Disney princesses have done.[41] However, for every feminist idea it presents, *Frozen* advances an undermining corrective.

*Frozen* engages the familiar trope of "princess in distress" but presents a new method of salvation. At the film's climatic end, Anna is frozen after sacrificing herself to save her sister. It is not a prince's kiss that brings her back to life, but her own willingness to die. That is the act of "true love" that breaks the spell. For a prince to rescue a princess, he must fight; but *Frozen* shows us that for a princess to rescue another princess, she must offer up her own life and die. In this way *Frozen* continues the anti-feminist trope perfectly. From Snow White's death and resurrection to Sleeping Beauty's curse, Cinderella's domestic slavery, and Belle's abduction by the Beast, the *magic* in the Magic Kingdom has come largely from female suffering. While women are presented as the ultimate problem for feminism in *Brave, Frozen* presents the sacrificial woman as the ultimate product of female empowerment.

Here in these Disney texts we can see the broader cultural struggle over what female empowerment looks like and what it may cost. The sacrificial role is one way female power can seemingly be undermined; another is representing powerful women as inherently lonely. Elsa is a benevolent queen, but her magical power estranges her from human relationships—she is, quite literally, frigid. When Elsa embraces her power, saying, "Let it go!" to the mechanisms of shame and control that policed her, she banishes herself to a lonely mountain and everyone nearly dies. The film conveys that Elsa's inability to control herself threatens the city she rules and everyone she loves. The politically and magically powerless Anna is the one who can save Elsa and her kingdom. Elsa eventually returns to her throne, but unlike powerless Anna, there is no romantic love on the horizon for her.

*Frozen* reveals an ambivalence in the broader culture about women and power. It would seem that that women should be empowered, but that they cannot stand in positions of power alone. They require a power source outside of themselves, but there is an increasing discomfort with communicating to young girls that men should be that source. Rather than whisking her off into the sunset, in *Frozen,* Anna's prince charming tries to kill her. Female power then must come from the sacrifices of other women. Finally, *Frozen* reifies the perception that if a woman is saved by the sacrifices of other women, *and* she manages to control herself, her powerful position still places her beyond the reach of romantic love. Here, *Frozen* enters the ongoing cultural debates about women "having it all." So are these new narratives feminist empowerment texts or the same old patriarchy in disguise? The answer is, yes. *Frozen* and *Brave* are neither inconsistent nor contradictory; rather, they are evidence of the multiple ongoing dialogues in American popular culture.

Since the 1950s, the Disney Universe has been a site of cultural and religious dialogue. In contemporary society, that universe is a locus for conversations on right and the left, from Marxist social critics to Southern Baptists and far beyond. The Disney Universe is more than a polarizing media producer; it is a site of negotiation that reveals and reifies religious and cultural tensions, ambiguities, and anxieties. In this chapter, we analyzed twenty-first century tensions dealing with nature versus technology and the roles of women. The Disney Universe is a space where people create meaning by engaging with these texts, narratives, theme parks, or consumables. The dialogues engendered by the Disney Universe evolve as religious and social currents change. Future Disney texts may wrestle with gender queering or racial justice issues. These may seem like heavy topics for the utopian Disney Universe, but so are colonialism and the roles of women in society. As sites of religious and cultural dialogue, Disney texts continue to mirror our contradictions, our bold steps and our undermining correctives, just as we continue to use them to make and unmake our religious and cultural imaginations.

## DISCUSSION QUESTIONS

1. Brehm and Rees consider several ways in which the Disney Universe has been a location for dialogue between religion and popular culture. One of those is that some religious groups

criticize Disney. What are they criticizing in the stories Disney tells and in the policies of the Disney parks? What ethical values led these groups to criticize Disney?

2. The chapter suggests that in Disney stories and parks two different religious themes arise, the first about futuristic technological progress and the second about a return to nature religion. Identify other examples of American popular culture that express these two ways of imagining the sacred. What tensions are inherent in these different visions? Are you drawn to one or the other?

3. The chapter also explores the way Disney has produced texts that reveal and reflect cultural and religious dialogues and anxieties about the role of women and girls, sometimes seeing them in quite traditional ways and at others dismantling gender norms and stereotypes. Identify examples of each within the Disney Universe. Why do you think Disney seems to want it both ways?

4. Discuss your own experience of Disney. How have you participated in the Disney Universe? What have those experiences meant to you? Do you share the concerns of some of Disney's critics? If so, which ones?

NOTES

1. Henry A. Giroux and Grace Pollock, *The Mouse That Roared: Disney and the End of Innocence* (1999; rev. ed., Lanham, MD: Rowman & Littlefield, 2010).

2. Jim Jones, "Southern Baptists: Convention Joins Disney Boycott," *Christianity Today,* July 14, 1997, www.christianitytoday.com/ct/1997/july14/7t8072.html; Dwayne Hastings, "AFA Ends Disney Boycott It Launched in Mid-1990s," *Baptist Press,* May 24, 2005, www.bpnews.net/20841/afa-ends-disney-boycott-it-launched-in-mid1990s; Tom Morganthau, "Baptists vs. Mickey: Why the Boycott against Disney Faces Steep Odds," *Newsweek,* June 30, 1997, www.highbeam.com/doc/1G1-19524034.html.

3. Scholars of religion and popular culture have studied Disney using a variety of lenses. Michael Mazur and Tara K. Koda use Mircea Eliade's theories on religion and myth to unpack how Disney functions as commoditized

religion, complete with pilgrimages to Disney's sacred spaces that take visitors "out of time." See Mazur and Koda, "The Happiest Place on Earth: Disney's America and the Commodification of Religion," in *God in the Details: American Religion in Popular Culture*, 2nd ed. (New York: Routledge, 2011), 307–21. Disney's powerful contributions to the creation and reification of American civil religion are noted in Robert B. Pettit, "One Nation Under Walt: Disney Theme Parks as Shrines of the American Civil Religion" (Popular Culture Association, Atlanta, GA, 1986), www.academia.edu/11811176/One_Nation_Under_Walt_Disney_Theme_Parks_as_Shrines_of_the_American_Civil_Religion. Finally, David Lyon uses Disney to problematize the "secularization thesis"—the theory that as cultures grow more technologically sophisticated, they grow more secular. See Lyon, *Jesus in Disneyland: Religion in Postmodern Times* (Malden, MA: Polity Press, 2000).

4. Nick Couldry, *Media Rituals: A Critical Approach* (New York: Routledge, 2005); Nick Couldry, *Media, Society, World: Social Theory and Digital Media Practice* (Malden, MA: Polity Press, 2012); David D. Hall, *Lived Religion in America: Toward A History of Practice* (Princeton, NJ: Princeton University Press, 1997); Stewart M Hoover and Knut Lundby, *Rethinking Media, Religion, and Culture* (Thousand Oaks, CA: Sage, 1997); Stewart M. Hoover, *Religion in the Media Age (Media, Religion and Culture)* (New York: Routledge, 2006); and Diane Winston, *Small Screen, Big Picture: Television and Lived Religion* (Waco, TX: Baylor University Press, 2009).

5. Couldry, *Media, Society, World*.

6. 1955 Disneyland Opening Day," ABC-TV, *Dateline Disneyland*, www.youtube.com/watch?v=JuzrZET-3Ew.

7. Matt. 5:14–16; Bruce M. Metzger and Roland E. Murphy, eds., *The New Oxford Annotated Bible* (New York: Oxford University Press, 1992).

8. Will Herberg, *Protestant, Catholic, Jew: An Essay in American Religious Sociology* (New York: Doubleday, 1956), 231. In Herberg's imagination, the ethnic and religious tensions of the prewar period had softened into a unity that made America stronger. As scholars would later point out, this supposed "unity" never really existed and any perception of it was predicated on liberal Protestant hegemony and American exceptionalism. See: Tracy Fessenden, *Culture and Redemption Religion, the Secular, and American Literature* (Princeton, NJ: Princeton University Press, 2007), For more on the critiques of Herberg, see Kevin M. Schultz, *Tri-Faith America: How Catholics and Jews Held Postwar America to Its Protestant Promise* (Oxford: Oxford University Press, 2013).

9. U.S. Department of Treasury, "History of 'In God We Trust,'" www.treasury.gov/about/education/Pages/in-god-we-trust.aspx.

10. Steven Watts, *The Magic Kingdom: Walt Disney and the American Way of Life* (1997; repr., Columbia, MO: University of Missouri Press, 2001).

11. "Neoliberalism" is not a term that easily maps onto the "conservative vs. liberal" political polarization of the United States. It refers to the resurgence of nineteenth-century laissez-faire capitalism and describes economic systems that favor privatization and deregulation and the dismantling of social (especially governmental) services and safety nets. Neoliberal cultural trends include using individual consumer choices to construct identity, looking for individual solutions to broader cultural problems, and equating consumer choice (as opposed to social justice or civic engagement) with "freedom" and "democracy."

12. Richard V. Francaviglia, "History after Disney: The Significance of 'Imagineered' Historical Places," *Public Historian* 17, no. 4 (1995): 69–74.

13. Johnson Cheu, ed., *Diversity in Disney Films: Critical Essays on Race, Ethnicity, Gender, Sexuality and Disability* (Jefferson, NC: McFarland, 2013).

14. See Hillary Warren, "Southern Baptists as Audience and Public: A Cultural Analysis of the Disney Boycott," in *Religion and Popular Culture*, ed. Daniel Stout and Judith Buddenbaum (Ames, IA: Wiley-Blackwell, 2001), 169–86. The Southern Baptist Convention is the largest organized body of evangelical Christian churches in the United States.

15. By 2005, broader evangelical interactions with media and popular culture had changed dramatically. Indeed, evangelical Christians adopted previously taboo forms, like rock and hip-hop music, and eventually, social media, and retooled them to express their values. Today, conservative Christians have successfully created satisfying and sophisticated alternatives to anything they might deem objectionable. What with the goofy characters in Christian-oriented animations such as *Veggie Tales* and *3-2-1 Penguins!* and high-budget non-Disney biblical feature films like *The Prince of Egypt*, evangelical families who choose not watch Disney products have myriad other options. For more, see Randall Balmer, *Mine Eyes Have Seen the Glory: A Journey into the Evangelical Subculture in America*, 4th ed. (New York: Oxford University Press, 2006).

16. Leef Smith, "Disney's Loin King? Group Sees Dirt in the Dust," *Washington Post*, September 1, 1995, www.washingtonpost.com/wp-srv/style/longterm/review96/flionking.htm.

17. Morgan Lee, "Joe Jonas Talks about Relationship with God, Frustration with Purity Rings in Raw, Revealing Interview," *Christian Post*, December 2, 2013, www.christianpost.com/news/joe-jonas-talks-about-relationship-with-god-frustration-with-purity-rings-in-raw-revealing-interview-109886.

18. For more on purity culture and American evangelicalism, including the True Love Waits movement, see Amy DeRogatis, *Saving Sex: Sexuality and*

370 / Religion and Popular Culture in Dialogue

Salvation in American Evangelicalism (New York: Oxford University Press, 2014), and Christine J. Gardner, *Making Chastity Sexy: The Rhetoric of Evangelical Abstinence Campaigns* (Berkeley: University of California Press, 2011).

19. "Culture wars" is a contested phrase, but one used often in American public discourse. It first appeared in James Davison Hunter's *Culture Wars: The Struggle to Define America* (New York: Basic Books, 1991), but work on the topic has grown exponentially in the twenty-five years since. For more, see Rhys H. Williams, *Cultural Wars in American Politics: Critical Reviews of a Popular Myth. Social Problems and Social Issues* (New York: Aldine de Gruyter, 1997); John Clifford Green, *Religion and the Culture Wars: Dispatches from the Front. Religious Forces in the Modern Political World* (Lanham, MD: Rowman & Littlefield, 1996); and Andrew Hartman, *A War for the Soul of America: A History of the Culture Wars* (Chicago: University of Chicago Press, 2015).

20. Bron Taylor, "Disney Worlds at War," in id., ed., *The Encyclopedia of Religion and Nature* (New York: Bloomsbury Academic, 2008), 489–93.

21. For definitions and examinations of "civil religion," see Robert N. Bellah, "Civil Religion in America," *Dædalus* 96, no. 1 (1967): 1–21; Tracy Fessenden, *Culture and Redemption Religion, the Secular, and American Literature* (Princeton, NJ: Princeton University Press, 2007); and Russell E. Richey and Donald G. Jones, eds., *American Civil Religion* (New York: Harper & Row, 1974).

22. Taylor, "Disney Worlds at War," 389.

23. Richard R. Beard, *Walt Disney's Epcot Center: Creating the New World of Tomorrow* (New York: Harry N. Abrams, 1982),13.

24. Beard, *Walt Disney's Epcot Center,* 29.

25. Stephen Kubiak, "A Guide to Drinking around the World at Disney's Epcot,"*Huffington Post,* www.huffingtonpost.com/visit-florida/a-guide-to-drinking-aroun_b_8192100.html.

26. Anna McCarthy, *The Citizen Machine: Governing by Television in 1950s America* (New York: New Press, 2010), 44; Nancy Langston, *Toxic Bodies: Hormone Disruptors and the Legacy of DES* (New Haven, CT: Yale University Press, 2010), 88.

27. For more on the idealization of returning to pastoral America, see Leo Marx, *The Machine in the Garden: Technology and the Pastoral Ideal in America* (New York: Oxford University Press, 1964).

28. David Whitely, *The Idea of Nature in Disney Animation* (Burlington, VT: Ashgate, 2008), 142.

29. Sylvester Johnson's work on modernity and colonialism frames much of our definition of the term. Johnson places studies of modernity at the center of concerns about natural rights, consumer capitalism, religious pluralism,

racialization, ethnic cleansing, popular sovereignty, and the democratization of spiritual power. This notion is akin the central argument in Bruno Latour's 1991 *We Have Never Been Modern,* which argues that the construction of "modernity" set up evaluative hierarchies that privileged the European scientific, intellectual, and institutional power systems. Johnson and Latour's work counters scholars like Charles Taylor, who consider modern people to be less connected to, or "buffered" from, the religious or mystical world. For more, see Sylvester A. Johnson, *African American Religions, 1500–2000: Colonialism, Democracy, and Freedom* (New York: Cambridge University Press, 2015); Bruno Latour, *We Have Never Been Modern,* trans. Catherine Porter (Cambridge, MA: Harvard University Press, 1993); and Charles Taylor, *A Secular Age* (Cambridge, MA: Belknap Press of Harvard University Press, 2007).

30. Catherine L. Albanese, *Nature Religion in America: From the Algonkian Indians to the New Age* (Chicago: University of Chicago Press, 1991); Catherine L. Albanese, *Reconsidering Nature Religion* (Harrisburg, PA: Bloomsbury T&T Clark, 2002); Richard Bohannon, ed., *Religions and Environments: A Reader in Religion, Nature and Ecology* (New York: Bloomsbury Academic, 2014); Belden C. Lane, *Landscapes of the Sacred: Geography and Narrative in American Spirituality* (Baltimore: Johns Hopkins University Press, 2001); Joanne Pearson, Richard H. Roberts, and Geoffrey Samuel, eds., *Nature Religion Today: Paganism in the Modern World,* (Edinburgh: Edinburgh University Press, 1998); *The Encyclopedia of Religion and Nature*, ed. Bron Taylor (New York: Bloomsbury Academic, 2008); and Bron Taylor, *Dark Green Religion: Nature Spirituality and the Planetary Future* (Berkeley: University of California Press, 2009).

31. Albanese, *Nature Religion in America.*

32. Mike Gabriel and Eric Goldberg, *Pocahontas,* (Walt Disney Feature Animation, 1995).

33. Taylor, "Disney Worlds at War."

34. *Snow White and the Seven Dwarfs* (Walt Disney Productions, 1937); and *Cinderella* (Walt Disney Productions, 1950).

35. Ron Clements and John Musker, *The Little Mermaid* (Walt Disney Pictures, 1989); Gary Trousdale and Kirk Wise, *Beauty and the Beast* (Walt Disney Feature Animation, 1991); and Ron Clements and John Musker, *Aladdin* (Walt Disney Feature Animation, 1992).

36. Other examples include the Dove "Love Your Body" campaign, Always' "Like a girl," and Special K's #OwnIt, all of which attempt to correct the antifeminist reputation of the diet and beauty industries by recasting their products as feminist symbols.

37. Sarah Banet-Weiser, "'Confidence You Can Carry!': Girls in Crisis and the Market for Girls' Empowerment Organizations," *Continuum: Journal of Media & Cultural Studies* 29, no. 2 (March 4, 2015): 182–93, doi:10.1080/10304312.20 15.1022938.

38. This is often dubbed "postfeminism." For more see Angela McRobbie, *Feminism and Youth Culture* (Basingstoke, England: Macmillan Education, 1991), and Yvonne Tasker and Diane Negra, *Interrogating Postfeminism: Gender and the Politics of Popular Culture* (Durham, NC: Duke University Press, 2007).

39. Mark Andrews, Brenda Chapman, and Steve Purcell, *Brave* (Pixar Animation/Walt Disney Pictures, 2012).

40. Kristen Howerton, "A Parent's Guide To 'Brave,'" *Huffington Post,* June 21, 2012, http://www.huffingtonpost.com/kristen-howerton/parents-guide-to-brave_b_1603208.html.

41. Chris Buck and Jennifer Lee, *Frozen* (Walt Disney Feature Animation 2013).

# CHAPTER EIGHTEEN

# Can Watching a Movie Be a Spiritual Experience?

ROBERT K. JOHNSTON

In 2012, the Oscars added a new component to their telecast. In addition to the jokes, the fashion, and the awards, they included a series of brief interviews with actors and actresses, asking them, "What is your favorite movie moment?" Christopher Plummer referenced Disney's *Snow White and the Seven Dwarfs* (1937). Janet McTeer cited Christopher Plummer for his role in *The Sound of Music* (1965). Several recalled a favorite movie moment from their childhood: seeing a car drive off a cliff, only for it to turn out to be a flying machine, in the British musical *Chitty Chitty Bang Bang* (1968). "It was a wonderful moment of cinema magic," Kenneth Branagh remembered. So too was Judy Garland singing "Over a Rainbow" in *The Wizard of Oz* (1939). Jessica Chastain confessed that it was while watching that movie that she "began my love affair with movies and me wanting to be a part of that wonder."[1]

Experiencing magic and wonder is something at the heart of the moviegoing experience—at least at its best. Viewers find themselves transported to another place or into the presence of another—perhaps even an Other. In the process, they explore life's possibilities and contradictions, testing out solutions and even finding themselves surprised by joy or sorrow, by love and pain, by life itself. Given such experiences, it should not be surprising that commentators have since film's early days explored the spiritual dimensions of this experience. In a pamphlet entitled *The Religious Possibilities of the Motion Picture* (1911), the Congregational minister Herbert Atchinson Jump compared the function of the movies to Jesus' use of parables.[2] "The real death in the photoplay is the ritualistic death and the real birth is the ritualistic birth, and the Cathedral mood of the motion picture which goes with these and is close to these in many of its phases, is an inexhaustible resource," the poet Vachel Lindsay believed, writing in 1915.[3]

Not all who have come after Lindsay and Jump have been as sure. But since the advent of Beta in 1979, which allowed for the re-viewing of film on demand, and the subsequent invention of the VCR, the DVD, Netflix, and now streaming, a growing number of commentators, both professional and lay, have continued the exploration of the depth and extent of film's spirituality.[4]

But as these claims have been being made, the question has also been asked with increasing frequency, "What exactly do we mean by 'God's presence' at the movies?" How is a movie's spirituality to be described? Or understood? In what way does God show up at the movies? (1) As only a "trace" or "echo," that is, as a reverberation of some past divine action? (2) Perhaps such claims are only human projections? Or (3) can such encounters be important, even foundational, to faith? Alternatively, (4) given human sin, is such spirituality destined to be simply confused and confusing? The questions come easily. They are the same questions that are asked concerning all claims regarding encountering God in everyday life.

## FINDING GOD IN THE CINEPLEX

So, eight years ago, I began asking students in my theology and film classes at Fuller Theological Seminary to write short papers offering their testimony concerning the most personally compelling spiritual experience they had had while watching a movie, and why? The numbers now approach four hundred. In making the assignment, I did not start with a given movie—*Field of Dreams* (1989), *Avatar* (2009), *Finding Nemo* (2003), or *The Shawshank Redemption* (1994), and ask, "Was this spiritually significant to you and why?" Instead, I reversed the flow and asked them to pick any movie they liked, but I wanted it to be the movie they felt was most spiritually significant to them. I also purposely left the meaning of the assignment ambiguous. Did I want them to speak of a movie that had deepened their theological understanding? Or one that had affected their spirits? Or was I perhaps asking for them to speak about a Transcendent experience, an encounter with God, that had happened to them while watching a movie? Was I after those experiences at the Cineplex that proved spiritually transformative? Or illumining? Or educational? Or directional? I did not say.

The reason for the vagueness of the question, of course, was to allow differentiations to surface. I wanted the student viewers themselves to shape the nature of their responses according to their own perception of their experience. And as might be expected, the responses varied greatly, with not all by any means sensing God's revealing presence at the movies. But though there was variety in their responses, they fell broadly into three groups, even as students moved freely back and forth between these differing meanings.

One group of papers centered on an experience of God's presence as mediated through/or experienced in the cinema. Some had a divine encounter, they said, an experience of the holy, the Transcendent, that was transformative in their lives. A second group of students wrote about how they perceived something greater, or other, or whole in their moviegoing experience. They experienced transcendence. They were unsure they had had a divine encounter, though the experience was spiritually formative. And still a third group were quite sure that they had not had a Spiritual encounter (that is, they had not encountered God directly), nor had their spirits been transformed, but nonetheless they told of learning a spiritual truth that had proven personally valuable to them. Examples from each group of students will illustrate these differing "reel" spiritualities.

*Deepening My Understanding*

Some students were quite sure that they had not had an encounter with the divine through watching a movie, but nonetheless believed that they had learned a spiritual truth, or a deeper understanding of one. A film had become a visual reminder of Christian truth, a metaphor of Christian theology that proved compelling. Often such "educational" experiences were in response to movies with religious, or quasi-religious, themes, such as *The Shawshank Redemption* (1994), *The Ultimate Gift* (2006), *The Passion of the Christ* (2004), *A Walk to Remember* (2002), *Lars and the Real Girl* (2007), *Lord of the Rings* (2001, 2002, 2003), *Simon Birch* (1998), *Signs* (2002), or movies that had clear Christ figures, like *The Green Mile* (1999), *The Dark Knight* (2008), and *Cool Hand Luke* (1967). But not always. *Forrest Gump* (1994), *The Kite Runner* (2007), even *Talladega Nights: The Ballad of Ricky Bobby* (2006) were also cited.

These students found such movies to function for them as theological parables. A sample of the language they used to describe the connection between the movie they saw and the experience they had makes clear the intellectual nature of the spiritual connection:

| | |
|---|---|
| "whispered truth" | "I learned from" |
| "was representative of" | "was deeply informative" |
| "was symbolic of" | "led to deep reflection" |
| "reminded me of" | "is telling me" |
| "allowed me to picture" | "provided space for theological reflection" |
| "helped me to understand" | "taught me" |
| "saw parallels with" | "allowed me to understand Scripture" |

For one student whose maternal great grandfather had escaped the pogroms of Eastern Europe in the early twentieth century, *Fiddler on the Roof* (1971) taught him that God was a character who weeps, not just an idea. For another, Hugh Jackman and Anne Hathaway in *Les Misérables* (2012) helped him understand the transforming power of generosity, love, and grace, helped him understand that God's "yes" is more primary than his "no." For Eric, the movie that gave picture and voice to that which was already inside him was *The Mission* (1986). The depiction of people laying down their lives for Jesus, the reminder that sin has consequences, and the scene where the native chooses not to slit the throat of Rodrigo Mendoza (Robert De Niro), showing the overwhelming reality of forgiveness, all helped "bring into focus Truth" for Eric. Though he had seen the movie only three times ( twenty-five, twenty, and fifteen years ago), he wrote of drawing on these moments many times since "as illustrations in discussions."

Representative as well was the testimony of one student's experience viewing David Lynch's *The Elephant Man* (1980). He related how that movie, based loosely on historical circumstance, allowed him to see more clearly, through eyes filled with tears, the God-given shape of the human. John Merrick is a badly deformed man, relegated to the circus sideshow in nineteenth-century England until he is rescued by Sir Frederick Treves, a medical doctor at the London Hospital. Through a series of circumstances, including Treves and his boss hearing John recite the 23rd Psalm, something his mother had taught him, Merrick becomes the talk of London society. When he is invited to have tea with Dr. Treves and his wife, he tells them that he wishes his mother could see him now with his lovely friends: "Perhaps she could love me as I am. I've tried so hard to be good." Mrs. Treves begins to cry uncontrollably, and so did my student. He wrote that every time he sees the scene, he realizes anew that John is a creation of God—that in fact, as Flannery O'Connor might say, "God is found most beautifully in the 'grotesque.'" For this student, John Merrick showed him "a full humanity: in suffering, in faith, in hope, and in love."

### Affecting My Spirit

Others wrote how they perceived through their moviegoing experience something greater, or other, or whole. T. S. Eliot calls this something "the still point of the turning world."[5] These viewers were not sure that they had had a divine encounter, but their experience had been enhancing to their own spirits. In fact, it had proven life-transforming. The language students used suggested that theirs was more of a "spiritual" insight through the story that had been discovered than a "Spiritual" experience, an encounter with an Other that was revealing something to them. But sometimes the language was ambiguous (no doubt like the experience itself). They spoke of a "profoundly human moment," of "tears of identification" related to a particular movie event as bringing "personal fulfillment" or change. Their experiences were often described as extraordinary and illuminating. For these viewers the world and/or their personal lives took on spiritual depth and texture because of a movie they had seen. But these moviegoers were reluctant to say they had actually met God at the movies.

For Glenn, re-watching *An Officer and a Gentleman* (1982) has continued to inspire him "to believe that I could rise above my personal reality," despite his dysfunctional family. For Andrew, *Up* (2009) allowed him to understand that his present life was not practice for some future well-being, but a wonderful gift to be enjoyed now. Struggling with his own social awkwardness and staunch introversion, and the realization that like Lars in *Lars and the Real Girl (2007),* he lacked community and a sense of belonging, Paul found in Lars a worthy hero, despite his shortcomings, a compelling example of the need to overcome his fear to be known. For Michelle, a woman suffering depression from not living up to her family's expectations of her, watching *The Perks of Being a Wallflower* (2012) allowed her to wake up the next morning with the veil of depression lifted, realizing that both God and her friends loved her and accepted her, messiness and all. Even the tenth viewing of *The Tree of Life* (2011) still affects Vince viscerally, the multiple parallels between his life and the O'Brien family helping him tap "into a universal well of life experiences," revealing that he is not alone.

Perhaps the most dramatic account of a movie's potential for spiritual transformation was the testimony of Carol, who in her twenties had been the victim of a home invasion robbery during the Christmas season. Raped, robbed, kidnapped, pistol-whipped, and shot, she was left for dead in an empty lot. Over the next five years, her life spiraled downward. Then, one Christmas, on the anniversary of her assault, she watched Frank Capra's *It's a Wonderful Life* (1946) on television. She had never seen it before. Watching, she identified with George Bailey (Jimmy Stewart), whose dreams have been dashed at every turn, though he has tried to help others all of his life. She too had always tried to be good, though living in a borderline-abusive household, but she could never live up to her parents' expectation. Like George, she had thought, "It would have been better if I had never been born."

However, in Capra's movie a gentle angel named Clarence shows George that all his simple acts of kindness have been important to the community where he lives, and my student said that her perspective on her own life also began to shift. "The gift this movie provided me with," she wrote, "was small hope." She explained,

> Following this period I no longer entertained thoughts of quitting life, but [had] a desire to find meaning in what had occurred to me. If the daily decisions that George Bailey made had such a profound influence on those around him, [maybe] the decisions that I was making, even the smallest, most insignificant, [might] have a profound influence on those around me."

Five years later, Carol was in seminary, sitting in my class, preparing to be a counsellor. She concluded her reflection by saying that though she was unsure whether the movie she experienced was "a divine encounter" or simply something that was "spiritually enhancing," she had no doubt that it was "life-transforming."

*Encountering God's Presence*

Carol was not sure whether viewing *It's a Wonderful Life* had been the occasion for an encounter with God, or whether it had simply been a profoundly moving experience of recentering and grounding her spirit. In the words of Avery Dulles, the line between "discovery" and "revelation" was blurred beyond recognition.[6] For Carol, her experience was perhaps a personal discovery. But for up to a third of my students, there was no doubt in their minds, as they described their movie-viewing experiences, that they had encountered God—that God had revealed Himself to them through the truth, beauty, and goodness portrayed on the screen, or through the lack of it. In each case, the movie's story had merged with their own stories, they said, resulting in an experience of the holy that had transformed their lives.

A few who wrote of their engagement with God's Spirit in and through a movie said it was difficult to only pick one, for there had been "so many profound experiences." They identified themselves as "extremely easily moved" and thus experienced "God's presence in nearly every film" they saw. But more typically, most said their encounter with God at the movies had been a rare experience. Jessica wrote, for example:

> I do not typically experience film in a deeply personal and spiritual way. However, last summer I was pleasantly surprised when I encountered God unexpectedly in, of all places, a children's film. Disney Pixar's *Toy Story 3* (2010) was the last place I expected to have a transcendent experience with a film, yet the unassuming packaging of a children's movie provided the perfect opportunity for an unexpected spiritual encounter.

What connected with Jessica in the film was the theme of growing up and moving on from one's childhood. She had been a fan of Woody, Buzz, and the rest of Andy's toys since as an eight-year-old she had seen the original *Toy Story* (1995). Expecting *Toy Story 3* to be only a fun, simple little movie, she instead experienced through Andy's character "a reflection of my own childhood and transition to adulthood." As Andy handed down his toys to little Bonnie, she said she "experienced a sudden and unexpected rush of emotions, which ultimately resulted in crying." For Jessica, too, was also about to embark on a major life transition of her own—she had just gotten engaged. "Seeing *Toy Story 3* allowed [me] to express and confront those bittersweet emotions associated with making a major life transition." Here, she said, was God's way of helping her process her feelings and telling her it was okay. "I learned from this experience," she wrote, "that God can speak to you and meet you in the most unexpected places, for who would have ever thought that a 23-year-old woman would have seen herself in a fictional, animated, 18-year-old boy who was giving his toys away."

One older student, John, recalled seeing *Easy Rider* (1969) with his friends three times one Saturday afternoon in 1969, soon after the movie came out. He spoke of the movie in detail some forty years after his viewing experience, writing, "I walked into the film as one person and exited virtually as another, awakened to new ideas and options." This iconic film about two counterculture bikers who travel cross-country from Los Angeles to Mardi Gras in New Orleans in search both of America and of meaning in their own lives is a classic road movie. Thus, there is not much plot, with meaning coming in the form of the interaction of the "buddies" both with each other and with those they meet along the way. Captain America (Peter Fonda) and Billy the Kid (Dennis Hopper) encounter hitchhikers, bigotry (given their counter-cultural lifestyle), jail, and even the death of a friend. They pick up a drunken lawyer played by Jack Nicholson (his breakout role). And they visit a gentle hippie religious commune in New Mexico.

There, they encounter a group of single adults and young families who have rejected the materialism and consumerism of their past (the American Dream) for a return to the earth. The travelers watch as the community puts on a costumed play and plants crops in dusty soil. They also observe those in the commune as they clasp hands, praying for "simple food for our simple tastes." My student wrote, watching the hippie commune, "I felt a remarkable sense of calm and well-being, as if a cool hand were put upon my brow." When Fonda leaves with Hopper "on a quest towards Mardi Gras nothingness," John wrote that he felt a "visceral sense of dread, what I would now describe as a panic attack, a tightening in my chest as if a hand squeezed my heart." Moreover, he said, "a voice in my head compelled me to say to a comrade, 'Man, they just blew it.'" Both his friend and this student were later startled when near the end of the film's uneasy ride, Captain America uses these identical words—speaking of "blowing it," of not finding that meaning they had set out to find.

Though *Easy Rider* leaves it ambiguous as to how the main characters precisely "blew it," it was crystal clear for this viewer. Though John had never lived communally and had no religious faith, the next day he boarded a bus in search of a similar community, a place where Jesus would live. "There was a depiction of faith that my spirit craved" in that movie, he says. its spiritually attuned hippies made such an impression on him that his journey toward Jesus began that day. Forty years later, he still lives communally and is now a Christian minister. *Easy Rider* had proven revelatory.

For Liz, the film that proved Transcendent for her was *Moulin Rouge!* (2001). The movie is a musical romance, telling the story of Christian, a penniless writer who falls in love with the beautiful courtesan Satine, winning her heart through song, poetry, and persistence. He loves her as opposed to simply desiring her, cares for her rather than lusts after her. Even though the jealous Duke expects her to be his lover, and even though Satine is dying of consumption, their love proves undying. Each has loved and been loved in return.

Liz wrote that she is not sure why the movie continues to move her so. Perhaps it is the fact that her life history has some connection with Satine's. Given their common brokenness, was it possible to be redeemed? *Moulin Rouge!* shouted "Yes." When Satine was found by Christian, Liz said, she was found:

> I was encountering God through this movie as I was given a vision of love conquering the past and conquering human sin and brokenness.... What the movie did uniquely was provide a context and an experience, which got past my analytical study brain (the brain that often kicks in when I read the Bible), to my emotions and heart. The power of the music, the images and the theatrical experience drew me in before my usual defenses and inner critic had time to react. I encountered the love of God and it changed me.

One last example must suffice. The movie *March of the Penguins* (2005) is a documentary about emperor penguins narrated in the English-language release by Morgan Freeman. Once every four years, the penguins return to their birthplace, waddling up to fifty miles over the ice to find a mate. Filmed by a French team who journeyed to Antarctica and endured temperatures that fell to −58°F for four months, the movie is thus both an unusual "love" story and a breathtaking chronicle about the miracle of life.

When one of my students saw the movie, it was during his last quarter of classes and he was weighing two possible ministry opportunities in churches once he graduated. One would be back in his hometown where the cost of housing was reasonable, his wife could stop working and be with their one-year-old child, they would be near family and friends, and he would be an assistant pastor. The other opportunity would be in the hip, downtown area of a large city where tens of thousands of young adults lived, and where a church wanted to start a ministry to connect spiritually with their lives. The problem was, the church did not have enough money to fund the position entirely, so his wife would still need to work, and there was no guarantee that things would succeed.

After seeing the movie with his wife, my student came in to class the next day wanting to talk with me. When I asked him what he wanted to share, he said, last night we saw *March of the Penguins* and drove home from the theater not speaking. Finally, we looked at each other and realized that God had spoken to us both while we were watching the movie. They had heard God say: "If I can take care of those stupid penguins, I can take care of you." Having encountered God at the movies, they were going to take the downtown church ministering to young adults.

## SOME CONCLUSIONS

What these student testimonials suggest is that a transcendent/spiritual experience through film—a "reel" spirituality, while remembered by most when asked, means different things to different people. Some remember a film experience that was Spiritual (capital "S"); others a movie that evoked a profound "spiritual" experience (small "s"); and still others found in the movie a parable of Christian truth that deepened their understanding of their faith. All three responses, though different, were significant. Though it is the case that most movies my students saw did not evoke such responses, all had had an occasional encounter, or encounters, with a "reel" spirituality that was indeed a real spirituality. In an analogous way to how Christians over the centuries have tried to describe natural theology, some of my students found in movies a support for the faithful; others, the occasion for spiritual growth; and still others, an encounter with the Divine. But whether the movie was thought transcendent, spiritual, or supportive of Christian truth, what stood out to all the students polled was the capacity of film to affect them deeply.

In an analogous way to how, in Proverbs 30 and 31, the sayings of the non-Israelites Agur and King Lemuel's mother are discovered by God's people to be God's revelation to them, and Paul finds the spiritual experiences of those on the Areopagos in Athens to be genuine, even if incomplete and partially mistaken (Acts 17), and in an analogous way to Pharaoh Neco hearing Elohim tell him to go to Josiah and tell Israel's king that God wanted him to let Neco pass through on his way to fight the Assyrians (2 Chron. 35), or Elijah hearing the sound of sheer silence (1 Kings 19), these students had spiritual experiences.[7] My students found in a movie either support for their belief, or the occasion for spiritual insight and growth, and/or an encounter with the Transcendent—occasionally all three together. Whether the movie was thought Transcendent, spiritual, or illuminating of Christian truth, what stood out for all the students polled was the capacity of film to touch them spiritually.

Moreover, though the reflection papers were each unique testimonies to one example of a spirituality of everyday life, there are also commonalities worth mentioning:

Personality type, while a factor, seems not to have been determinative as to whether someone had a numinous experience. What was important, instead, was the deep resonance the viewer felt between something in the film narrative (or image or music) and the viewer's own life. A connection was experienced.

The theme of the movie that proved significant in the lives of these adult viewers was sometimes religious and sometimes not. The movie's "religious" content seems not to have been the critical factor, though it sometimes was present, particularly for those who found their understanding of their faith deepened.

Many of the movies that became transparent to the divine were classics that will endure, including *Wings of Desire* (1987), *The Tree of Life* (2001), *Star Wars* (1977), *Up* (2009), *Finding Nemo* (2003), *The Shawshank Redemption* (1994), *Fight Club* (1999), *Life Is Beautiful* (1997), and Carl Theodor Dreyer's film about a Danish Lutheran priest, *Ordet* (*The Word; 1955*). But others had little artistic significance, among them *I Heart Huckabees* (2004), *Matrix: Reloaded* (2003), *The Green Mile* (1999), *The Ultimate Gift* (2006), *A Walk to Remember* (2002), *As Good as It Gets* (1997).

In their reflections on movies that proved spiritually significant to them, some of the viewers made clear use of the language of Christian theology. That is, though Christians can for purposes of theological discussion disconnect the Spirit's revealing presence in the church and through Scripture from that which occurs outside the church and without direct reference to the Christian faith, Christian theology recognizes that there is but one Spirit. Church and world, special and general revelation, intersect and merge in the lives of Christian believers.

And beyond these particulars, there are also wider observations that seem apropos, and which might serve as a conclusion, even as these narratives invite deeper cultural, biblical and theological probing.

First, few in the Christian church have been encouraged to think theologically about our encounters with God which take place outside the church and its Scripture. The result has been a growing disconnect between how the church continues to speak formally concerning spiritual experience and how those who are not Christians speak of that same reality. Typically, Christian theologians continue to downplay the importance of God's presence through the arts, finding in such knowledge (and for them it is knowledge, not divine encounter) at best a mere echo or trace of the divine presence, or perhaps a projection of divine reality, something unable to provide sufficient insight or to compel obedience and devotion.

Those outside the Christian church, on the other hand, often respond to numinous encounters and spiritual experiences by describing them as foundational and even transformative in their lives. While the church has feared idolatry and self-deception (you don't whisper "God" by shouting "wo/man"), those outside the church have often described their responses in terms of humility and awe. Such disparity, though long-standing, has simply multiplied as our culture has embraced what some label "neoromanticism," where spirituality is once again considered a public virtue.

Secondly, rather than affirming with our brothers and sisters God's presence throughout God's world, Christians have too often been pouring cold water on that spark. The unfortunate result has been twofold: on the one side, there has been a loss of opportunity for dialogue and witness for those of us in the Christian church. If Christians are uninterested in their neighbors' spirituality, why should they be interested in ours? And on the other side, turning from what might be labeled "witness" to that which is often termed "discipleship," if a divine presence has been revealed to others through the arts, then Christians are impoverishing themselves in their relationship with and knowledge of God to the degree that they are insensitive to this expression of a spirituality of everyday life.

Lastly, an interest by Christians in spirituality and the arts is being triggered by larger changes that are going on in Western culture, particularly around the theological ordering given to what are historically labeled life's transcendentals—truth, beauty, and goodness. In the 1960s, Christianity's theological orientation circled around notions of truth, for as a culture we would have ordered the transcendentals as first truth, then goodness, and finally beauty. By the 1970s and 1980s, however, our Western culture, having lived through the Vietnam War and having seen the assassinations of John and Robert Kennedy and Martin Luther King Jr., had reordered these verities. And so too the Western church. Christians now began with the need for goodness, before moving on to truth, and finally to beauty. But as modernity came to an end in the West, and the millennium dawned, with the sterility of the West's rationalism imploding in on itself, the cultural ordering of the transcendentals again changed. With the West now well into the new century, increasing numbers are saying that we should begin with beauty, and then move to goodness, before considering truth. All three are fundamental, but the epistemological ordering has changed.

Such seismic shifts in the cultural plates of the West have deep implications for Christian theology. One of these is surely the ever-increasing openness to a neoromanticism in our culture. And with this comes a growing societal openness to spirituality, particularly as it is mediated through culture and the arts.

### DISCUSSION QUESTIONS

1. Johnston describes compelling spiritual experiences that his students report in watching movies, including many that are not religious in obvious ways. Have you had such an experience while watching a movie? Would it fit one or more of the categories described in the chapter?

2. In such experiences, is the dialogue between religion and popular culture located in the film itself, or in the audience? Why do you say so? What does your answer suggest about the movie-watching experience and the way people make meaning out of the popular culture they engage?

3. Many people understand some films to function religiously as parables. What is the value of making such a comparison and what are potential pitfalls?

4. Johnston is an ordained minister in the Evangelical Covenant Church, and much of his earlier work has focused on encouraging evangelicals, who have sometimes been suspicious of whether film and popular culture can be ethically appropriate experiences, to be open to a wider reflection on the popular arts. Do you see evidence of that distrust of popular culture in Johnston's reports of his students' responses? Have you seen evidence of it in other places? Is there evidence, in the essay or in your own experience, of a greater openness to popular culture among evangelicals or other religious groups? Why might that be happening? What is its impact on religious cultures?

NOTES

Parts of this chapter were first given as a plenary address to the Western section of the Society of Biblical Literature, Santa Clara, CA, March 25, 2012; as lectures at Dallas Theological Seminary, October 2014, and at Pepperdine University, January 2015. Readers are also directed to my chapter 38, "The Film Viewer and Natural Theology: God's 'Presence' at the Movies," in *The Oxford Handbook of Natural Theology,* ed. Russell Re Manning (Oxford: Oxford University Press, 2013), 595–610, as well as to the Preface and chapter 3 of my book *God's Wider Presence: Reconsidering General Revelation* (Grand Rapids, MI: Baker Academic, 2014), xii–xix, 42–66.

1. The 84th Annual Academy Awards, February 26, 2012, www.iwannawatch .to/2014/09/the-84th-annual-academy-awards-2012.

2. Herbert Jump, *The Religious Possibilities of the Motion Picture* (New Britain, CT: South Congregational Church, private distribution, 1911), repr. in Terry

Lindvall, *The Silents of God: Selected Issues and Documents in Silent American Film and Religion, 1908–1925* (Lanham, MD: Scarecrow Press, 2001), 54–78.

3. Vachel Lindsay, *The Art of the Moving Picture* (1915; repr. New York: Modern Library, 2000), 176–77.

4. Michael Bird's chapter "Film as Hierophany" in *Religion in Film*, ed. John R. May and Michael Bird (1982), found the Lutheran theologian Paul Tillich helpful in understanding film's spiritual possibilities. Joel Martin and Conrad Ostwald edited *Screening the Sacred* (1995); Andrew Greeley and Albert Bergeson wrote on *God in the Movies* (2000); Ken Gire's popular study from 2000 was entitled *Reflections on the Movies: Hearing God in the Unlikeliest Places;* and my own book *Reel Spirituality* also appeared first in 2000, followed by its second edition in 2006. Gareth Higgins's personal reflection entitled *How Movies Helped Save My Soul* followed in 2003. A study guide Catherine Barsotti and I wrote in 2004 is entitled *Finding God in the Movies.* Eric Christianson edited *Cinema Divinité* with two colleagues in 2005; the subtitle of Chris Deacy and Gaye Ortiz's 2008 book *Theology and Film: Challenging the Sacred/Secular Divide. Seeing the Sacred in the Best Films of the 21st Century,* the subtitle of Craig Detweiler's *Into the Dark,* published in the same year, is even more direct. Roy Anker's 2010 book *Of Pilgrims and Fire* is subtitled *When God Shows Up at the Movies.* And the list has continued.

5. T. S. Eliot, "Burnt Norton," *Four Quartets,* in *The Complete Poems and Plays, 1909–1950* (New York: Harcourt, Brace & World, 1971), 119.

6. Avery Dulles, "Revelation and Discovery," in *Theology and Discovery: Essays in Honor of Karl Rahner, S.J.,* ed. William J. Kelly (Milwaukee: Marquette University Press, 1980), 1–29.

7. For a fuller discussion of the spiritual experiences of biblical characters that happened outside of the formal religious structures and often outside of Israel's community of faith, see Johnston, *God's Wider Presence,* 67–119.

# CHAPTER NINETEEN

# Rap Music and Its Message

## On Interpreting the Contact between Religion and Popular Culture

ANTHONY PINN

George Clinton and Parliament would be in town doing some of their classic cuts—"Flashlight," and so on. My friends were going and part of me wanted to attend, but, as a good "church boy," I was torn. Should a Christian attend such a "worldly" event, listening to songs that did not address themes of spiritual uplift? Granted, I did on occasion listen to these songs, but I had always believed that this was somehow wrong. Could there be a relationship between these two worlds? Initially I thought not. My friends went to the concert, and I stayed home. It would be years before I would see George Clinton live, only after I was able to recognize and appreciate the natural conversation or convergence between popular culture and religiosity.

Media sources tend to highlight the negative and reactionary interaction between religious ideologies and popular culture; one need only think about the friction between Rev. Calvin Butts and several "gangsta" rap artists. The former argues that this form of musical production erodes moral values and religious sensibilities; the artists respond that they are speaking of reality and are misunderstood and disrespected. This, however, is only one form of interaction between religion and popular culture. On another level, Paul Tillich is correct; they work in harmony revising and rethinking each other, interpreting each other for the benefit of larger communities. As Bruce David Forbes writes in the introduction: "Because popular culture surrounds us, it seems reasonable to assume that its messages and subtle themes influence us as well as reflecting us. If popular culture reflects values we already hold, that reflection also serves to reinforce our values and deepen our commitment to them." This essay is my attempt to discuss this form of interaction between religion and popular culture. The question is, how do those who are interested in understanding and exploring the connections between these two worldviews interpret the dialogue? My goal is not to outline or rehearse the conversation, but rather to provide a methodology for exploring this conversation, a method growing out of the source material. I have labeled this approach "nitty-gritty hermeneutics."

## "NITTY-GRITTY HERMENEUTICS" DEFINED

The term "nitty-gritty" denotes a hard and concrete orientation in which the "raw natural facts" are of tremendous importance, irrespective of their ramifications. While serving to confine vision and orientation to certain parameters of roughness, it also uncompromisingly expands the meaning and possibility of life to its full limits. Thus nitty-gritty hermeneutics seeks a clear and unromanticized understanding of a hostile world, and entails "telling it like it is" and taking risks. Embedded in this method of interpretation is a sense that paradox and tension aren't necessarily problems but rather can serve as opportunities to explore dimensions of cultural life that we might otherwise overlook or downplay. This way of approaching cultural life begins with an understanding that human life is messy, complex, and layered.

Aspects of this hermeneutic include a sense of heuristic rebelliousness, as well as raw and uncompromised insight. This hermeneutical approach takes the material of life that goes unspoken and hidden, and expresses it. In Foucault's terms, this hermeneutic ruptures American dialogue both by bringing to the surface "subjugated knowledge," which dismantles false perceptions and harmful practices, and by altering popular perceptions and life values.[1]

Defined by its nitty-gritty character, nitty-gritty hermeneutics exhibits a sense of nonconformity. It ridicules interpretations and interpreters who seek to inhibit or restrict liberative movement and hard inquiries into the problems of life. The nitty-gritty "thang," so to speak, forces a confrontation with the "funky stuff" of life, and, oddly enough, finds strength in the challenge posed. These two principles—rootedness in rebelliousness and raw, uncompromising insight—not only give shape to this hermeneutic but are also found in cultural expressions such as the blues. That is to say, the blues illustrates the nature and function of nitty-gritty hermeneutics.[2] I do not mean to suggest an endorsement of oppressive opinions held within the blues or other forms of musical expression such as rap. However, I am not willing to reject these forms of expression simply because they contain some of the misguided tendencies of the larger society. Rather, I am suggesting that the positive expressions of this music (i.e., the examples of this music which have a constructive intention) suggest a hermeneutic that is worthy of investigation and implementation by those interested in the connections between religion and popular culture, because it already entails this very conversation between religious realities and cultural production.

## NITTY-GRITTY HERMENEUTICS IN ACTION: THE BLUES

The historical origin of the blues as a musical form is virtually impossible to pinpoint. It is, however, safe to say that blues songs took form long before their actual recording, and likely developed alongside spirituals and secular work songs. Consequently, existential and musical contexts informing work songs and spirituals determined the content, shape, and sound of the blues. Yet whereas the spirituals—"religious songs"—tell the story of black life in terms of a collective reality, blues songs shift to an individualized, personal accounting of existence in a hostile society.[3]

In these songs, the promises of the spirituals were weighed and tested in light of life's controlling hardships, and utopian ideals were found wanting. Hence the blues as a musical form is concerned with truth as it arises out of experience. That is, for blues artists "truth is experience and experience is the truth."[4] The blues' commitment to the unpolished expression of black life made some segments of the black community uncomfortable. For example, the blues met with the disapproval of black churches because the lyrical content and "seductive" nature of the music fell outside of the norms, values, and morality advocated by black church tradition. Raw or "gutbucket" experiences were poetically presented, critiqued, and synthesized, yet unapologetically understood as real and unavoidable. The body within the blues, unlike within black church theologies, was not a problem to control, to render docile so as to tame its wickedness. Rather the blues body is a source of pain and pleasure, and what we know about life is premised on the movement of that body through time and space. It, the blues body, isn't to be despised, but rather enjoyed. No subject was taboo, although most were shrouded in metaphorical language. The rejection of the blues stems from the "hard living" and hard questioning noted in the lyrics. In this manner, blues performers openly discussed aspects of life that church folk would just as soon have kept hidden, and challenged espoused yet unpracticed principles of religion.[5]

Blues artists often found traditionally religious interpretations of life fundamentally flawed and unproductive. The blues critiqued the hypocrisy and inactivity of black churches and used this as fuel for significations and sarcasm. John T. "Funny Papa" Smith makes this point in the following lyrics:

> Some of the good Lawd's children, some of them aint no good,
> Some of the good Lawd's children, some of them aint no good.

Some of them are the devil, ooh, well, well,
  and won't help you if they could.
Some of the good Lawd's children kneel upon their knees and pray,
Some of the good Lawd's children kneel upon their knees and pray.
You serve the devil in the night, ooh, well
  and serve the Lawd in the day.[6]

Smith's questioning of banal theological formulations and sarcasm about hyper-optimistic religiosity when he sings about the traditional notion of a good God held by black Christian religion is also typical of the blues. He sings:

I used to ask God questions, then answer that question my self,
I used to ask God questions, then answer that question my self,
'Bout when I was born, wonder was there any mercy left?
You know it must be the devil I'm servin', I know it can't be Jesus Christ,
You know it must be the devil I'm servin', I know it can't be Jesus Christ,
'Cause I ask him to save me and look like he tryin' to take my life.[7]

Looking over the course of his life, Smith is unable to accept traditional conceptions of God (as compassionate and historically involved), nor is he willing to explain his continual hardship through divine mystery. Taking a hard look at his condition and Christian faith, Smith raises subtle questions concerning the evidence of God's involvement in the world and one's ability to decipher this involvement.

The blues forces a rethinking of what religion is and what it means to be religious. In this way, blues players expanded the narrow perceptions of religiosity beyond the confines of mainstream black traditional approaches. Hence, with respect to the blues, it is unacceptable to limit religion and religiosity to traditional black Christian (or theistic) models. Consider the following lines:

Yes I went out on the mountain, looked over in Jerusalem,
Yes I went out on the mountain, looked over in Jerusalem,
Well, I see them hoodoo women, ooh Lord, makin' up in their
  low-down tents.

Well I'm going to Newport to see Aunt Caroline Dye,
Well I'm going to Newport to see Aunt Caroline Dye,
She's a fortune-teller, oh Lord, she sure don't tell no lie.[8]

Productive religiosity comes to mean a religiosity whose principles have felt consequences for daily life. Doctrinal and theological "purity" pale in comparison to existential need. Usable religion must not place abstraction and neat theological categories above human experience: only that which is proven by experience holds value. Religious expression is here defined by its commitment to human accountability, and responsibility for human occurrences. To a large extent, productive religiosity is fluid, in that its dynamics alter with the existential situation; thus it avoids dilemmas of applicability resulting from the rigid demands and dictates of tradition.

The nitty-gritty hermeneutics surfacing in the blues interprets religion based upon complex black life as a tool, by which humans are encouraged to remove psychologically comforting theological "crutches" and develop themselves as liberators. Ralph Ellison captures this meaning in "Richard Wright's Blues":

> The blues is an impulse to keep the painful details and episodes of a brutal experience alive in one's aching consciousness, to finger its jagged edge and to transcend it, not by the consolation of philosophy [or religious constructs] but by squeezing from it a near-tragic, near-comic lyricism. As a form, the blues is an autobiographical chronicle of personal catastrophe expressed lyrically.... [Blues songs'] attraction lies in this, that they at once express both the agony of life and the possibility of conquering it through sheer toughness of spirit. They fall short of tragedy only in that they provide no solution, offer no scapegoat but the self.[9]

There is a sense in which blues tones, such as those mentioned above, carve out a space of creativity and ingenuity in the middle of oppressive circumstances, and this space belongs to both those who sing and those who listen. I believe there is much for academics to learn from the contours of this made space.

NITTY GRITTY HERMENEUTICS
IN ACTION: RAP

Blues songs make use of the same creative and existential materials as the spirituals, thereby creating a continuum of musical expression. But perpetual hardship, and the need to respond creatively to it, continues into the present, resulting in a new musical exploration that is both continuous with the earlier one, and appropriate to current conditions and contexts. This new form is rap music. Consequently, the substance of this nascent method of interpretation—nitty gritty hermeneutics—also appears in rap.[10]

An accurate history of rap music must understand it in connection to the larger development of hip-hop culture. Hip-hop first emerges as a cultural and creative response to the matrix of industrial decline, social isolation, and political decay endemic to the Bronx in New York City.[11] Faced with declining opportunities for socioeconomic mobility, and the accompanying marginality, young artists made use of their creative resources to establish an alternative "way of being" in the world, complete with a vocabulary, style of dress, visual artistic expression (graffiti art as early as 1971), and dance (break dancing as early as 1973) uniquely their own.[12]

In essence, hip-hop culture and its musical voice—rap—signal both cultural resistance and, in keeping with this essay's theme, a continued dialogue with religious ideals and institutions. The music behind rap lyrics, with its sampling and strong beats, rethinks traditional understandings of proper musical formation, and finds pleasure in the sounds the music industry labeled undesirable. As Tricia Rose insightfully points out,

> Although famous rock musicians have used recognizable samples from other prominent musicians as part of their album material, for the most part, samples were used to "flesh out" or accent.... Rap producers have inverted this logic, using samples as a point of reference, as a means by which the process of repetition and recontextualization can be highlighted and privileged.[13]

On another level, rap lyrics—the verbal expression of hip-hop's more general affirmation of identity and critique of the larger society—present a "postmodern" articulation of themes, lifestyles, and behaviors found in black oral traditions. Rap music has roots in African musical techniques and African-influenced oral practices, and uses folk heroes such as "Bad Niggers," Brer Rabbit, Signifying Monkey, Stagolee, and Dolemite as models in order to develop ways of outsmarting and temporarily gaining the upper hand over the dominant society while still rehearsing the realities of black urban life. More recent influences include storytellers such as the Last Poets and Gil Scott-Heron, as well as mid-twentieth-century radio personalities such as Douglas "Jocko" Henderson.[14]

Most rap music aficionados mark the emergence of what became contemporary rap with the arrival of DJ Kool Herc in New York City from Jamaica in 1972. DJ Kool Herc used the Jamaican tradition of toasting or speaking over extended beats and, like Afrika Bambaataa and Grandmaster Flash, began holding open-air parties in the Bronx. In 1979, "Rapper's Delight" was recorded by the Sugar Hill Gang (on Sugar Hill Records) and sold millions of copies.[15] The Sugar Hill Gang, from New Jersey, brought rap to a larger audience by making it available to groups outside select New York circles. Prior to this, MCs and DJs distributed their goods using dubbing devices and cassette players known as "boom boxes," but with the success of "Rapper's Delight," the commercialization of rap music was under way.

In the early 1980s, East Coast hip-hop made its way to the West Coast, where Soul Sonic Force and Afrika Bambaataa toured in 1980. Captured by the rap music craze, Los Angeles residents used two skating rinks, "World on Wheels" and "Skateland," as rapper training camps, where contests sponsored by radio station KDAY were held. This style gave way to the creativity of Eazy E, Dr. Dre (formerly of the World Class Wreckin' Crew), Ice Cube, and the other members of N.W.A. (Niggaz With Attitude). N.W.A. firmly established a style of rap based upon the hard facts of LA gang and hustler life. Granted, Schooly

D and KRS-One (with Scott La Rock) on the East Coast and Ice-T ("Six in the Morning" and "Colors") on the West Coast had already pioneered this hard-life form of rap music, and I do not mean to downplay the national attention they gained. Yet it was not until N.W.A. recorded "Straight Outta Compton" (as a Macola Company / Ruthless record production for sale out of car trunks) and successfully adopted "gangsta" personae that this style gained a large audience. As Brian Cross says: "N.W.A. placed themselves on the hiphop map with authenticity, capturing the aggression and anger of the streets of South Central in their intonation and timbre. This places the listener in an intimate position relative to their rhymes. Ice-T sounds like a narrator by comparison."[16]

The raw aggression and reckless lifestyle portrayed by this form of rap caught the attention of rap fans and defined the West Coast as the center of "realism" rap or gangsta rap.[17] New York's rap was "flavored" by the dynamics of hip-hop culture, and so West Coast rap highlighted, in response, its culture's own defining features, most prominently gang culture. Compton was in direct competition with the Bronx.[18] The reputation of West Coast rap has been enhanced, in recent years, by the work of Cypress Hill, Snoop Doggy Dogg, Dr. Dre, Warren G., Ice Cube, and Yo-Yo.

The above history, although brief, presents the social and cultural context, creative dynamics, and scope—East Coast and West Coast—of rap music's development. What is needed at this point is a typology to clarify the thematic structure of rap's lyrical content. I argue that there are three major (at times overlapping) categories of rap music: "status" rap, "gangsta" rap, and "progressive" rap.

The "status" strand of rap first appears in the Sugar Hill Gang's "Rapper's Delight." This cut consists of braggadocio's rhythms and mild signification, which denote a strong concern with "status" and social prowess. At one point in this rap, "Big Bank Hank" outlines his superior skills and sexual attractiveness. He boasts that a

Reporter stopped me for an interview
She said, she's heard stories and she's heard fables
That I'm vicious on the mic and the turntables.
This young reporter I did adore,
So I rocked the mike like I never did before,
She said damn fly-guy I'm in love with you,
the Casanova legend must have been true.
I said by the way baby what's your name,
She said I go by the name of Lois Lane.
She said you can be my boyfriend, you surely can,
Just let me quit my boyfriend called Superman.[19]

This style of rap music, emerging early, is concerned with distinguishing artists from their competitors. "Status" rap, combined with breakdance movements, served as the major tool within this struggle for artistic dominance. Both cultural expressions highlighted competitor's flaws and shortcomings while emphasizing the rapper's or dancer's own prowess. The social critique offered in this brand of rap is usually limited to the assertion of self in opposition to a society that is seeking black nonexistence. This rupture is often expressed sexually and overtly, such as in the lyrics of New York's Heavy D. The following lines are from "Mr. Big Stuff" (1990):

I'm a fly girl lover and a woman pleaser
Girls say, "Heavy, let me squeeze you"
An incredible
Overweight, huggable Prince of poetry
That's why I'm so lovable.[20]

Groups such as Salt-N-Pepa effectively brought black women into the rap world beyond roles as sexual objects and targets for male aggression and distrust, highlighting the personal value and strength of black women. Salt-N-Pepa (the trio of "Salt" [Cheryl James], "Pepa" [Sandy Denton], and "Spinderella" [the DJ Dee Dee Roper]) argue for self appreciation—the creation of strong and assertive individuals—and, in so doing, promote the value of human personality. "It's About Expression" (1991):

> You know life is all about expression
> You only live once, you're not coming back
> So express yourself...
> Express yourself
> You gotta be you and only you, baby
> Express yourself
> Let me be me
> Express yourself
> Don't tell me what I cannot do, baby
> Express yourself.[21]

More recent artists such as Lil' Kim and Foxy Brown also signify and challenge sexual stereotypes.

Although "status" rap contains an implicit political agenda, it explicitly discusses the social "living of life." As Michael Eric Dyson recounts, rap of this nature allows rappers, and by extension their listeners, to momentarily move beyond physical demise and enjoy the material benefits of the American Dream.[22] Unfortunately, this struggle for individual, ontological, and material "space" often results in counterproductive and oppressive tendencies, which can be seen in the sexism, patriarchal ideals, and problematic consumerism that much "status" rap expresses. On one level, this brand of rap strikes at the dehumanizing tendencies of American society; on another level, it buys into the structures and attitudes fostering such dehumanizing practices.

"Gangsta" rap presents this dual message in even stronger terms, responding to the same dehumanizing effects of life in the United States with much more overt intracommunal and extracommunal aggression. The first major gangsta group, N.W.A., consciously plays out America's nightmare, depicting itself as ruthlessly dominating its environment. However, one notices an implied critique of American racism. Take, for example, N.W.A.'s controversial rap "Fuck Tha Police" (1989):

Fuck the police, comin' straight from the underground
A young nigga got it bad because I'm brown
And not the other color. Some police think
They have the authority to kill a minority
Fuck that shit 'cause I ain't the one
For a punk motherfucker with a badge and a gun.[23]

The members of this group point out the manner in which "law and order" operates on principles that encourage the victimizing of young people based upon style of dress and skin color. Whereas some acquiesce to this treatment, N.W.A. promotes resistance to such practices in order to maintain a sense of self-worth and importance.

If N.W.A. is correct in its analysis, the anger and violence expressed in gangsta rap is reflective of American society in general. In other words, violence and crime do not originate with rap music, but are part of the American fabric and merely magnified by musical expression.

We ain't the problems, we ain't the villains
Its the suckers deprivin' the truth from our children
You can't hide the fact, Jack
There's violence in the streets everyday
Any fool can recognize that
But you try to lie and lie
And say America's some motherfuckin' apple pie.[24]

Dr. Dre uses the "Americanness" of gangsta rap's lyrics to justify the violence of his album *The Chronic* (1993). In an interview with *Rolling Stone,* he said:

People are always telling me my records are violent[,] … that they say bad things about women, but those are the topics they bring up themselves…. They don't want to talk about the good shit because that doesn't interest them, and it's not going to interest their readers…. If I'm promoting violence, they're doing it just as much as I am by focusing on it in the article. That really bugs me out—you know, if it weren't going on, I couldn't talk about it.[25]

In addition to pointing out the oppressive nature of American society, gangsta rap outlines the practices within the "hood" that allow survival. As with "status" rap, gangsta style often entails using counter-productive tools in order to achieve identity and material comfort. A consequence of this is the sexist and misogynistic attitude glorified in the music. Women are often viewed as the enemy, the ones who destroy black manhood and thereby call into question the gangsta's survival.[26] As a result of this assumed threat, women are dealt with harshly; they are stopped at all cost from ending the G's quest for success. Rappers, without question, must be held responsible for the oppression supported in their music. At the same time, however, critics and fans must recognize that gangsta rap echoes oppressive precepts acknowledged and encouraged by the larger society.[27] That is to say, the attitudes and activities often chronicled in gangsta rap do not originate with these artists. Rather they mimic the desire for the American Dream using the tools available to them, tools put in place long before their birth.

Even with these flaws, gangsta rap (and to a lesser extent status rap) provides a brief glimpse of the interpretative honesty, roughness, and concern for personal identity inherent in nitty-gritty hermeneutics. The appeal to reality at all cost, and despite the possibility of more comfortable agendas, is clear in these two forms of rap. Still, this critical insight is most forcefully presented in the "progressive" strain of rap. Aware of the same existential hardships and contradictions as gangsta rap, progressive rap seeks to address these concerns without intracommunal aggression and in terms of political and cultural education, providing an interpretation of American society and a constructive agenda (e.g., self respect, knowledge, pride, and unity) for the uplift of black America. One also encounters a more overt dialogue with and interpretation of black religiosity in progressive rap.[28]

Nascent progressive rap gained popular attention with "The Message" (1982) by the New York rappers Grand Master Flash and the Furious Five. Using a portrait of life amid industrial decline, social alienation, and political corruption, this rap interprets the cycle of poverty and dehumanization producing limited life options and despair. It speaks to the destructiveness of systemically imposed "ghetto" existence.

You'll grow in the ghetto living second-rate
And your eyes will sing a song of deep hate
The places you play and where you stay
Looks like one great big alleyway.[29]

Grand Master Flash and the Furious Five's appeal stemmed, in part, from the group's uncompromising attention to the "underbelly" of U.S. economic and sociopolitical structures. Yet implicit within this depiction of daily hardships in urban centers was an understanding that knowledge might produce the struggle necessary for transformation.

Progressive rap seeks, first, to change the system, using black history and cultural developments as well as a critique of social structures to point out the intrinsic value of black life and increase positive black self-expression. The group Public Enemy classically represents this agenda. Its lead rapper, Chuck D, understands rap music as an arena for the exchange of vital information. Rap deciphers the muddled ideologies of political, economic, and social institutions and makes listeners aware of necessary steps leading to self-determination.[30]

As the self-proclaimed "prophet of rage," Chuck D sees the meaning of American society as centering around the control and destruction of black minds and bodies. Through raps such as "Fight the Power," "Bring the Noise," "Shut 'Em Down," "Party for Your Right to Fight," and "White Heaven/Black Hell," Public Enemy outlines this control and the methods for breaking its grip. Public Enemy's interpretive eye is not focused solely upon the larger society and its flaws, but also chastises African Americans for the role they play in their own destruction.

Of more direct interest here is Chuck D's insight into black religion. He argues that black religion should contribute to the liberation of black people. The meaning of black religion is found in its support of black identity and consciousness, and its rejection of status quo politics, economics, and social relations. Chuck D's support of the Nation of Islam suggests that black churches, as representative of majority black religious expression, are not in line with religion's ultimate purpose and that the "Nation's" praxis better fulfills the meaning of religion.

Public Enemy understands the Nation of Islam as redemptive because it provides the quest for African American progress with a vivifying spiritual base. The 1990 album *Fear of a Black Planet* presents a musical interpretation of the Nation of Islam, inspiring critics to make comments such as this:

> [Public Enemy] has become the spokesperson for a new wave of African American consciousness shaped in the tradition of Elijah Muhammad, Malcolm X, and Louis Farrakhan. [It] is not the only rap group influenced by the symbols and rhetoric of the Nation of Islam, [but] they are [sic] by far its most significant and most consistent proponents.[31]

Through its Islam-influenced lyrics and rebellious beats, Public Enemy provided a "jeremiad" calling attention to the hypocrisy of white America. Chuck D also reprimanded African Americans for involvement in their own oppression, while pointing out their potential for liberative action. Such a thick and layered message is the hallmark of progressive rap.

Although Public Enemy is generally the primary example used to define the nature and content of progressive rap, it is my opinion that some of the best progressive rap in the 1990s was been produced by Arrested Development (from Atlanta), notwithstanding the lack of attention given the group in academic treatments. AD, as the group is commonly called, exhibits a hybridization of Afrocentrism and the 1960s black aesthetic. In keeping with the interpretation of American society provided by Public Enemy, AD sees the fundamental meaning of U.S. institutions and ideologies as demarcated by the ontological and epistemological demise of black individuals and communities. Through raps such as "People Everday" and "Ache'n for Acres," Arrested Development illustrates the self-destructive and community-eroding effects of consumerism and sociopolitical alienation. Seeing through the ideological platforms aimed at the extirpation of black life, Arrested Development offers a regenerative program based upon pan-African cultural nationalism, social cohesion, economic cooperation, and proactive politics.

In stronger terms than the other groups mentioned, AD provides a critique of religiosity that demonstrates the tenacity of nitty-gritty hermeneutics. A clear example of this is the rap "Fishin' 4 Religion," from its album *3 Years, 5 Months and 2 Days in the Life of . . .* (Chrysalis Records, 1992). In this rap, AD critiques black ministers' promotion of passivity as a sign of righteousness, as well as the lack of sustained and direct community involvement by black churches. In part, this involves an attack upon the symbolic and imagistic grounding of black religion, by critiquing the inconsistencies between the demands for liberation and the conception of God peddled by black Christian churches. Using liberation as a theological norm, AD determines that many black churches do not embody the true nature and meaning of black religion's objective. Black religion must promote ontological and epistemological "blackness" and thereby encourage the holistic survival of the black community. Unfortunately, however, black churches are "praising a God that watches you weep, and doesn't want you to do a damn thing about it." Thus the activism suggested by black religion is actually counterproductive, because it does not extend beyond emotional outbursts and spiritual platitudes. Resolutions of this nature have no relationship to temporal and proactive plans for social transformation; they are far too spiritualized to be of any worldly good.

> When they want change the preacher says shout it,
> Does shoutin' bring about the change, I doubt it.
> All shoutin' does is make you lose your voice.

In the words of MC Speech (the group's leader), black churches fail to "nurture" African Americans; instead, they enslave them within a web of opiatic eschatology and debilitating consternation. In this way, the essence or genuine meaning of religion is transmuted into a plea for religiously coded banality and "turn-the-other-cheek" benignancy. AD expresses this while relaying a particular church scene:

... sitting in church hearing legitimate woes.
Pastor tells the lady it'll be alright,
Just pray so you can see the pearly gates so white.
The Lady prays and prays, prays, prays, it's everlasting.
There's nothing wrong with prayin', it's what she's askin'.

According to this critique, many black churches are unwilling to address the hard issues of life. Therefore, in Marx's phrase, they are the opium of the people. Individualistic and indolent religiosity promoted by churches is a major factor in the underdevelopment of black America.

Arrested Development musically outlines a religiosity committed to the hands-on deliverance of black people from a profusion of existential dilemmas, without respect to traditional theology and doctrine. In AD's constructive project, one sees another aspect of nitty-gritty hermeneutics: the uncovering and revitalizing of religion outside the confines of long-standing but ineffectual theological tradition. It is a project steeped in realism, in the primacy of experience over doctrine.

For example, in keeping with traditional African religions,[32] Arrested Development extols the earth and calls union with the earth a "divine" source of power and a chief objective of any vibrant religious system. Such a religious system is constructed from the rudimentary and rather Manichean treatment of certain life principles, for example, in the rap "Washed Away." Here, the delusion of righteousness and goodness is metaphorically depicted as the destruction of a seashore by demonic tides. AD urges humans to fight the trickster serpent's efforts to destroy the seashore:

Why do we let them wash it away
Why are we allowing them to take what's good
Why won't we teach our children what is real
Why don't we collect and save what is real
Look very hard and swim the ocean
We must find what needs to be found.
Look all around and find a wise man
To feed us the truth and keep us sound.

From this sense of connectedness to a scene much larger than oneself comes the inspiration for transformation. That is, the proper working of a religion must involve both collective efforts to identify the sources of oppression, and the storing up (and sharing) of vital, self-affirming cultural information. Only a religiosity that participates in and affirms the cultural life of the community, and speaks plainly to pressing issues without paying tribute to unproved theological assertions—no new wine in old skins—is in keeping with the meaning of religion. Think about it this way, if religion involves the human effort to find the meaning in life, to wrestle with the fundamental questions of human existence—Who are we? What are we? Why are we? When are we? Where are we?—it informs and influences dimensions of our individual and collective lives well beyond the boundaries of official organizations, doctrines, and creeds. Religion, then, informs but is also informed by cultural production. It is our effort to shape and speak to the world.

The interaction between religious ideals and popular culture is extremely important because it says something about who we are and what is of fundamental importance to us. But how are we to unpack this interaction, this dialogue? The answer lies in the interaction itself, in the contact; it is present in the depictions of life, the raw facts of existence exposed by the coming together of worldviews represented by religion and popular culture. I have labeled the interpretative process involved nitty-gritty hermeneutics. Scholars of religious studies need to recognize, among other things, that there are more than riddles in rap rhymes.

DISCUSSION QUESTIONS

1. Religious groups often critique popular culture. This chapter moves in the other direction; Pinn argues that a particular aspect of popular culture, rap music, critiques traditional religion. Can you think of other examples of popular culture that offer critiques of traditional forms of religion in some way?

2. The author asserts that one message of rap music is that black churches fail to deal adequately with the history of suffering by African Americans, thus avoiding the hard realities of life. What evidence would you give to support this critique or to respond to it?

3. What is it about rap music that meets needs in the black community unmet by black churches? Play one or more examples of the music discussed in the chapter. What is your bodily experience of listening to this music? What is the difference between listening to the music and reading the lyrics printed on the page. How would you describe the feelings and emotions evoked by listening?

4. One overarching theme in this volume is that popular culture both reflects us and shapes us. Is that true of rap music as well? How?

## NOTES

This essay is an altered version of chapter 5 in Anthony Pinn's book *Why Lord?: Suffering and Evil in Black Theology* (New York: Continuum, 1995).

1. See Michel Foucault, *Power/Knowledge: Selected Interviews and Other Writings, 1972–1977* (New York: Pantheon Books, 1980).

2. I thank Abraham Wheeler, one of my students, for valuable information on certain blues figures.

3. See LeRoi Jones, *Blues People: The Negro Experience in White America and the Music That Developed from It* (New York: Morrow Quill, 1963), 63–68. For a more detailed history of the blues, see William Barlow, *"Looking Up at Down": The Emergence of Blues Culture* (Philadelphia: Temple University Press, 1989); Charles Keil, *Urban Blues*, 2d ed. (Chicago: University of Chicago Press, 1969 ); Paul Oliver, *Blues Fell This Morning: The Meaning of the Blues*, 2d ed., foreword by Richard Wright (New York: Cambridge University Press, 1990); and Jon Michael Spencer, *Blues and Evil* (Knoxville: University of Tennessee Press, 1993).

4. James Cone, *The Spirituals and the Blues: An Interpretation* (New York: Seabury Press, 1972), 78.

5. Part of this critique involves the sarcastic lampooning of repressive Christian sex codes. The blues responds to this aspect of black religion by openly celebrating expressed sexuality as a vital component of freedom. Using easily deciphered metaphors such as "jelly rolling," blues artists promoted sexuality as a vital and invaluable aspect of humanity. In this way, blues figures such as Ma Rainey, Robert Johnson, Muddy Waters, Koko Taylor, and others moved away from provincial (church-inspired) ethical codes and restraining sensibilities and embraced the full depiction of their being in the world. This implies a hermeneutic, or norm of interpretation, that examines tradition and rejects religion's allegiance to the nineteenth-century codes of conduct that problematized black sexuality, thereby denying African Americans a full range of human expression. Nitty-gritty hermeneutics, as expressed in the blues, interprets religious conduct codes as properly encouraging the full expression of one's humanity as a symbol of freedom. Religious systems and practices that hamper full human expression are thus inherently hypocritical.

6. James Cone, "The Blues: A Secular Spiritual," in *Sacred Music of the Secular City: From Blues to Rap,* ed. Jon Michael Spencer (Durham, NC: Duke University Press, 1992), 68–97, song quoted on p. 93. This volume is a special issue of *Black Sacred Music: A Journal of Theomusicology* 6, no. 1 (Spring 1992). And see also *Handbook of Texas Online,* Carlyn Copeland, "Smith, John T. [Funny Papa]," www.tshaonline.org/handbook/online/articles/fsm96.

7. Quoted in Oliver, *Blues Fell This Morning,* 118.

8. Quoted in ibid., 128.

9. Quoted in Jerry G. Watts, Heroism and the *Black Intellectual: Ralph Ellison, Politics, and Afro-American Intellectual Life* (Chapel Hill: University of North Carolina Press, 1994), 54–55.

10. This blues-rap continuum extends the spiritual-blues impulse discussed by Cornel West in the article "On Afro-American Popular Music: From Bebop to Rap," in his *Prophetic Fragments* (Grand Rapids, MI: William B. Eerdmans, 1988), 177–88, esp. 182–83.

11. See Tricia Rose, *Black Noise: Rap Music and Black Culture in Contemporary America* (Hanover, NH: University Press of New England, 1994), 21–25. For a more detailed and complete history and analysis of rap music than that presented in this essay, see, in addition to Rose, Mark Costello and David Foster, *Signifying Rappers: Rap and Race in the Urban Present* (New York: Ecco, 1990); Brian Cross, *It's Not about a Salary: Rap, Race and Resistance in Los Angeles* (New York: Verso, 1993); William Eric Perkins, ed., *Droppin' Science: Critical Essays on Rap Music and Hip Hop Culture* (Philadelphia: Temple University Press, 1996).

12. Break dancing and graffiti art did not remain exclusively within the black community. Movies such as *Breakin'* (1984) and *Wild Style* (1983) commercialized these art forms and brought them to a larger audience. Rapper Fab 5 Freddy's graffiti art, for example, was eventually displayed in New York City galleries.

13. Rose, *Black Noise*, 73. An analysis of the musical element of rap is beyond the scope of this essay; for further information, see Thomas Schumacher, "'This Is a Sampling Sport': Digital Sampling, Rap Music and the Law in Cultural Production," *Media, Culture and Society* 17, no. 2 (April 1995): 253–63; "Rap: Taking It from the Streets," *Keyboard* 14, no. 2 (November 1988): 32–45. See also Tricia Rose, "Soul Sonic Forces: Technology, Orality, and Black Cultural Practices in Rap Music," in *Sounding Off: Music as Subversion/Resistance/Revolution,* ed. Ron Sakolsky and Fred Wei-Han Ho (Brooklyn: Autonomedia, 1995), 97–108, a version of *Black Noise,* chap. 3.

Jon Michael Spencer is aware of the manner in which analysis of the music is often missing from discussions of rap music and other forms of musical expression. In much of his early work, Spencer developed a method for exploring both music and lyrics, as a way of better understanding the religious and theological importance of musical developments. He named this approach "theomusicology." Information on his approach might prove helpful for readers: see Jon Michael Spencer, ed., *Theomusicology,* a special issue of *Black Sacred Music: A Journal of Theomusicology* 8, no. 1 (Spring 1994).

14. Douglas "Jocko" Henderson was a disk jockey known for his rhythmic sign-on. For an example of this, see Mel Watkins, *On the Real Side: Laughing, Lying, and Signifying; The Underground Tradition of African-American Humor That Transformed American Culture, from Slavery to Richard Pryor* (New York: Simon & Schuster, 1994), 297. Stagolee (or Staggerlee) is a major figure in African American folklore. He is a "badman" whose activities carve out a space of independence while also causing destruction within the African American communities he touches. For additional information, see ibid., chapter 11, especially 461–69.

15. It should be noted that other rap songs were recorded during this early period, including "King Tim III" by Fatback. However, this and others like it were small releases that did not have the same impact as "Rapper's Delight."

16. Cross, *It's Not about a Salary,* 37. See chap. 1 for a history of rap music on the West Coast.

17. Ibid., 24. Houston's Geto Boys also present a strong example of gangsta rap. Scarface, formerly of the Geto Boys, continues this image as a solo artist in, e.g., *Mr. Scarface Is Bak* (1991), *The Diary* (1994), and *The Untouchables* (1997).

18. The distinction between the two schools of rap should not be too strongly stated, since the line between East Coast and West Coast is blurred as a result of rapid growth and blending of styles.

19. Quoted in B. Adler and Janette Beckman, eds., *Rap: Portraits and Lyrics of a Generation of Black Rockers* (New York: St. Martin's Press, 1991), 41.

20. Quoted in ibid., 59.

21. Quoted in ibid., 55.

22. Michael Eric Dyson, "Rap Culture, the Church, and American Society," in Spencer, *Sacred Music of the Secular City*, 268–73, esp. 270.

23. N.W.A., "Fuck Tha Police," *Straight Outta Compton* (Priority Records, 1989).

24. Quoted in *Body Count* (Los Angeles: One-on-One Recorders, 1992), 75, from "Freedom of Speech" (1990) by L.A.'s Ice-T.

25. Jonathan Gold, "Dr. Dre and Snoop Doggy Dogg: One Nation Under a G Thang," *Rolling Stone*, September 30, 1993, 38–43, quotation from p. 124. There are certainly examples of this "gangsta" attitude, including the deceased Tupac and The Notorious B.I.G. However, Dr. Dre and *The Chronic* mark a major turning point in the marketing of gangsta rap and, as a result, continue to serve as a useful example.

26. I continue this line of argument in "'Gettin' Grown': Notes on Gangsta Rap Music and Notions of Manhood," *Journal of African American* Men 2, no. 1 (Summer 1996): 61–73.

27. bell hooks makes this argument in "Gangsta Culture-Sexism and Misogyny: Who Will Take the Rap," in *Outlaw Culture* (New York: Routledge, 1994), 115–23, esp. 117.

28. For examples of this sort of explicit critique in gangsta rap, see pieces such as Ice Cube's "When I Get to Heaven" and Scarface's "Mind Playin' Tricks on Me," 1994.

29. Quoted in Adler and Beckman, *Rap*, 19.

30. See Robert Christagau and Gret Tate, "Chuck D All Over the Map," *Village Voice, Rock & Roll Quarterly* (Fall 1991): 12–18. For more in-depth information, see Chuck D with Yusuf Jah, *Fight the Power: Rap, Race, and Reality* (New York: Delacorte Press, 1997).

31. William Eric Perkins, "Nation of Slam Ideology in the Rap of Public Enemy," in *The Emergency of Black and the Emergence of Rap*, ed. Jon Michael Spencer (Durham, NC: Duke University Press, 1992), 41–50, quotation from pp. 41–42. This volume is a special issue of *Black Sacred Music: A Journal of Theomusicology* 5, no. 1 (Spring 1991). Other rap groups such as Poor Righteous Teachers embrace the philosophy of the 5% Nation, a Nation of Islam splinter group formed by Clarence 13X. This group argues that 85 percent of the

people are ignorant, 10 percent are capable of initiating liberation but fail to do so, and 5 percent have the truth and are poor righteous teachers.

32. The African basis of AD's religiosity is hinted at in the group's make-up, which includes the Baba (Ojay) figures. This name—Baba—is given to African spiritual advisors.

# CHAPTER TWENTY

# Broadswords and Face Paint

*Why Braveheart Still Matters*

CURTIS D. COATS AND STEWART M. HOOVER

For ten years we have been involved in a major research project on Christian masculinity with particular attention to the attitudes and understanding of evangelical men. One of our surprise discoveries was the continued resonance of *Braveheart,* a film from 1995 directed by Mel Gibson, for the men we interviewed. In some white, U.S. evangelical Christian circles, no other film inspired the same devotion as *Braveheart.* Sometimes, the film came up unsolicited. For example, Clark Caldwell, an evangelical pastor, noted:

> You go to *Braveheart,* and you see a man who has a cause. He has a passion; he has something he is willing to die for.... That's kind of the Braveheart mentality. You go out. You believe something strongly. You're willing to stand up and paint your face blue and do whatever it takes because injustice needs to know that it's wrong.

Other times, a lively discussion emerged when we brought up the film. The following example is from a group of white, thirty-something evangelical men at an "emerging" evangelical church. After showing them the image of Mel Gibson's William Wallace, the men responded:

FRANCIS: I've watched it like ten times.

INTERVIEWER: Is this a positive image of masculinity?

(Many nods and murmurs to the affirmative)

COLIN: Let me just say that like for ten–fifteen years, lead pastor–that was his most referenced movie.

FRANCIS: Especially in Christian circles too . . . I was in Campus Crusade in college and whenever we had like men's time, [the film was] always mentioned. Like there was even one time when we like painted our faces blue . . . like a really random thing, but—a little over the top.

BOBBY: So, behind it, like right at the beginning when they asked him to fight? And he says, "No. Didn't I just stand up for it? Didn't I just prove it?" And then later he does fight because it's for his family, for his values, sticking up for his country, and not just trying to kill somebody to show his manliness.

INTERVIEWER: So a reluctant hero—is that what resonates with men?

COLIN: I don't think he was reluctant.

ELLIOT: I think he was principled, so when it came to the point where fighting was his choice, then he fought. But up until then, fighting wasn't a necessity.

DAVIS: He was able to control his emotions and use them for the greater good.

ELLIOT: Yeah. And tapped into them when need be.

GREG: The idea of him standing up for what he believes in and willing to sacrifice so much for that. I think that's kind of what I picture a man doing.

Evangelical men outside of our study have expressed similar sentiments, especially when reflecting on the twentieth anniversary of the film in 2015. For example, J. E. Eubanks Jr., writing for the blog *Christ & Pop Culture,* talked about how the film taught him to love, to be a noble man, to have family and friendships based on "relationships that can be true and real, with a raw honesty that sets aside pretense," and to fight with passion and conviction.[1]

Christopher West, founder of The Cor Project, shared these sentiments as well, noting:

Men love *Braveheart* because it gives them something noble to aspire to as men. We don't admire William Wallace. We want to *be* William Wallace. We want to be the kind of man who's courageous enough to fight, to lay it all down, to endure the most gruesome, bloody death for the sake of ... [his wife] Murron.[2]

West notes that whereas many claim that Wallace is fighting for freedom, for him the enduring story is that Wallace is fighting and dying for his wife, who "bears the most affirming countenance of gratitude and appreciation" as Wallace is killed, and for his "son," Robert the Bruce, whom Wallace metaphorically fathers, demonstrating the "possibility of second chances, of redemption after failure."

It is by now firmly established that *Braveheart* resonates with a segment of white American evangelical culture that connects to the essentialist narratives of patriarchy embedded in the film.[3] What remains to be done is a more careful analysis of *why* this film matters. We therefore want to analyze the context of the film and the visual structure of the film itself. This exercise is necessary because *Braveheart* cannot still ring true simply because of its narrative arc. If this were the case, then many films in the action, drama, Western, fantasy and action biopic genres should resonate in the same way. Indeed, many men, religious and secular, do connect with these kinds of stories, but the connection to *Braveheart* is a connection of a different kind. *Braveheart* achieves iconic status as a film by which a certain type of white, thirty- or fortysomething, heterosexual, evangelical Christian man marks his life.

In the pages that follow, we begin with context. We work with the narratives offered to us in our study of Christian masculinity to establish the memory of *Braveheart,* and we explore the religious and broader contexts in which this film is situated. Then we engage the film itself, exploring some of its visual and structural components that connect to audience narratives about the film.

## CONTEXT

The context of *Braveheart* is multitemporal and multilocal. The optimum place to begin is with the stories of the people we've interviewed. Recall the comments by Caldwell, the men's group, and the bloggers quoted above. Mel Gibson as William Wallace exudes nobility, integrity and commitment. He demonstrates, even through his death, the three perceived elementals of masculinity—provision, protection, and purpose.[4] Gibson's Wallace fights when he must, sacrifices always, and loves fully—his wife, his men, and his country.

In addition to the powerful narrative of manhood that Gibson's Wallace offers these men, the film serves as a moral touchstone for evangelical families as they negotiate what they will watch *and* what they will allow their kids to watch. Despite its graphic violence, *Braveheart* and other films like it are more acceptable to this audience than many "sexualized" films because films like *Braveheart* are perceived as morally instructive and "real."

The notion of historical realism has been the subject of scholarly discussion about films like *Braveheart*.[5] Certainly, the film is not historically accurate, but for these audiences, the "real" is mainly connected to the "truth" in *Braveheart*. For example, in a film review from the Christian review site, *Movieguide,* the reviewer notes, "*Braveheart* is a rallying cry for the supremacy of God's law."[6] Thus, the violence in *Braveheart* is justified because it is couched in a story that speaks to some higher truth that, in fact, makes the violence necessary. It is telling, of course, that films with graphic sexual content cannot speak to these higher truths with this audience because of their moral ideas about sex.

Discussions about the portrayals of violence and sex are an important moment (and, often, the singular moment) when our respondents (both evangelical and "ecumenical" Protestants)[7] turn the conversation away from the basic narrative elements of a film to its visual components, which we take up below in exploring the text. However, in terms of context, this moment in the discussion with respondents is an important place where white, heterosexual American Protestants are in dialogue with visual media.

The Protestant discomfort (and fascination) with visual portrayals of any kind has a long history, a history on which our respondents implicitly draw.[8] And the concern with visual portrayals of sex and violence in film has been a key area of discussion among religious people, film producers, and government regulators for more than a century.[9]

For most of our evangelical respondents, these broader historical discourses about sex and violence connect to dominant, essentialized gender discourses about portrayals of sex and the power of these portrayals over men, a power that can be so strong that it can damage a man's personal relationship with Christ and his ability to be the spiritual head of the family.[10] The evangelical version of the discourse we are discussing notes that visual sexual portrayals cannot be redeemed, whereas violence can be redeemed by the *truth* of the story. This is particularly important in our discussion of *Braveheart*, because sex is essential to the story, a point to which we will return in the next section.

Before moving to the film itself, it is important to further situate *Braveheart* in its historical moment—the United States in 1995. The 1990s were a decade of considerable ferment in Christianity in the United States, marking the renewal of old concerns about men in the church.[11] Many of the contemporary calls to Christian masculine renewal find their footing in the United States in the 1990s. Of particular note, this decade is the high tide mark for evangelical men's groups like Promise Keepers.

*Braveheart* was released amid this ferment. Its story clearly resonated with key parts of the audience as a story of unquestioned, "pure" masculinity, filled with medieval violence, heterosexual love, rites of passage, male bonding, and freedom from tyranny. It should not be surprising that the film remained in theaters for 387 days or that it debuted at #1 on Billboard's Top DVD sales list on September 16, 2000, and remained in the top fifteen on that list at the end of the year.[12]

As one of the men in the focus group mentioned above, many Christian men in their formative college years were encouraged to live like Wallace, to act out his characteristics, to embody and perform his look and mannerisms. And they watched Gibson's Wallace again and again—in whole and in part. In a sort of mimicry of the film's story where Wallace's body was quartered and sent to different parts of the kingdom, inspiring revolution, the film itself has been carved up and displayed in different parts of the U.S. Christian kingdom throughout the 1990s and 2000s to inspire a revolution in Christian masculinity.

Some men so quickly recall William Wallace's iconic blue paint in the film because they've painted their own faces as a symbolic ritual in a men's group. Men recall Wallace's inspirational battle speech because it has been played back to them in sermons for twenty years. Men recall the powerful movement of white male bodies through sweeping landscapes because those parts of the film have been repackaged in texts like John Eldredge's book *Wild At Heart: Discovering the Secret of a Man's Soul* (2001) or in men's retreats where men are encouraged to find authentic purpose and community among other men in similar real and imagined landscapes.

Further, for these men, *Braveheart* gives them a powerful touchstone in popular culture, a watershed moment where themes from the Bible, according to them, burst forth on the silver screen. *Braveheart* gave these men a way to be masculine *and* Christian. Note this comment from Eldredge on the Christian Broadcast Network:

> There is a story written on every human heart. It is the same story—good and evil, love, romance, danger, sacrifice. It is all there. Jack dies in *Titanic* so that Rose may live. Wallace dies in *Braveheart* to set Scotland free. Maximus dies in *Gladiator* that the people might be free. See the themes? *The Return of the King*, it is all borrowing from the gospel. If we can give the gospel back to people in Technicolor, if we can give it back to them in its full beauty, that is what I want to do.[13]

*Braveheart* also holds its cultural power because it is the rebirth of the historical epic film,[14] giving a generation of white men what Charlton Heston gave a different generation of men in William Wyler's film *Ben Hur* in 1959. *Braveheart*'s power may be even more palpable because of the way it has been remixed, repackaged, and reperformed—in theaters, with other men in home groups, in books, and at men's retreats. The remixing and replaying of *Braveheart* in intimate settings with other *men* is a powerful, contextual marker of the film's lasting impact on white, heterosexual evangelical men's gender-identity narratives, a marker that is particular to this digital age.

TEXT

In this section we discuss how *Braveheart* works structurally and visually as a domestic and epic drama and how it portrays sex and violence in a way that justifies the latter and allows collective amnesia about the former.

### *Braveheart: Epic and Domestic*

We argue that *Braveheart* is a domestic drama because it presents the story of William Wallace as an ideal family man, a man who wanted a wife to love, children to nurture, and soil to till. When cruel forces shattered his domestic vision, he found a different cause—to save Scotland, which makes this film epic as well. Structurally, however, his purpose doesn't change. In the film the fate of Scotland is tied to the fate of family and vice versa. The film is structured so as to unite the domestic and the nation, carrying both from beginning to end in harmony.

The first forty-five minutes of this film build the interconnection between Wallace, family, and Scotland, culminating in the brutal murder of Wallace's wife, Murron (Catherine McCormack). In the first two minutes, we watch Young William (James Robinson) walk into a room of Scottish men and their sons hanging from the rafters of a cottage. Shots of the hanging men are angled sharply upward, so the audience can see as Young William sees these grotesque figures. The scene soon cuts to eye-level shots of Young William in the arms of his father, who comforts him through this grotesque scene. The scene cuts back to a young boy hanging from the rafters, again at a sharp angle, then back to a close-up on William's face, which fades to the next scene, where William is dreaming and the young boy hanging from the rafters calls to him (4:45). In the first five minutes, this film shows Scotland to the audience through the faces of dead fathers and sons and through the eyes of its hero, William Wallace. Early on, the audience is cued that this is not simply a domestic drama. It is an epic, one where the fate of a nation rests on a young hero.

Around the seven-minute mark, we see an early shot of the lone hero walking back to his cottage, when he pauses to listen. The camera focuses on the boy at eye level as he looks into the growing dark. The shot shifts behind William, still at eye level, yet at a wide angle where this small boy stands alone in the rainy dusk among the Scottish highlands. This is the first moment in the film where William feels his family torn from him, a moment where he is by himself surrounded by the towering landscape of Scotland. There is intimacy in this shot (shooting at his eye level, focusing on his searching eyes). Yet there is also a broader visual narrative here—a national and heroic one—Wallace alone, Scottish, centered in the shot among the highlands, wide angle.

Juxtaposed with these images of the lone William amidst graphic violence are scenes with his love interest, Murron, who is introduced to the viewer as a young girl at William's father's funeral. She comforts William through the death of his father and returns in the end of the film as an apparition (seen only by the audience and Wallace) during William's own death at the hands of the king of England, Edward I, remembered in the film as the brutal "Longshanks" (Patrick McGoohan). If Wallace is the ideal man (to this audience), then Murron is the ideal woman—helper, comforter, nurturer.

These bookend moments with Murron in the first and last minutes of the film are especially striking when compared to the loneliness she feels at her own death (45:15), shown through close-ups of her face, fearful and tearful, which cut to a panning shot of the horizon, allowing the audience to search frantically for Wallace through her eyes. This moment of her death, and Wallace's inability to save her, drives him through the film until he can return to her.

Scotland stands in for Murron as the one he protects, the one he longs to free from the bondage of tyranny. Yet, in the first act, even while the narrative points to a longing for what we call the "domestic ideal,"[15] Murron stands in for Scotland as well, free in her love for William, searching for her hero, then bound and helpless before the ruthless nobility, in need of protection. She and Scotland unite in giving

William purpose. Even after she is killed, she shows up in key moments of the film, compelling Wallace to his national purpose and comforting him in his death.

The film connects the domestic and the nation in a way that yields synthesis, not discordance. The story works because of Murron's death. This is the central pivot point in the film. Yet the story also works because Scotland is feminized through Murron. Both are the bodies for which Wallace provides and protects and through which he gains purpose. The narrative does not simply pivot from Murron to Scotland upon her death, thereby suggesting tension between Wallace's domestic and national purposes. Rather, Murron and Scotland are together throughout the film in key moments. The film uses effective editing, visual juxtaposition, camera perspective, and musical score to tie the stories together.[16]

Our respondents rarely mentioned the audio-visual work done in the film to carry the narrative. What they remembered and discussed were scenes like the pivotal battle speech, where we first see Wallace in his blue face paint, or the concluding scene where a tortured Wallace cries, "Freedom!" Although one might imagine visual images to be in the heads of respondents as they narrated *Braveheart*'s story to us, they never described the film from a *visual* standpoint. Rather, they merely recalled glimpses of the film.

From respondents' stories, it is difficult to grasp the ways in which religion and the *visual* narrative are in dialogue. What we have done thus far is combine their narratives about the film with the visual and narrative structure of the film to better understand *why* a film might be remembered in a certain way. In the opening of this chapter, we saw men expressing an ideal masculinity that captured both a domestic ideal and a national (or at least broader) purpose. *Braveheart,* as an audio-visual experience, captures both. It does so with creative tension captured through narrative, audio, and visual means—leaving the audience to wonder if Wallace will lose Scotland as he lost Murron. But the tension is resolved as Scotland unites in rebellion, as Wallace lives on through his child in the princess's womb, and as Wallace and

Murron reconnect, her death but a momentary sting and not a lasting lapse of Wallace's duty to protect.

## Visual Violence/Invisible Sex

If the dialogue between religion and visual narrative is obscure in audience retellings of films, there is one area where the dialogue is explicit: discussions about sex and violence. The evangelicals we interviewed did not casually embrace violence. They rejected what they saw as unnecessary violence in revenge films like *Saw* or horror films. But the violence of *Braveheart*, *Gladiator*, or *Saving Private Ryan* was accepted as historical realism.

Visually, *Braveheart* is a feast of stylized violence. Viewers see multiple gruesome acts shot in vivid close-up detail—close-up shots of the young boys hanging from the rafters of the cottage, Wallace crushing a man's skull with a battle hammer (50:00), or Wallace cutting a nobleman's throat in vivid, cold detail (52:50). The film is rated R for graphic violence, and it lives up to the rating.

What makes the stylized violence of *Braveheart* acceptable?

There is a sense from our respondents that the violence in *Braveheart* is historically real. But we suggest that this notion of "real" violence plays a minor role in the acceptance of violence, even though it is often the first defense mentioned by respondents.

Instead, the more significant justifications are that the violence is necessary for some greater truth, and that it is portrayed with what we call gendered restraint. Wallace's violence is simply necessary to a greater good, at least to fans of the film. England has brutally oppressed Scotland, and this plays out specifically on Wallace's family—first his father and brother, then his wife. In light of this we can see how audiences might demand an Old Testament vengeance. Anything less would be unmanly and, possibly, un-Christian (in their view). The other justification—restraint—may seem contradictory in a film like *Braveheart*, given its heavy dose of violence, but we point to two scenes in this film that show Gibson's gendered restraint: Murron's death scene and that of the nobleman who killed her.

The scene of Murron's execution (45:31) is a quick eight-shot sequence. The noble draws his knife. The film cuts to a close-up of a guard who tried to rape Murron. The camera cuts back to the noblemen walking toward Murron then quickly to an over-the-shoulder shot of him drawing the knife across her throat. The audience hears but does not see the knife cut through flesh. Instead, the film cuts back to a close-up of her face as she dies. The shot quickly cuts back to the over-the-shoulder shot of the nobleman wiping his knife clean then back to a tight close-up of her face as she dies, focusing on her eyes. Finally, the film cuts back to the over-the-shoulder shot, her head hanging lifeless as the noble says, "Now, let this scrapper come to me." The entire sequence is less than twenty seconds long, and the longest shot is a close-up of her dying face.

Though the type of execution is the same, the death of the nobleman is very different. In this six-shot, eighteen-second sequence (52:30), Wallace pins the nobleman to a wooden post. The shot is a tight over-the-shoulder shot, closer than the over-the-shoulder shot in Murron's execution. The audience hears Wallace draw a knife. In a quick three-shot sequence, the film shows a tight head shot with the knife against the nobleman's throat, a cut to a head shot of Wallace's face, and a cut back to the nobleman as Wallace draws the knife across his throat. Rather than a tight shot on the nobleman's eyes—the shot technique used in Murron's execution—the audience sees a cropped shoulder shot revealing the gash in the nobleman's throat, bleeding out, followed by another cut to Wallace's face. The sequence concludes with a longer shot of the nobleman's body falling forward, brushing the dispassionate Wallace on its way to the ground (signified by a hard "thud").

The differences between these scenes show restraint in the way in which Gibson chose to display identical forms of execution. The scene of Murron's execution is relatively bloodless and focuses on her eyes as she dies. The nobleman's execution is more graphic, focusing on the gaping gash in his throat. "Realistic violence" requires graphic, masochistic violence *among men*,[17] but when perpetrated against women, it must be handled less graphically and avenged narratively.

Such restraint highlights Laura Mulvey's feminist critique of portrayals of women in Hollywood film. Gibson's gendered restraint of violence protects the female body from graphic, violent display, preserving her "to-be-looked-at-ness ... as erotic spectacle."[18] While evangelical discourse *verbally* negates the "erotic spectacle," it embraces the preservation of the female body through its discourse of protection.

If portrayals of violence can be justified, portrayals of sex must be rejected or, if evident in a powerful film like *Braveheart*, forgotten (or unspoken). In our conversations with respondents about *Braveheart*, no one ever mentioned the sexual narratives coursing through the film. Yet *Braveheart* is a film with prominent, relatively graphic sex and nudity. These elements should arguably make a film off-limits to evangelical audiences, who, in our interviews with them, repeatedly warn that *seeing* sex in Hollywood films is dangerous to their marital and spiritual lives. Yet, the portrayals of sex in *Braveheart* are forgotten or, at least, avoided in respondents' narratives. Always.

Sex, sexual orientation and sexual bodies are not trivial in this film. The homosexual orientation of the English king's son makes an important symbolic point. The sex scene with Murron is critical, celebrating the consummation of her union with Wallace both by confirming their connection and signaling that Wallace would not have to yield her to the nobleman on their wedding night. The extramarital sex scene with Princess Isabelle (Sophie Marceau) is crucial in the triumph of Wallace—that his line is continued through the line of kings, while Longshanks, line dies with his son. Finally, a scene with frontal male nudity is important as comedic relief and showing symbolic rebellion.

Despite what Gibson must have considered the necessity of these different expressions of sex to carry the plot, they have all been lost in the memories (or at least in the expression of those memories) of the film's fans we interviewed. The reasons for this, we suggest, are twofold. First, they take up relatively little space in the film. The longest of the scenes, the sex scene between William and Murron, is a little more than a minute long. Second, all of the sexual acts and nude bodies in the film fit into the narrative of a good, strong, Christian man and can thus serve as background to more pressing narratives of provision, protection, and purposefulness on the part of good, strong Christian men in general.

The most notable instance of sex is the scene between William and Murron on their wedding night. Gibson chose to shoot Catherine McCormack (Murron) from the waist up, showing her breasts, first in moonlight silhouette, then clearly nude. This nudity is concerning to evangelical audiences.[19] While the shot lingers on her breasts as she and Gibson come together, the scene only shows their tender embrace, not prolonged sexual intercourse. We assume this visual restraint might make such an expression palatable, if still offensive, to the religious sensibilities of this audience. If not, given the way the film is consumed now, this quick sequence can easily be skipped. Further, this sex scene follows a prolonged private wedding ceremony with a clergyman, which situates the sex scene in a sanctified, Christian marriage. Gibson certainly could have shot this sex scene in a way that showed even more restraint, but clearly his choices did not create enough dissonance with the audience for them to avoid or criticize this film or to significantly mark their memories of it. It is also possible that this scene provided a moment of "guilty pleasure" for the heterosexual, evangelical male audience, a pleasure that must remain unspoken, if not forgotten.

The sex scene with Marceau (Princess Isabelle) did not cause comment either. Whereas the scene with Murron was a *visual* issue (female nudity), the problem with Marceau's scene is narrative in nature—portrayal of extramarital sex. This scene is even shorter than the scene with McCormack, and it shows no nudity. Gibson opted for a cropped shoulder shot of the two of them lying in bed. The scene also binds Isabelle with Murron through the musical score. The music for Gibson's scene with Marceau is the same in the sex scene with Murron and in Wallace's death scene, which cuts from Isabelle crying to Murron smiling as she welcomes Wallace "home" to her. Further, this sex scene with

Isabelle is followed by cuts to Robert the Bruce's father dying in bed
and a scene of Longshanks alone, dying by the fire. The purpose of the
scene with Marceau is clearly to immortalize Wallace through his seed
(and to symbolically slay his enemies) and to connect Isabelle, by proxy
even, to Murron, through music, through the juxtaposition between the
women in the Wallace death scene, and through a scene where the
ghost of Murron wakes Wallace from a dream to meet Isabelle (104:00).[20]

These portrayals of sex, like the violence, would seem justifiable for
similar reasons—sex is restrained and necessary for the plot. We suggest that these scenes are forgotten or ignored because of the artistic
choices made by the director *and* because the dialogue about sex among
evangelicals *requires* that they ignore or forget these elements to avoid
complicating the iconic status of this film.

That Gibson showed gendered restraint again as a director should
not be underplayed here either. He pushed the boundaries of this audience's sensibilities, but not too far, offering glimpses of "sin" and perhaps thus affording some guilty pleasure through the cinematic gaze
while at the same time establishing a kind of realism of the tributes
afforded to male heroes, i.e. a need for sex and love.

Two other sexual elements in the film should, on the face of it, be
troubling to evangelical audiences. Firstly, a scene of full frontal male
nudity (83:00), and secondly, Prince Edward's sexual orientation.

The male nudity in the film occurs in a battle scene following Wallace's iconic call to battle. While male genitalia are clearly evident,
they are shot from afar, are not sexualized, and fit structurally with the
sentiments of Wallace's "freedom" speech. If there were any confusion
that freedom-loving revolutionary activity is both gendered masculine
*and* biologically male, Gibson erases that confusion through this "lad-
dish" scene, used to show fearlessness and to offer comedic relief.

Prince Edward's sexuality would also be troubling to evangelical
audiences. Evangelical narratives about homosexuality tend to resent
the mere representation of homosexuality in media. There is, of course,
an air of historical accuracy in this portrayal, but we suggest Gibson

stylized Edward's homosexuality to reproduce a heteronormative narrative through the veneer of historical accuracy.[21] Edward can be forgotten because his only purpose is to reinforce Wallace's *true* masculinity. And, as with the female nudity, Prince Edward's sexuality could also carry a hint of a "guilty pleasure" gaze.

## CONCLUSION

We hope this close reading of the text and shifting contexts of audience perceptions of *Braveheart* helps the reader understand *Braveheart* and its place in the white, heterosexual, American evangelical male imagination. *Braveheart* revitalized a film genre connected to Bible epics in earlier Hollywood cinema. The film was released during a period when Christian masculinity was in question and where evangelical men's groups like Promise Keepers emerged in response. *Braveheart* allowed men to talk about Christian masculinity through a popular media product that resonated at some level with the broader culture. It also helped create spaces for male bonding and intimacy, allowing men to "be men," to talk about their longing to have purpose, to have meaningful social bonds, to perform as warriors, protectors, and providers with purpose. *Braveheart* helped make a version of *Christian* masculinity relevant and desirable. Because of this, *Braveheart* has been remixed and replayed for two decades, focusing and amplifying certain parts of the story at the expense of others.

This context is part of why *Braveheart* works as a powerful symbolic resource for evangelical men, but the film itself is also part of this story. Clearly, the story resonates. This is in evident in the ways in which evangelical men connect *Braveheart* to their positive sense of masculinity. But films are not simply stories that are told; they are seen and heard. The close reading of the structure of this film and its scenes of violence and sex, coupled with the context we've discussed, should provide better understanding of how certain elements of the film are recalled and reexperienced twenty years later, while other powerful elements of the film are forgotten or ignored. The film is structured in a way, and the camera structures the gaze in a way, that shapes how the film is experienced. These elements—text and context—help explain why this film still matters to some evangelical men two decades after its release.

## DISCUSSION QUESTIONS

1. What questions about organized religion and about masculinity lead the evangelical men that Coats and Hoover study to turn to *Braveheart?* How is the film helpful to them? How does it help them talk about gender, their relationships with their wives and children, and their own identify in the family, society, and the church? What do we learn about their dialogue between religion and culture though this study?

2. The authors suggest the men they interviewed had personal experiences of the film, that evangelical leaders showed excerpts in sermons and small group meetings, and that the men recalled the story and used it to talk about issues of masculine identity and purpose. In what ways might these experiences of retelling, excerpting, and interpreting a media text influence how the text is experienced or remembered?

3. In contrast to authors who offer us their own interpretations of particular movies or other examples of popular culture, these authors root their interpretation of the film, and the use a particular audience makes of it, in interviews with the men they are studying. What does that add to our understanding? What problems might there be in such an approach?

4. Are there particular films that have provided you with images of what it means to be male or female? Have these images been helpful or harmful to you in thinking about your own gender identity and expression?

## NOTES

1. http://christandpopculture.com/not-every-man-really-lives-the-20-year-impact-of-braveheart.

2. http://corproject.com/58-braveheart-and-the-need-for-heroic-fatherhood.

3. See James R. Keller, "Masculinity and Marginality in *Rob Roy* and *Braveheart*," *Journal of Popular Film & Television* 24, no. 4 (1997): 146–51; William Luhr, "Mutilating Mel. Martyrdom and Masculinity in *Braveheart*," in *Mythologies of Violence in Postmodern Media*, ed. Christopher Sharrett (Detroit, MI: Wayne State University Press, 1999), 227–46; Jeffrey A. Brown, "The Tortures of Mel Gibson: Masochism and the Sexy Male Body," *Men and Masculinities* 5, no. 2 (2002): 123–43.

4. Stewart M. Hoover and Curtis D. Coats, *Does God Make the Man? Media, Religion, and the Crisis of Masculinity* (New York: New York University Press, 2015), 19.

5. Colin McArthur, *Brigadoon, Braveheart and the Scots: Distortions of Scotland in Hollywood Cinema* (New York: I. B. Tauris, 2003); Tim Edensor, "Reading *Braveheart*: Representing and Contesting Scottish Identity," *Scottish Affairs* 21, no 1 (1997): 135–58.

6. https://www.movieguide.org/reviews/braveheart.html.

7. See David A. Hollinger, *After Cloven Tongues of Fire: Protestant Liberalism in Modern American History* (Princeton, NJ: Princeton University Press, 2013), 4.

8. See, e.g., David Morgan, *The Lure of Images: A History of Religion and Visual Media in America* (London: Routledge, 2007); Terry Lindvall, *Sanctuary Cinema: Origins of the Christian Film Industry* (New York: New York University Press, 2011).

9. Alexander McGregor, *The Catholic Church and Hollywood: Censorship and Morality in 1930s Cinema* (New York: I. B. Tauris, 2013); Leonard J. Leff and Jerold L. Simmons, *The Dame in the Kimono: Hollywood, Censorship, and the Production Code* (Lexington: University Press of Kentucky, 2013); Lindvall, *Sanctuary Cinema*; Leonard J. Leff, "The Breening of America," *PMLA* 106, no. 3 (1991): 432–45.

10. For an example of this type of essentialized discourse about sex, see Fred Stoeker and Steve Arterburn, *Every Man's Battle: Strategies for Victory in the Real World of Sexual Temptation* (Colorado Springs, CO: Waterbrook Press, 2000).

11. For more about these "old concerns," see work on "muscular Christianity," e.g., Donald E. Hall, *Muscular Christianity: Embodying the Victorian Age* (Cambridge: Cambridge University Press, 2006); Dane S. Claussen, *The*

*Promise Keepers: Essays on Masculinity and Christianity* (Jefferson, NC: McFarland, 2000); Michael S. Kimmel and Amy Aronson, *Men and Masculinities: A Social, Cultural, and Historical Encyclopedia, Volume 1: A–J* (Santa Barbara, CA: ABC-CLIO, 2004); Michael A. Messner, *Politics of Masculinities: Men in Movements* (Lanham, MD: Rowman & Littlefield, 1997).

12. *Billboard* 112, no. 52 (Dec. 23, 2000), 60, and no. 38 (Sept. 16, 2000), 74.

13. http://www1.cbn.com/biblestudy/john-eldredge-speaks-on-ransoming-hearts.

14. Robert Burgoyne, *The Hollywood Historical Film* (Hoboken, NJ: Wiley-Blackwell, 2008), 38.

15. Hoover and Coats, *Does God Make the Man?*, 111.

16. See McArthur, *Brigadoon, Braveheart and the Scots*.

17. Brown, "Tortures of Mel Gibson."

18. Laura Mulvey, "Visual Pleasure and Narrative Cinema," in *Media and Cultural Studies: KeyWorks*, ed. Meenakshi Gigi Durham and Douglas M. Kellner (Oxford: Blackwell, 2006), 346.

19. See, e.g., this Christian review, www.movieguide.org/reviews/braveheart.html.

20. See also, McArthur, *Brigadoon, Braveheart and the Scots*, 154–60.

21. See also Sid Ray, "Hunks, History, and Homophobia: Masculinity Politics in *Braveheart* and *Edward II*," *Film and History: An Interdisciplinary Journal of Film and Television Studies* 29, nos. 3–4 (1999): 22–31.

# CONTRIBUTORS

*Sophia Rose Arjana* is visiting assistant professor of Islamic studies at the Iliff School of Theology in Denver, Colorado. Her monograph *Muslims in the Western Imagination* was published in 2015, and she is also the author of articles and book chapters on liberation theology, Islamic pilgrimage, Islamophobia, and Orientalism. Her global study of Muslim pilgrimage practices, *Pilgrimage in Islam: Traditions and Modern Practices*, 2017. A coauthored project focused on female Muslim comic and cartoon superheroines, titled *Veiled Heroes: Muslim Women, Liberation, and Popular Culture*, will be published in 2018.

*Jason C. Bivins* is professor of religious studies at North Carolina State University in Raleigh. A specialist in the religions of the United States, he is the author of *The Fracture of Good Order: Christian Antiliberalism and the Challenge to American Politics* (2003); *Religion of Fear: The Politics of Horror in Conservative Evangelicalism* (2008); and *Spirits Rejoice! Jazz and American Religion* (2015), in addition to multiple essays and book chapters on political religions, theory and method, religion and popular culture, and new religious movements.

*Stephanie Brehm* is a doctoral candidate at Northwestern University in Evanston, Illinois. Her research interests include religion, popular culture, American studies and media studies. Her current project looks at the intersection of religion and humor in the twenty-first century, specifically Catholic humor, in the case study of Stephen Colbert.

*Dan W. Clanton Jr.* is associate professor of religious studies at Doane University in Crete, Nebraska. His research interests include aesthetic interpretations of biblical literature as well as the intersection between religion and (popular) culture. Along with Terry Ray Clark, he is to co-editor of the forthcoming *Oxford Handbook to the Bible and Popular Culture in America*. In addition to spending time with his family and reading comic books, he enjoys collecting and listening to jazz and classical music, and watching far too much television.

*Curtis D. Coats* is Lecturer in the Department of Communication at Seattle University. He is the coauthor of *Does God Make the Man? Media, Religion, and the Crisis of Masculinity* (2015) and co-editor of *Practical Spiritualities in a Media Age* (2015). He is currently working with Richard Boada on a collaborative photography/poetry project entitled *Urban Ecosystems: Living Tensions in Jackson, Mississippi*, and on a documentary with Scott Ramsey about New Age tourism in Sedona, Arizona.

*Nabil Echchaibi* is associate professor of media studies and associate director of the Center for Media, Religion and Culture at the University of Colorado Boulder. His research focuses on religion and the role of media in shaping and reflecting modern religious identities among Muslims in the Middle East and in Western societies. His work on diasporic media, Muslim media cultures, and Islamic alternative modernity has appeared in various journals and in many book publications. He is the author of *Voicing Diasporas: Ethnic Radio in Paris and Berlin between Culture and Renewal* (2011) and the co-editor with Adrienne Russell of *International Blogging: Identity, Politics and Networked Publics* (2009). He has also written opinion columns in the popular press, including the *Guardian, Forbes Magazine, Salon, Al Jazeera, Huffington Post, Religion Dispatches,* and *Open Democracy*.

*Bruce David Forbes,* co-editor of the two previous editions of this volume (2005, 2000), is professor of religious studies at Morningside College in Sioux City, Iowa. His publications include *Christmas: A Candid History* (2008), *America's Favorite Holidays: Candid Histories* (2015), and other essays. He has served on the national board of the American Academy of Religion and was with Jeffrey Mahan founding co-chair of the AAR Religion and Popular Culture Group.

*Shreena Niketa Gandhi* is assistant professor of religion at Michigan State University in East Lansing. Her current book project, *A Cultural History of Yoga in the U.S.,* is under review. Her teaching focuses on religion, race, and capitalism in the Americas.

*Gregory Price Grieve* is head of the Religious Studies Department at the University of North Carolina, Greensboro. He researches and teaches at the intersection of digital media, Buddhism, and the study of critical media practices. His monograph *Cyber Zen: Imagining Authentic Buddhist Identity, Community and Religious Practice in the Virtual World of Second Life* (2016) explores how people use digital media to practice popular forms of religion and makes conspicuous ideal forms of contemporary spirituality.

*Rachel B. Gross* is John and Marcia Goldman Professor of American Jewish Studies in the Department of Jewish Studies at San Francisco State University. In 2014 to 2016, she was a visiting assistant professor in the Department of Religion and Culture at Virginia Tech in Blacksburg. She contributed to *Religion, Food and Eating in North America* (2014) and is currently working on a book that examines the religious nature of contemporary nostalgic representations of American Jewish immigration history.

*Stewart M. Hoover* is an internationally recognized expert on media and religion and the author or editor of twelve books, including *Media, Home, and Family* (2004), with Lynn Schofield Clark and Diana F. Alters; *Religion in the Media Age* (2006); and *Does God Make the Man?* (2015), with Curtis D. Coats. His field of scholarship covers media audience research, media history, and the social and political impact of the media. He directs the Center for Media, Religion, and Culture at the University of Colorado Boulder, where he is professor of media studies and religious studies.

*Jane Naomi Iwamura* is associate professor and chair of the Religious Studies Department at the University of the West in Rosemead, California. Her research focuses on Asian American religions and race and popular culture in the United States (with an emphasis on visual culture). Her publications include *Revealing the Sacred in Asian and Pacific America,* co-edited with Paul R. Spickard (2003), and *Virtual Orientalism: Religion and American Popular Culture.* (2011). She has also written on Japanese American lived religions, as well as the intersection of religion and Asian American literary production. She co-founded the Asian Pacific American Religions Research Initiative (APARRI), a national scholarly network advancing the interdisciplinary study of Asian Pacific Americans and their religions.

*Michael Jindra* is a research scholar in the Center for the Study of Religion and Society and an adjunct associate professor in the Department of Anthropology at the University of Notre Dame. His main interest is in what drives people to become involved in different activities. He has written about large funeral celebrations in Africa, video gaming, and fan phenomena and is currently writing about how lifestyle diversity influences outcomes like inequality, and also on how nonprofit organizations try to assist the poor through "relational work."

*Jessica Johnson* is a lecturer at the University of Washington in Seattle in the Departments of Anthropology and Gender, Women, and Sexuality Studies. She is writing a book based on a decade of ethnographic research on Mars Hill Church entitled *Biblical Porn: Sex, Affect and Evangelical Empire*. Her publications based on this research include the articles "The Citizen-Soldier: Masculinity, War, and Sacrifice at an Emerging Church in Seattle, Washington" (2010) and "Porn Again Christian? Mark Driscoll, Mars Hill Church, and a Pornification of the Pulpit" (2015).

*Robert K. Johnston*, a past president of the American Theological Society and an ordained minister in the Evangelical Covenant Church, is professor of theology and culture at Fuller Theological Seminary, Pasadena, California, and co-director of Fuller's Reel Spirituality Institute. He is the author or editor of fifteen books, including *The Christian at Play* (1983; reprint 1997); *Useless Beauty: Ecclesiastes through the Lens of Contemporary Film* (2004); *Finding God in the Movies*, co-authored with Catherine Barsotti (2004); *Reel Spirituality: Theology and Film in Dialogue* (2000, 2006); and *God's Wider Presence: Reconsidering General Revelation* (2014).

*Michelle M. Lelwica* is professor of religion at Concordia College in Moorhead, Minnesota, where she teaches courses that explore the intersections of religion, gender, culture, and the body. She is the author of *Starving for Salvation: The Spiritual Dimensions of Eating Problems among American Girls and Women* (1999); *The Religion of Thinness* (2009); and *Shameful Bodies: Religion and the Culture of Physical Improvement* (2017), as well as many scholarly articles and popular blogs relating to women's conflicted relationships with food and their bodies. She has also published articles and taught courses that focus on engaged/embodied pedagogy and mindfulness practice.

*Jeffrey H. Mahan*, co-editor of the two previous editions of this volume (2005, 2000), holds the Ralph E. and Norma E. Peck Chair in Religion and Public Communication at the Iliff School of Theology in Denver, Colorado. His publications include *American Television Genres*, with Stuart Kaminsky (1985); *Shared Wisdom: A Guide to Case Study Reflection in Ministry*, with Barbara B Troxell and Carol J Allen (1993); and *Media, Religion and Culture: An Introduction* (2014), as well as various chapters and articles on media, religion and popular culture.

With Bruce Forbes he was founding co-chair of the American Academy of Religion's Religion and Popular Culture Group.

*Kristin M. Peterson* is a doctoral candidate in media studies and a research fellow for the Center for Media, Religion and Culture at the University of Colorado Boulder. Her research focuses on Islam in North America, specifically examining how young Muslims engage with online media sites such as YouTube, Instagram, and blogs as spaces to explore different discourses, aesthetic styles, and affects. She is interested in the role that aesthetics and affects play in the constitution of religious subjects and the formation of religious communities. Her other research interests include the use of Arabic in social media, Islamic fashion, feminism and religion, and discourses around authenticity.

*Anthony Pinn* is Agnes Cullen Arnold Professor of Humanities and professor of religion at Rice University, where he is also the founding director of the Center for Engaged Research and Collaborative Learning. He is also director of research for the Institute for Humanist Studies and either the author or the editor of over thirty-five books, including *Humanism: Essays on Race, Religion and Popular Culture* (2015) and *Religion in Hip Hop: Mapping the New Terrain in the US,* jointly edited with Monica R. Miller and Bernard "Bun B" Freeman (2015).

*Joseph L. Price* is Genevieve S. Connick Professor of Religious Studies at Whittier College, in Whittier, California. His long-standing interest in sports and religion is reflected in *Rounding the Bases: Baseball and Religion in America* (2005) and his edited volume *From Season to Season: Sports as American Religion* (2001). He serves as general editor for the Mercer University Press series Sports and Religion.

*Myev Rees* is a doctoral candidate at Northwestern University in Evanston, Illinois. Her work examines American religion, media, and popular culture, particularly evangelicalism, reality television, and digital media. She is interested in questions related to gender and the body, as well as mediated religious constructions of motherhood, childhood, family, and the home.

*Elijah Siegler* is associate professor and chair of the Department of Religious Studies at the College of Charleston, where teaches courses on Religion and Film and Religion and Popular Culture, among many others. He coauthored *New Religious Movements* (2006), and has published articles on the film director David Cronenberg, the TV producer Tom Fontana, cop shows, American

Daoism, and religious studies pedagogy. He recently edited *Coen: Framing Religion in Amoral Order* (2016) and coauthored *Dream Trippers: Global Daoism and the Predicament of Modern Spirituality* (2017)

*Sarah Mcfarland Taylor* is an associate professor of religious studies at Northwestern University in Evanston, Illinois. Her current book project, *Restorying Earth: Media, Environment, and Popular Moral Engagement* (NYU Press, forthcoming), analyzes diverse representations of environmental moral engagement in contemporary mediated popular culture. Her book *Green Sisters: A Spiritual Ecology* (2007) won the Catholic Press Association's first prizes for best book on gender issues and best book on social concerns. Taylor is pursuing an additional advanced degree in Media Studies at The New School in New York City, where she is a candidate in the Media History, Criticism, and Philosophy graduate track. As a member of the American Academy of Religion's national board of directors and its Midwest regional director, Taylor directed a task force working to reduce the AAR's ecological "footprint."

*Pete Ward* is professorial fellow in ecclesiology and ethnography in the Department of Theology and Religion at Durham University in Durham, England, and professor of practical theology at the Norwegian School of Theology in Oslo. He has written on popular culture and the church in *Liquid Church* (2002), on the economics and culture of contemporary Christian worship songs in *Selling Worship* (2005), and on celebrity worship in *Gods Behaving Badly: Media Religion and Celebrity Culture* (2011).

# INDEX

Protestant, 161, 203, 270–71, 348;
    aesthetics, 245, 203, 223; chaplain,
    354; prayer, 355; reformation, 123
*Protestant, Catholic, Jew* (Herberg), 354
Puder, Glen D. (Rev.), 354
Purim, 186–87
*Purim Superhero, The* (Kushner),
    186–87
purity rings, 357
*"Purpose"* (Beiber), 317–18

quasi-religion, 233, 263, 267, 291, 376. *See
    also* parareligion

racism, 347, 400
rap, 152, 335, 390–407. *See also* gangsta
    rap; progressive rap; status rap
"Rapper's Delight" (Sugar Hill Gang),
    397–98
Raschke, Carl, 106
Ray, Darrel, 248
*Real Marriage* (Driscoll), 160, 165–69
Real, Michael, 7
Rees, Myev , 334, 435
*Religion and Sports* (Albert), 292
Religion: definition, 10, 190, 218, 220–21;
    formal definitions, 17, 217, 220;
    functional definitions, 16–17, 217;
    substantive definitions, 16, 217
*Religious Possibilities of the Motion Picture,
    The* (Jump), 374
Rev. Billy. *See* Tallen, Bill
ritual, 264–67, 297–98; consumption,
    243; cultural, 266; drama, 18; fandom,
    231–35; Jewish, 180, 182–84, 186–87;
    men's, 418; public, 17; resistance, 251;
    ritualization, 197, 202–4; sacrifice,
    102, 274–75; satanic, 107, 109; Shinto,
    281; space, 298; sports, 291, 295–97,
    302; time, 298
*Ritual Theory/Ritual Practice* (Bell), 203
Ritzer, George, 245–6
Roddenberry, Gene, 228, 230
Rose, Tricia, 396
*Rounding the Bases* (Price), 292, 435

rules, 197, 205; moral, 275; religious, 145,
    273; sports, 293, 297–98, 303, 306
Russell, Bertrand, 248

sacred: absence of, 102, 108–9; buyos-
    phere, 243–47, 253–54; consumption,
    221; history, 71–81; in nature, 361–62;
    projects, 228; rituals,178, 264–67; self,
    323–5; space, 202, 205, 242; in sports,
    291–92; system, 123; text, 28, 122–23,
    219; time, 74; truth, 263. *See also*
    profane
Saeed, Sana, 144–45
Said, Edward, 86
Saint Nicholas/Santa Claus, 136–37,
    141
Salt-n-Pepa, 399
*Sammy Spider's First Book of Jewish
    Holidays,* 183
Sandler, Winnie, 188
Santayana, George, 290
Sapp, D. Gregory, 292
Sartre, Jean-Paul, 299
Satan, 89, 197, 202; Satanic, 101–2, 103,
    107–9; Satanism, 102, 108–10, 114
Saturnalia, Roman, 130, 132
Scharoun, Lisa, 245–56
Schenck, Ken, 43–44
Schmidt, Leigh, 244–45
Schwartz, Hillel, 271
science fiction, 226–27, 29
science, faith in, 237
Scooby Doo, 71–72, 79–80
Scott-Heron, Gil, 397
secular, 442–43, 153–55, 218, 264–67,
    274–75; culture, 145, 153; Jews, 179;
    practices, 337; rituals, 264–67;
    secularization, 13, 23, 179, 231, 269;
    spaces, 246
Seid, Roberta Pollack, 271
*Selling God* (Moore), 21, 246
sexism, 332, 364, 400, 402
sexual, 93, 145, 166, 398; assault, 106;
    codes, 409; imagery, 352; objects,
    399; sin, 166; stereotypes, 400